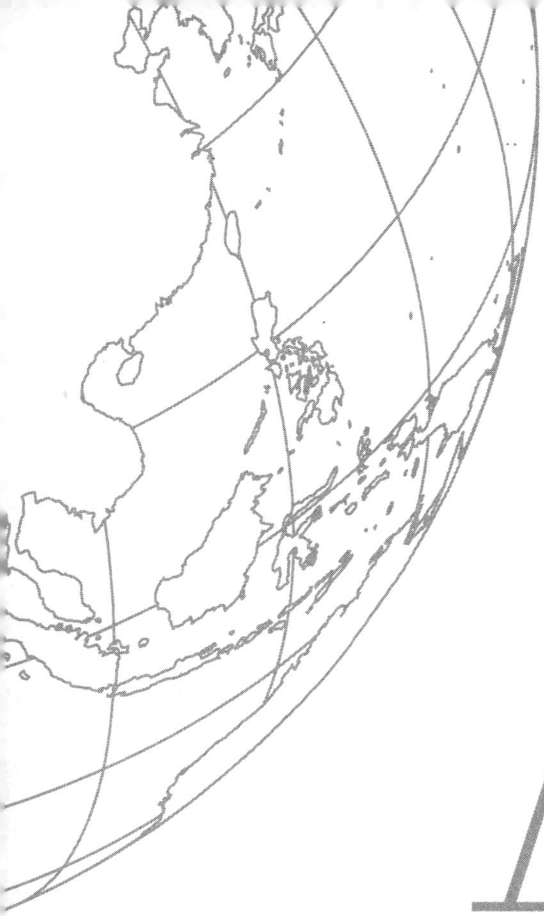

HAMMOND

PORTABLE

Atlas

OF THE WORLD

Contents

Interpreting Maps

Designed to enhance your knowledge and enjoyment of the atlas, these pages explain map principles, scales, symbology and how to locate information quickly.

3 Map Projections
4-5 Using This Atlas

Geographic Comparisons

These eight pages contain flags and important facts about each independent country, plus dimensions of the earth's major mountains, longest rivers and largest lakes and islands.

6-11 World Flags & Reference Guide
12-13 World Statistics

Maps of the World

New maps, derived from a computer database, accurately present political detail while proprietary map projections show the most distortion-free views of the continents.

14-15 World - Physical Map
16-17 World - Political Map 1:82M

Europe and Northern Asia

18 Europe 1:17.5M
19 Metropolitan London, Paris 1:587K
20 Scandinavia, Finland 1:7M; Iceland 1:7M
21 United Kingdom, Ireland 1:3.5M
22-23 Northeastern Ireland, Northern England and Wales 1:1.17M
24-25 Southern England and Wales 1:1.17M
26-27 North Central Europe 1:3.5M
28-29 Netherlands, Northwestern Germany 1:1.17M
30-31 Belgium, Northern France, Western Germany 1:1.17M
32-33 West Central Europe 1:3.5M
34-35 Spain, Portugal 1:3.5M; Barcelona, Madrid, Lisbon 1:1.17M, Azores, Canary Islands, Madeira 1:7M
36-37 Central Alps Region 1:1.17M
38-39 Southern Italy, Albania, Greece 1:3.5M; Athens 1:1.17M
40-41 Hungary, Northern Balkan States 1:3.5M
42-43 Northeastern Europe 1:7M; St. Petersburg, Moscow 1:1.17M
44-45 Southeastern Europe 1:7M
46-47 Russia and Neighboring Countries 1:21M

Asia

48 Asia 1:49M
49 Eastern Mediterranean 1:3.5M; Central Israel and West Bank 1:1.17M
50-51 Northern Middle East 1:7M; Istanbul 1:1.17M
52-53 Southwestern Asia 1:10.5M
54-55 Eastern Asia 1:10.5M
56-57 Central and Southern Japan 1:3.5M; Tokyo, Osaka-Nagoya 1:1.17M
58 Korea 1:3.5M; Seoul 1:1.17M
59 Northeastern China 1:7M; Beijing-Tianjin, Shanghai 1:3.5M
60-61 Southeastern China, Burma 1:7M
62-63 Southern Asia 1:10.5M
64 Punjab Plain 1:3.5M; Southern India 1:3.5M
65 Eastern Burma, Thailand, Indochina 1:7M
66-67 Southeastern Asia 1:10.5M

Pacific, Australia

68-69 Central Pacific Ocean 1:31.5M; New Caledonia, Fiji 1:7M, Samoa, Tahiti 1:3.5M
70-71 Australia 1:14M; New Zealand 1:10.5M
72 Northeastern Australia 1:7M; Brisbane, Sydney 1:1.17M
73 Southeastern Australia 1:7M; Melbourne 1:1.17M

Africa, Antarctica

74 Africa 1:31.5M
75 Northern Morocco, Algeria, Tunisia 1:3.5M
76-77 Northern Africa 1:17.5M
78-79 West Africa 1:7M
80-81 South Africa 1:7M; Cape Region, Witwatersrand, Mauritius and Réunion 1:3.5M Madagascar 1:7M
82 Southern Africa 1:17.5M
83 Antarctica 1:28M

North America

84 North America 1:35M
85 Alaska 1:10.5M
86-87 Canada 1:14M
88-89 United States 1:14M; Hawaii 1:3.5M, Oahu 1:1.17M
90-91 Southwestern Canada, Northwestern United States 1:7M
92-93 Southwestern United States 1:7M
94-95 Southeastern Canada, Northeastern United States 1:7M; Montreal, Toronto-Buffalo 1:1.17M
96-97 Southeastern United States 1:7M
98 Los Angeles; New York-Philadelphia; Washington 1:1.17M
99 Seattle-Tacoma; Sacramento-San Francisco-San Jose; Detroit; Chicago-Milwaukee 1:1.17M
100-101 Northern and Central Mexico 1:7M; Mexico City-Veracruz 1:3.5M, Distrito Federal 1:1.17M
102-103 Southern Mexico, Central America, Western Caribbean 1:7M
104 Eastern Caribbean, Bahamas 1:7M

South America

105 South America 1:28M
106-107 Northern South America 1:15M
108 Southeastern Brazil 1:7M; São Paulo-Rio de Janeiro 1:3.5M
109 Southern South America 1:15M

Index

A 6,000-entry A to Z index lists major places and geographic features in the atlas, complete with page numbers and easy-to-use alpha-numeric references.

110-120 Index of the World

ISBN 1-56865-079-5

Map Projections

Simply stated, the mapmaker's challenge is to project the earth's curved surface onto a flat plane. To achieve this elusive goal, cartographers have developed map projections — equations which govern this conversion of geographic data.

This section explores some of the most widely used projections. It also introduces a new projection, the Hammond Optimal Conformal.

General Principles and Terms

The earth rotates around its axis once a day. Its end points are the North and South poles; the line circling the earth midway between the poles is the equator. The arc from the equator to either pole is divided into 90 degrees of latitude. The equator represents 0° latitude. Circles of equal latitude, called parallels, are traditionally shown at every fifth or tenth degree.

The equator is divided into 360 degrees. Lines circling the globe from pole to pole through the degree points on the equator are called meridians, or great circles. All meridians are equal in length, but by international agreement the meridian passing through the Greenwich Observatory near London has been chosen as the prime meridian or 0° longitude. The distance in degrees from the prime meridian to any point east or west is its longitude.

While meridians are all equal in length, parallels become shorter as they approach the poles. Whereas one degree of latitude represents approximately 69 miles (112 km.) anywhere on the globe, a degree of longitude varies from 69 miles (112 km.) at the equator to zero at the poles. Each degree of latitude and longitude is divided into 60 minutes. One minute of latitude equals one nautical mile (1.15 land miles or 1.85 km.).

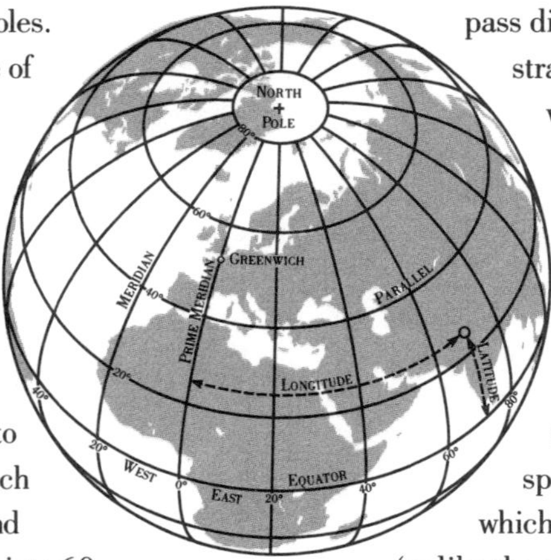

How to Flatten a Sphere: The Art of Controlling Distortion

There is only one way to represent a sphere with absolute precision: on a globe. All attempts to project our planet's surface onto a plane unevenly stretch or tear the sphere as it flattens, inevitably distorting shapes, distances, area (sizes appear larger or smaller than actual size), angles or direction.

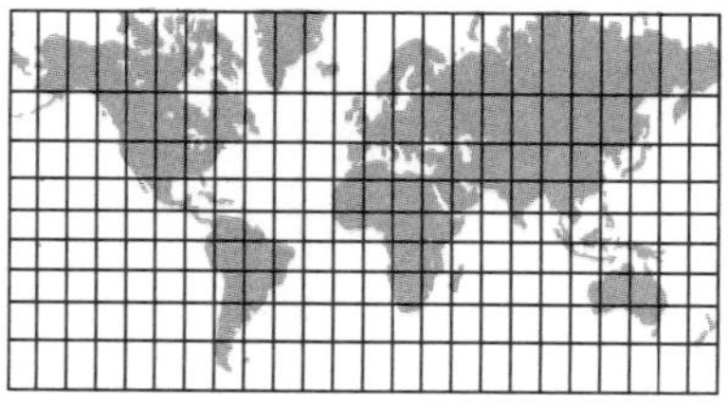

Figure 1 **Mercator Projection**

Since representing a sphere on a flat plane always creates distortion, only the parallels or the meridians (or some other set of lines) can maintain the same length as on a globe of corresponding scale. All other lines must be either too long or too short. Accordingly, the scale on a flat map cannot be true everywhere; there will always be different scales in different parts of a map. On world maps or very large areas, variations in scale may be extreme. Most maps seek to preserve either true area relationships (equal area projections) or true angles and shapes (conformal projections); some attempt to achieve overall balance.

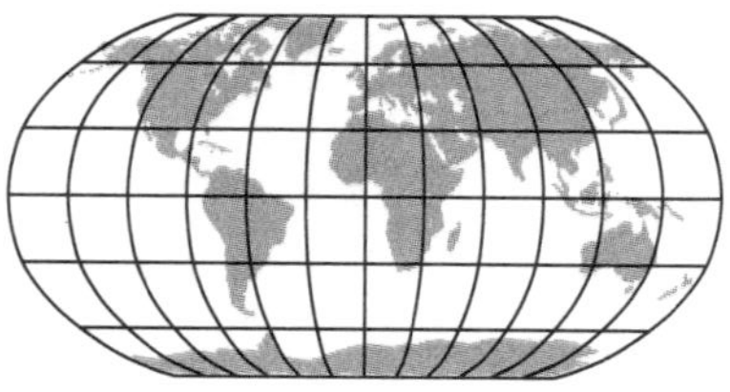

Figure 2 **Robinson Projection**

Projections: Selected Examples

Mercator (Fig. 1): This projection is especially useful because all compass directions appear as straight lines, making it a valuable navigational tool. Moreover, every small region conforms to its shape on a globe — hence the name conformal. But because its meridians are evenly-spaced vertical lines which never converge (unlike the globe), the horizontal parallels must be drawn farther and farther apart at higher latitudes to maintain a correct relationship. Only the equator is true to scale, and the size of areas in the higher latitudes is dramatically distorted.

Robinson (Fig. 2): To create the thematic maps in Global Relationships and the two-page world map in the Maps of the World section, the Robinson projection was used. It combines elements of both conformal and equal area projections to show the whole earth with relatively true shapes and reasonably equal areas.

Conic (Fig. 3): This projection has been used frequently for air navigation charts and to create most of the national and regional maps in this atlas. (See text in margin at left).

Hammond's Optimal Conformal

As its name implies, this new conformal projection (Fig. 4) presents the optimal view of an area by reducing shifts in scale over an entire region to the minimum degree possible. While conformal maps generally preserve all small shapes, large shapes can become very distorted because of varying scales, causing considerable inaccuracy in distance measurements. The concept underlying the Optimal Conformal is that for any region on the globe, there is an ideal projection for which scale variation can be made as small as possible. Consequently, unlike other projections, the Optimal Conformal does not use one standard formula to construct a map. Each map is a unique projection — the optimal projection for that particular area.

After a cartographer defines the subject area, a sophisticated computer program evaluates the size and shape of the region, projecting the most distortion-free map possible. All of the continent maps in this atlas, except Antarctica, have been drawn using the Optimal projection.

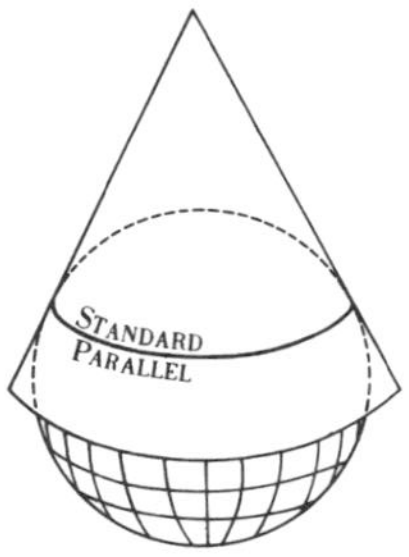

Figure 3
Conic Projection
The original idea of a conic projection is to cap the globe with a cone, and then project onto the cone from the planet's center the lines of latitude and longitude (the parallels and meridians). To produce a working map, the cone is simply cut open and laid flat. The conic projection used here is a modification of this idea. A cone can be made tangent to any standard parallel you choose. One popular version of a conic projection, the Lambert Conformal Conic, uses two standard parallels near the top and bottom of the map to further reduce errors of scale.

Figure 4
Hammond's Optimal Conformal Projection
Like all conformal maps, the Optimal projection preserves angles exactly and minimizes distortion in shapes. This projection is more successful than any previous projection at spreading curvature across the entire map, producing the most distortion-free map possible.

Using This Atlas

How to Locate Information Quickly
Our Maps of the World section is organized by continent. If you're looking for a major region of the world, consult the Contents on page two.

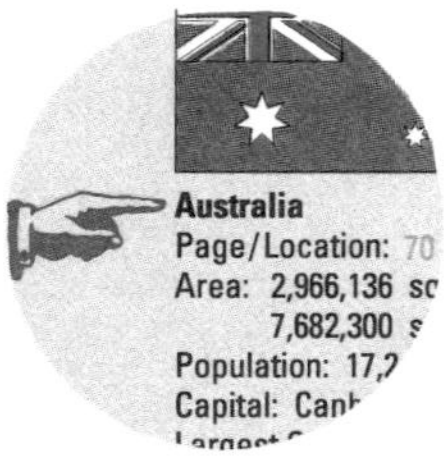

World Reference Guide
This concise guide lists the countries of the world alphabetically. If you're looking for the largest scale map of any country, you'll find a page and alpha-numeric reference at a glance, as well as information about each country, including its flag.

Master Index
When you're looking for a specific place or physical feature, your quickest route is the Master Index. This 6,000-entry alphabetical index lists both the page number and alpha-numeric reference for major places and features in Maps of the World.

This new atlas is created from a unique digital database, and its computer-generated maps represent a new phase in map-making technology.

How Computer-Generated Maps Are Made

To build a digital database capable of generating this world atlas, the latitude and longitude of every significant town, river, coastline, natural and political border, transportation network and peak elevation was researched and digitized. Hundreds of millions of data points describing every important geographic feature are organized into thousands of different map feature codes.

There are no maps in this unique system. Rather, it consists entirely of coded points, lines and polygons. To create a map, cartographers simply determine what specific information they wish to show, based upon considerations of scale, size, density and importance of different features.

New technology developed by mathematical physicist Mitchell Feigenbaum uses fractal geometry to describe and re-configure coastlines, borders and mountain ranges to fit a variety of map scales and projections. Dr. Feigenbaum has also created a computerized type placement program which allows thousands of map labels to be placed accurately in minutes. After these steps have been completed, the computer then draws the final map.

Each section of this atlas has been designed to be both easy and enjoyable to use. Familiarizing yourself with its organization will help you to benefit fully from its use.

World Flags and Reference Guide

This colorful section portrays each nation of the world, its flag, important geographical data, such as size, population and capital, and its location in the Maps of the World section.

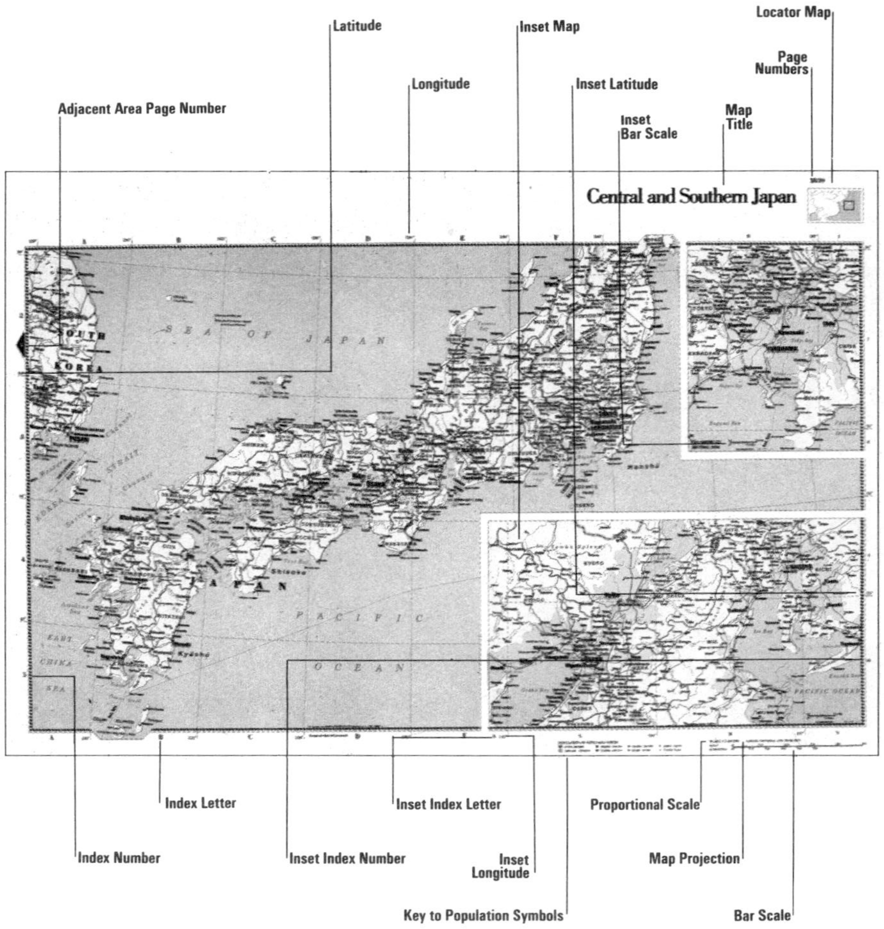

Symbols Used on Maps of the World

First Order (National) Boundary	City and Urban Area Limits	Rome — First Order (National) Capital
First Order Water Boundary	Demilitarized Zone	Belfast — Second Order (Internal) Capital
First Order Disputed Boundary	National Park/Preserve/Scenic Area	Hull — Third Order (Internal) Capital
Second Order (Internal) Boundary	National Forest/Forest Reserve	Neighborhood
Second Order Water Boundary	National Wilderness/Grassland	Pass
Second Order Disputed Boundary	National Recreation Area/Monument	Ruins
Third Order (Internal) Boundary	National Seashore/Lakeshore	Falls
Undefined Boundary	National Wildlife/Wilderness Area	Rapids
International Date Line	Native Reservation/Reserve	Dam
Shoreline, River	Military/Government Reservation	Point Elevation
Intermittent River	Lake, Reservoir	Park
Canal/Aqueduct	Intermittent Lake	Wildlife Area
Continental Divide	Dry Lake	Point of Interest
Highways/Roads	Salt Pan	Well
Railroads	Desert/Sand Area	International Airport
Ferries	Swamp	Other Airport
Tunnels (Road, Railroad)	Lava Flow	Air Base
Ancient Walls	Glacier	Naval Base

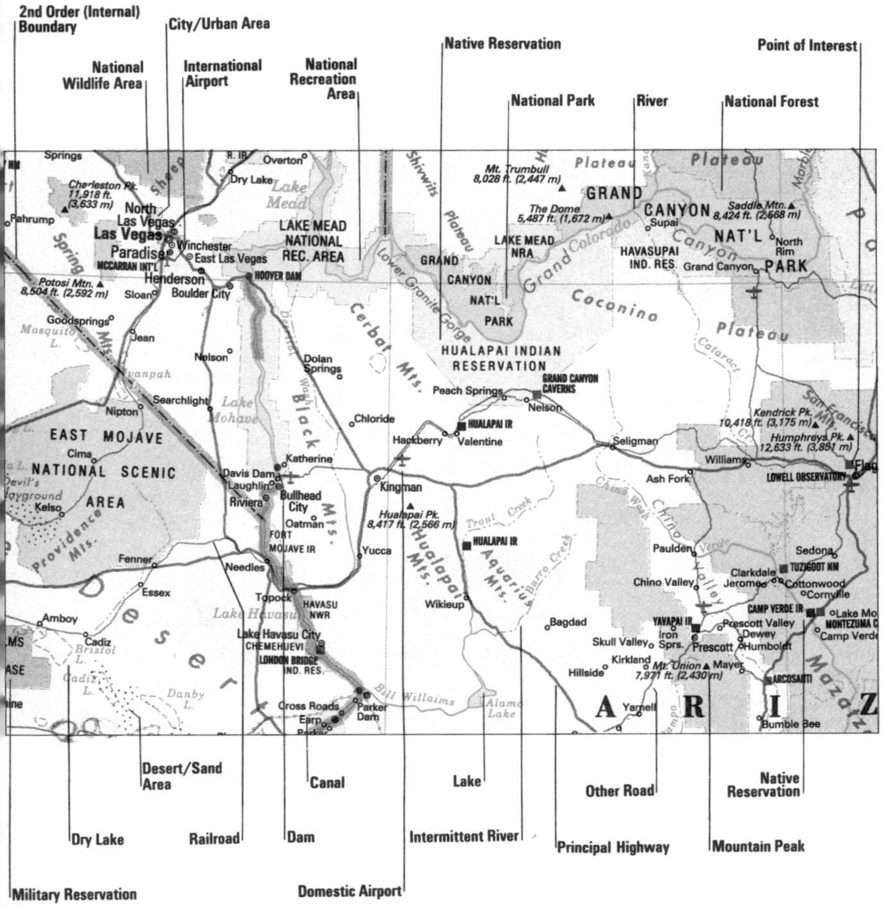

Principal Map Abbreviations

Abor. Rsv.	Aboriginal Reserve	Ind. Res.	Indian Reservation	NWR	National Wildlife Reserve
Admin.	Administration	Int'l	International	Obl.	Oblast
AFB	Air Force Base	IR	Indian Reservation	Occ.	Occupied
Amm. Dep.	Ammunition Depot	Isth.	Isthmus	Okr.	Okrug
Arch.	Archipelago	Jct.	Junction	Par.	Parish
Arpt.	Airport	L.	Lake	Passg.	Passage
Aut.	Autonomous	Lag.	Lagoon	Pen.	Peninsula
B.	Bay	Lakesh.	Lakeshore	Pk.	Peak
Bfld.	Battlefield	Mem.	Memorial	Plat.	Plateau
Bk.	Brook	Mil.	Military	PN	Park National
Bor.	Borough	Miss.	Missile	Pref.	Prefecture
Br.	Branch	Mon.	Monument	Prom.	Promontory
C.	Cape	Mt.	Mount	Prov.	Province
Can.	Canal	Mtn.	Mountain	Prsv.	Preserve
Cap.	Capital	Mts.	Mountains	Pt.	Point
C.G.	Coast Guard	Nat.	Natural	R.	River
Chan.	Channel	Nat'l	National	RA	Recreation Area
Co.	County	Nav.	Naval	Ra.	Range
Cr.	Creek	NB	National Battlefield	Rec.	Recreation(al)
Ctr.	Center	NBP	National Battlefield Park	Ref.	Refuge
Dep.	Depot	NBS	National Battlefield Site	Reg.	Region
Depr.	Depression	NHP	National Historical Park	Rep.	Republic
Dept.	Department	NHPP	National Historical Park and Preserve	Res.	Reservoir, Reservation
Des.	Desert	NHS	National Historic Site	Rvwy.	Riverway
Dist.	District	NL	National Lakeshore	Sa.	Sierra
DMZ	Demilitarized Zone	NM	National Monument	Sd.	Sound
Dpcy.	Dependency	NMEMP	National Memorial Park	Seash.	Seashore
Eng.	Engineering	NMILP	National Military Park	So.	Southern
Est.	Estuary	No.	Northern	SP	State Park
Fd.	Fiord, Fjord	NP	National Park	Spr., Sprs.	Spring, Springs
Fed.	Federal	NPP	National Park and Preserve	St.	State
Fk.	Fork	NPRSV	National Preserve	Sta.	Station
Fld.	Field	NRA	National Recreation Area	Stm.	Stream
For.	Forest	NRSV	National Reserve	Str.	Strait
Ft.	Fort	NS	National Seashore	Terr.	Territory
G.	Gulf			Tun.	Tunnel
Gov.	Governor			Twp.	Township
Govt.	Government			Val.	Valley
Gd.	Grand			Vill.	Village
Gt.	Great			Vol.	Volcano
Har.	Harbor			Wild.	Wildlife, Wilderness
Hd.	Head			Wtr.	Water
Hist.	Historic(al)				
Hts.	Heights				
I., Is.	Island(s)				

World Statistics

World Statistics lists the dimensions of the earth's principal mountains, islands, rivers and lakes, along with other useful geographic information.

Maps of the World

These detailed regional maps are arranged by continent, and introduced by a political map of that continent. The continent maps, which utilize Hammond's new Optimal Conformal projection, are distinguished by individual colors for each country to highlight political divisions.

On the regional maps, different colors and textures highlight distinctive features such as parks, forests, deserts and urban areas. These maps also provide considerable information concerning geographic features and political divisions.

Master Index

This is an A-Z listing of names found on the political maps. It also has its own abbreviation list which, along with other Index keys, appears on page 110.

Map Scales

A map's scale is the relationship of any length on the map to an identical length on the earth's surface. A scale of 1:3,000,000 means that one inch on the map represents 3,000,000 inches (47 miles, 76 km.) on the earth's surface. Thus, a 1:1,000,000 scale is larger than 1:3,000,000, just as 1/1 is larger than 1/3.

The most densely populated areas are shown at a scale of 1:1,170,000, while selected metropolitan areas are covered at either 1:587,000 or 1:1,170,000. Other populous areas are presented at 1:3,500,000 and 1:7,000,000, allowing you to accurately compare areas and distances of similar regions. Remaining regions are scaled at 1:10,500,000. The continent maps, as well as the United States, Canada, Russia, Pacific and World have smaller scales.

Boundary Policies

This atlas observes the boundary policies of the U.S. Department of State. Boundary disputes are customarily handled with a special symbol treatment, but de facto boundaries are favored if they seem to have any degree of permanence, in the belief that boundaries should reflect current geographic and political realities. The portrayal of independent nations in the atlas follows their recognition by the United Nations and/or the United States government.

Hammond also uses accepted conventional names for certain major foreign places. Usually, space permits the inclusion of the local form in parentheses. To make the maps more readily understandable to English-speaking readers, many foreign physical features are translated into more recognizable English forms.

A Word About Names

Our source for all foreign names and physical names in the United States is the decision lists of the U.S. Board of Geographic Names, which contain hundreds of thousands of place names. If a place is not listed, the Atlas follows the name form appearing on official foreign maps or in official gazetteers of the country concerned. For rendering domestic city, town and village names, this atlas follows the forms and spelling of the U.S. Postal Service.

World Flags and Reference Guide

Afghanistan
Page/Location: 53/H2
Area: 250,775 sq. mi.
649,507 sq. km.
Population: 16,450,000
Capital: Kabul
Largest City: Kabul
Highest Point: Noshaq
Monetary Unit: afghani

Albania
Page/Location: 39/F2
Area: 11,100 sq. mi.
28,749 sq. km.
Population: 3,335,000
Capital: Tiranë
Largest City: Tiranë
Highest Point: Korab
Monetary Unit: lek

Algeria
Page/Location: 76/F2
Area: 919,591 sq. mi.
2,381,740 sq. km.
Population: 26,022,000
Capital: Algiers
Largest City: Algiers
Highest Point: Tahat
Monetary Unit: Algerian dinar

Andorra
Page/Location: 35/F1
Area: 188 sq. mi.
487 sq. km.
Population: 53,000
Capital: Andorra la Vella
Largest City: Andorra la Vella
Highest Point: Coma Pedrosa
Monetary Unit: Fr. franc, Sp. peseta

Angola
Page/Location: 82/C3
Area: 481,351 sq. mi.
1,246,700 sq. km.
Population: 8,668,000
Capital: Luanda
Largest City: Luanda
Highest Point: Morro de Môco
Monetary Unit: kwanza

Antigua and Barbuda
Page/Location: 104/F3
Area: 171 sq. mi.
443 sq. km.
Population: 64,000
Capital: St. John's
Largest City: St. John's
Highest Point: Boggy Peak
Monetary Unit: East Caribbean dollar

Argentina
Page/Location: 109/C4
Area: 1,072,070 sq. mi.
2,776,661 sq. km.
Population: 32,664,000
Capital: Buenos Aires
Largest City: Buenos Aires
Highest Point: Cerro Aconcagua
Monetary Unit: Argentine peso

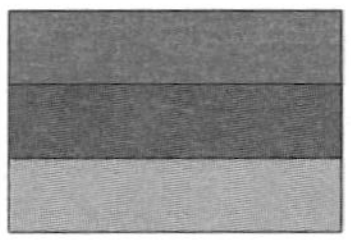

Armenia
Page/Location: 45/H5
Area: 11,506 sq. mi.
29,800 sq. km.
Population: 3,283,000
Capital: Yerevan
Largest City: Yerevan
Highest Point: Alagez
Monetary Unit: Armenian ruble

Australia
Page/Location: 70
Area: 2,966,136 sq. mi.
7,682,300 sq. km.
Population: 17,288,000
Capital: Canberra
Largest City: Sydney
Highest Point: Mt. Kosciusko
Monetary Unit: Australian dollar

Austria
Page/Location: 33/L3
Area: 32,375 sq. mi.
83,851 sq. km.
Population: 7,666,000
Capital: Vienna
Largest City: Vienna
Highest Point: Grossglockner
Monetary Unit: schilling

Azerbaijan
Page/Location: 45/H4
Area: 33,436 sq. mi.
86,600 sq. km.
Population: 7,029,000
Capital: Baku
Largest City: Baku
Highest Point: Bazardyuzyu
Monetary Unit: manat

Bahamas
Page/Location: 104/B2
Area: 5,382 sq. mi.
13,939 sq. km.
Population: 252,000
Capital: Nassau
Largest City: Nassau
Highest Point: 207 ft. (63 m)
Monetary Unit: Bahamian dollar

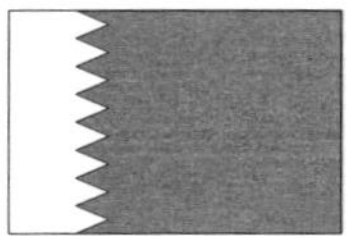

Bahrain
Page/Location: 52/F3
Area: 240 sq. mi.
622 sq. km.
Population: 537,000
Capital: Manama
Largest City: Manama
Highest Point: Jabal Dukhān
Monetary Unit: Bahraini dinar

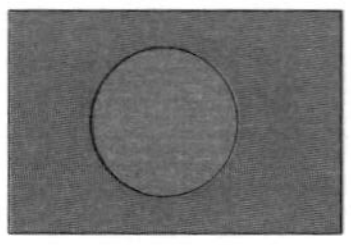

Bangladesh
Page/Location: 60/E3
Area: 55,126 sq. mi.
142,776 sq. km.
Population: 116,601,000
Capital: Dhaka
Largest City: Dhaka
Highest Point: Keokradong
Monetary Unit: taka

Barbados
Page/Location: 104/G4
Area: 166 sq. mi.
430 sq. km.
Population: 255,000
Capital: Bridgetown
Largest City: Bridgetown
Highest Point: Mt. Hillaby
Monetary Unit: Barbadian dollar

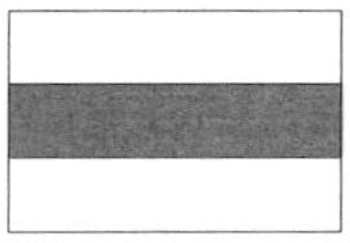

Belarus
Page/Location: 18/F3
Area: 80,154 sq. mi.
207,600 sq. km.
Population: 10,200,000
Capital: Minsk
Largest City: Minsk
Highest Point: Dzerzhinskaya
Monetary Unit: Belarusian ruble

Belgium
Page/Location: 30/C2
Area: 11,781 sq. mi.
30,513 sq. km.
Population: 9,922,000
Capital: Brussels
Largest City: Brussels
Highest Point: Botrange
Monetary Unit: Belgian franc

Belize
Page/Location: 102/D2
Area: 8,867 sq. mi.
22,966 sq. km.
Population: 228,000
Capital: Belmopan
Largest City: Belize City
Highest Point: Victoria Peak
Monetary Unit: Belize dollar

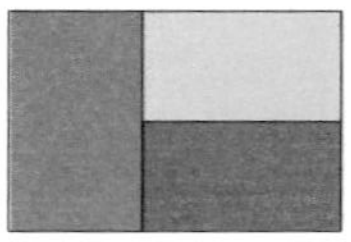

Benin
Page/Location: 79/F4
Area: 43,483 sq. mi.
112,620 sq. km.
Population: 4,832,000
Capital: Porto-Novo
Largest City: Cotonou
Highest Point: Nassoukou
Monetary Unit: CFA franc

Bhutan
Page/Location: 62/E2
Area: 18,147 sq. mi.
47,000 sq. km.
Population: 1,598,000
Capital: Thimphu
Largest City: Thimphu
Highest Point: Kula Kangri
Monetary Unit: ngultrum

Bolivia
Page/Location: 106/F7
Area: 424,163 sq. mi.
1,098,582 sq. km.
Population: 7,157,000
Capital: La Paz; Sucre
Largest City: La Paz
Highest Point: Nevado Ancohuma
Monetary Unit: Bolivian peso

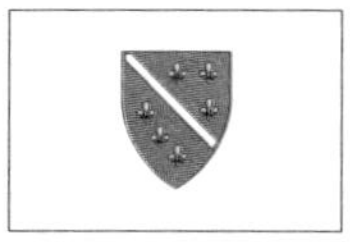

Bosnia and Herzegovina
Page/Location: 40/C3
Area: 19,940 sq. mi.
51,645 sq. km.
Population: 4,124,256
Capital: Sarajevo
Largest City: Sarajevo
Highest Point: Maglič
Monetary Unit: —

Botswana
Page/Location: 52/D5
Area: 224,764 sq. mi.
582,139 sq. km.
Population: 1,258,000
Capital: Gaborone
Largest City: Gaborone
Highest Point: Tsodilo Hills
Monetary Unit: pula

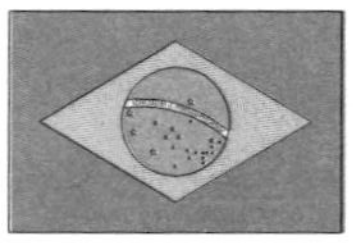

Brazil
Page/Location: 105/D3
Area: 3,284,426 sq. mi.
8,506,663 sq. km.
Population: 155,356,000
Capital: Brasília
Largest City: São Paulo
Highest Point: Pico da Neblina
Monetary Unit: cruzeiro real

Brunei
Page/Location: 66/D2
Area: 2,226 sq. mi.
5,765 sq. km.
Population: 398,000
Capital: Bandar Seri Begawan
Largest City: Bandar Seri Begawan
Highest Point: Bukit Pagon
Monetary Unit: Brunei dollar

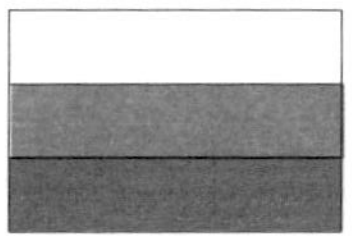

Bulgaria
Page/Location: 41/G4
Area: 42,823 sq. mi.
110,912 sq. km.
Population: 8,911,000
Capital: Sofia
Largest City: Sofia
Highest Point: Musala
Monetary Unit: lev

Burkina Faso
Page/Location: 79/E3
Area: 105,869 sq. mi.
274,200 sq. km.
Population: 9,360,000
Capital: Ouagadougou
Largest City: Ouagadougou
Highest Point: 2,405 ft. (733 m)
Monetary Unit: CFA franc

Burma
Page/Location: 63/G3
Area: 261,789 sq. mi.
678,034 sq. km.
Population: 42,112,000
Capital: Rangoon
Largest City: Rangoon
Highest Point: Hkakabo Razi
Monetary Unit: kyat

Burundi
Page/Location: 82/E1
Area: 10,747 sq. mi.
27,835 sq. km.
Population: 5,831,000
Capital: Bujumbura
Largest City: Bujumbura
Highest Point: 8,760 ft. (2,670 m)
Monetary Unit: Burundi franc

Cambodia
Page/Location: 65/D3
Area: 69,898 sq. mi.
181,036 sq. km.
Population: 7,146,000
Capital: Phnom Penh
Largest City: Phnom Penh
Highest Point: Phnum Aoral
Monetary Unit: riel

Cameroon
Page/Location: 76/H7
Area: 183,568 sq. mi.
475,441 sq. km.
Population: 11,390,000
Capital: Yaoundé
Largest City: Douala
Highest Point: Mt. Cameroon
Monetary Unit: CFA franc

Canada
Page/Location: 86
Area: 3,851,787 sq. mi.
9,976,139 sq. km.
Population: 27,296,859
Capital: Ottawa
Largest City: Toronto
Highest Point: Mt. Logan
Monetary Unit: Canadian dollar

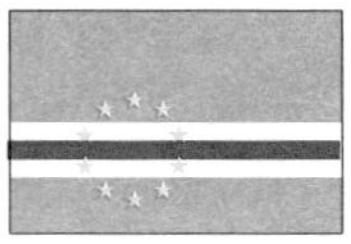

Cape Verde
Page/Location: 74/K9
Area: 1,557 sq. mi.
4,033 sq. km.
Population: 387,000
Capital: Praia
Largest City: Praia
Highest Point: 9,282 ft. (2,829 m)
Monetary Unit: Cape Verde escudo

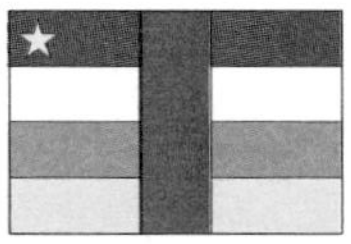

Central African Republic
Page/Location: 77/J6
Area: 242,000 sq. mi.
626,780 sq. km.
Population: 2,952,000
Capital: Bangui
Largest City: Bangui
Highest Point: Mt. Kayagangiri
Monetary Unit: CFA franc

Chad
Page/Location: 77/J4
Area: 495,752 sq. mi.
1,283,998 sq. km.
Population: 5,122,000
Capital: N'Djamena
Largest City: N'Djamena
Highest Point: Emi Koussi
Monetary Unit: CFA franc

Chile
Page/Location: 109/B3
Area: 292,257 sq. mi.
756,946 sq. km.
Population: 13,287,000
Capital: Santiago
Largest City: Santiago
Highest Point: Nevado Ojos del Salado
Monetary Unit: Chilean peso

China
Page/Location: 48/J6
Area: 3,691,000 sq. mi.
9,559,690 sq. km.
Population: 1,151,487,000
Capital: Beijing
Largest City: Shanghai
Highest Point: Mt. Everest
Monetary Unit: yuan

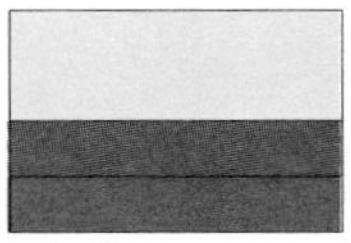

Colombia
Page/Location: 106/D3
Area: 439,513 sq. mi.
1,138,339 sq. km.
Population: 33,778,000
Capital: Bogotá
Largest City: Bogotá
Highest Point: Pico Cristóbal Colón
Monetary Unit: Colombian peso

Comoros
Page/Location: 74/G6
Area: 719 sq. mi.
1,862 sq. km.
Population: 477,000
Capital: Moroni
Largest City: Moroni
Highest Point: Karthala
Monetary Unit: Comorian franc

Congo
Page/Location: 74/D5
Area: 132,046 sq. mi.
342,000 sq. km.
Population: 2,309,000
Capital: Brazzaville
Largest City: Brazzaville
Highest Point: Lékéti Mts.
Monetary Unit: CFA franc

Costa Rica
Page/Location: 103/F4
Area: 19,575 sq. mi.
50,700 sq. km.
Population: 3,111,000
Capital: San José
Largest City: San José
Highest Point: Cerro Chirripó Grande
Monetary Unit: Costa Rican colón

Croatia
Page/Location: 40/C3
Area: 22,050 sq. mi.
57,110 sq. km.
Population: 4,601,469
Capital: Zagreb
Largest City: Zagreb
Highest Point: Veliki Troglav
Monetary Unit: Croatian dinar

Cuba
Page/Location: 103/F1
Area: 44,206 sq. mi.
114,494 sq. km.
Population: 10,732,000
Capital: Havana
Largest City: Havana
Highest Point: Pico Turquino
Monetary Unit: Cuban peso

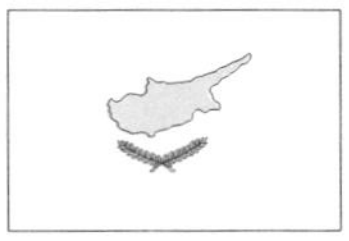

Cyprus
Page/Location: 49/C2
Area: 3,473 sq. mi.
8,995 sq. km.
Population: 709,000
Capital: Nicosia
Largest City: Nicosia
Highest Point: Olympus
Monetary Unit: Cypriot pound

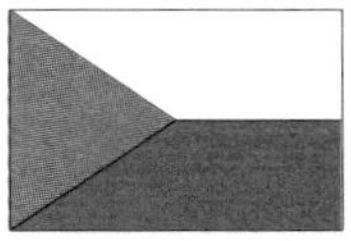

Czech Republic
Page/Location: 27/H4
Area: 30,449 sq. mi.
78,863 sq. km.
Population: 10,291,927
Capital: Prague
Largest City: Prague
Highest Point: Sněžka
Monetary Unit: Czech koruna

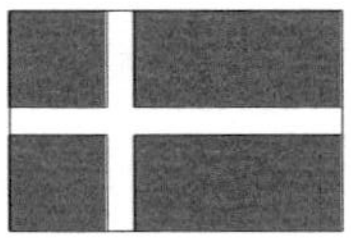

Denmark
Page/Location: 20/C5
Area: 16,629 sq. mi.
43,069 sq. km.
Population: 5,133,000
Capital: Copenhagen
Largest City: Copenhagen
Highest Point: Yding Skovhøj
Monetary Unit: Danish krone

Djibouti
Page/Location: 77/P5
Area: 8,880 sq. mi.
23,000 sq. km.
Population: 346,000
Capital: Djibouti
Largest City: Djibouti
Highest Point: Moussa Ali
Monetary Unit: Djibouti franc

Dominica
Page/Location: 104/F4
Area: 290 sq. mi.
751 sq. km.
Population: 86,000
Capital: Roseau
Largest City: Roseau
Highest Point: Morne Diablotin
Monetary Unit: Dominican dollar

Dominican Republic
Page/Location: 104/D3
Area: 18,704 sq. mi.
48,443 sq. km.
Population: 7,385,000
Capital: Santo Domingo
Largest City: Santo Domingo
Highest Point: Pico Duarte
Monetary Unit: Dominican peso

Ecuador
Page/Location: 106/C4
Area: 109,483 sq. mi.
283,561 sq. km.
Population: 10,752,000
Capital: Quito
Largest City: Guayaquil
Highest Point: Chimborazo
Monetary Unit: sucre

Egypt
Page/Location: 77/L2
Area: 386,659 sq. mi.
1,001,447 sq. km.
Population: 54,452,000
Capital: Cairo
Largest City: Cairo
Highest Point: Mt. Catherine
Monetary Unit: Egyptian pound

El Salvador
Page/Location: 102/D3
Area: 8,260 sq. mi.
21,393 sq. km.
Population: 5,419,000
Capital: San Salvador
Largest City: San Salvador
Highest Point: Santa Ana
Monetary Unit: Salvadoran colón

Equatorial Guinea
Page/Location: 76/G7
Area: 10,831 sq. mi.
28,052 sq. km.
Population: 379,000
Capital: Malabo
Largest City: Malabo
Highest Point: Pico de Santa Isabel
Monetary Unit: CFA franc

Eritrea
Page/Location: 77/N4
Area: 36,170 sq. mi.
93,679 sq. km.
Population: 3,500,000
Capital: Āsmera
Largest City: Āsmera
Highest Point: Soira
Monetary Unit: birr

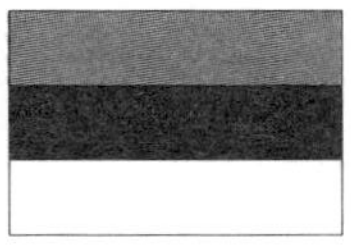

Estonia
Page/Location: 42/E4
Area: 17,413 sq. mi.
45,100 sq. km.
Population: 1,573,000
Capital: Tallinn
Largest City: Tallinn
Highest Point: Munamägi
Monetary Unit: kroon

Ethiopia
Page/Location: 77/N6
Area: 435,606 sq. mi.
1,128,220 sq. km.
Population: 51,617,000
Capital: Addis Ababa
Largest City: Addis Ababa
Highest Point: Ras Dashen Terara
Monetary Unit: birr

Fiji
Page/Location: 68/G6
Area: 7,055 sq. mi.
18,272 sq. km.
Population: 744,000
Capital: Suva
Largest City: Suva
Highest Point: Tomaniivi
Monetary Unit: Fijian dollar

Finland
Page/Location: 20/H2
Area: 130,128 sq. mi.
337,032 sq. km.
Population: 4,991,000
Capital: Helsinki
Largest City: Helsinki
Highest Point: Kahperusvaara
Monetary Unit: markka

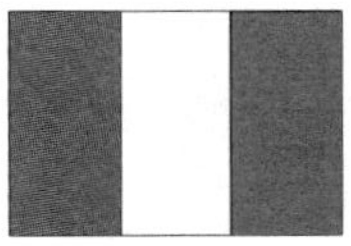

France
Page/Location: 32/D3
Area: 210,038 sq. mi.
543,998 sq. km.
Population: 58,073,553
Capital: Paris
Largest City: Paris
Highest Point: Mont Blanc
Monetary Unit: French franc

Gabon
Page/Location: 76/H7
Area: 103,346 sq. mi.
267,666 sq. km.
Population: 1,080,000
Capital: Libreville
Largest City: Libreville
Highest Point: Mt. Iboundji
Monetary Unit: CFA franc

Gambia
Page/Location: 78/B3
Area: 4,127 sq. mi.
10,689 sq. km.
Population: 875,000
Capital: Banjul
Largest City: Banjul
Highest Point: 98 ft. (30 m)
Monetary Unit: dalasi

Georgia
Page/Location: 45/G4
Area: 26,911 sq. mi.
69,700 sq. km.
Population: 5,449,000
Capital: Tbilisi
Largest City: Tbilisi
Highest Point: Kazbek
Monetary Unit: lari

Germany
Page/Location: 26/E3
Area: 137,753 sq. mi.
356,780 sq. km.
Population: 79,548,000
Capital: Berlin
Largest City: Berlin
Highest Point: Zugspitze
Monetary Unit: Deutsche mark

Ghana
Page/Location: 79/E4
Area: 92,099 sq. mi.
238,536 sq. km.
Population: 15,617,000
Capital: Accra
Largest City: Accra
Highest Point: Afadjoto
Monetary Unit: cedi

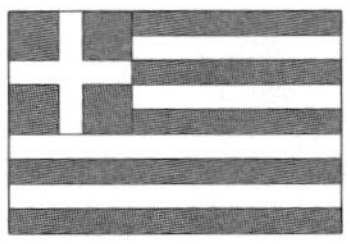

Greece
Page/Location: 39/G3
Area: 50,944 sq. mi.
131,945 sq. km.
Population: 10,043,000
Capital: Athens
Largest City: Athens
Highest Point: Mt. Olympus
Monetary Unit: drachma

Grenada
Page/Location: 104/F5
Area: 133 sq. mi.
344 sq. km.
Population: 84,000
Capital: St. George's
Largest City: St. George's
Highest Point: Mt. St. Catherine
Monetary Unit: East Caribbean dollar

World Flags and Reference Guide

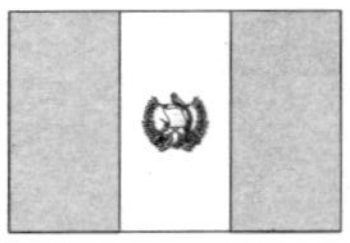

Guatemala
Page/Location: 102/D3
Area: 42,042 sq. mi.
108,889 sq. km.
Population: 9,266,000
Capital: Guatemala
Largest City: Guatemala
Highest Point: Tajumulco
Monetary Unit: quetzal

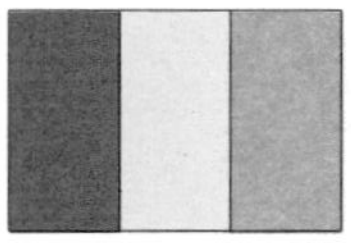

Guinea
Page/Location: 78/C4
Area: 94,925 sq. mi.
245,856 sq. km.
Population: 7,456,000
Capital: Conakry
Largest City: Conakry
Highest Point: Mt. Nimba
Monetary Unit: Guinea franc

Guinea-Bissau
Page/Location: 78/B3
Area: 13,948 sq. mi.
36,125 sq. km.
Population: 943,000
Capital: Bissau
Largest City: Bissau
Highest Point: 689 ft. (210 m)
Monetary Unit: Guinea-Bissau peso

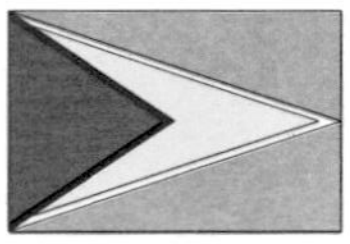

Guyana
Page/Location: 106/G2
Area: 83,000 sq. mi.
214,970 sq. km.
Population: 1,024,000
Capital: Georgetown
Largest City: Georgetown
Highest Point: Mt. Roraima
Monetary Unit: Guyana dollar

Haiti
Page/Location: 103/H2
Area: 10,694 sq. mi.
27,697 sq. km.
Population: 6,287,000
Capital: Port-au-Prince
Largest City: Port-au-Prince
Highest Point: Pic la Selle
Monetary Unit: gourde

Honduras
Page/Location 102/E3
Area: 43,277 sq. mi.
112,087 sq. km.
Population: 4,949,000
Capital: Tegucigalpa
Largest City: Tegucigalpa
Highest Point: Cerro de las Minas
Monetary Unit: lempira

Hungary
Page/Location: 40/D2
Area: 35,919 sq. mi.
93,030 sq. km.
Population: 10,558,000
Capital: Budapest
Largest City: Budapest
Highest Point: Kékes
Monetary Unit: forint

Iceland
Page/Location: 20/N7
Area: 39,768 sq. mi.
103,000 sq. km.
Population: 260,000
Capital: Reykjavík
Largest City: Reykjavík
Highest Point: Hvannadalshnúkur
Monetary Unit: króna

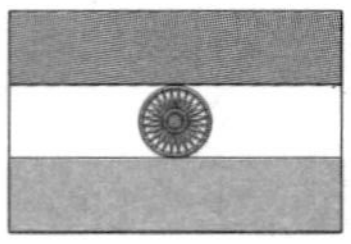

India
Page/Location: 62/C3
Area: 1,269,339 sq. mi.
3,287,588 sq. km.
Population: 869,515,000
Capital: New Delhi
Largest City: Calcutta
Highest Point: Nanda Devi
Monetary Unit: Indian rupee

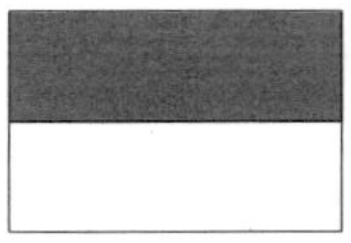

Indonesia
Page/Location: 67/E4
Area: 788,430 sq. mi.
2, 042,034 sq. km.
Population: 19,560,000
Capital: Jakarta
Largest City: Jakarta
Highest Point: Puncak Jaya
Monetary Unit: rupiah

Iran
Page/Location: 51/H3
Area: 636,293 sq. mi.
1,648,000 sq. km.
Population: 59,051,000
Capital: Tehran
Largest City: Tehran
Highest Point: Qolleh-ye Damāvand
Monetary Unit: Iranian rial

Iraq
Page/Location: 50/E3
Area: 172,476 sq. mi.
446,713 sq. km.
Population: 19,525,000
Capital: Baghdad
Largest City: Baghdad
Highest Point: Haji Ibrahim
Monetary Unit: Iraqi dinar

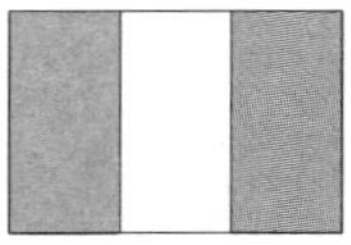

Ireland
Page/Location: 21/A4
Area: 27,136 sq. mi.
70,282 sq. km.
Population: 3,489,000
Capital: Dublin
Largest City: Dublin
Highest Point: Carrantuohill
Monetary Unit: Irish pound

Israel
Page/Location: 49/D3
Area: 7,847 sq. mi.
20,324 sq. km.
Population: 4,558,000
Capital: Jerusalem
Largest City: Tel Aviv-Yafo
Highest Point: Har Meron
Monetary Unit: shekel

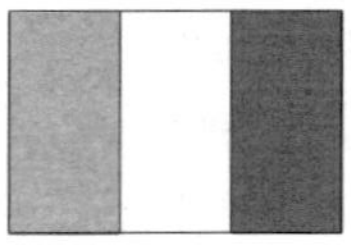

Italy
Page/Location: 18/E4
Area: 116,303 sq. mi.
301,225 sq. km.
Population: 57,772,000
Capital: Rome
Largest City: Rome
Highest Point: Monte Rosa
Monetary Unit: Italian lira

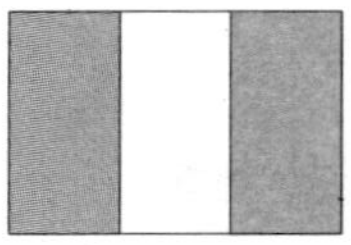

Ivory Coast
Page/Location: 78/D5
Area: 124,504 sq. mi.
322,465 sq. km.
Population: 12,978,000
Capital: Yamoussoukro
Largest City: Abidjan
Highest Point: Mt. Nimba
Monetary Unit: CFA franc

Jamaica
Page/Location: 103/G2
Area: 4,411 sq. mi.
11,424 sq. km.
Population: 2,489,000
Capital: Kingston
Largest City: Kingston
Highest Point: Blue Mountain Pk.
Monetary Unit: Jamaican dollar

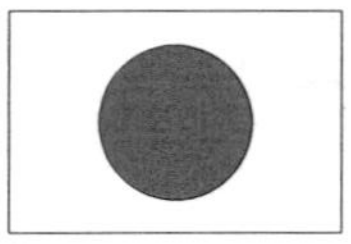

Japan
Page/Location: 55/M4
Area: 145,730 sq. mi.
377,441 sq. km.
Population: 124,017,000
Capital: Tokyo
Largest City: Tokyo
Highest Point: Fujiyama
Monetary Unit: yen

Jordan
Page/Location: 49/E4
Area: 35,000 sq. mi.
90,650 sq. km.
Population: 3,413,000
Capital: Amman
Largest City: Amman
Highest Point: Jabal Ramm
Monetary Unit: Jordanian dinar

Kazakhstan
Page/Location: 46/G5
Area: 1,048,300 sq. mi.
2,715,100 sq. km.
Population: 16,538,000
Capital: Alma-Ata
Largest City: Alma-Ata
Highest Point: Khan-Tengri
Monetary Unit: Kazakhstani ruble

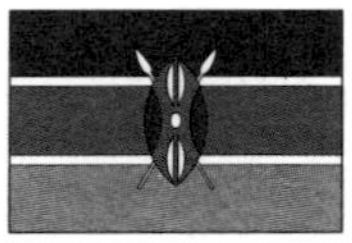

Kenya
Page/Location: 77/M7
Area: 224,960 sq. mi.
582,646 sq. km.
Population: 25,242,000
Capital: Nairobi
Largest City: Nairobi
Highest Point: Mt. Kenya
Monetary Unit: Kenya shilling

Kiribati
Page/Location: 69/H5
Area: 291 sq. mi.
754 sq. km.
Population: 71,000
Capital: Bairiki
Largest City: —
Highest Point: Banaba Island
Monetary Unit: Australian dollar

Korea, North
Page/Location: 58/D2
Area: 46,540 sq. mi.
120,539 sq. km.
Population: 21,815,000
Capital: P'yŏngyang
Largest City: P'yŏngyang
Highest Point: Paektu-san
Monetary Unit: North Korean won

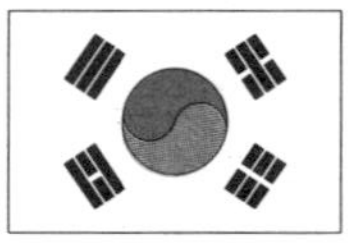

Korea, South
Page/Location: 58/D4
Area: 38,175 sq. mi.
98,873 sq. km.
Population: 43,134,000
Capital: Seoul
Largest City: Seoul
Highest Point: Halla-san
Monetary Unit: South Korean won

Kuwait
Page/Location: 51/F4
Area: 6,532 sq. mi.
16,918 sq. km.
Population: 2,204,000
Capital: Al Kuwait
Largest City: Al Kuwait
Highest Point: 951 ft. (290 m)
Monetary Unit: Kuwaiti dinar

Kyrgyzstan
Page/Location: 46/H5
Area: 76,641 sq. mi.
198,500 sq. km.
Population: 4,291,000
Capital: Bishkek
Largest City: Bishkek
Highest Point: Pik Pobedy
Monetary Unit: som

Laos
Page/Location: 65/C2
Area: 91,428 sq. mi.
236,800 sq. km.
Population: 4,113,000
Capital: Vientiane
Largest City: Vientiane
Highest Point: Phou Bia
Monetary Unit: kip

Latvia
Page/Location: 42/E4
Area: 24,595 sq. mi.
63,700 sq. km.
Population: 2,681,000
Capital: Riga
Largest City: Riga
Highest Point: Gaizina Kalns
Monetary Unit: lats

Lebanon
Page/Location: 49/D3
Area: 4,015 sq. mi.
10,399 sq. km.
Population: 3,385,000
Capital: Beirut
Largest City: Beirut
Highest Point: Qurnat as Sawdā
Monetary Unit: Lebanese pound

Lesotho
Page/Location: 80/E3
Area: 11,720 sq. mi.
30,355 sq. km.
Population: 1,801,000
Capital: Maseru
Largest City: Maseru
Highest Point: Thabana-Ntlenyana
Monetary Unit: loti

Liberia
Page/Location: 78/C4
Area: 43,000 sq. mi.
111,370 sq. km.
Population: 2,730,000
Capital: Monrovia
Largest City: Monrovia
Highest Point: Mt. Wuteve
Monetary Unit: Liberian dollar

Libya
Page/Location: 77/J2
Area: 679,358 sq. mi.
1,759,537 sq. km.
Population: 4,353,000
Capital: Tripoli
Largest City: Tripoli
Highest Point: Picco Bette
Monetary Unit: Libyan dinar

Liechtenstein
Page/Location: 37/F3
Area: 61 sq. mi.
158 sq. km.
Population: 28,000
Capital: Vaduz
Largest City: Vaduz
Highest Point: Grauspitz
Monetary Unit: Swiss franc

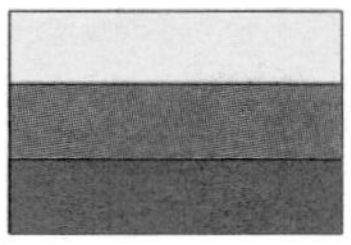

Lithuania
Page/Location: 42/D5
Area: 25,174 sq. mi.
65,200 sq. km.
Population: 3,690,000
Capital: Vilnius
Largest City: Vilnius
Highest Point: Nevaišių
Monetary Unit: litas

Luxembourg
Page/Location: 31/F4
Area: 999 sq. mi.
2,587 sq. km.
Population: 388,000
Capital: Luxembourg
Largest City: Luxembourg
Highest Point: Ardennes Plateau
Monetary Unit: Luxembourg franc

Macedonia
Page/Location: 39/G2
Area: 9,889 sq. mi.
25,612 sq. km.
Population: 1,909,136
Capital: Skopje
Largest City: Skopje
Highest Point: Korab
Monetary Unit: denar

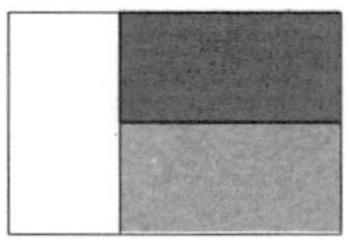

Madagascar
Page/Location: 81/H8
Area: 226,657 sq. mi.
587,041 sq. km.
Population: 12,185,000
Capital: Antananarivo
Largest City: Antananarivo
Highest Point: Maromokotro
Monetary Unit: Malagasy franc

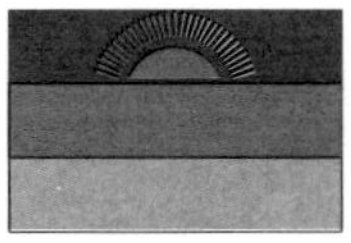

Malawi
Page/Location: 82/F3
Area: 45,747 sq. mi.
118, 485 sq. km.
Population: 9,438,000
Capital: Lilongwe
Largest City: Blantyre
Highest Point: Mulanje Mts.
Monetary Unit: Malawi kwacha

Malaysia
Page/Location: 67/C2
Area: 128,308 sq. mi.
332,318 sq. km.
Population: 17,982,000
Capital: Kuala Lumpur
Largest City: Kuala Lumpur
Highest Point: Gunung Kinabalu
Monetary Unit: ringgit

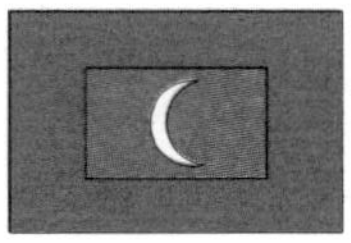

Maldives
Page/Location: 48/G9
Area: 115 sq. mi.
298 sq. km.
Population: 226,000
Capital: Male
Largest City: Male
Highest Point: 20 ft. (6 m)
Monetary Unit: rufiyaa

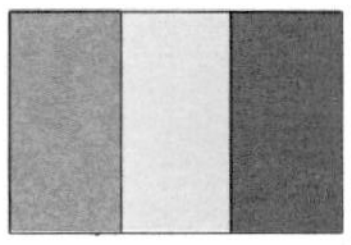

Mali
Page/Location: 76/E4
Area: 464,873 sq. mi.
1,204,021 sq. km.
Population: 8,339,000
Capital: Bamako
Largest City: Bamako
Highest Point: Hombori Tondo
Monetary Unit: CFA franc

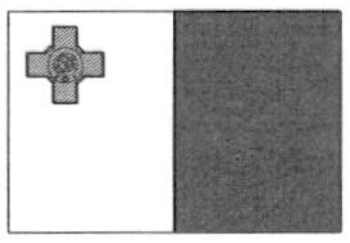

Malta
Page/Location: 38/D5
Area: 122 sq. mi.
316 sq. km.
Population: 356,000
Capital: Valletta
Largest City: Sliema
Highest Point: 830 ft. (253 m)
Monetary Unit: Maltese lira

Marshall Islands
Page/Location: 68/G3
Area: 70 sq. mi.
181 sq. km.
Population: 48,000
Capital: Majuro
Largest City: —
Highest Point: 20 ft. (6 m)
Monetary Unit: U.S. dollar

Mauritania
Page/Location: 76/C4
Area: 419,229 sq. mi.
1,085, 803 sq. km.
Population: 1,996,000
Capital: Nouakchott
Largest City: Nouakchott
Highest Point: Kediet Ijill
Monetary Unit: ouguiya

Mauritius
Page/Location: 81/S15
Area: 790 sq. mi.
2,046 sq. km.
Population: 1,081,000
Capital: Port Louis
Largest City: Port Louis
Highest Point: 2,713 ft. (827 m)
Monetary Unit: Mauritian rupee

Mexico
Page/Location: 84/G7
Area: 761,601 sq. mi.
1,972,546 sq. km.
Population: 90,007,000
Capital: Mexico City
Largest City: Mexico City
Highest Point: Citlaltépetl
Monetary Unit: Mexican peso

Micronesia
Page/Location: 68/D4
Area: 271 sq. mi.
702 sq. km.
Population: 108,000
Capital: Kolonia
Largest City: —
Highest Point: —
Monetary Unit: U.S. dollar

Moldova
Page/Location: 41/J2
Area: 13,012 sq. mi.
33,700 sq. km.
Population: 4,341,000
Capital: Chişinău
Largest City: Chişinău
Highest Point: 1,408 ft. (429 m)
Monetary Unit: leu

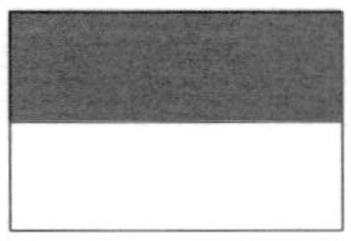

Monaco
Page/Location: 33/G5
Area: 368 acres
149 hectares
Population: 30,000
Capital: Monaco
Largest City: —
Highest Point: —
Monetary Unit: French franc

Mongolia
Page/Location: 54/D2
Area: 606,163 sq. mi.
1,569, 962 sq. km.
Population: 2,247,000
Capital: Ulaanbaatar
Largest City: Ulaanbaatar
Highest Point: Tavan Bogd Uul
Monetary Unit: tughrik

Morocco
Page/Location: 76/C1
Area: 172,414 sq. mi.
446,550 sq. km.
Population: 26,182,000
Capital: Rabat
Largest City: Casablanca
Highest Point: Jebel Toubkal
Monetary Unit: Moroccan dirham

Mozambique
Page/Location: 82/G4
Area: 303,769 sq. mi.
786,762 sq. km.
Population: 15,113,000
Capital: Maputo
Largest City: Maputo
Highest Point: Monte Binga
Monetary Unit: metical

Namibia
Page/Location: 82/C5
Area: 317,827 sq. mi.
823,172 sq. km.
Population: 1,521,000
Capital: Windhoek
Largest City: Windhoek
Highest Point: Brandberg
Monetary Unit: rand

Nauru
Page/Location: 68/F5
Area: 7.7 sq. mi.
20 sq. km.
Population: 9,000
Capital: Yaren (district)
Largest City: —
Highest Point: 230 ft. (70 m)
Monetary Unit: Australian dollar

Nepal
Page/Location: 62/D2
Area: 54,663 sq. mi.
141,577 sq. km.
Population: 19,612,000
Capital: Kathmandu
Largest City: Kathmandu
Highest Point: Mt. Everest
Monetary Unit: Nepalese rupee

Netherlands
Page/Location: 28/B5
Area: 15,892 sq. mi.
41,160 sq. km.
Population: 15,022,000
Capital: The Hague; Amsterdam
Largest City: Amsterdam
Highest Point: Vaalserberg
Monetary Unit: Netherlands guilder

New Zealand
Page/Location: 71/Q10
Area: 103,736 sq. mi.
268,676 sq. km.
Population: 3,309,000
Capital: Wellington
Largest City: Auckland
Highest Point: Mt. Cook
Monetary Unit: New Zealand dollar

Nicaragua
Page/Location: 103/E3
Area: 45,698 sq. mi.
118,358 sq. km.
Population: 3,752,000
Capital: Managua
Largest City: Managua
Highest Point: Pico Mogotón
Monetary Unit: córdoba

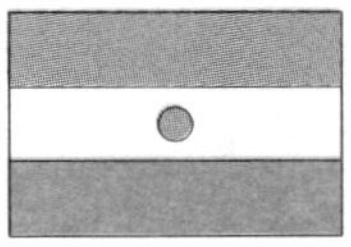

Niger
Page/Location: 76/G4
Area: 489,189 sq. mi.
1,267,000 sq. km.
Population: 8,154,000
Capital: Niamey
Largest City: Niamey
Highest Point: Bagzane
Monetary Unit: CFA franc

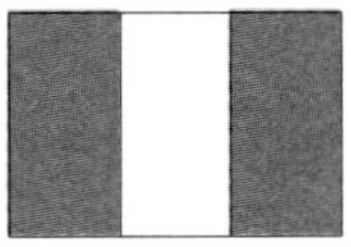

Nigeria
Page/Location: 76/G6
Area: 357,000 sq. mi.
924,630 sq. km.
Population: 122,471,000
Capital: Abuja
Largest City: Lagos
Highest Point: Dimlang
Monetary Unit: naira

Norway
Page/Location: 20/C3
Area: 125,053 sq. mi.
323,887 sq. km.
Population: 4,273,000
Capital: Oslo
Largest City: Oslo
Highest Point: Glittertjnden
Monetary Unit: Norwegian krone

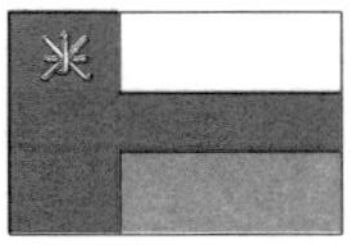

Oman
Page/Location: 53/G4
Area: 120,000 sq. mi.
310,800 sq. km.
Population: 1,534,000
Capital: Muscat
Largest City: Muscat
Highest Point: Jabal ash Shām
Monetary Unit: Omani rial

Pakistan
Page/Location: 53/H3
Area: 310,403 sq. mi.
803,944 sq. km.
Population: 117,490,000
Capital: Islamabad
Largest City: Karachi
Highest Point: K2 (Godwin Austen)
Monetary Unit: Pakistani rupee

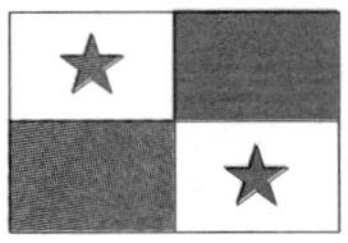

Panama
Page/Location: 103/F4
Area: 29,761 sq. mi.
77,082 sq. km.
Population: 2,476,000
Capital: Panamá
Largest City: Panamá
Highest Point: Barú
Monetary Unit: balboa

Papua New Guinea
Page/Location: 68/D5
Area: 183,540 sq. mi.
475,369 sq. km.
Population: 3,913,000
Capital: Port Moresby
Largest City: Port Moresby
Highest Point: Mt. Wilhelm
Monetary Unit: kina

Paraguay
Page/Location: 105/D5
Area: 157,047 sq. mi.
406,752 sq. km.
Population: 4,799,000
Capital: Asunción
Largest City: Asunción
Highest Point: Sierra de Amambay
Monetary Unit: guaraní

World Flags and Reference Guide

Peru
Page/Location: 106/C5
Area: 496,222 sq. mi.
1,285,215 sq. km.
Population: 22,362,000
Capital: Lima
Largest City: Lima
Highest Point: Nevado Huascarán
Monetary Unit: nuevo sol

Philippines
Page/Location: 48/M8
Area: 115,707 sq. mi.
299,681 sq. km.
Population: 65,759,000
Capital: Manila
Largest City: Manila
Highest Point: Mt. Apo
Monetary Unit: Philippine peso

Poland
Page/Location: 27/K2
Area: 120,725 sq. mi.
312,678 sq. km.
Population: 37,800,000
Capital: Warsaw
Largest City: Warsaw
Highest Point: Rysy
Monetary Unit: zloty

Portugal
Page/Location: 34/A3
Area: 35,549 sq. mi.
92,072 sq. km.
Population: 10,388,000
Capital: Lisbon
Largest City: Lisbon
Highest Point: Serra da Estrela
Monetary Unit: Portuguese escudo

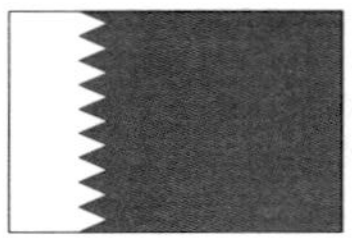

Qatar
Page/Location: 52/F3
Area: 4,247 sq. mi.
11,000 sq. km.
Population: 518,000
Capital: Doha
Largest City: Doha
Highest Point: Dukhān Heights
Monetary Unit: Qatari riyal

Romania
Page/Location: 41/F3
Area: 91,699 sq. mi.
237,500 sq. km.
Population: 23,397,000
Capital: Bucharest
Largest City: Bucharest
Highest Point: Moldoveanul
Monetary Unit: leu

Russia
Page/Location: 46/H3
Area: 6,592,812 sq. mi.
17,075,400 sq. km.
Population: 147,386,000
Capital: Moscow
Largest City: Moscow
Highest Point: El'brus
Monetary Unit: Russian ruble

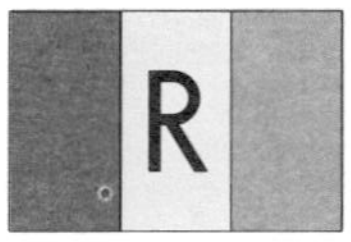

Rwanda
Page/Location: 82/E1
Area: 10,169 sq. mi.
26,337 sq. km.
Population: 7,903,000
Capital: Kigali
Largest City: Kigali
Highest Point: Karisimbi
Monetary Unit: Rwanda franc

Saint Kitts and Nevis
Page/Location: 104/F3
Area: 104 sq. mi.
269 sq. km.
Population: 40,000
Capital: Basseterre
Largest City: Basseterre
Highest Point: Mt. Misery
Monetary Unit: East Caribbean dollar

Saint Lucia
Page/Location: 104/F4
Area: 238 sq. mi.
616 sq. km.
Population: 153,000
Capital: Castries
Largest City: Castries
Highest Point: Mt. Gimie
Monetary Unit: East Caribbean dollar

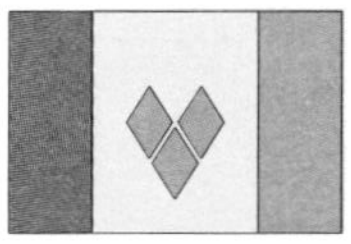

Saint Vincent and the Grenadines
Page/Location: 104/F4
Area: 150 sq. mi.
388 sq. km.
Population: 114,000
Capital: Kingstown
Largest City: Kingstown
Highest Point: Soufrière
Monetary Unit: East Caribbean dollar

San Marino
Page/Location: 33/K5
Area: 23.4 sq. mi.
60.6 sq. km.
Population: 23,000
Capital: San Marino
Largest City: San Marino
Highest Point: Monte Titano
Monetary Unit: Italian lira

São Tomé and Príncipe
Page/Location: 76/G7
Area: 372 sq. mi.
963 sq. km.
Population: 128,000
Capital: São Tomé
Largest City: São Tomé
Highest Point: Pico de São Tomé
Monetary Unit: dobra

Saudi Arabia
Page/Location: 104/F3
Area: 829,995 sq. mi.
2,149,687 sq. km.
Population: 17,870,000
Capital: Riyadh
Largest City: Riyadh
Highest Point: Jabal Sawdā'
Monetary Unit: Saudi riyal

Senegal
Page/Location: 78/B3
Area: 75,954 sq. mi.
196,720 sq. km.
Population: 7,953,000
Capital: Dakar
Largest City: Dakar
Highest Point: Fouta Djallon
Monetary Unit: CFA franc

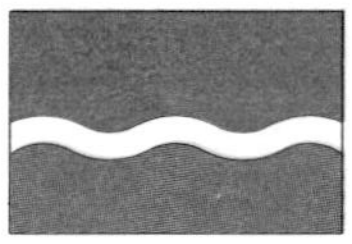

Seychelles
Page/Location: 74/H5
Area: 145 sq. mi.
375 sq. km.
Population: 69,000
Capital: Victoria
Largest City: Victoria
Highest Point: Morne Seychellois
Monetary Unit: Seychellois rupee

Sierra Leone
Page/Location: 78/B4
Area: 27,925 sq. mi.
72,325 sq. km.
Population: 4,275,000
Capital: Freetown
Largest City: Freetown
Highest Point: Loma Mansa
Monetary Unit: leone

Singapore
Page/Location: 66/B3
Area: 226 sq. mi.
585 sq. km.
Population: 2,756,000
Capital: Singapore
Largest City: Singapore
Highest Point: Bukit Timah
Monetary Unit: Singapore dollar

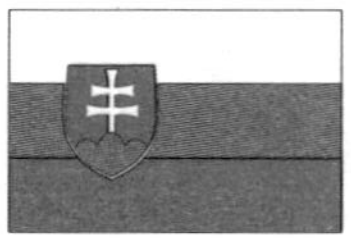

Slovakia
Page/Location: 27/K4
Area: 18,924 sq. mi.
49,013 sq. km.
Population: 4,991,168
Capital: Bratislava
Largest City: Bratislava
Highest Point: Gerlachovský Štít
Monetary Unit: Slovak koruna

Slovenia
Page/Location: 40/B3
Area: 7,898 sq. mi.
20,456 sq. km.
Population: 1,891,864
Capital: Ljubljana
Largest City: Ljubljana
Highest Point: Triglav
Monetary Unit: tolar

Solomon Islands
Page/Location: 68/E6
Area: 11,500 sq. mi.
29,785 sq. km.
Population: 347,000
Capital: Honiara
Largest City: Honiara
Highest Point: Mt. Makarakomburu
Monetary Unit: Solomon Islands dollar

Somalia
Page/Location: 77/Q6
Area: 246,200 sq. mi.
637,658 sq. km.
Population: 6,709,000
Capital: Mogadishu
Largest City: Mogadishu
Highest Point: Shimber Berris
Monetary Unit: Somali shilling

South Africa
Page/Location: 80/C3
Area: 455,318 sq. mi.
1,179,274 sq. km.
Population: 40,601,000
Capital: Cape Town; Pretoria
Largest City: Johannesburg
Highest Point: Injasuti
Monetary Unit: rand

Spain
Page/Location: 34/C2
Area: 194,881 sq. mi.
504,742 sq. km.
Population: 39,385,000
Capital: Madrid
Largest City: Madrid
Highest Point: Pico de Teide
Monetary Unit: peseta

Sri Lanka
Page/Location: 62/D6
Area: 25,332 sq. mi.
65,610 sq. km.
Population: 17,424,000
Capital: Colombo
Largest City: Colombo
Highest Point: Pidurutalagala
Monetary Unit: Sri Lanka rupee

Sudan
Page/Location: 77/L5
Area: 967,494 sq. mi.
2,505,809 sq. km.
Population: 27,220,000
Capital: Khartoum
Largest City: Omdurman
Highest Point: Jabal Marrah
Monetary Unit: Sudanese pound

Suriname
Page/Location: 107/G3
Area: 55,144 sq. mi.
142,823 sq. km.
Population: 402,000
Capital: Paramaribo
Largest City: Paramaribo
Highest Point: Juliana Top
Monetary Unit: Suriname guilder

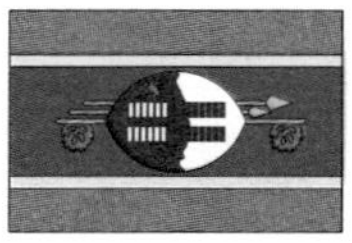

Swaziland
Page/Location: 81/E2
Area: 6,705 sq. mi.
17,366 sq. km.
Population: 859,000
Capital: Mbabane
Largest City: Mbabane
Highest Point: Emlembe
Monetary Unit: lilangeni

Sweden
Page/Location: 20/E3
Area: 173,665 sq. mi.
449,792 sq. km.
Population: 8,564,000
Capital: Stockholm
Largest City: Stockholm
Highest Point: Kebnekaise
Monetary Unit: krona

Switzerland
Page/Location: 36/D4
Area: 15,943 sq. mi.
41,292 sq. km.
Population: 6,784,000
Capital: Bern
Largest City: Zürich
Highest Point: Dufourspitze
Monetary Unit: Swiss franc

Syria
Page/Location: 50/D3
Area: 71,498 sq. mi.
185,180 sq. km.
Population: 12,966,000
Capital: Damascus
Largest City: Damascus
Highest Point: Jabal ash Shaykh
Monetary Unit: Syrian pound

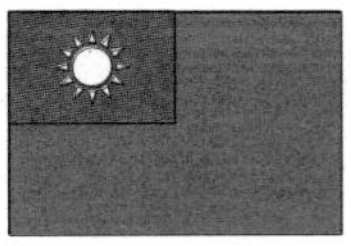

Taiwan
Page/Location: 61/J3
Area: 13,971 sq. mi.
36,185 sq. km.
Population: 16,609,961
Capital: Taipei
Largest City: Taipei
Highest Point: Yü Shan
Monetary Unit: new Taiwan dollar

Tajikistan
Page/Location: 46/H6
Area: 55,251 sq. mi.
143,100 sq. km.
Population: 5,112,000
Capital: Dushanbe
Largest City: Dushanbe
Highest Point: Communism Peak
Monetary Unit: Tajik ruble

Tanzania
Page/Location: 82/F2
Area: 363,708 sq. mi.
942,003 sq. km.
Population: 26,869,000
Capital: Dar es Salaam
Largest City: Dar es Salaam
Highest Point: Kilimanjaro
Monetary Unit: Tanzanian shilling

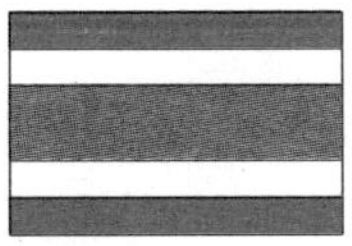

Thailand
Page/Location: 65/C3
Area: 198,455 sq. mi.
513,998 sq. km.
Population: 56,814,000
Capital: Bangkok
Largest City: Bangkok
Highest Point: Doi Inthanon
Monetary Unit: baht

Togo
Page/Location: 79/F4
Area: 21,622 sq. mi.
56,000 sq. km.
Population: 3,811,000
Capital: Lomé
Largest City: Lomé
Highest Point: Mt. Agou
Monetary Unit: CFA franc

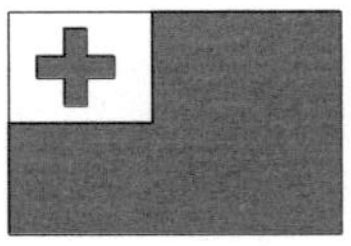

Tonga
Page/Location: 69/H7
Area: 270 sq. mi.
699 sq. km.
Population: 102,000
Capital: Nuku'alofa
Largest City: Nuku'alofa
Highest Point: Kao Island
Monetary Unit: pa'anga

Trinidad and Tobago
Page/Location: 104/F5
Area: 1,980 sq. mi.
5,128 sq. km.
Population: 1,285,000
Capital: Port-of-Spain
Largest City: Port-of-Spain
Highest Point: El Cerro del Aripo
Monetary Unit: Trin. & Tobago dollar

Tunisia
Page/Location: 76/G1
Area: 63,378 sq. mi.
164,149 sq. km.
Population: 8,276,000
Capital: Tunis
Largest City: Tunis
Highest Point: Jabal ash Sha'nabī
Monetary Unit: Tunisian dinar

Turkey
Page/Location: 50/C2
Area: 300,946 sq. mi.
779,450 sq. km.
Population: 58,581,000
Capital: Ankara
Largest City: Istanbul
Highest Point: Mt. Ararat
Monetary Unit: Turkish lira

Turkmenistan
Page/Location: 46/F6
Area: 188,455 sq. mi.
488,100 sq. km.
Population: 3,534,000
Capital: Ashkhabad
Largest City: Ashkhabad
Highest Point: Rize
Monetary Unit: manat

Tuvalu
Page/Location: 68/G5
Area: 9.78 sq. mi.
25.33 sq. km.
Population: 9,000
Capital: Fongafale
Largest City: —
Highest Point: 16 ft. (5 m)
Monetary Unit: Australian dollar

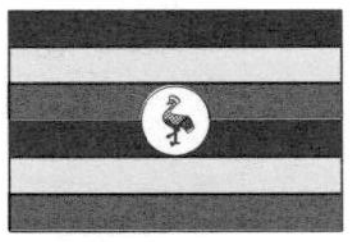

Uganda
Page/Location: 77/M7
Area: 91,076 sq. mi.
235,887 sq. km.
Population: 18,690,000
Capital: Kampala
Largest City: Kampala
Highest Point: Margherita Peak
Monetary Unit: Ugandan shilling

Ukraine
Page/Location: 44/D2
Area: 233,089 sq. mi.
603,700 sq. km.
Population: 51,704,000
Capital: Kiev
Largest City: Kiev
Highest Point: Goverla
Monetary Unit: grivna

United Arab Emirates
Page/Location: 52/F4
Area: 32,278 sq. mi.
83,600 sq. km.
Population: 2,390,000
Capital: Abu Dhabi
Largest City: Dubayy
Highest Point: Hajar Mts.
Monetary Unit: Emirian dirham

United Kingdom
Page/Location: 21
Area: 94,399 sq. mi.
244,493 sq. km.
Population: 57,515,000
Capital: London
Largest City: London
Highest Point: Ben Nevis
Monetary Unit: pound sterling

United States
Page/Location: 88
Area: 3,623,420 sq. mi.
9,384,658 sq. km.
Population: 252,502,000
Capital: Washington
Largest City: New York
Highest Point: Mt. McKinley
Monetary Unit: U.S. dollar

Uruguay
Page/Location: 109/E3
Area: 72,172 sq. mi.
186,925 sq. km.
Population: 3,121,000
Capital: Montevideo
Largest City: Montevideo
Highest Point: Cerro Catedral
Monetary Unit: Uruguayan peso

Uzbekistan
Page/Location: 46/G5
Area: 173,591 sq. mi.
449,600 sq. km.
Population: 19,906,000
Capital: Tashkent
Largest City: Tashkent
Highest Point: Khodzha-Pir'yakh
Monetary Unit: Uzbek ruble

Vanuatu
Page/Location: 68/F6
Area: 5,700 sq. mi.
14,763 sq. km.
Population: 170,000
Capital: Vila
Largest City: Vila
Highest Point: Tabwemasana
Monetary Unit: vatu

Vatican City
Page/Location: 38/C2
Area: 108.7 acres
44 hectares
Population: 1,000
Capital: —
Largest City: —
Highest Point: —
Monetary Unit: Italian lira

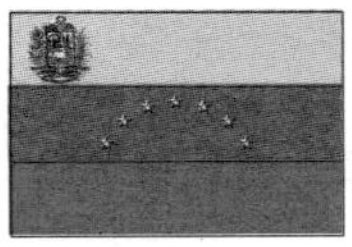

Venezuela
Page/Location: 106/E2
Area: 352,143 sq. mi.
912,050 sq. km.
Population: 20,189,000
Capital: Caracas
Largest City: Caracas
Highest Point: Pico Bolívar
Monetary Unit: bolívar

Vietnam
Page/Location: 65/D2
Area: 128,405 sq. mi.
332,569 sq. km.
Population: 67,568,000
Capital: Hanoi
Largest City: Ho Chi Minh City
Highest Point: Fan Si Pan
Monetary Unit: dong

Western Samoa
Page/Location: 69/H6
Area: 1,133 sq. mi.
2,934 sq. km.
Population: 190,000
Capital: Apia
Largest City: Apia
Highest Point: Mt. Silisili
Monetary Unit: tala

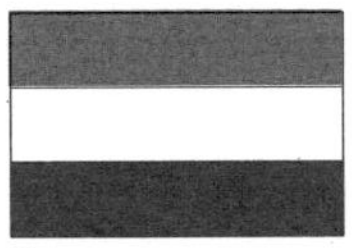

Yemen
Page/Location: 52/E5
Area: 188,321 sq. mi.
487,752 sq. km.
Population: 10,063,000
Capital: Sanaa
Largest City: Aden
Highest Point: Nabī Shu'ayb
Monetary Unit: Yemeni rial

Yugoslavia
Page/Location: 40/E3
Area: 38,989 sq. mi.
100,982 sq. km.
Population: 11,371,275
Capital: Belgrade
Largest City: Belgrade
Highest Point: Đaravica
Monetary Unit: Yugoslav new dinar

Zaire
Page/Location: 74/E5
Area: 905,063 sq. mi.
2,344,113 sq. km.
Population: 37,832,000
Capital: Kinshasa
Largest City: Kinshasa
Highest Point: Margherita Peak
Monetary Unit: zaire

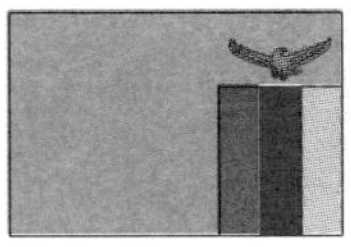

Zambia
Page/Location: 82/E3
Area: 290,586 sq. mi.
752,618 sq. km.
Population: 8,446,000
Capital: Lusaka
Largest City: Lusaka
Highest Point: Sunzu
Monetary Unit: Zambian kwacha

Zimbabwe
Page/Location: 82/E4
Area: 150,803 sq. mi.
390,580 sq. km.
Population: 10,720,000
Capital: Harare
Largest City: Harare
Highest Point: Inyangani
Monetary Unit: Zimbabwe dollar

World Statistics

Elements of the Solar System

	Mean Distance from Sun: in Miles	in Kilometers	Period of Revolution around Sun	Period of Rotation on Axis	Equatorial Diameter in Miles	in Kilometers	Surface Gravity (Earth = 1)	Mass (Earth = 1)	Mean Density (Water = 1)	Number of Satellites
Mercury	35,990,000	57,900,000	87.97 days	59 days	3,032	4,880	0.38	0.055	5.5	0
Venus	67,240,000	108,200,000	224.70 days	243 days†	7,523	12,106	0.90	0.815	5.25	0
Earth	93,000,000	149,700,000	365.26 days	23h 56m	7,926	12,755	1.00	1.00	5.5	1
Mars	141,730,000	228,100,000	687.00 days	24h 37m	4,220	6,790	0.38	0.107	4.0	2
Jupiter	483,880,000	778,700,000	11.86 years	9h 50m	88,750	142,800	2.87	317.9	1.3	16
Saturn	887,130,000	1,427,700,000	29.46 years	10h 39m	74,580	120,020	1.32	95.2	0.7	23
Uranus	1,783,700,000	2,870,500,000	84.01 years	17h 24m†	31,600	50,900	0.93	14.6	1.3	15
Neptune	2,795,500,000	4,498,800,000	164.79 years	17h 50m	30,200	48,600	1.23	17.2	1.8	8
Pluto	3,667,900,000	5,902,800,000	247.70 years	6.39 days(?)	1,500	2,400	0.03(?)	0.01(?)	0.7(?)	1

† Retrograde motion

Dimensions of the Earth

	Area in: Sq. Miles	Sq. Kilometers
Superficial area	196,939,000	510,073,000
Land surface	57,506,000	148,941,000
Water surface	139,433,000	361,132,000
	Distance in: Miles	**Kilometers**
Equatorial circumference	24,902	40,075
Polar circumference	24,860	40,007
Equatorial diameter	7,926.4	12,756.4
Polar diameter	7,899.8	12,713.6
Equatorial radius	3,963.2	6,378.2
Polar radius	3,949.9	6,356.8
Volume of the Earth	2.6×10^{11} cubic miles	10.84×10^{11} cubic kilometers
Mass or weight	6.6×10^{21} short tons	6.0×10^{21} metric tons
Maximum distance from Sun	94,600,000 miles	152,000,000 kilometers
Minimum distance from Sun	91,300,000 miles	147,000,000 kilometers

Oceans and Major Seas

	Area in: Sq. Miles	Sq. Kms.	Greatest Depth in: Feet	Meters
Pacific Ocean	64,186,000	166,241,700	36,198	11,033
Atlantic Ocean	31,862,000	82,522,600	28,374	8,648
Indian Ocean	28,350,000	73,426,500	25,344	7,725
Arctic Ocean	5,427,000	14,056,000	17,880	5,450
Caribbean Sea	970,000	2,512,300	24,720	7,535
Mediterranean Sea	969,000	2,509,700	16,896	5,150
South China Sea	895,000	2,318,000	15,000	4,600
Bering Sea	875,000	2,266,250	15,800	4,800
Gulf of Mexico	600,000	1,554,000	12,300	3,750
Sea of Okhotsk	590,000	1,528,100	11,070	3,370
East China Sea	482,000	1,248,400	9,500	2,900
Yellow Sea	480,000	1,243,200	350	107
Sea of Japan	389,000	1,007,500	12,280	3,740
Hudson Bay	317,500	822,300	846	258
North Sea	222,000	575,000	2,200	670
Black Sea	185,000	479,150	7,365	2,245
Red Sea	169,000	437,700	7,200	2,195
Baltic Sea	163,000	422,170	1,506	459

The Continents

	Area in: Sq. Miles	Sq. Kms.	Percent of World's Land
Asia	17,128,500	44,362,815	29.5
Africa	11,707,000	30,321,130	20.2
North America	9,363,000	24,250,170	16.2
South America	6,875,000	17,806,250	11.8
Antarctica	5,500,000	14,245,000	9.5
Europe	4,057,000	10,507,630	7.0
Australia	2,966,136	7,682,300	5.1

Major Ship Canals

	Length in: Miles	Kms.	Minimum Depth in: Feet	Meters
Volga-Baltic, Russia	225	362	–	–
Baltic-White Sea, Russia	140	225	16	5
Suez, Egypt	100.76	162	42	13
Albert, Belgium	80	129	16.5	5
Moscow-Volga, Russia	80	129	18	6
Volga-Don, Russia	62	100	–	–
Göta, Sweden	54	87	10	3
Kiel (Nord-Ostsee), Germany	53.2	86	38	12
Panama Canal, Panama	50.72	82	41.6	13
Houston Ship, U.S.A.	50	81	36	11

Largest Islands

	Area in: Sq. Miles	Sq. Kms.
Greenland	840,000	2,175,600
New Guinea	305,000	789,950
Borneo	290,000	751,100
Madagascar	226,400	586,376
Baffin, Canada	195,928	507,454
Sumatra, Indonesia	164,000	424,760
Honshu, Japan	88,000	227,920
Great Britain	84,400	218,896
Victoria, Canada	83,896	217,290
Ellesmere, Canada	75,767	196,236
Celebes, Indonesia	72,986	189,034
South I., New Zealand	58,393	151,238
Java, Indonesia	48,842	126,501
North I., New Zealand	44,187	114,444
Newfoundland, Canada	42,031	108,860
Cuba	40,533	104,981
Luzon, Philippines	40,420	104,688
Iceland	39,768	103,000
Mindanao, Philippines	36,537	94,631
Ireland	31,743	82,214
Sakhalin, Russia	29,500	76,405
Hispaniola, Haiti & Dom. Rep.	29,399	76,143

	Area in: Sq. Miles	Sq. Kms.
Hokkaido, Japan	28,983	75,066
Banks, Canada	27,038	70,028
Ceylon,Sri Lanka	25,332	65,610
Tasmania, Australia	24,600	63,710
Svalbard, Norway	23,957	62,049
Devon, Canada	21,331	55,247
Novaya Zemlya (north isl.), Russia	18,600	48,200
Marajó, Brazil	17,991	46,597
Tierra del Fuego, Chile & Argentina	17,900	46,360
Alexander, Antarctica	16,700	43,250
Axel Heiberg, Canada	16,671	43,178
Melville, Canada	16,274	42,150
Southhampton, Canada	15,913	41,215
New Britain, Papua New Guinea	14,100	36,519
Taiwan, China	13,836	35,835
Kyushu, Japan	13,770	35,664
Hainan, China	13,127	33,999
Prince of Wales, Canada	12,872	33,338
Spitsbergen, Norway	12,355	31,999
Vancouver, Canada	12,079	31,285
Timor, Indonesia	11,527	29,855
Sicily, Italy	9,926	25,708

	Area in: Sq. Miles	Sq. Kms.
Somerset, Canada	9,570	24,786
Sardinia, Italy	9,301	24,090
Shikoku, Japan	6,860	17,767
New Caledonia, France	6,530	16,913
Nordaustlandet, Norway	6,409	16,599
Samar, Philippines	5,050	13,080
Negros, Philippines	4,906	12,707
Palawan, Philippines	4,550	11,785
Panay, Philippines	4,446	11,515
Jamaica	4,232	10,961
Hawaii, United States	4,038	10,458
Viti Levu, Fiji	4,010	10,386
Cape Breton, Canada	3,981	10,311
Mindoro, Philippines	3,759	9,736
Kodiak, Alaska, U.S.A.	3,670	9,505
Cyprus	3,572	9,251
Puerto Rico, U.S.A.	3,435	8,897
Corsica, France	3,352	8,682
New Ireland, Papua New Guinea	3,340	8,651
Crete, Greece	3,218	8,335
Anticosti, Canada	3,066	7,941
Wrangel, Russia	2,819	7,301

Principal Mountains

	Height in : Feet	Meters
Everest, Nepal-China	29,028	8,848
K2 (Godwin Austen), Pakistan-China	28,250	8,611
Makalu, Nepal-China	27,789	8,470
Dhaulagiri, Nepal	26,810	8,172
Nanga Parbat, Pakistan	26,660	8,126
Annapurna, Nepal	26,504	8,078
Rakaposhi, Pakistan	25,550	7,788
Kongur Shan, China	25,325	7,719
Tirich Mir, Pakistan	25,230	7,690
Gongga Shan, China	24,790	7,556
Communism Peak, Tajikistan	24,590	7,495
Pobedy Peak, Kyrgyzstan	24,406	7,439
Chomo Lhari, Bhutan-China	23,997	7,314
Muztag, China	23,891	7,282
Cerro Aconcagua, Argentina	22,831	6,959
Ojos del Salado, Chile-Argentina	22,572	6,880
Bonete, Chile-Argentina	22,546	6,872
Tupungato, Chile-Argentina	22,310	6,800
Pissis, Argentina	22,241	6,779
Mercedario, Argentina	22,211	6,770
Huascarán, Peru	22,205	6,768

	Height in : Feet	Meters
Llullaillaco, Chile-Argentina	22,057	6,723
Nevada Ancohuma, Bolivia	21,489	6,550
Chimborazo, Ecuador	20,561	6,267
McKinley, Alaska	20,320	6,194
Logan, Yukon, Canada	19,524	5,951
Cotopaxi, Ecuador	19,347	5,897
Kilimanjaro, Tanzania	19,340	5,895
El Misti, Peru	19,101	5,822
Pico Cristóbal Colón, Colombia	18,947	5,775
Huila, Colombia	18,865	5,750
Citlaltépetl (Orizaba), Mexico	18,701	5,700
Damavand, Iran	18,606	5,671
El'brus, Russia	18,510	5,642
St. Elias, Alaska, U.S.A.-Yukon, Canada	18,008	5,489
Dykh-tau, Russia	17,070	5,203
Batian (Kenya), Kenya	17,058	5,199
Ararat, Turkey	16,946	5,165
Vinson Massif, Antarctica	16,864	5,140
Margherita (Ruwenzori), Africa	16,795	5,119
Kazbek, Georgia-Russia	16,558	5,047
Puncak Jaya, Indonesia	16,503	5,030

	Height in : Feet	Meters
Blanc, France	15,771	4,807
Klyuchevskaya Sopka, Russia	15,584	4,750
Fairweather, Br. Col., Canada	15,300	4,663
Dufourspitze (Mte. Rosa), Italy-Switzerland	15,203	4,634
Ras Dashen, Ethiopia	15,157	4620
Matterhorn, Switzerland	14,691	4,478
Whitney, California, U.S.A.	14,494	4,418
Elbert, Colorado, U.S.A.	14,433	4,399
Rainier, Washington, U.S.A.	14,410	4,392
Shasta, California, U.S.A.	14,162	4,317
Pikes Peak, Colorado, U.S.A.	14,110	4,301
Finsteraarhorn, Switzerland	14,022	4, 274
Mauna Kea, Hawaii, U.S.A.	13,796	4,205
Mauna Loa, Hawaii, U.S.A.	13,677	4,169
Jungfrau, Switzerland	13,642	4,158
Grossglockner, Austria	12,457	3,797
Fujiyama, Japan	12,389	3,776
Cook, New Zealand	12,349	3,764
Etna, Italy	10,902	3,323
Kosciusko, Australia	7,310	2,228
Mitchell, North Carolina, U.S.A.	6,684	2,037

Longest Rivers

	Length in : Miles	Kms.
Nile, Africa	4,145	6,671
Amazon, S. America	3,915	6,300
Chang Jiang (Yangtze), China	3,900	6,276
Mississippi-Missouri-Red Rock, U.S.A.	3,741	6,019
Ob'-Irtysh-Black Irtysh, Russia-Kazakhstan	3,362	5,411
Yenisey-Angara, Russia	3,100	4,989
Huang He (Yellow), China	2,877	4,630
Amur-Shilka-Onon, Asia	2,744	4,416
Lena, Russia	2,734	4,400
Congo (Zaire), Africa	2,718	4,374
Mackenzie-Peace-Finlay,Canada	2,635	4,241
Mekong, Asia	2,610	4,200
Missouri-Red Rock, U.S.A.	2,564	4,125
Niger, Africa	2,548	4,101
Paraná-La Plata, S. America	2,450	3,943
Mississippi, U.S.A.	2,348	3,778
Murray-Darling, Australia	2,310	3,718
Volga, Russia	2,194	3,531
Madeira, S. America	2,013	3,240
Purus, S. America	1,995	3,211
Yukon, Alaska-Canada	1,979	3,185
St. Lawrence, Canada-U.S.A.	1,900	3,058
Rio Grande, Mexico-U.S.A.	1,885	3,034
Syrdar'ya-Naryn, Asia	1,859	2,992
São Francisco, Brazil	1,811	2,914

	Length in : Miles	Kms.
Indus, Asia	1,800	2,897
Danube, Europe	1,775	2,857
Salween, Asia	1,770	2,849
Brahmaputra, Asia	1,700	2,736
Euphrates, Asia	1,700	2,736
Tocantins, Brazil	1,677	2,699
Xi (Si), China	1,650	2,601
Amudar'ya, Asia	1,616	2,601
Nelson-Saskatchewan, Canada	1,600	2,575
Orinoco, S. America	1,600	2,575
Zambezi, Africa	1,600	2,575
Paraguay, S. America	1,584	2,549
Kolyma, Russia	1,562	2,514
Ganges, Asia	1,550	2,494
Ural, Russia-Kazakhstan	1,509	2,428
Japurá, S. America	1,500	2,414
Arkansas, U.S.A.	1,450	2,334
Colorado, U.S.A.-Mexico	1.450	2,334
Negro, S. America	1,400	2,253
Dnieper, Russia-Belarus-Ukraine	1,368	2,202
Orange, Africa	1,350	2,173
Irrawaddy, Burma	1,325	2,132
Brazos, U.S.A.	1,309	2,107
Ohio-Allegheny, U.S.A.	1,306	2,102
Kama, Russia	1,252	2,031

	Length in : Miles	Kms.
Don, Russia	1,222	1,967
Red, U.S.A.	1,222	1,966
Columbia, U.S.A.-Canada	1,214	1,953
Saskatchewan, Canada	1,205	1,939
Peace-Finlay, Canada	1,195	1,923
Tigris, Asia	1,181	1,901
Darling, Australia	1,160	1,867
Angara, Russia	1,135	1,827
Sungari, Asia	1,130	1,819
Pechora, Russia	1,124	1,809
Snake, U.S.A.	1,038	1,670
Churchill, Canada	1,000	1,609
Pilcomayo, S. America	1,000	1,609
Uruguay, S. America	994	1.600
Platte-N. Platte, U.S.A.	990	1,593
Ohio, U.S.A.	981	1,578
Magdalena, Colombia	956	1,538
Pecos, U.S.A.	926	1,490
Oka, Russia	918	1,477
Canadian, U.S.A.	906	1,458
Colorado, Texas, U.S.A.	894	1,439
Dniester, Ukraine-Moldova	876	1,410
Fraser, Canada	850	1,369
Rhine, Europe	820	1,319
Northern Dvina, Russia	809	1,302

Principal Natural Lakes

	Area in: Sq. Miles	Sq. Kms.	Max. Depth in: Feet	Meters
Caspian Sea, Asia	143,243	370,999	3,264	995
Lake Superior, U.S.A.-Canada	31,820	82,414	1,329	405
Lake Victoria, Africa	26,724	69,215	270	82
Lake Huron, U.S.A.-Canada	23,010	59,596	748	228
Lake Michigan, U.S.A.	22,400	58,016	923	281
Aral Sea, Kazakhstan-Uzbekistan	15,830	41,000	213	65
Lake Tanganyika, Africa	12,650	32,764	4,700	1,433
Lake Baykal, Russia	12,162	31,500	5,316	1,620
Great Bear Lake, Canada	12,096	31,328	1,356	413
Lake Nyasa (Malawi), Africa	11,555	29,928	2,320	707
Great Slave Lake, Canada	11,031	28,570	2,015	614
Lake Erie, U.S.A.-Canada	9,940	25,745	210	64
Lake Winnipeg, Canada	9,417	24,390	60	18
Lake Ontario, U.S.A.-Canada	7,540	19,529	775	244
Lake Ladoga, Russia	7,104	18,399	738	225
Lake Balkhash, Kazakhstan	7,027	18,200	87	27
Lake Maracaibo, Venezuela	5,120	13,261	100	31
Lake Chad, Africa	4,000 –	10,360 –		
	10,000	25,900	25	8
Lake Onega, Russia	3,710	9,609	377	115

	Area in: Sq. Miles	Sq. Kms.	Max. Depth in: Feet	Meters
Lake Eyre, Australia	3,500-0	9,000-0	–	–
Lake Titicaca, Peru-Bolivia	3,200	8,288	1, 000	305
Lake Nicaragua, Nicaragua	3,100	8,029	230	70
Lake Athabasca, Canada	3,064	7,936	400	122
Reindeer Lake, Canada	2,568	6,651	–	–
Lake Turkana (Rudolf), Africa	2,463	6,379	240	73
Issyk-Kul', Kyrgyzstan	2,425	6,281	2,303	702
Lake Torrens, Australia	2,230	5,776	–	–
Vänern, Sweden	2,156	5,584	328	100
Nettilling Lake, Canada	2,140	5,543	–	–
Lake Winnipegosis, Canada	2,075	5,374	38	12
Lake Mobutu Sese Seko (Albert), Africa	2,075	5,374	160	49
Kariba Lake, Zambia-Zimbabwe	2,050	5,310	295	90
Lake Nipigon, Canada	1,872	4,848	540	165
Lake Mweru, Zaire-Zambia	1,800	4,662	60	18
Lake Manitoba, Canada	1,799	4,659	12	4
Lake Taymyr, Russia	1,737	4,499	85	26
Lake Khanka, China-Russia	1,700	4,403	33	10
Lake Kioga, Uganda	1,700	4,403	25	8
Lake of the Woods, U.S.A.-Canada	1,679	4,349	70	21J2

ARCTIC OCEAN
CANADA BASIN
Beaufort Sea
Wrangel I.
Pt. Barrow
Banks I.
Chukchi Sea
QUEEN ELIZABETH ISLANDS
Ellesmere I.
Devon I.
Victoria I.
GREENLAND
Baffin Bay
Baffin Island
Arctic Circle
Denmark Str.
Iceland
Great Britain
Ireland
Yukon
Mt. McKinley
MacKenzie
Great Bear L.
Great Slave L.
Peace
Rocky Mountains
Great Plains
Hudson Bay
NORTH AMERICA
Bering Sea
ALEUTIAN BASIN
ALEUTIAN ISLANDS
ALEUTIAN TRENCH
Gulf of Alaska
LABRADOR BASIN
IRMINGER BASIN
ICELAND BASIN
CHARLIE-GIBBS FRACTURE ZONE
Newfoundland
C. Race
Great Lakes
Appalachian Mts.
Missouri
Ohio
Mississippi
C. Hatteras
Colorado
Rio Grande
MENDOCINO FRACTURE ZONE
C. Mendocino
HAWAIIAN ISLANDS
HAWAIIAN RIDGE
MOLOKAI FRACTURE ZONE
Tropic of Cancer
Lower California
Gulf of Mexico
ATLANTIC
MID-ATLANTIC RIDGE
Cuba
WEST INDIES
Caribbean Sea
−28,232 ft. (−8605 m)
C. Verde
Atlas Mts.
CLIPPERTON FRACTURE ZONE
CENTRAL PACIFIC BASIN
PACIFIC
Equator
GUATEMALA BASIN
Orinoco
Negro
Amazon
Madeira
São Francisco
ROMANCHE FRACTURE ZONE
C. de São Roque
BRAZIL BASIN
OCEAN
SOUTH AMERICA
Andes Mountains
PERU-CHILE TRENCH
PERU BASIN
NAZCA RIDGE
−26,457 ft. (−8064 m)
CHILE BASIN
Cerro Aconcagua
Paraná
EAST PACIFIC RISE
OCEAN
TONGA TRENCH
Tropic of Capricorn
KERMADEC TRENCH
SOUTHWEST PACIFIC BASIN
ARGENTINE BASIN
Falkland Is.
Tierra del Fuego
C. Horn
Drake Passage
−27,313 ft. (−8325 m)
SOUTH SANDWICH TRENCH
PACIFIC-ANTARCTIC RIDGE
Antarctic Circle
AMUNDSEN ABYSSAL PLAIN
Antarctic Peninsula
WEDDELL ABYSSAL PLAIN
Bellingshausen Sea
Weddell Sea
Ross Sea
ANTARCTICA

World

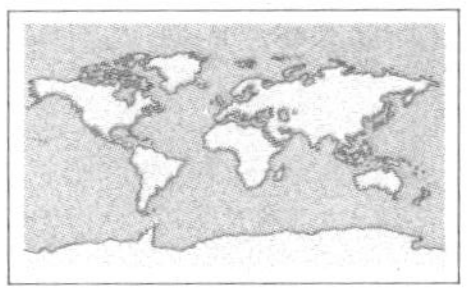

ARCTIC OCEAN
−17,881 ft. (−5450 m)
FRANZ JOSEF LAND
SEVERNAYA ZEMLYA
NEW SIBERIAN IS.
SVALBARD
NOVAYA ZEMLYA
Kara Sea
Barents Sea
Laptev Sea
Wrangel I.
Nordkapp
Kjölen
Baltic Sea
L. Ladoga
Ural Mountains
Siberia
Yenisey
Ob'
Angara
Lena
Aldan
Bering Sea
ALEUTIAN BASIN
ALEUTIAN ISLANDS
ALEUTIAN TRENCH
Kamchatka Pen.
Sea of Okhotsk
Irtysh
Volga
L. Baykal
EUROPE
ASIA
Dnieper
Amur
Sakhalin
KURIL-KAMCHATKA TRENCH
Danube
Black Sea
Caspian Sea
Aral Sea
L. Balkhash
Gobi
Sea of Japan
Honshu
NORTHWEST PACIFIC BASIN
JAPAN TRENCH
Mediterranean Sea
Euphrates
Kunlun
Huang
East China Sea
Himalaya
Mt. Everest
Indus
Ganges
Chang
PACIFIC OCEAN
Tropic of Cancer
AFRICA
Nile
Red Sea
Arabian Sea
ARABIAN BASIN
Bay of Bengal
Salween
Mekong
Taiwan
PHILIPPINE BASIN
MARIANA IS.
MARIANA TRENCH
Luzon
South China Sea
Challenger Deep −36,198 ft. (−11,033 m)
MARSHALL IS.
CENTRAL PACIFIC BASIN
CARLSBERG RIDGE
C. Comorin
Ceylon
Mindanao
Borneo
CAROLINE IS.
MELANESIAN BASIN
Equator
L. Victoria
Kilimanjaro
Congo
SOMALI BASIN
CENTRAL INDIAN RIDGE
CEYLON PLAIN
NINETYEAST RIDGE
Sumatra
Java
JAVA TRENCH
24,443 ft. (−7450 m)
Celebes
New Guinea
INDIAN OCEAN
Zambezi
Madagascar
Coral Sea
Fiji Is.
Great Barrier Reef
Tropic of Capricorn
AUSTRALIA
BROKEN PLATEAU
Orange
CAPE BASIN
C. of Good Hope
AGULHAS RIDGE
C. Leeuwin
Tasman Sea
North Cape
North I.
South I.
S. AUSTRALIA BASIN
Tasmania
SOUTHWEST INDIAN RIDGE
SOUTHEAST INDIAN RIDGE
KERGUELEN PLATEAU
ENDERBY ABYSSAL PLAIN
AUSTRALIAN-ANTARCTIC BASIN
Antarctic Circle
C. Adare
Amery Ice Shelf
Ross Sea
ANTARCTICA

ARCTIC OCEAN
NORTH AMERICA
CANADA
UNITED STATES
MEXICO
GREENLAND (KALAALLIT NUNAAT)
ALASKA (U.S.)
ASIA
EUROPE
SOUTH AMERICA
BRAZIL
ARGENTINA
PERU
BOLIVIA
COLOMBIA
VENEZUELA
CHILE
URUGUAY
PARAGUAY
ECUADOR
GUYANA
SURINAME
FRENCH GUIANA
NORTH PACIFIC OCEAN
NORTH ATLANTIC OCEAN
SOUTH PACIFIC OCEAN
SOUTH ATLANTIC OCEAN
BERING SEA
Hudson Bay
Gulf of Mexico
CARIBBEAN SEA
West Indies
Greater Antilles
Lesser Antilles
LABRADOR SEA
WEDDELL SEA
ROSS SEA
Drake Passage
HAWAIIAN ISLANDS (U.S.)
ALEUTIAN IS.
KIRIBATI
LINE ISLANDS
PHOENIX IS.
COOK ISLANDS
FRENCH POLYNESIA
MARQUESAS IS.
TUAMOTU ARCH.
SOCIETY IS. (FR.)
TUBUAI IS. (FR.)
Tropic of Cancer
Equator
Tropic of Capricorn
Arctic Circle
Antarctic Circle
International Date Line
Mexico City
New York
Washington
Chicago
Los Angeles
Toronto
Montréal
Ottawa
Havana
Bogotá
Caracas
Lima
Quito
La Paz
Santiago
Buenos Aires
Montevideo
São Paulo
Rio de Janeiro
Brasília
Reykjavík
Lisbon
Dakar
Mt. McKinley 20,320 ft. (6,194 m)
Cerro Aconcagua 6,959 m
Vinson Massif 5,140 m

World

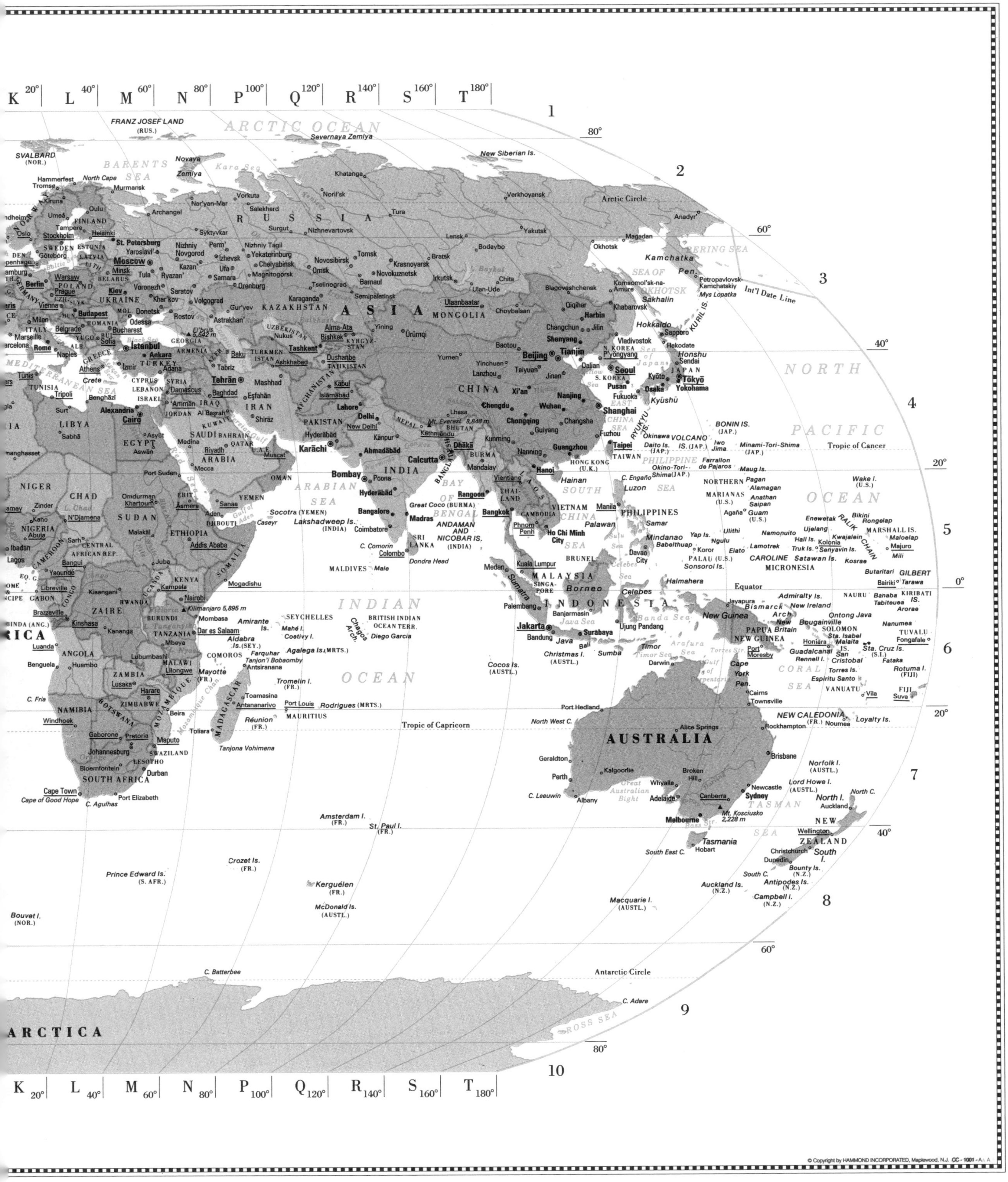

POPULATION OF CITIES AND TOWNS
- OVER 5,000,000
- 2,000,000 - 4,999,999
- 500,000 - 1,999,999
- UNDER 500,000

SCALE 1:81,700,000 ROBINSON PROJECTION STANDARD PARALLELS 38°N AND 38°S

MILES 0 1000 2000 3000 4000

KILOMETERS 0 1000 2000 3000 4000

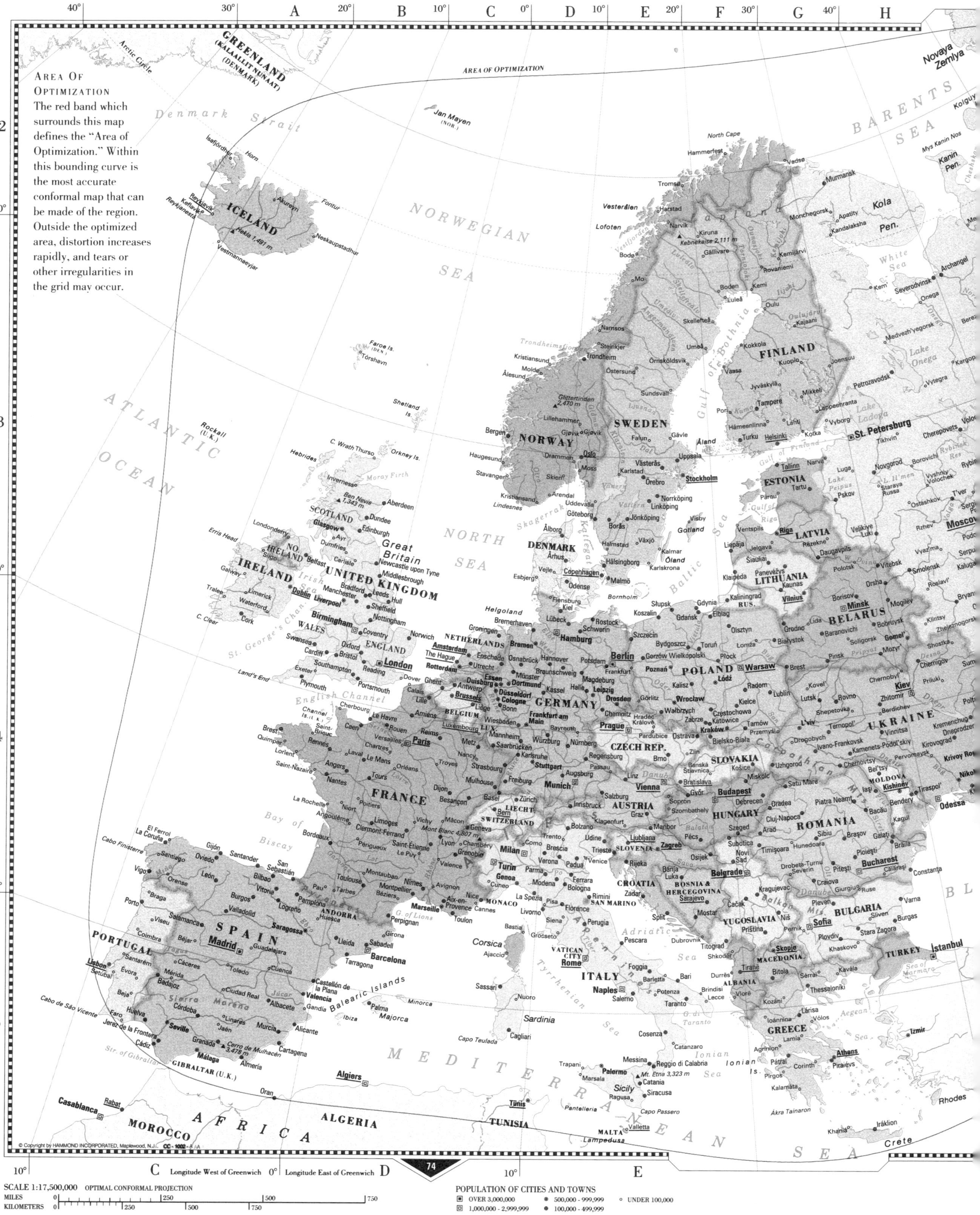

AREA OF OPTIMIZATION

The red band which surrounds this map defines the "Area of Optimization." Within this bounding curve is the most accurate conformal map that can be made of the region. Outside the optimized area, distortion increases rapidly, and tears or other irregularities in the grid may occur.

Europe

SCALE 1:587,000 LAMBERT CONFORMAL CONIC PROJECTION

MILES 0 10 20

KILOMETERS 0 10 20

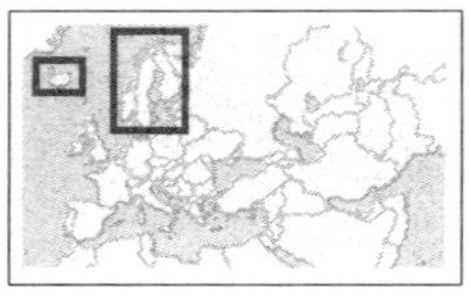

Scandinavia and Finland, Iceland

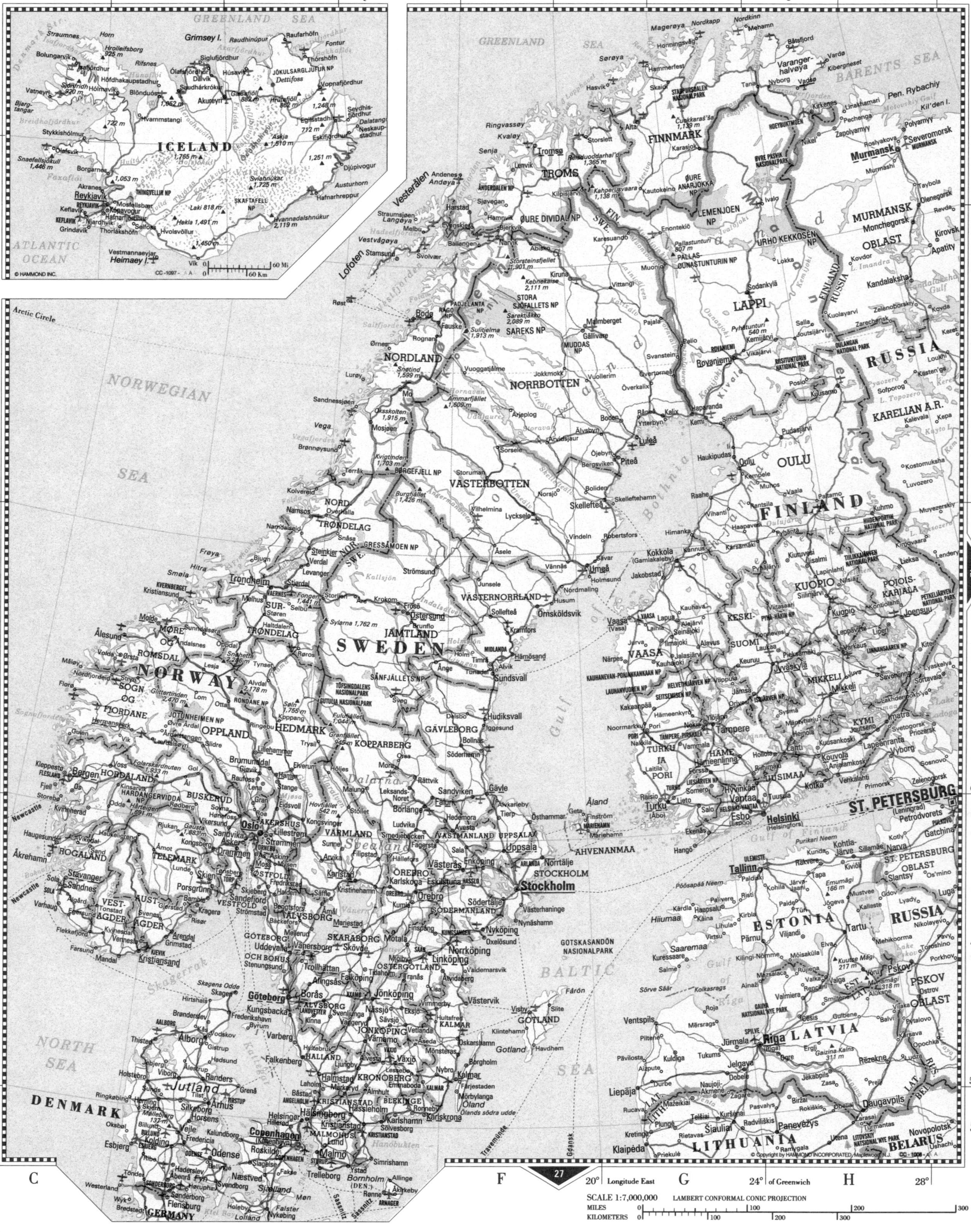

United Kingdom, Ireland

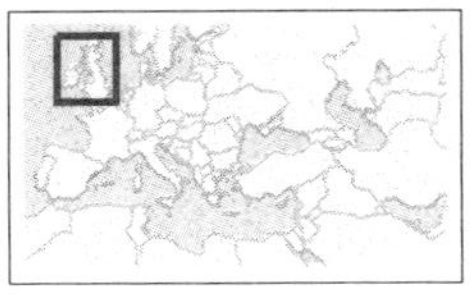

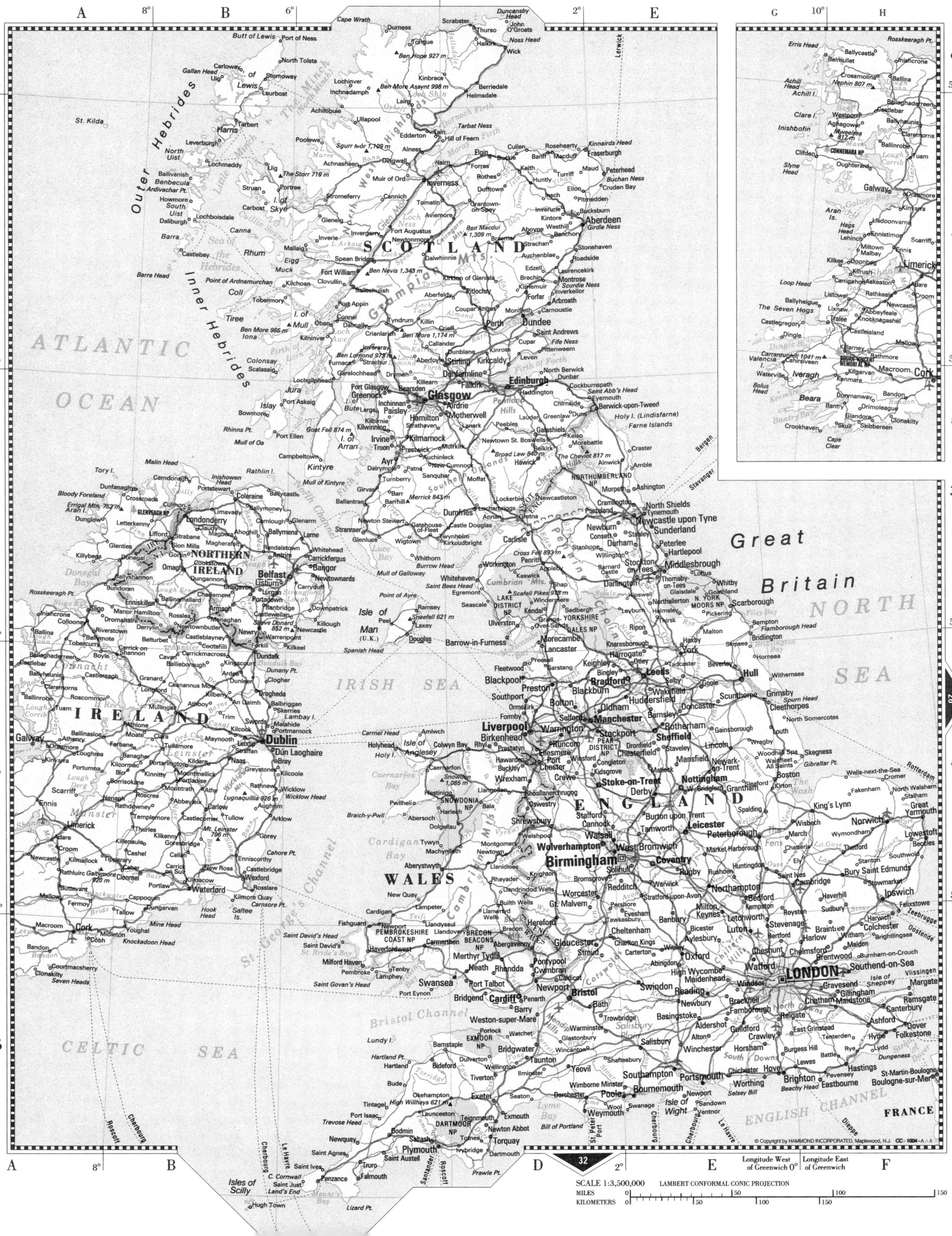

NORTHERN IRELAND
IRELAND
SCOTLAND
Isle of Man
(U.K.)
IRISH SEA
North Channel
St. George's Channel
UNITED KINGDOM
IRELAND
Firth of Clyde
Solway Firth
Cardigan Bay
Dublin
Belfast
DONEGAL
LONDONDERRY
LIMAVADY
COLERAINE
BALLYMONEY
MOYLE
LARNE
BALLYMENA
MAGHERAFELT
STRABANE
OMAGH
COOKSTOWN
ANTRIM
NEWTOWNABBEY
CARRICKFERGUS
NORTH DOWN
ARDS
LISBURN
CRAIGAVON
DUNGANNON
ARMAGH
BANBRIDGE
DOWN
NEWRY
MOURNE
FERMANAGH
MONAGHAN
CAVAN
LOUTH
MEATH
WESTMEATH
DUBLIN
OFFALY
KILDARE
LAOIS
(LEIX)
WICKLOW
CARLOW
WEXFORD
KILKENNY
STRATHCLYDE
DUMFRIES
GWYNEDD
SNOWDONIA
NAT'L PARK
Anglesey
Lleyn Pen.
Inishowen
Kintyre
Ulster
Leinster
Lough Neagh
The Rhinns
The Machars
Southern Uplands
Cambrian Mts.
21

Northeastern Ireland, Northern England and Wales

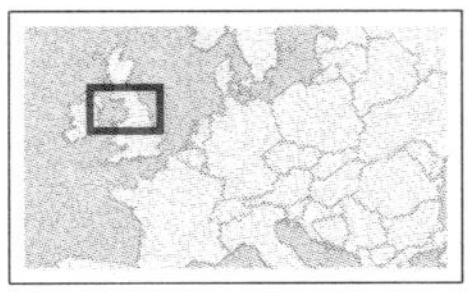

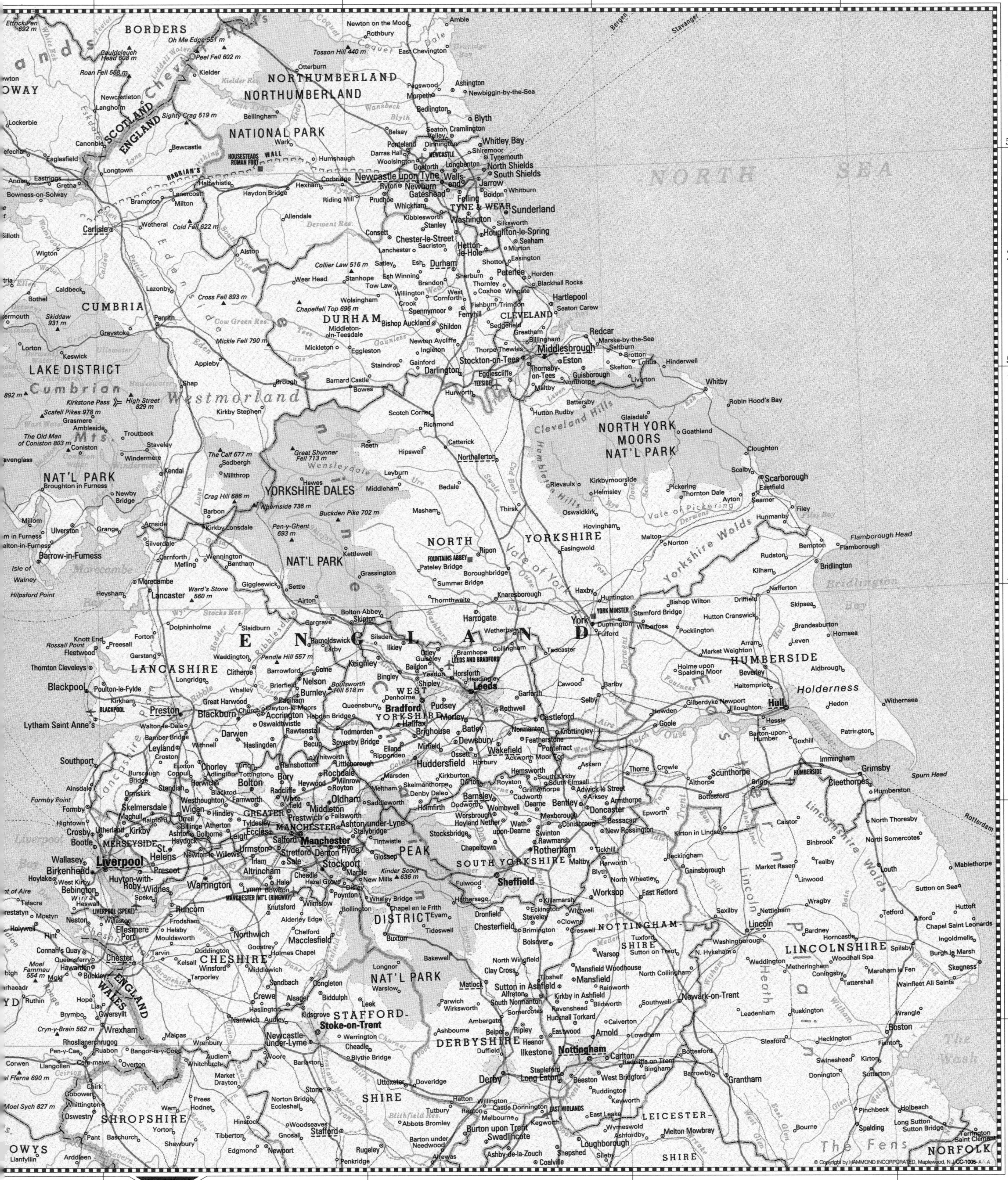

POPULATION OF CITIES AND TOWNS
- OVER 2,000,000
- 1,000,000 - 1,999,999
- 500,000 - 999,999
- 250,000 - 499,999
- 100,000 - 249,999
- 30,000 - 99,999
- 10,000 - 29,999
- UNDER 10,000

SCALE 1:1,170,000 LAMBERT CONFORMAL CONIC PROJECTION

MILES 0 10 20 30 40 50

KILOMETERS 0 10 20 30 40 50

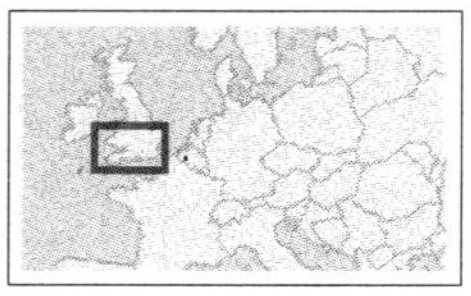

Southern England and Wales

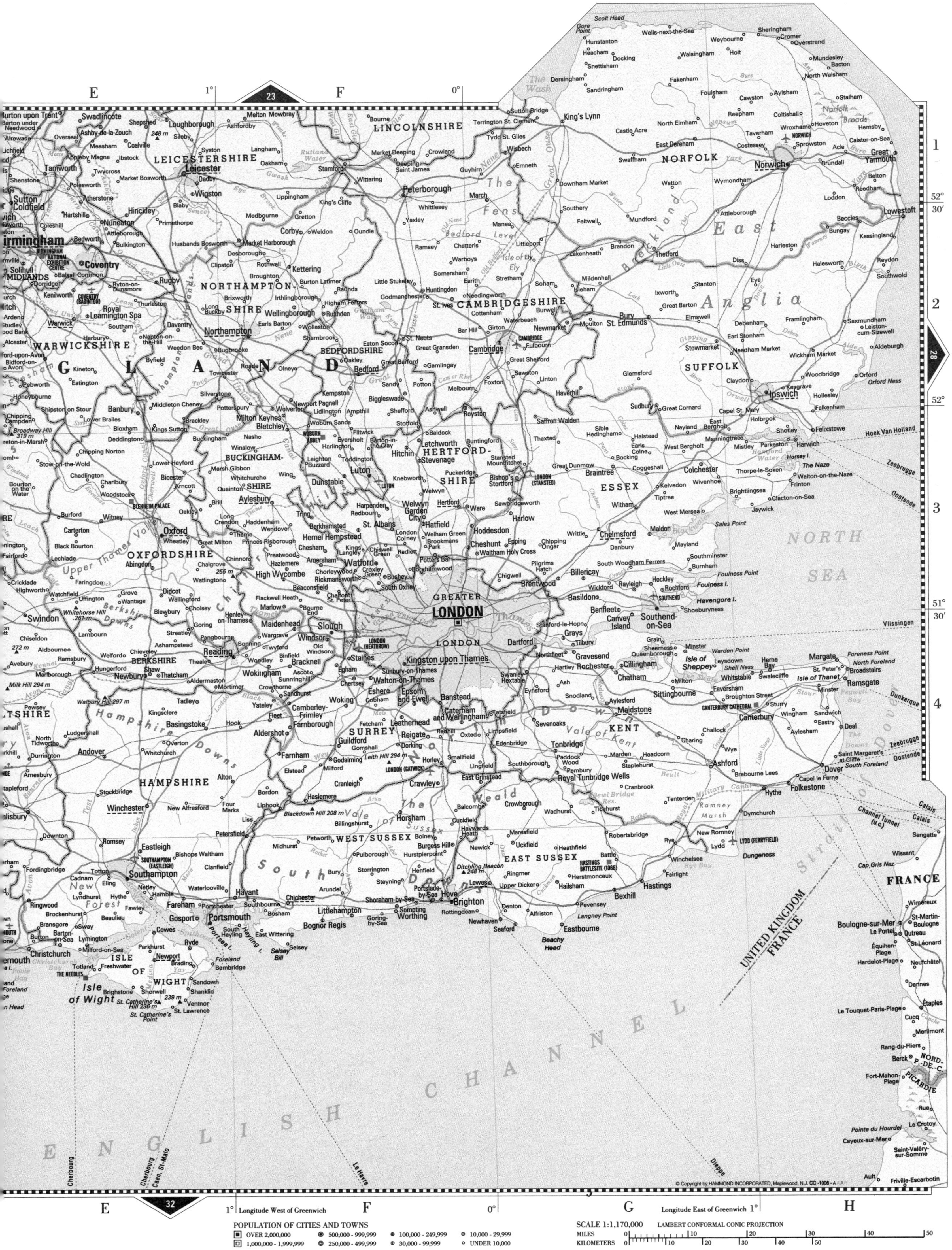

POPULATION OF CITIES AND TOWNS

- OVER 2,000,000
- 1,000,000 - 1,999,999
- 500,000 - 999,999
- 250,000 - 499,999
- 100,000 - 249,999
- 30,000 - 99,999
- 10,000 - 29,999
- UNDER 10,000

SCALE 1:1,170,000 LAMBERT CONFORMAL CONIC PROJECTION

MILES 0 10 20 30 40 50

KILOMETERS 0 10 20 30 40 50

NORTH SEA
DENMARK
GERMANY
NETHERLANDS
BELGIUM
FRANCE
LUXEMBOURG
SWITZERLAND
AUSTRIA
U.K.
Great Britain
North Frisian Islands
East Frisian Islands
West Frisian Islands
LOWER SAXONY
NORTH RHINE-WESTPHALIA
HESSE
RHINELAND-PALATINATE
SAARLAND
BADEN-WÜRTTEMBERG
BAVARIA
THURINGIA
SAXONY-ANHALT
MECKLENBURG-WES
SCHLESWIG-HOLSTEIN
ALSACE
LORRAINE
CHAMPAGNE-ARDENNE
PICARDIE
NORD-PAS-DE-CALAIS
ILE-DE-FRANCE
CENTRE
BOURGOGNE
FRANCHE-COMTÉ
Amsterdam
The Hague
Rotterdam
Brussels
PARIS
Hamburg
Bremen
Hannover
Frankfurt am Main
Cologne
Düsseldorf
Stuttgart
Munich
Leipzig
Longitude East of Greenwich

North Central Europe

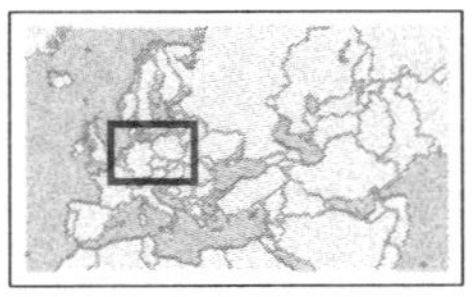

POPULATION OF CITIES AND TOWNS

OVER 2,000,000	500,000 - 999,999	100,000 - 249,999	10,000 - 29,999
1,000,000 - 1,999,999	250,000 - 499,999	30,000 - 99,999	UNDER 10,000

SCALE 1:3,500,000 LAMBERT CONFORMAL CONIC PROJECTION

MILES 0 50 100 150

KILOMETERS 0 50 100 150

Netherlands, Northwestern Germany

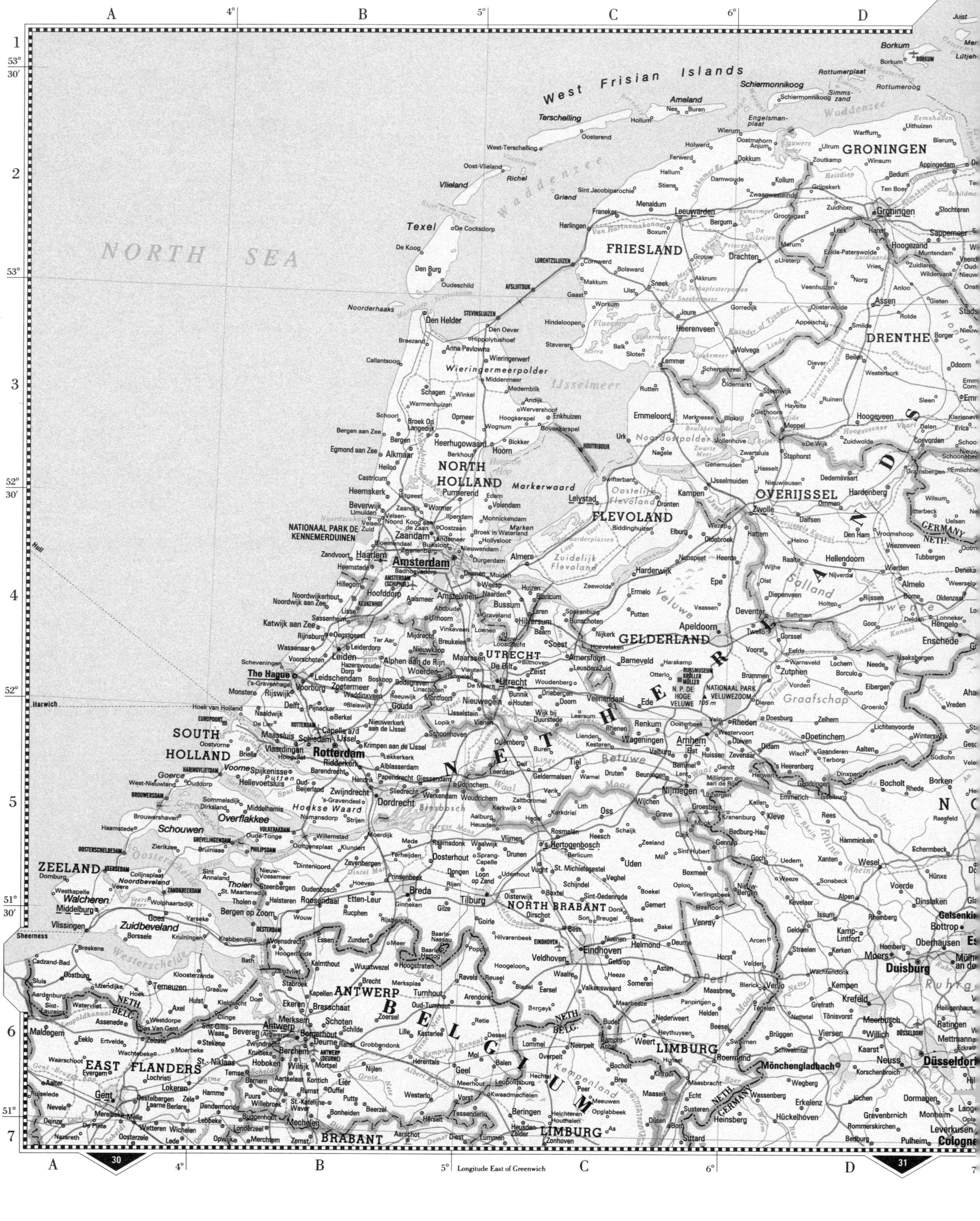

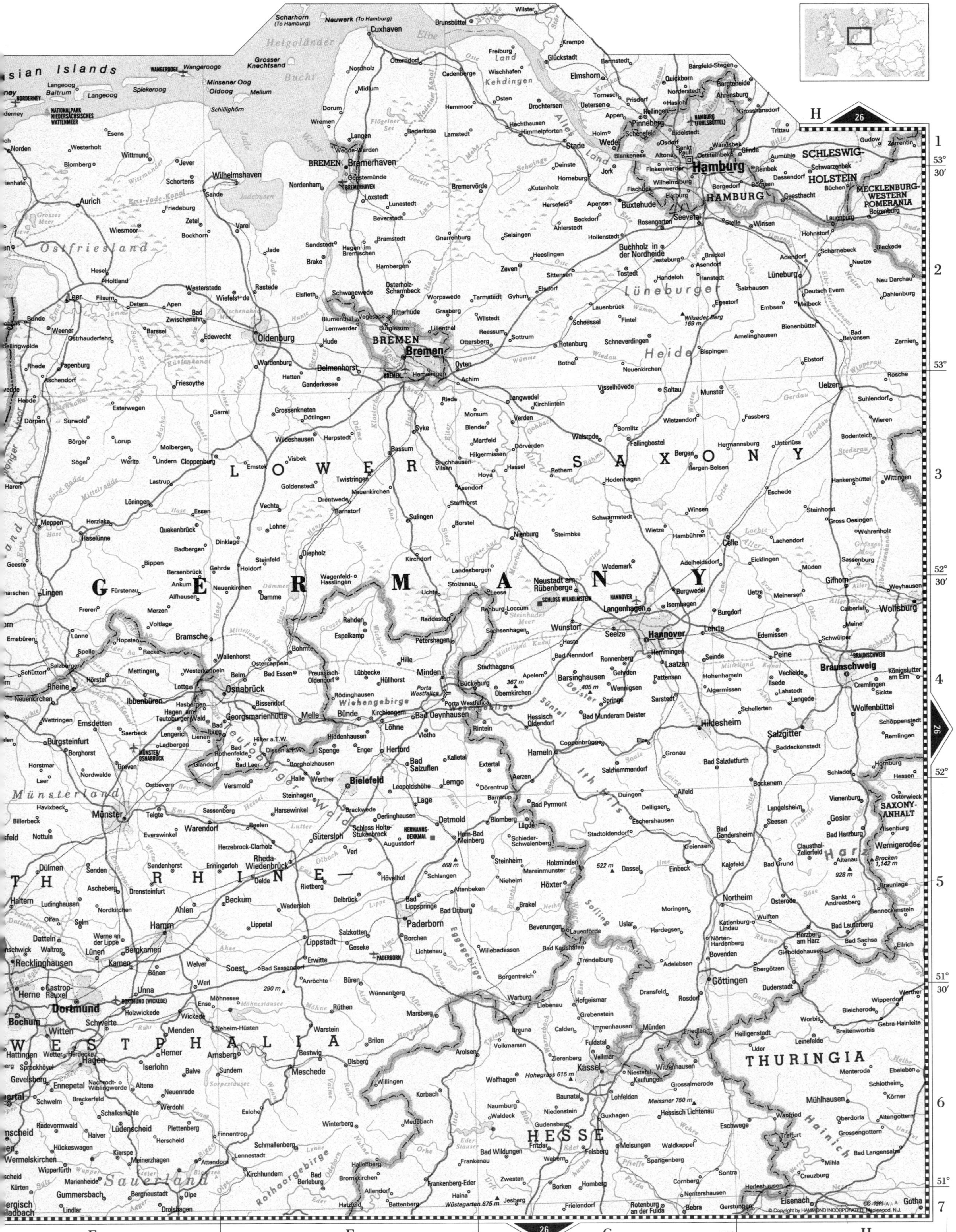

POPULATION OF CITIES AND TOWNS

OVER 2,000,000	500,000 - 999,999	100,000 - 249,999	10,000 - 29,999
1,000,000 - 1,999,999	250,000 - 499,999	30,000 - 99,999	UNDER 10,000

SCALE 1:1,170,000 LAMBERT CONFORMAL CONIC PROJECTION

MILES 0 10 20 30 40 50

KILOMETERS 0 10 20 30 40 50

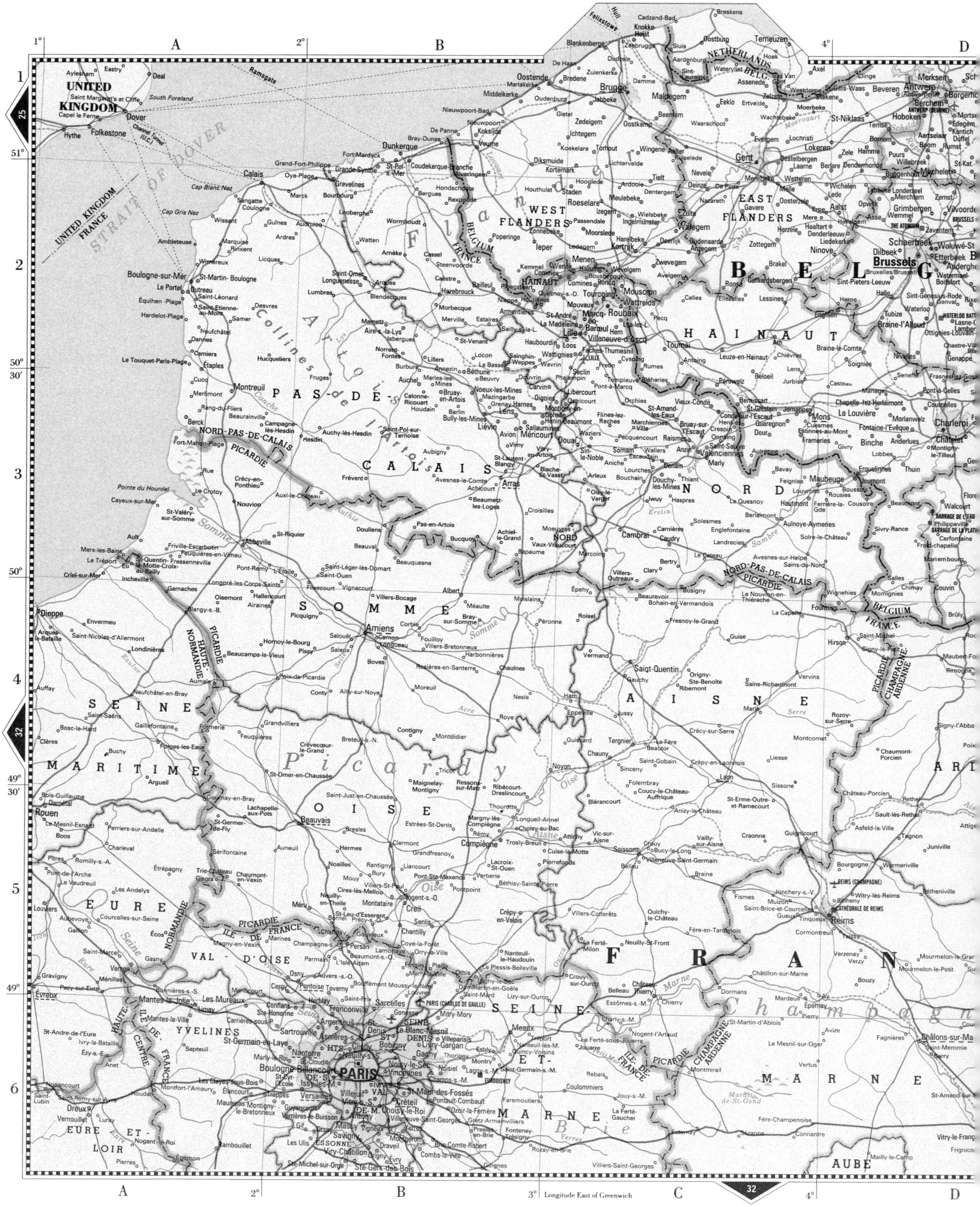
UNITED KINGDOM
FRANCE
BELGIUM
NETHERLANDS
STRAIT OF DOVER
WEST FLANDERS
EAST FLANDERS
HAINAUT
NORD-PAS-DE-CALAIS
PICARDIE
HAUTE-NORMANDIE
ILE-DE-FRANCE
CHAMPAGNE-ARDENNE
CENTRE
PAS-DE-CALAIS
NORD
SOMME
AISNE
OISE
SEINE-MARITIME
EURE
VAL-D'OISE
YVELINES
SEINE-ET-MARNE
MARNE
EURE-ET-LOIR
ESSONNE
AUBE
Picardy
Artois
Collines de l'Artois
Flanders
Champagne
Brie
Paris
Brussels
Lille
Amiens
Reims
Rouen
Calais
Dover
Dunkerque
Boulogne-sur-Mer
Beauvais
Compiègne
Saint-Quentin
Arras
Valenciennes
Gent
Brugge
Antwerp
Mons
Charleroi
Longitude East of Greenwich
1°
2°
3°
4°
51°
50° 30′
50°
49° 30′
49°
A
B
C
D
1
2
3
4
5
6
25
32

Belgium, Northern France, Western Germany

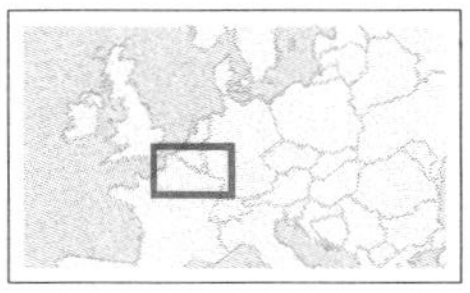

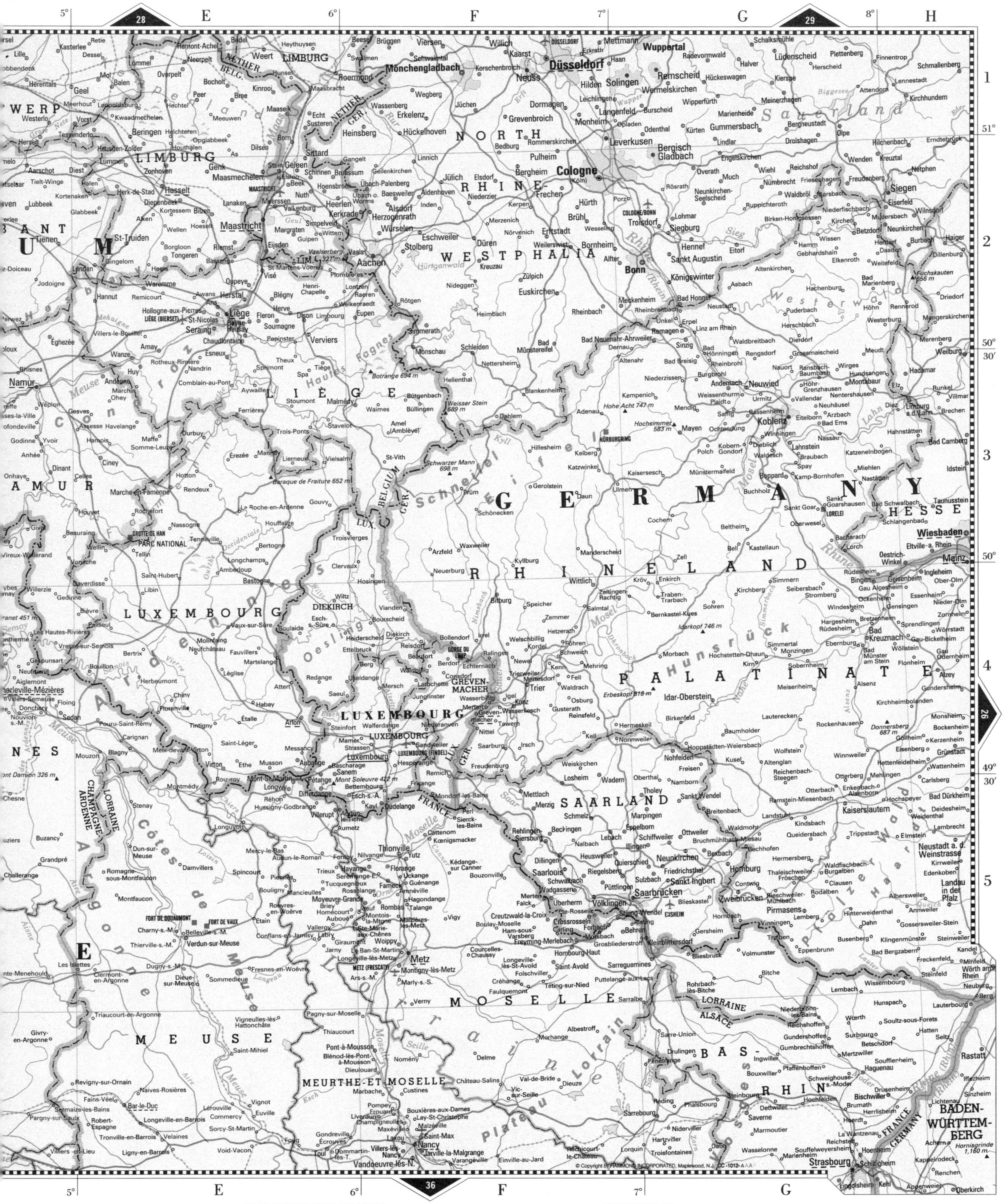

POPULATION OF CITIES AND TOWNS

■ OVER 2,000,000	◉ 500,000 - 999,999	● 100,000 - 249,999	⊙ 10,000 - 29,999
▣ 1,000,000 - 1,999,999	◎ 250,000 - 499,999	• 30,000 - 99,999	○ UNDER 10,000

SCALE 1:1,170,000 LAMBERT CONFORMAL CONIC PROJECTION

MILES 0 10 20 30 40 50

KILOMETERS 0 10 20 30 40 50

FRANCE
BELGIUM
SPAIN
PARIS
Brussels
Marseille
BAY OF BISCAY
English Channel
Gulf of Lions
NORD-PAS-DE-CALAIS
PICARDIE
HAUTE-NORMANDIE
BASSE-NORMANDIE
ILE-DE-FRANCE
CHAMPAGNE-ARDENNE
BOURGOGNE
CENTRE
BRETAGNE
PAYS DE LA LOIRE
POITOU-CHARENTES
LIMOUSIN
AUVERGNE
RHONE-ALPES
AQUITAINE
MIDI-PYRÉNÉES
LANGUEDOC-ROUSSILLON
ANDORRA
CATALONIA
ARAGON
NAVARRE
BASQUE PROVS.
CANTABRIA
CASTILE & LEON
LA RIOJA
Channel Islands (U.K.)
U.K.
FRANCE
Massif Central
Longitude East of Greenwich
Longitude West of Greenwich
26
34
35

West Central Europe

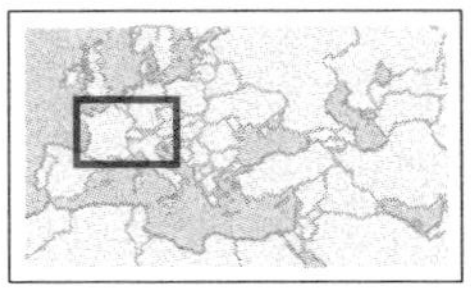

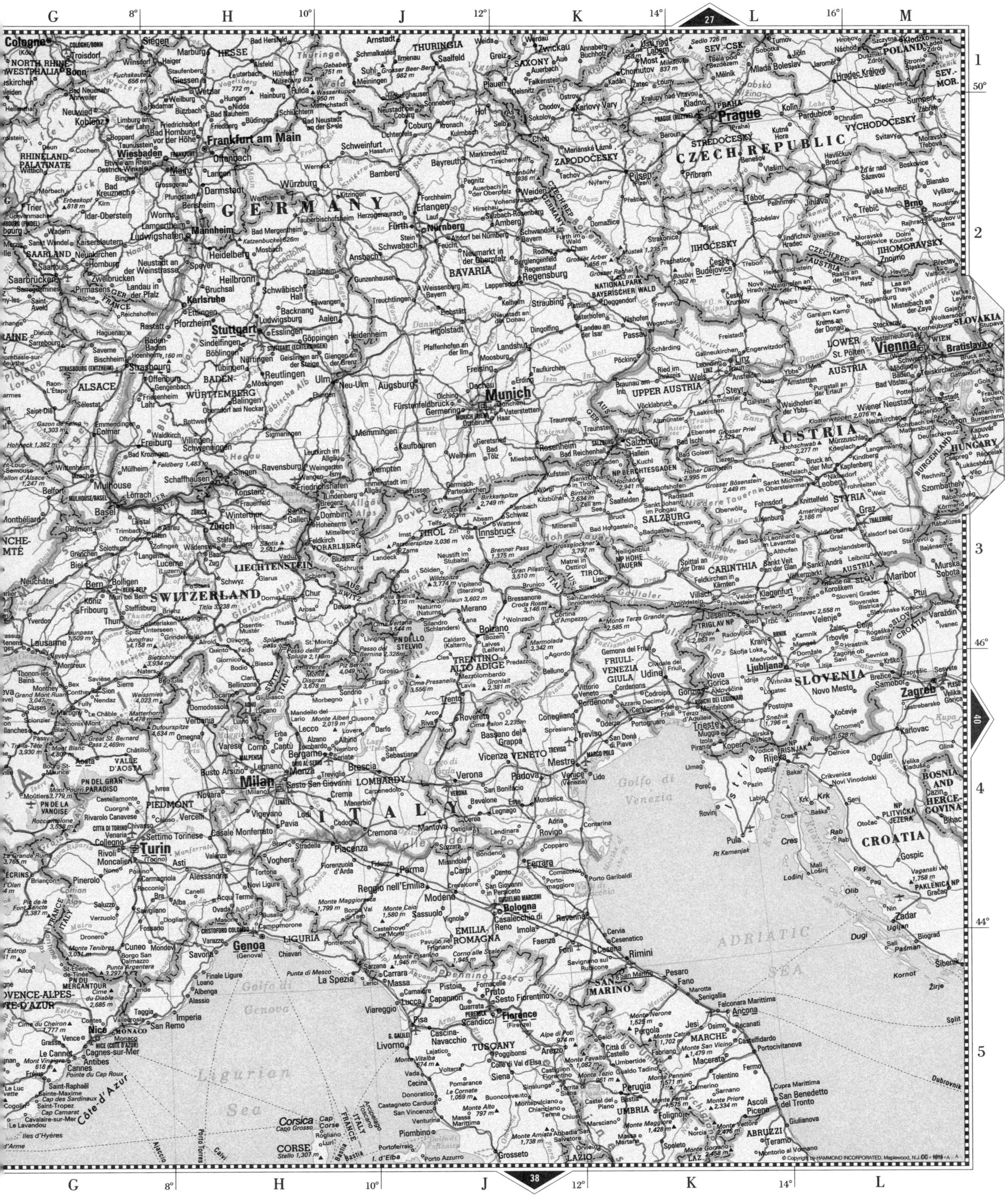

POPULATION OF CITIES AND TOWNS

OVER 2,000,000	500,000 - 999,999	100,000 - 249,999	10,000 - 29,999
1,000,000 - 1,999,999	250,000 - 499,999	30,000 - 99,999	UNDER 10,000

SCALE 1:3,500,000 LAMBERT CONFORMAL CONIC PROJECTION

MILES 0 50 100 150

KILOMETERS 0 50 100 150

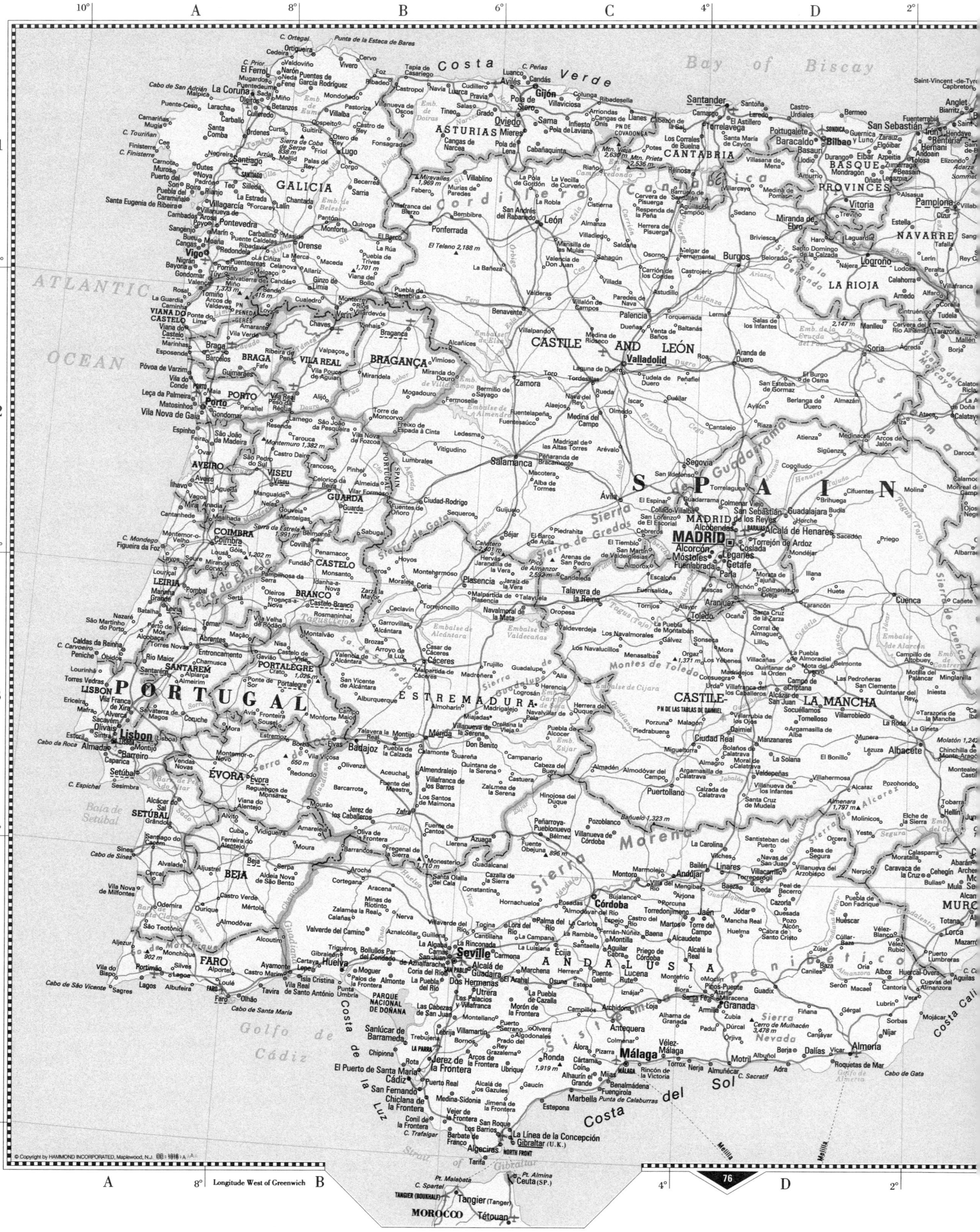
Bay of Biscay
Costa Verde
ATLANTIC OCEAN
SPAIN
PORTUGAL
GALICIA
ASTURIAS
CANTABRIA
BASQUE PROVINCES
NAVARRE
LA RIOJA
CASTILE AND LEÓN
MADRID
CASTILE-LA MANCHA
ESTREMADURA
ANDALUSIA
Cordillera Cantábrica
Sierra de Gredos
Sierra de Guadarrama
Sierra Morena
Sistema Penibético
Sierra Nevada
Montes de Toledo
Golfo de Cádiz
Costa de la Luz
Costa del Sol
Strait of Gibraltar
MOROCCO
Gibraltar (U.K.)
Ceuta (SP.)
Lisbon
Porto
Madrid
Seville
Córdoba
Granada
Málaga
Valladolid
Salamanca
Bilbao
Santander
Oviedo
La Coruña
Vigo
Toledo
Badajoz
Cádiz
Almería
Albacete
Cuenca
Burgos
León
Tangier
Tétouan
Longitude West of Greenwich
76

Spain, Portugal

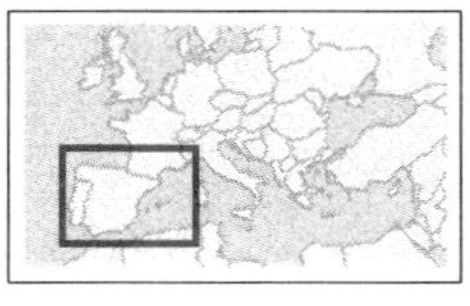

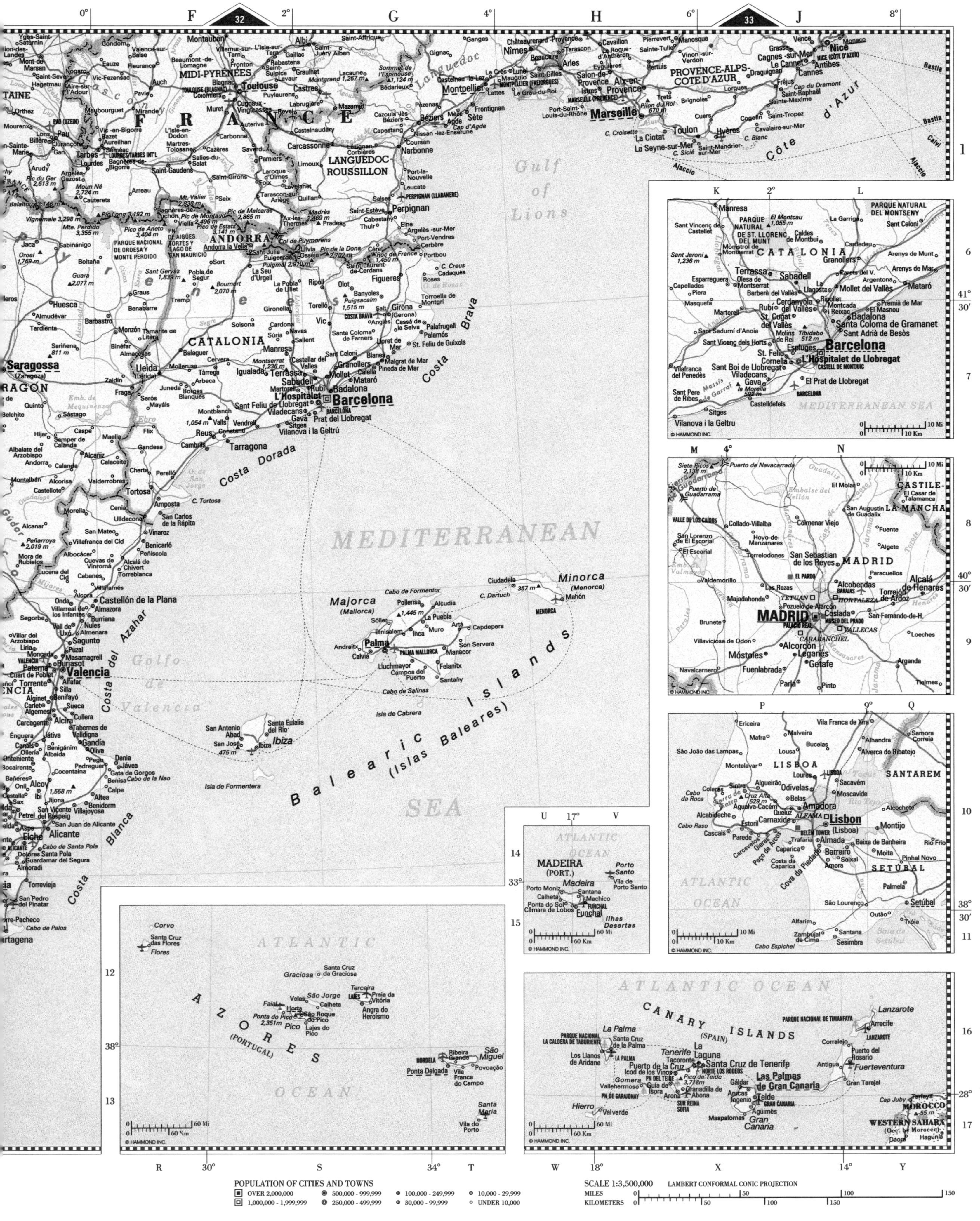

POPULATION OF CITIES AND TOWNS
- OVER 2,000,000
- 1,000,000 - 1,999,999
- 500,000 - 999,999
- 250,000 - 499,999
- 100,000 - 249,999
- 30,000 - 99,999
- 10,000 - 29,999
- UNDER 10,000

SCALE 1:3,500,000 LAMBERT CONFORMAL CONIC PROJECTION

MILES 0 50 100 150

KILOMETERS 0 50 100 150

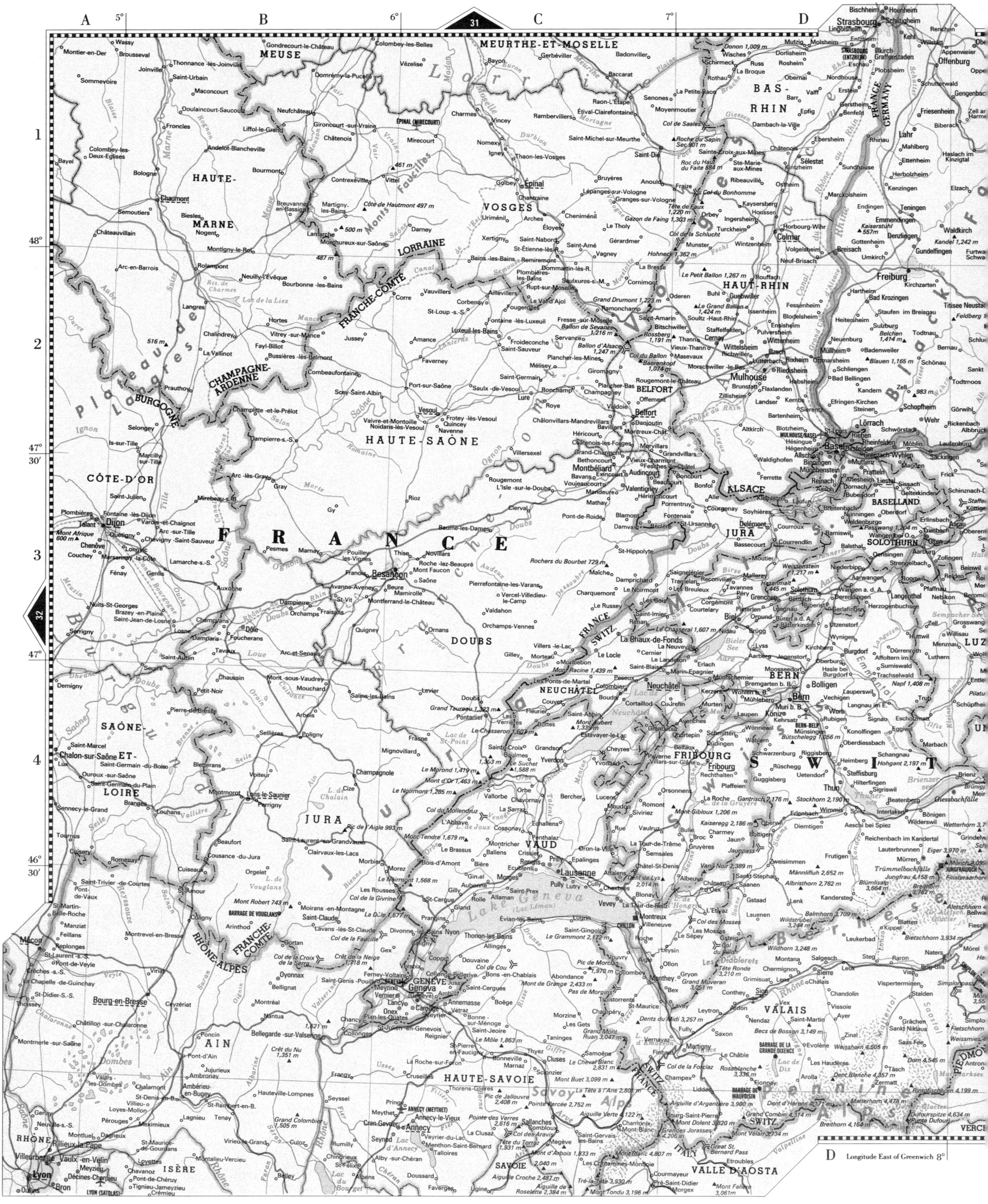
FRANCE
SWITZ.
GERMANY
ITALY
MEURTHE-ET-MOSELLE
MEUSE
HAUTE-MARNE
BAS-RHIN
HAUT-RHIN
VOSGES
LORRAINE
FRANCHE-COMTÉ
CHAMPAGNE-ARDENNE
BURGOGNE
HAUTE-SAÔNE
CÔTE-D'OR
DOUBS
JURA
SAÔNE-ET-LOIRE
AIN
RHÔNE-ALPES
HAUTE-SAVOIE
SAVOIE
ISÈRE
RHÔNE
ALSACE
BELFORT
BASELLAND
SOLOTHURN
NEUCHÂTEL
BERN
FRIBOURG
VAUD
VALAIS
VALLE D'AOSTA
Lake Geneva (Lac Léman)
Plateau de Langres
Black Forest
Bernese Alps
Pennine Alps
Strasbourg
Colmar
Mulhouse
Freiburg
Basel
Belfort
Épinal
Vesoul
Dijon
Besançon
Neuchâtel
Bern
Fribourg
Lausanne
Genève
Annecy
Lons-le-Saunier
Bourg-en-Bresse
Mâcon
Lyon
Chaumont
A B C D
1 2 3 4
5° 6° 7°
48° 47°30′ 47° 46°30′
31
32
Longitude East of Greenwich 8°

Central Alps Region

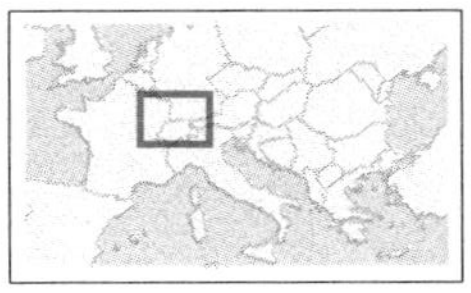

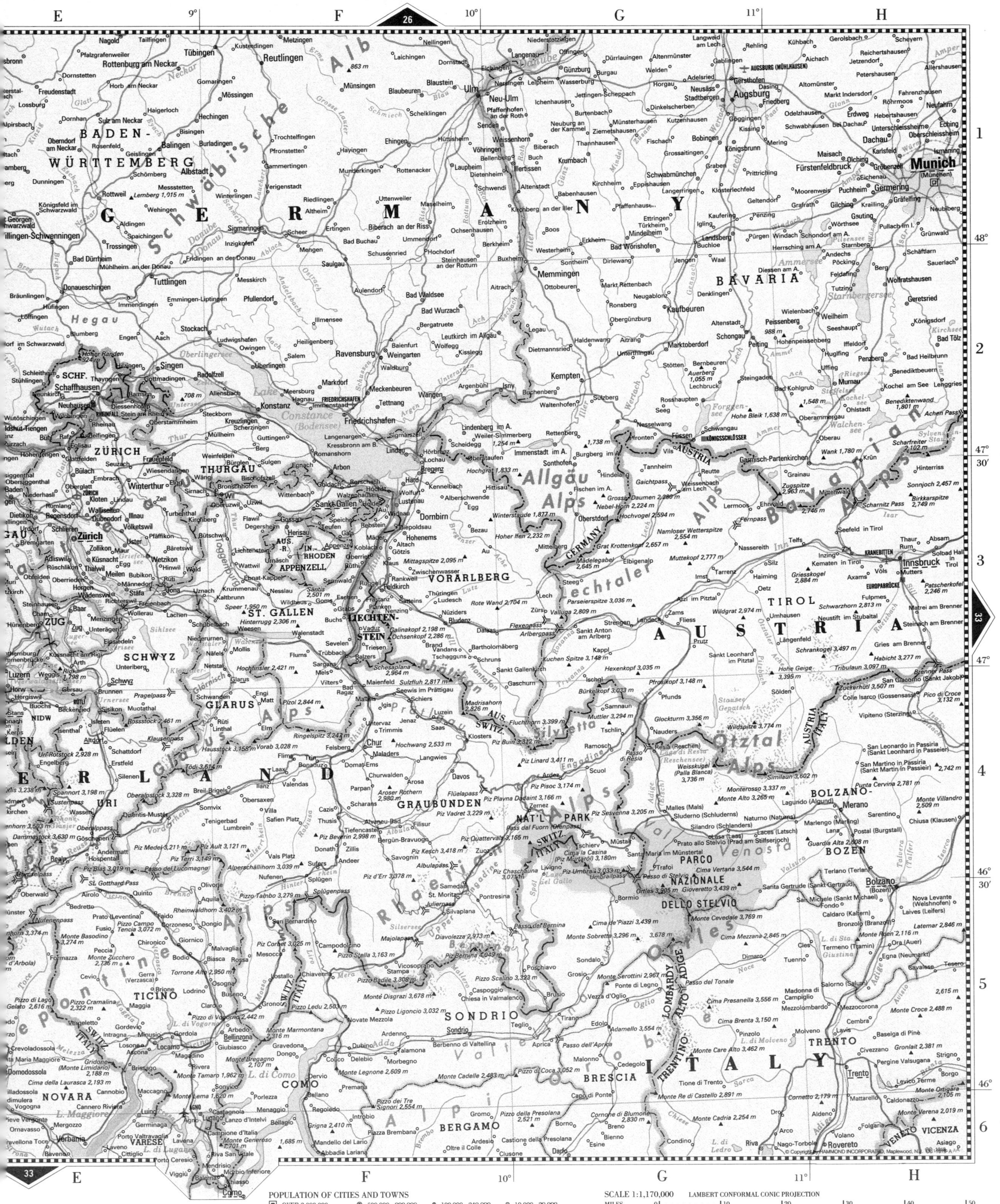

POPULATION OF CITIES AND TOWNS

- OVER 2,000,000
- 1,000,000 - 1,999,999
- 500,000 - 999,999
- 250,000 - 499,999
- 100,000 - 249,999
- 30,000 - 99,999
- 10,000 - 29,999
- UNDER 10,000

SCALE 1:1,170,000 LAMBERT CONFORMAL CONIC PROJECTION

MILES 0 10 20 30 40 50

KILOMETERS 0 10 20 30 40 50

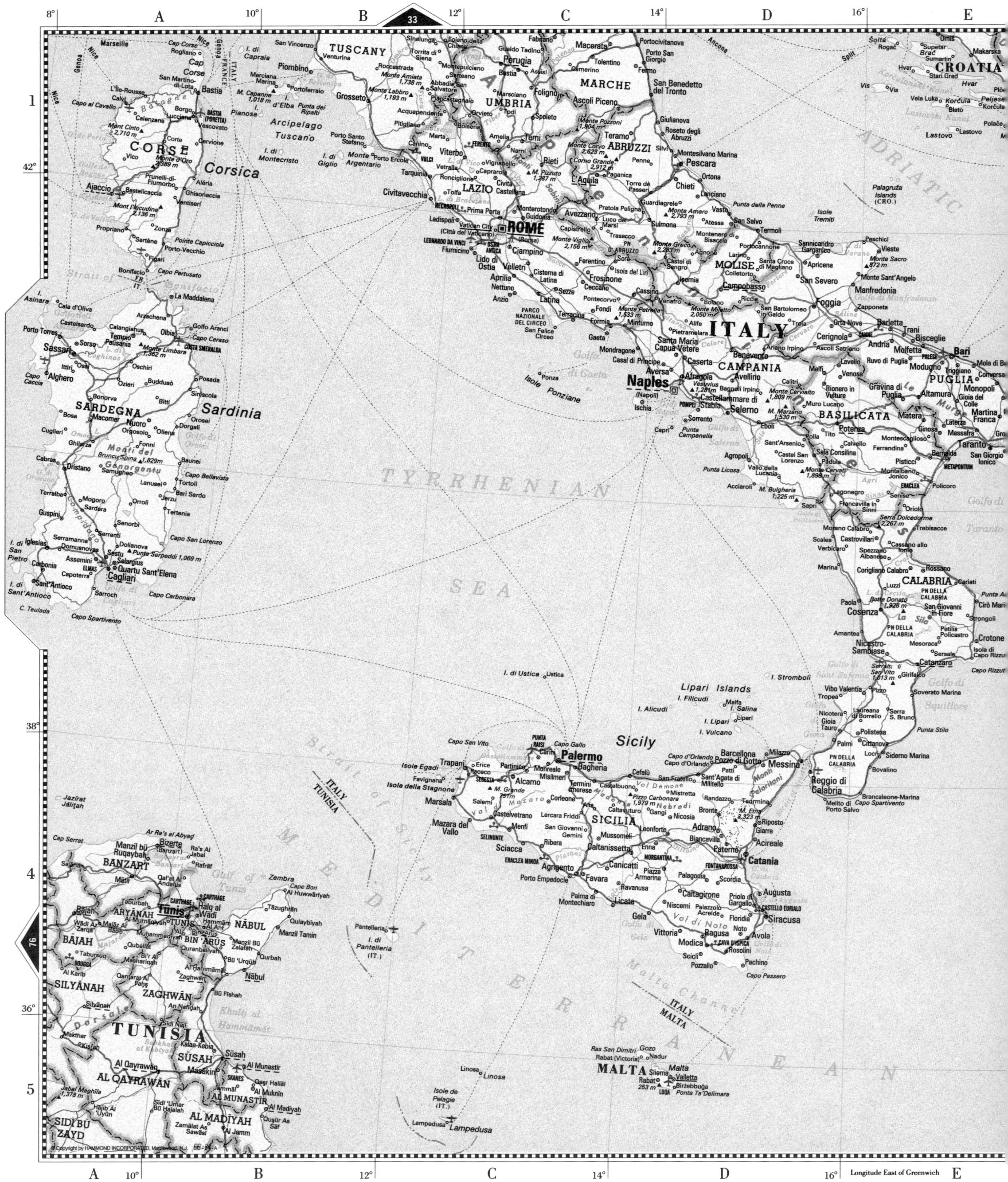

SCALE 1:3,500,000 LAMBERT CONFORMAL CONIC PROJECTION

MILES 0 50 100 150

KILOMETERS 0 50 100 150

POPULATION OF CITIES AND TOWNS

■ OVER 2,000,000	◉ 500,000 - 999,999	● 100,000 - 249,999	◎ 10,000 - 29,999
▣ 1,000,000 - 1,999,999	◉ 250,000 - 499,999	● 30,000 - 99,999	○ UNDER 10,000

Southern Italy, Albania, Greece

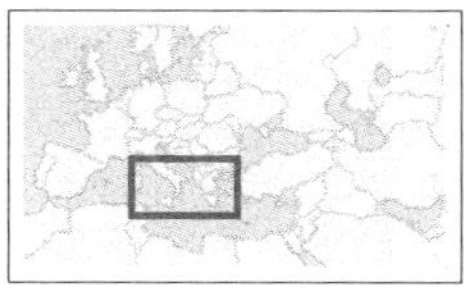

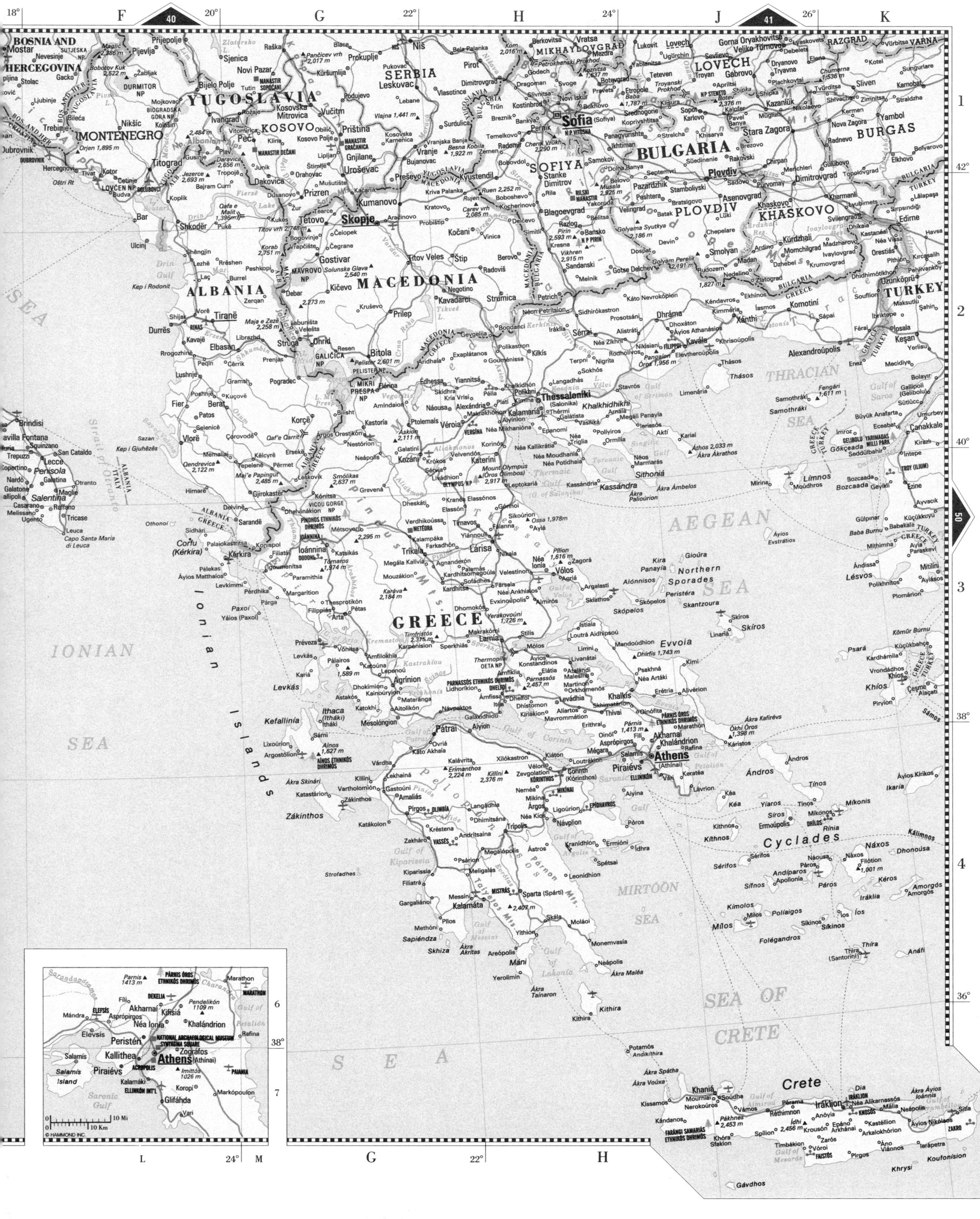

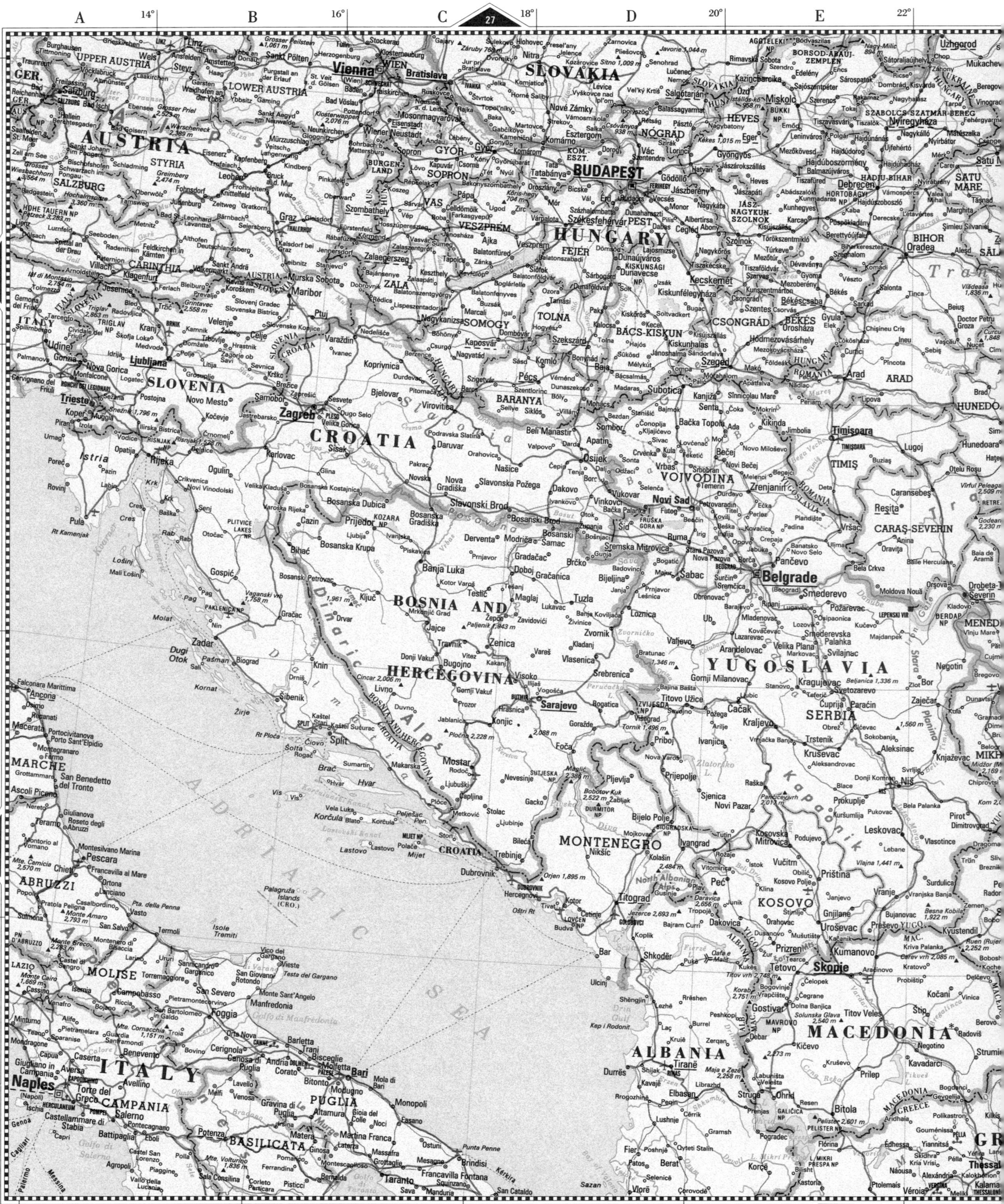

SCALE 1:3,500,000 LAMBERT CONFORMAL CONIC PROJECTION

POPULATION OF CITIES AND TOWNS

OVER 2,000,000	500,000 - 999,999	100,000 - 249,999	10,000 - 29,999
1,000,000 - 1,999,999	250,000 - 499,999	30,000 - 99,999	UNDER 10,000

* WHILE THERE IS NO OTHER OFFICIALLY RECOGNIZED NAME FOR THIS AREA, THE NAME "MACEDONIA" DERIVES FROM ITS FORMER STATUS AS A YUGOSLAV REPUBLIC, AND IS NOT RECOGNIZED BY MANY NATIONS.

Hungary, Northern Balkan States

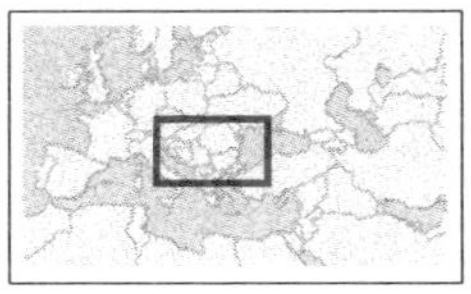

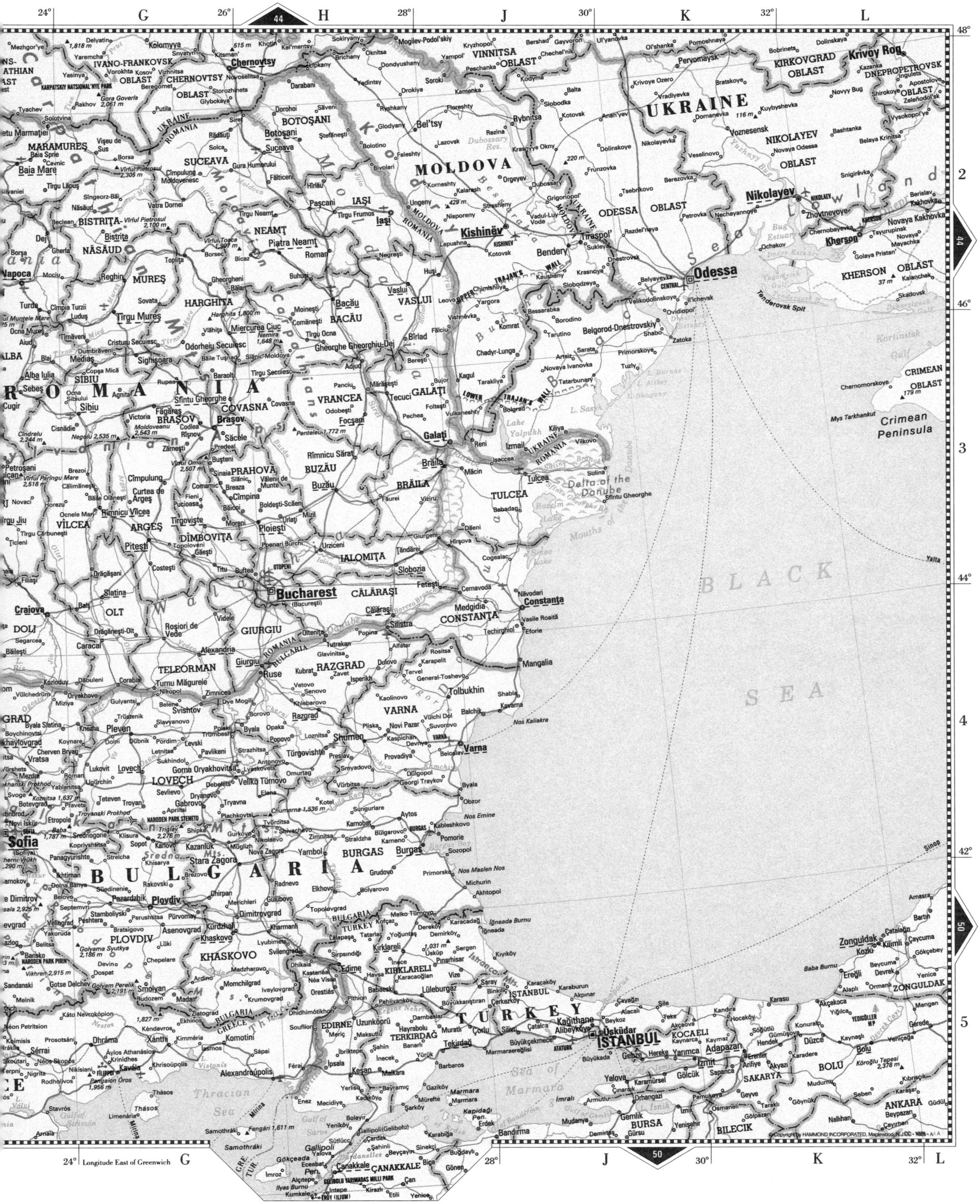

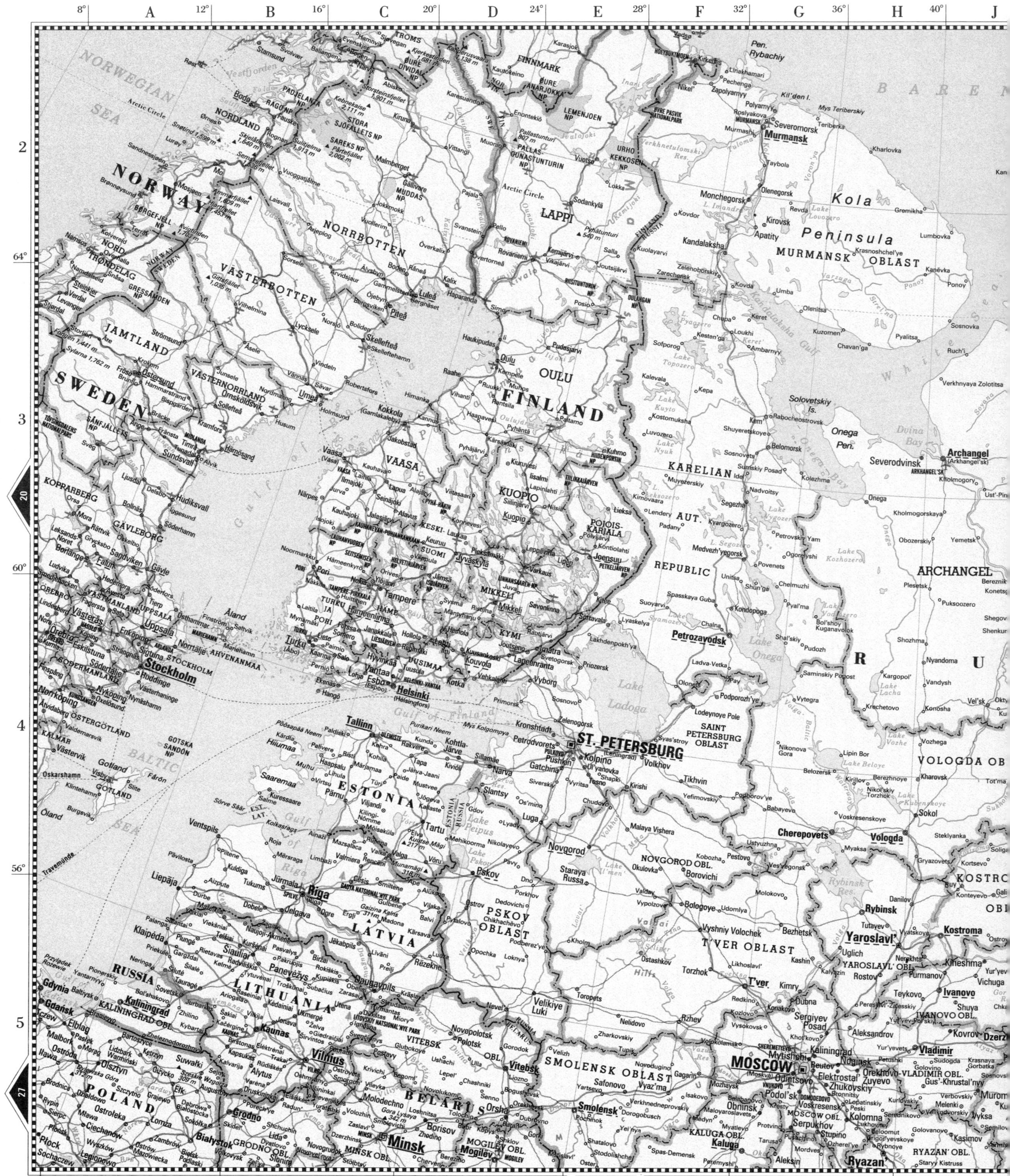
NORWEGIAN SEA
NORWAY
SWEDEN
FINLAND
ESTONIA
LATVIA
LITHUANIA
BELARUS
POLAND
RUSSIA
Kola Peninsula
MURMANSK OBLAST
KARELIAN AUT. REPUBLIC
ARCHANGEL
VOLOGDA OB
SAINT PETERSBURG OBLAST
NOVGOROD OBL.
PSKOV OBLAST
TVER OBLAST
SMOLENSK OBLAST
YAROSLAVL' OBL.
MOSCOW OBL.
KALUGA OBL.
VLADIMIR OBL.
IVANOVO OBL.
RYAZAN' OBL.
MINSK OBL.
MOGILEV OBL.
VITEBSK OBL.
GRODNO OBL.
KALININGRAD OBL.
Gulf of Bothnia
Gulf of Finland
Gulf of Riga
BALTIC SEA
White Sea
Onega Bay
Lake Ladoga
Lake Onega
Lake Peipus
Murmansk
Archangel
Oulu
Vaasa
Turku
Helsinki
Tampere
Stockholm
Uppsala
Tallinn
Riga
Vilnius
Kaunas
Minsk
ST. PETERSBURG
Novgorod
Pskov
Petrozavodsk
Vologda
Yaroslavl'
T'ver
MOSCOW
Smolensk
Kaliningrad
Gdańsk
Białystok
Grodno
Vitebsk
Mogilev
Kaluga
Ryazan'
Ivanovo
Kostroma
Rybinsk
Cherepovets
Longitude East of Greenwich
8° 12° 16° 20° 24° 28° 32° 36° 40°
A B C D E F G H J
2 3 4 5
64° 60° 56°
20
21
44

Northeastern Europe

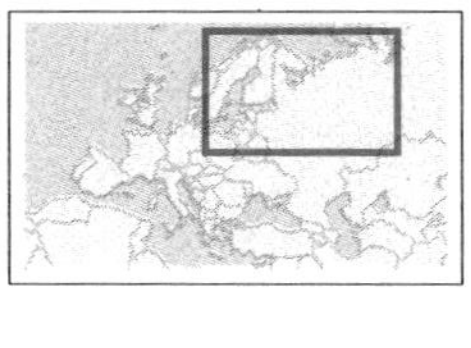

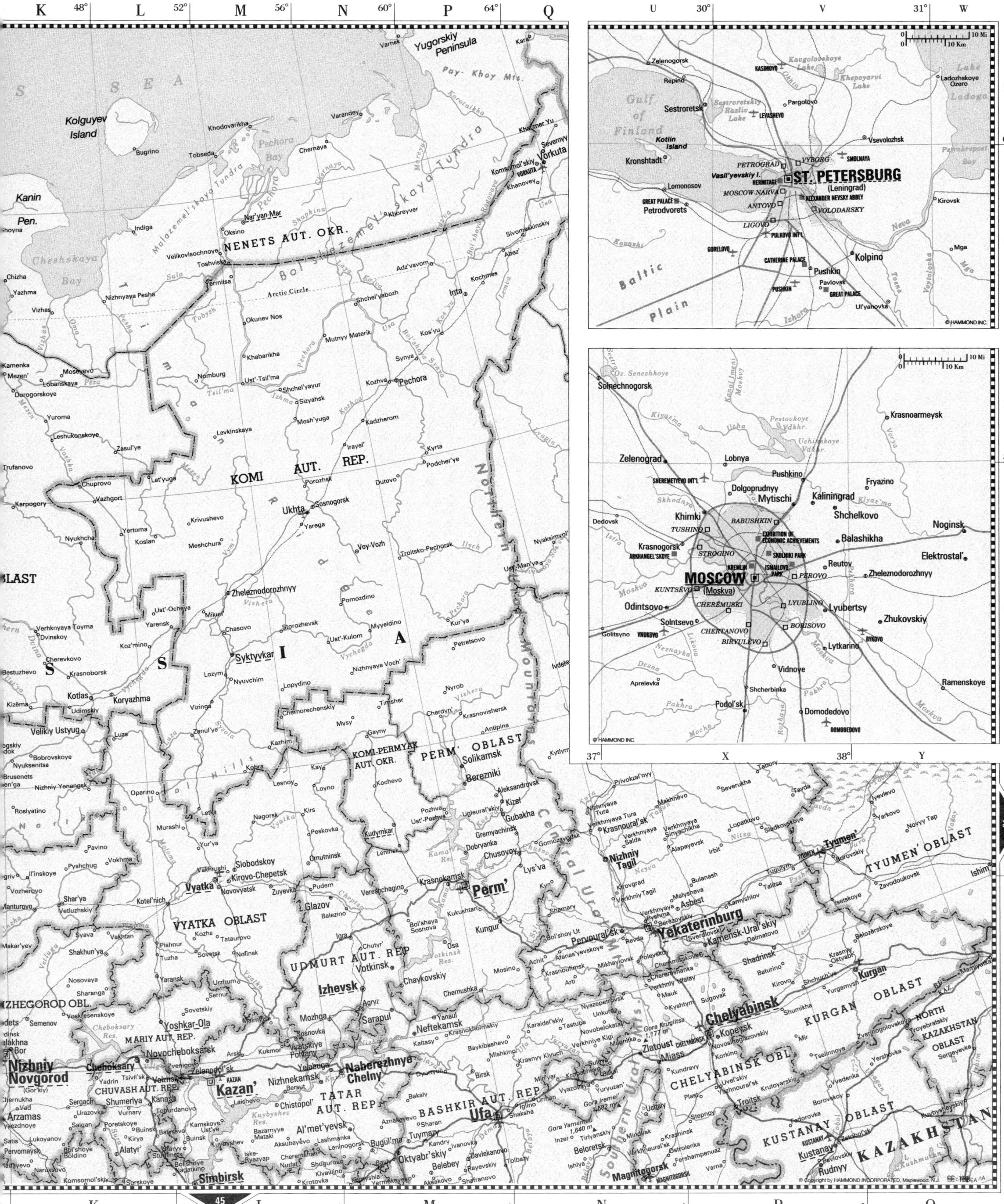

POPULATION OF CITIES AND TOWNS
- OVER 2,000,000
- 1,000,000 - 1,999,999
- 500,000 - 999,999
- 250,000 - 499,999
- 100,000 - 249,999
- 30,000 - 99,999
- 10,000 - 29,999
- UNDER 10,000

SCALE 1:7,000,000 LAMBERT CONFORMAL CONIC PROJECTION
MILES 0 100 200 300
KILOMETERS 0 100 200 300

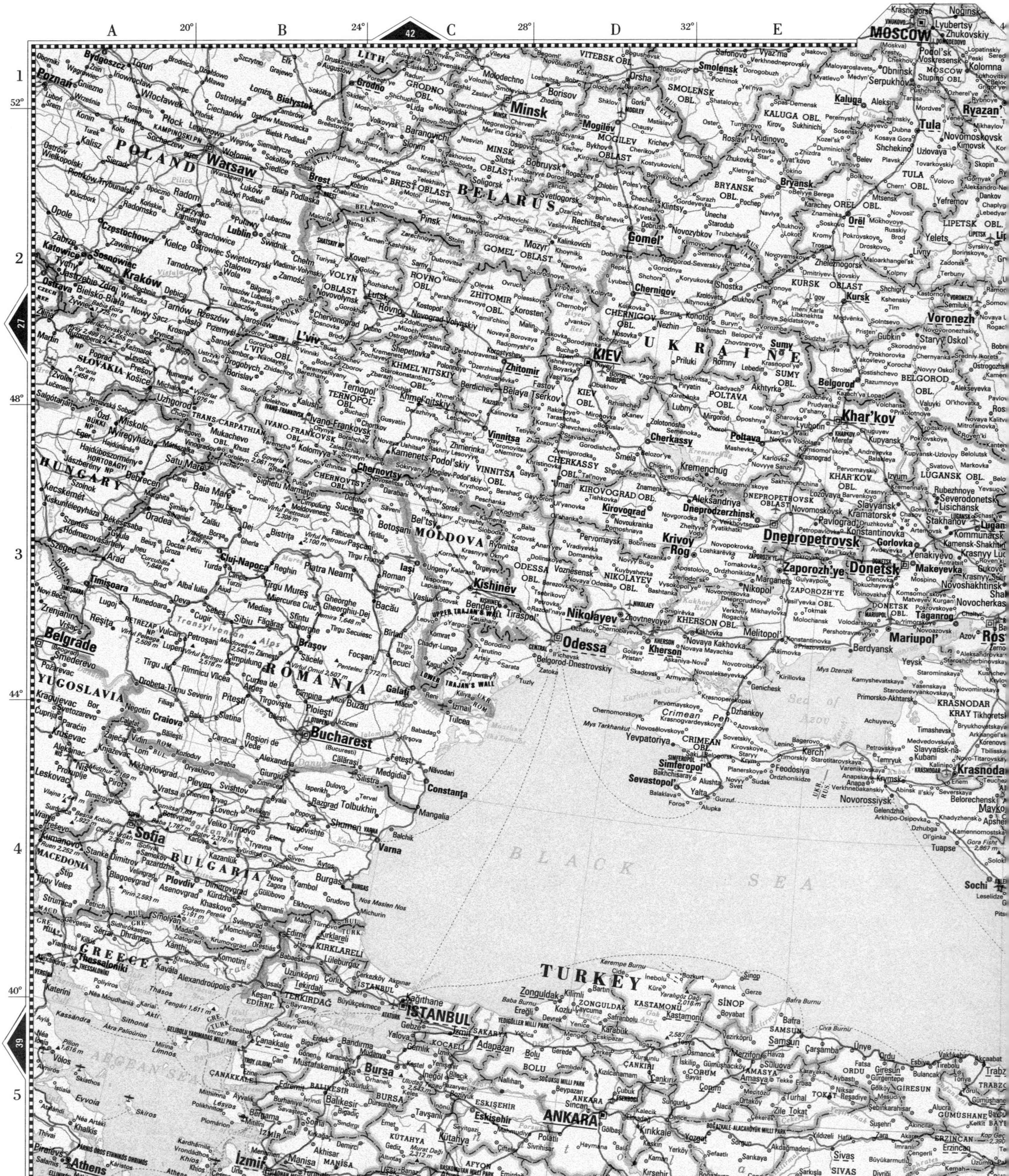

SCALE 1:7,000,000 LAMBERT CONFORMAL CONIC PROJECTION

MILES 0 100 200 300

KILOMETERS 0 100 200 300

Longitude East 28° of Greenwich

POPULATION OF CITIES AND TOWNS

- OVER 2,000,000
- 1,000,000 - 1,999,999
- 500,000 - 999,999
- 250,000 - 499,999
- 100,000 - 249,999
- 30,000 - 99,999
- 10,000 - 29,999
- UNDER 10,000

Southeastern Europe

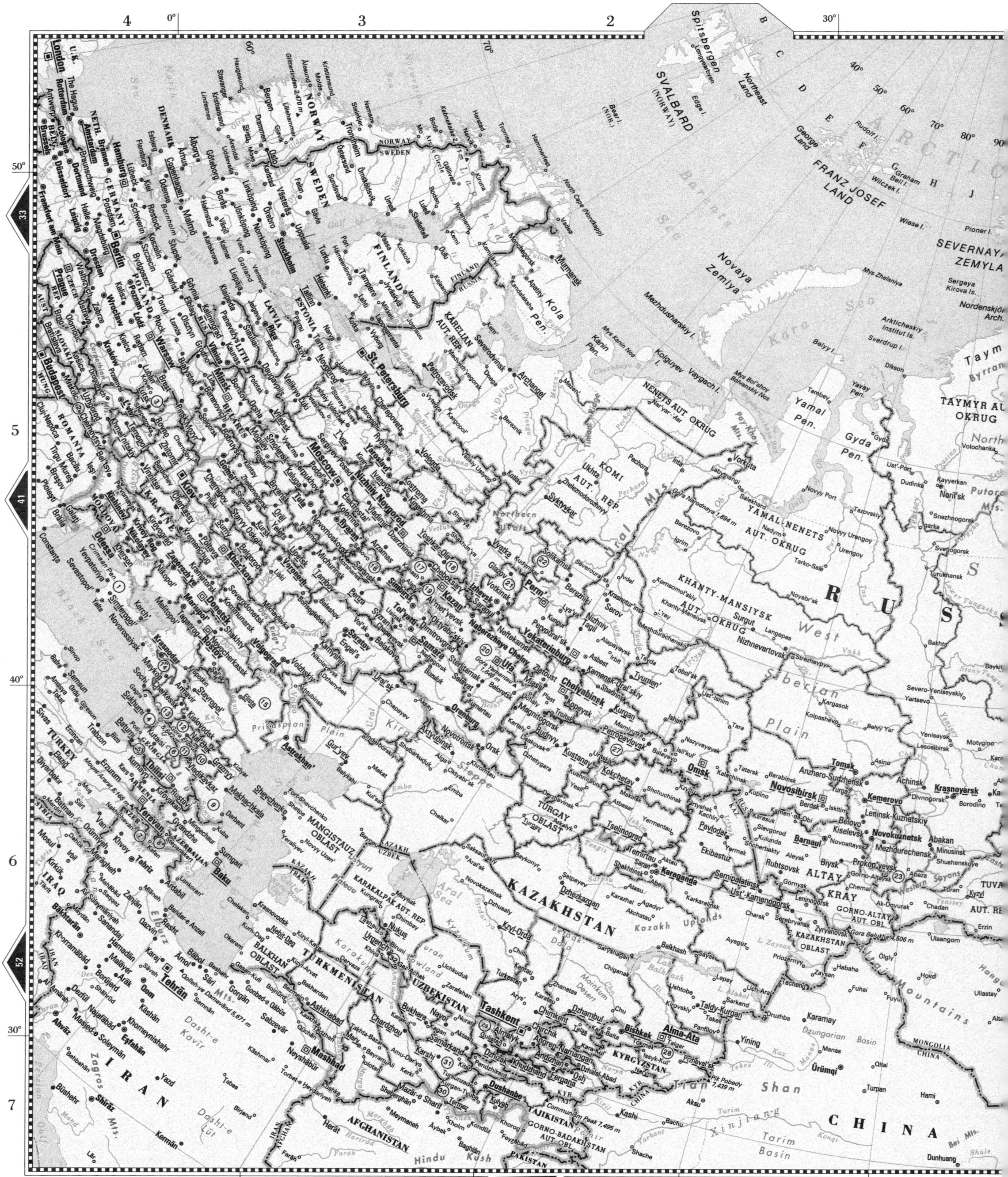
ARCTIC
FRANZ JOSEF LAND
SEVERNAYA ZEMLYA
SVALBARD (NORWAY)
Spitsbergen
Northeast Land
Barents Sea
Kara Sea
Novaya Zemlya
Kola Pen.
White Sea
Yamal Pen.
Gyda Pen.
TAYMYR AUT. OKRUG
NENETS AUT. OKRUG
YAMAL-NENETS AUT. OKRUG
KHANTY-MANSIYSK AUT. OKRUG
KOMI AUT. REP.
KARELIAN AUT. REP.
Ural Mts.
West Siberian Plain
RUSSIA
NORWAY
SWEDEN
FINLAND
DENMARK
ESTONIA
LATVIA
LITH.
POLAND
GERMANY
NETH.
BELG.
U.K.
CZECH REP.
SLOVAKIA
HUNG.
AUST.
ROMANIA
MOLDOVA
UKRAINE
BELARUS
TURKEY
GEORGIA
ARMENIA
AZERBAIJAN
SYRIA
IRAQ
IRAN
TURKMENISTAN
UZBEKISTAN
KAZAKHSTAN
KYRGYZSTAN
TAJIKISTAN
AFGHANISTAN
PAKISTAN
CHINA
MONGOLIA
Black Sea
Caspian Sea
Aral Sea
London
Amsterdam
Berlin
Prague
Budapest
Warsaw
Oslo
Stockholm
Helsinki
Tallinn
Riga
Vilnius
Minsk
Kiev
Moscow
St. Petersburg
Tehrān
Baku
Tbilisi
Yerevan
Tashkent
Alma-Ata
Bishkek
Dushanbe
Ashkhabad
Novosibirsk
Omsk
Yekaterinburg
Kazakh Uplands
Tian Shan
Hindu Kush
Zagros Mts.
Elburz Mts.
Altay Mountains
Tarim Basin
Dzungarian Basin
Longitude East of Greenwich

Russia and Neighboring Countries

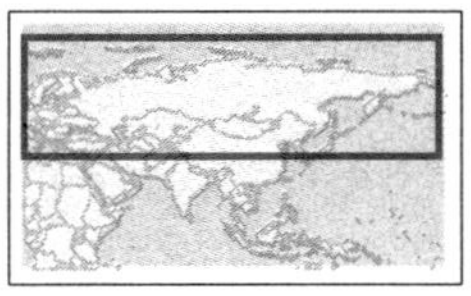

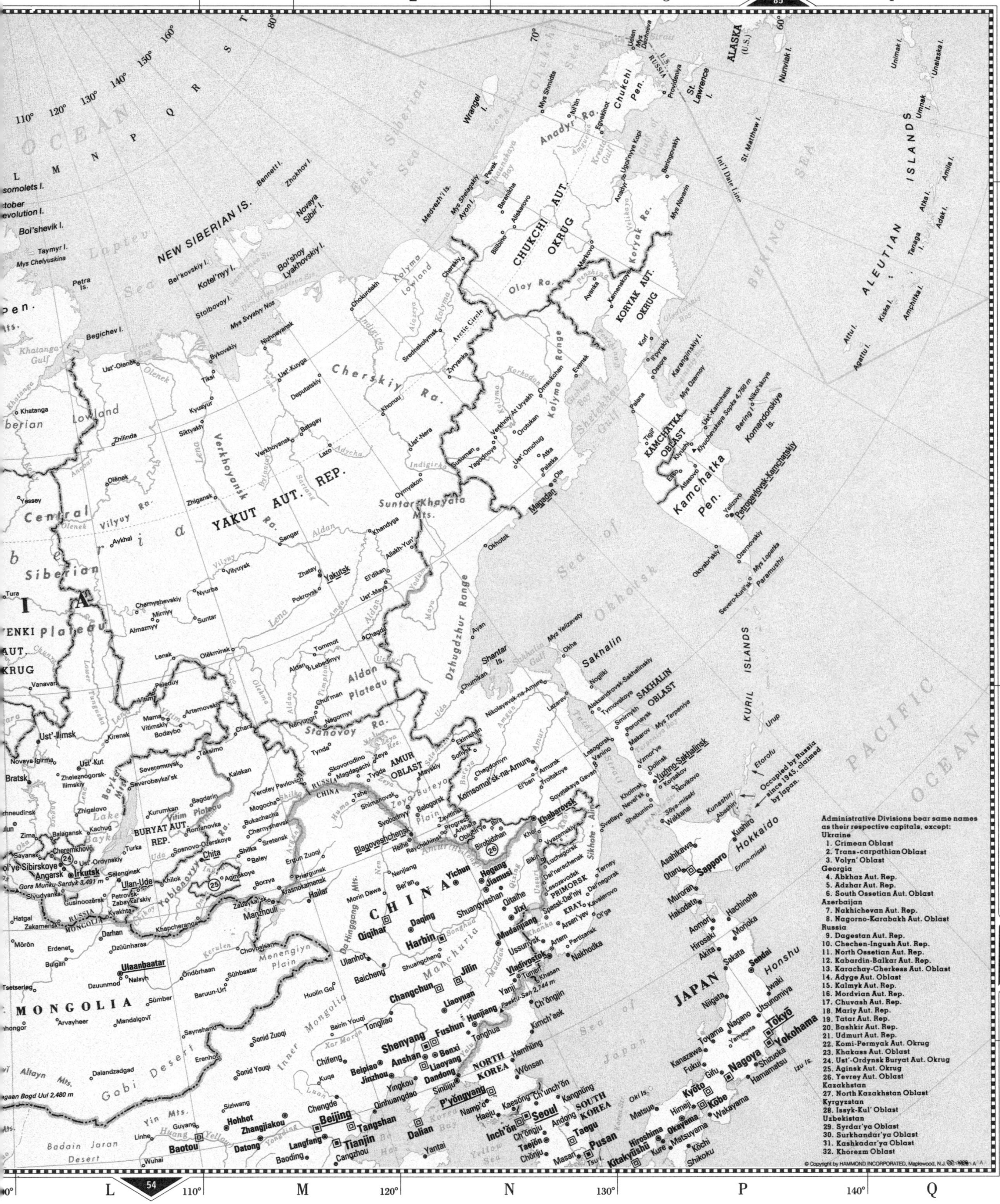

POPULATION OF CITIES AND TOWNS
- OVER 2,000,000
- 1,000,000 - 1,999,999
- 500,000 - 999,999
- 100,000 - 499,999
- 50,000 - 99,999
- UNDER 50,000

SCALE 1:21,000,000 LAMBERT CONFORMAL CONIC PROJECTION

MILES 0 300 600 900

KILOMETERS 0 300 600 900

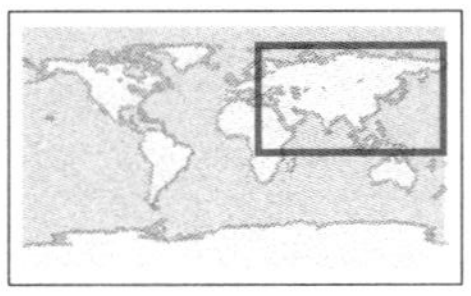

Asia

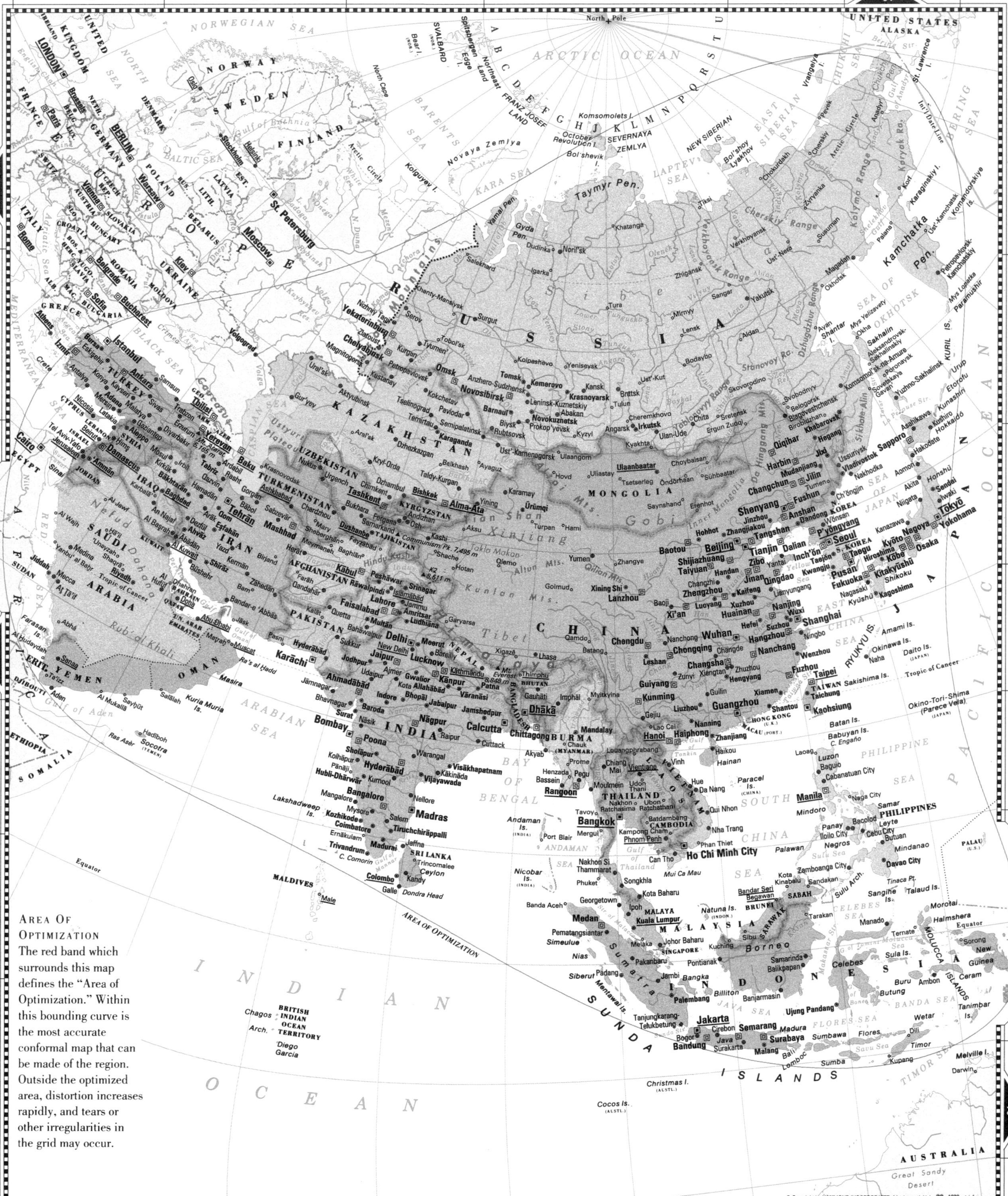

AREA OF OPTIMIZATION

The red band which surrounds this map defines the "Area of Optimization." Within this bounding curve is the most accurate conformal map that can be made of the region. Outside the optimized area, distortion increases rapidly, and tears or other irregularities in the grid may occur.

Longitude East F of Greenwich

SCALE 1:49,000,000 OPTIMAL CONFORMAL PROJECTION

MILES 0 700 1400 2100

KILOMETERS 0 700 1400 2100

POPULATION OF CITIES AND TOWNS

- OVER 3,000,000
- 1,000,000 - 2,999,999
- 500,000 - 999,999
- 100,000 - 499,999
- UNDER 100,000

Eastern Mediterranean Region

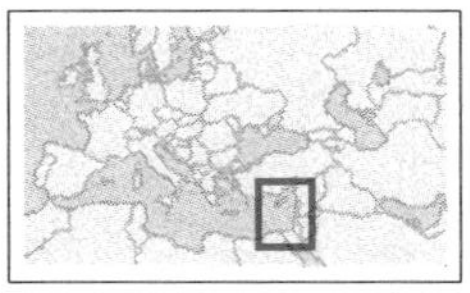

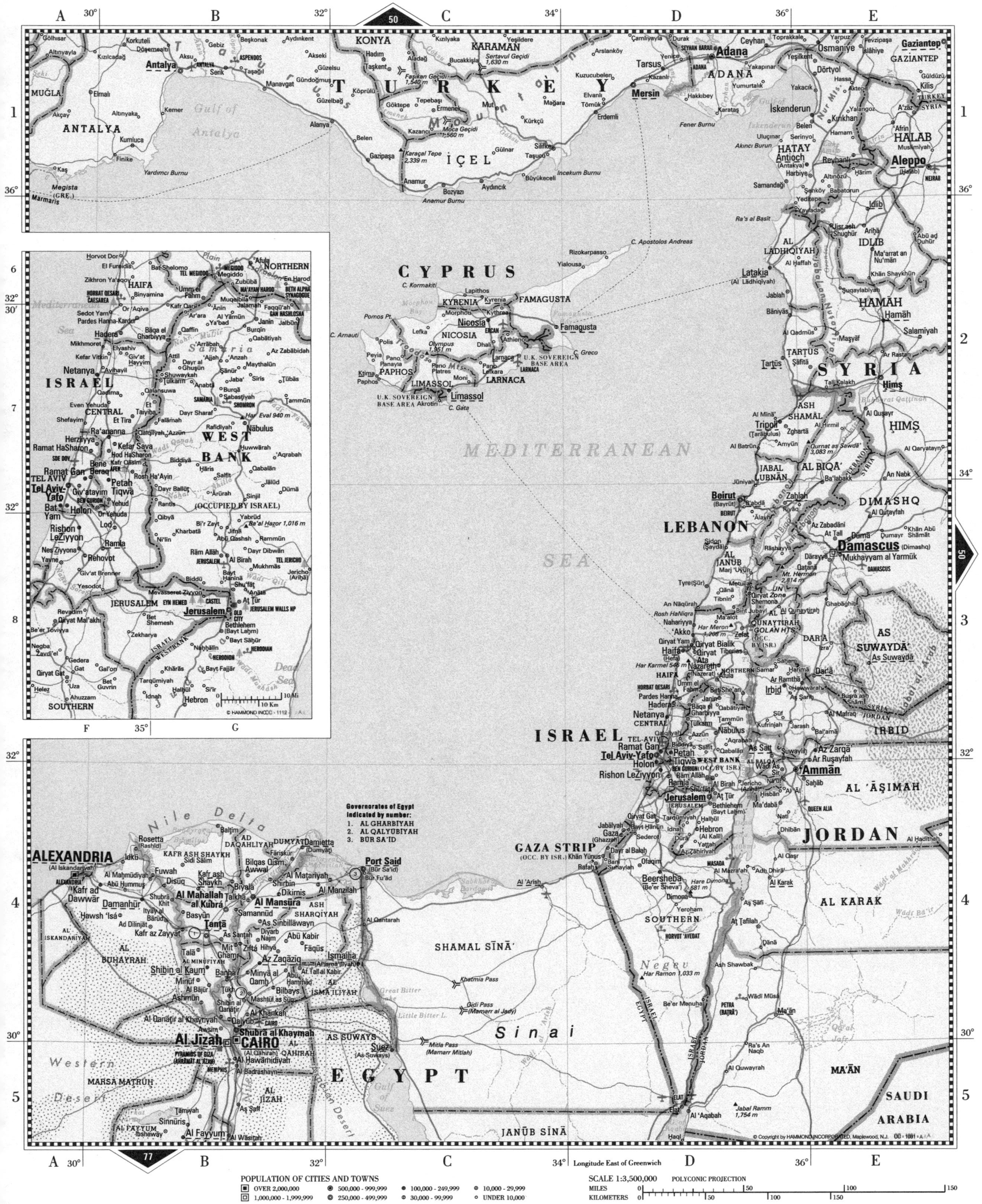

POPULATION OF CITIES AND TOWNS

- OVER 2,000,000
- 1,000,000 - 1,999,999
- 500,000 - 999,999
- 250,000 - 499,999
- 100,000 - 249,999
- 30,000 - 99,999
- 10,000 - 29,999
- UNDER 10,000

SCALE 1:3,500,000 POLYCONIC PROJECTION

MILES 0 50 100 150

KILOMETERS 0 50 100 150

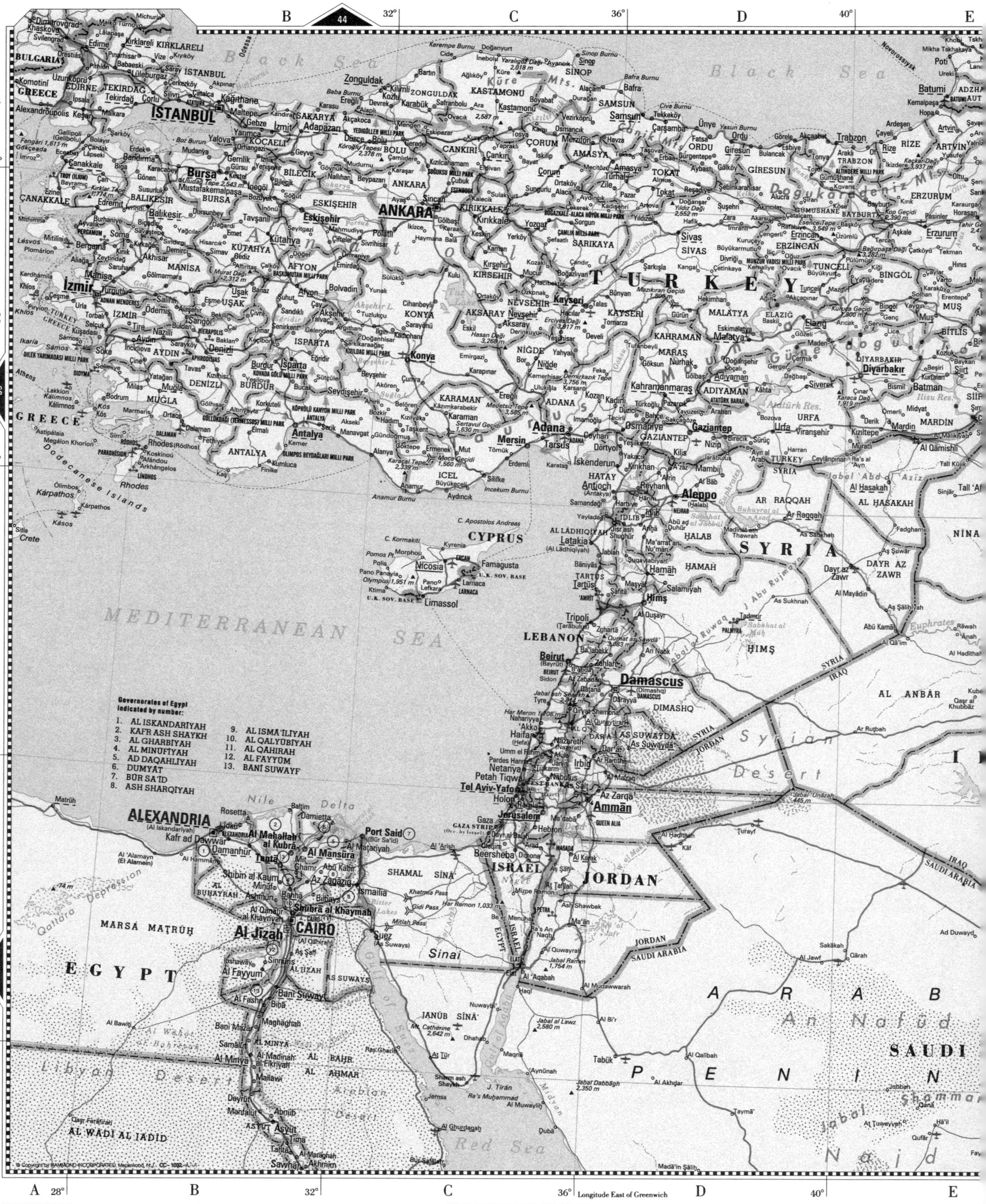

Longitude East of Greenwich

SCALE 1:7,000,000 LAMBERT CONFORMAL CONIC PROJECTION

MILES 0 100 200 300

KILOMETERS 0 100 200 300

POPULATION OF CITIES AND TOWNS

- OVER 2,000,000
- 1,000,000 - 1,999,999
- 500,000 - 999,999
- 250,000 - 499,999
- 100,000 - 249,999
- 30,000 - 99,999
- 10,000 - 29,999
- UNDER 10,000

Northern Middle East

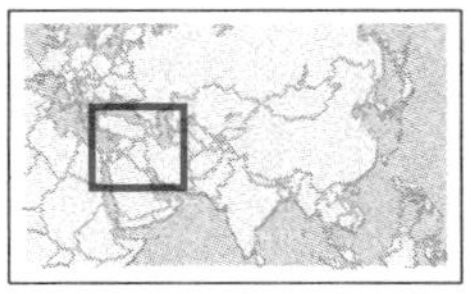

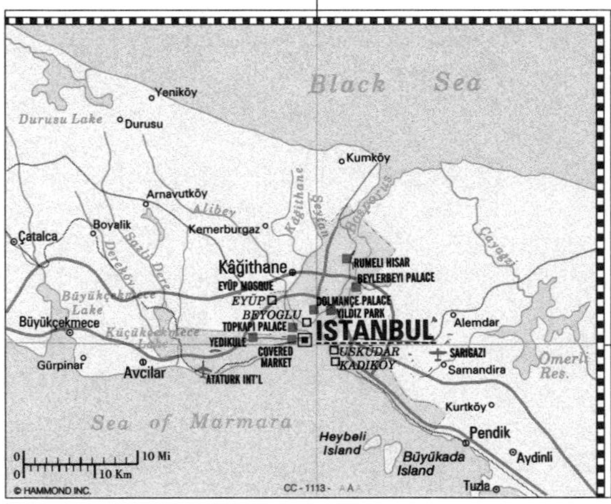

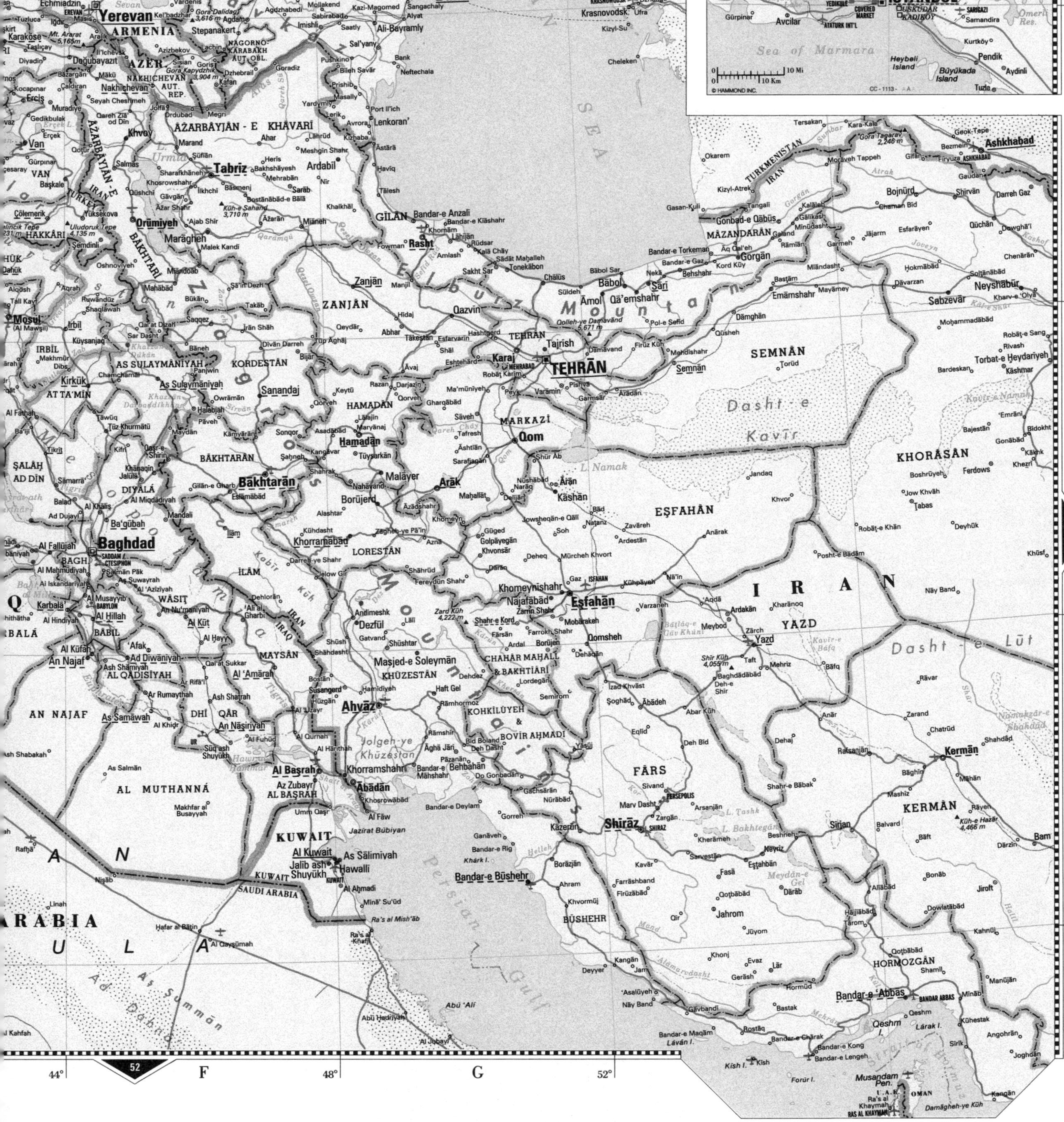

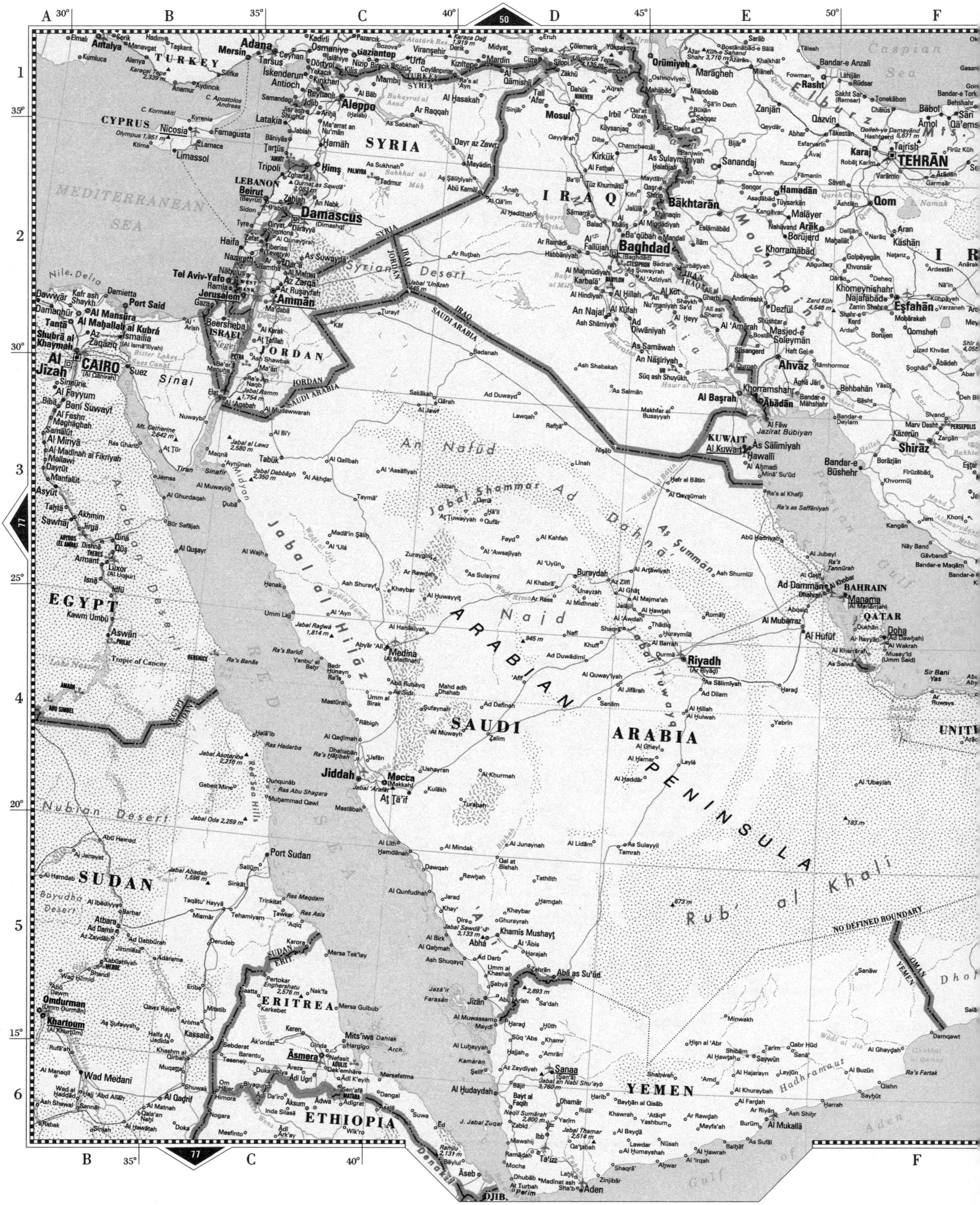

TURKEY
CYPRUS
SYRIA
LEBANON
ISRAEL
JORDAN
IRAQ
KUWAIT
IRAN
SAUDI ARABIA
EGYPT
SUDAN
ERITREA
ETHIOPIA
YEMEN
OMAN
BAHRAIN
QATAR
DJIB.
MEDITERRANEAN SEA
Caspian Sea
RED SEA
Persian Gulf
Gulf of Aden
ARABIAN PENINSULA
Syrian Desert
An Nafūd
Ad Dahnā'
As Summān
Najd
Jabal al Hijāz
Jabal Shammar
Jabal Tuwayq
Rub' al Khālī
Hadhramaut
Arabian Desert
Nubian Desert
Bayudha Desert
Sinai
Mesopotamia
Zagros Mountains
Elburz Mts.
Red Sea Hills
Tropic of Cancer
NO DEFINED BOUNDARY
Ankara
Adana
Mersin
Antalya
Aleppo
Damascus
Beirut
Tel Aviv-Yafo
Jerusalem
Ammān
Baghdad
Mosul
Al Başrah
Al Kuwayt
TEHRĀN
Qom
Eşfahān
Shīrāz
Ahvāz
Bākhtarān
Tabrīz
Orūmīyeh
Riyadh
Medina
Mecca
Jiddah
Ad Dammām
Manama
Doha
Sanaa
Aden
CAIRO
Al Jīzah
Port Said
Suez
Aswān
Port Sudan
Khartoum
Omdurman
Āsmera
Nicosia
Limassol
A
B
C
D
E
F
1
2
3
4
5
6
30°
35°
40°
45°
50°
25°
20°
15°
50
77

Southwestern Asia

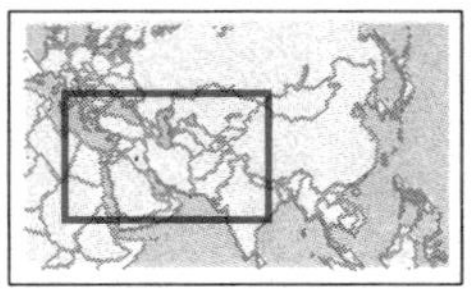

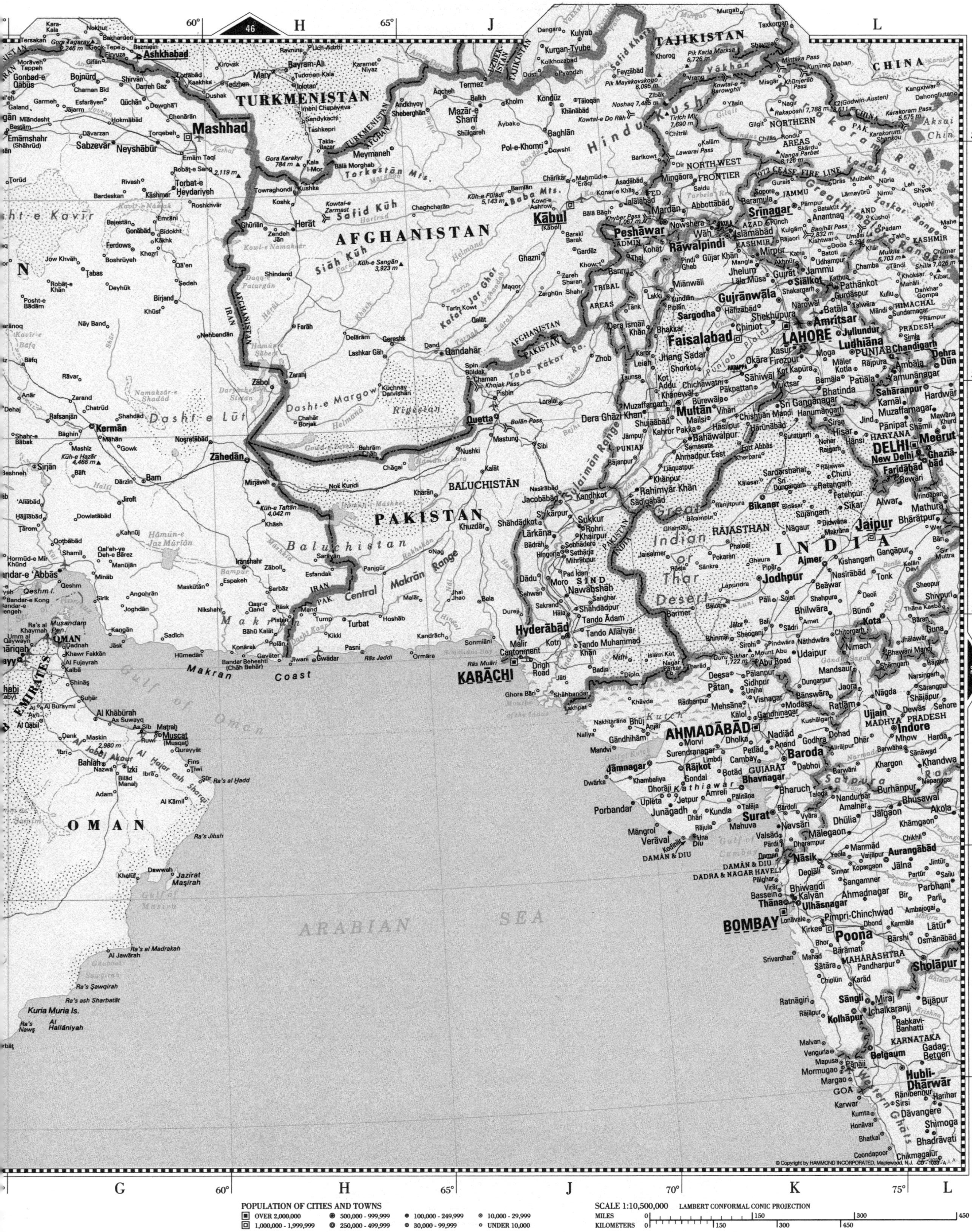

POPULATION OF CITIES AND TOWNS

▣ OVER 2,000,000	◉ 500,000 - 999,999	● 100,000 - 249,999	◉ 10,000 - 29,999
◻ 1,000,000 - 1,999,999	◎ 250,000 - 499,999	● 30,000 - 99,999	○ UNDER 10,000

SCALE 1:10,500,000 LAMBERT CONFORMAL CONIC PROJECTION

MILES 0 150 300 450

KILOMETERS 0 150 300 450

46
63
Longitude East of Greenwich
RUSSIA
MONGOLIA
CHINA
KAZAKHSTAN
INDIA
Ulaanbaatar
BEIJING
XI'AN
CHENGDU
WUHAN
Irkutsk
Ulan-Ude
Chita
Ürümqi
Lanzhou
Xining
Baotou
Hohhot
Taiyuan
Zhengzhou
Shijiazhuang
Lake Baykal
Gobi Desert
Govi Altayn Mts.
Hangayn Mts.
Altun Mountains
Kunlun Mts.
Qilian Mts.
Yablonovyy Range
Western Sayan
Eastern Sayan
Tarim Basin
Dzungarian Basin
Badain Jaran Desert
Tengger Desert
Ordos
Tibet
Bayan Har Mountains

Eastern Asia

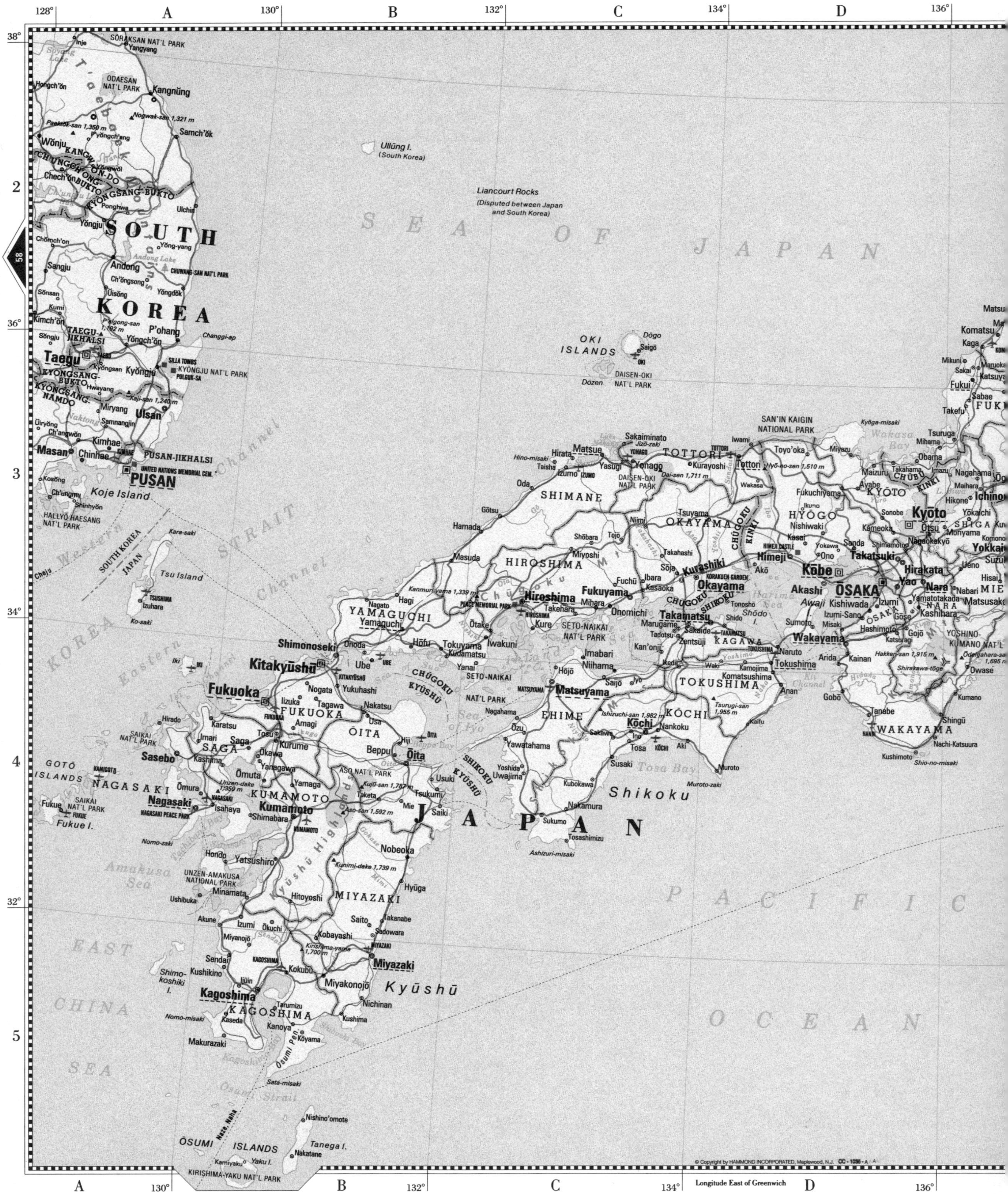
SEA OF JAPAN
SOUTH KOREA
JAPAN
PACIFIC OCEAN
EAST CHINA SEA
KOREA STRAIT
Western Channel
Eastern Channel
Shikoku
Kyūshū
OKI ISLANDS
Ullŭng I. (South Korea)
Liancourt Rocks (Disputed between Japan and South Korea)
Tsu Island
Koje Island
GOTŌ ISLANDS
ŌSUMI ISLANDS
Tanega I.
Yaku I.
Fukue I.
SAN'IN KAIGIN NATIONAL PARK
DAISEN-OKI NAT'L PARK
SETO-NAIKAI NAT'L PARK
ASO NAT'L PARK
UNZEN-AMAKUSA NATIONAL PARK
SAIKAI NAT'L PARK
KIRISHIMA-YAKU NAT'L PARK
YOSHINO-KUMANO NAT'L PARK
SŎRAKSAN NAT'L PARK
ODAESAN NAT'L PARK
CHUWANG-SAN NAT'L PARK
KYŎNGJU NAT'L PARK
HALLYŎ HAESANG NAT'L PARK
PUSAN
Taegu
Ulsan
Masan
Kyŏngju
P'ohang
Andong
Kangnŭng
Wŏnju
Kitakyūshū
Fukuoka
Shimonoseki
Nagasaki
Kumamoto
Kagoshima
Miyazaki
Ōita
Hiroshima
Okayama
Matsue
Tottori
Matsuyama
Kōchi
Takamatsu
Tokushima
Kōbe
Himeji
ŌSAKA
Kyōto
Nara
Wakayama
SHIMANE
YAMAGUCHI
HIROSHIMA
OKAYAMA
TOTTORI
HYŌGO
KYŌTO
ŌSAKA
NARA
WAKAYAMA
EHIME
KŌCHI
KAGAWA
TOKUSHIMA
FUKUOKA
SAGA
NAGASAKI
KUMAMOTO
ŌITA
MIYAZAKI
KAGOSHIMA
128°
130°
132°
134°
136°
38°
36°
34°
32°
A
B
C
D
2
3
4
5
58
© Copyright by HAMMOND INCORPORATED, Maplewood, N.J.
Longitude East of Greenwich

Central and Southern Japan

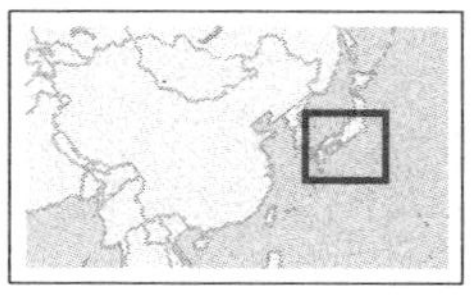

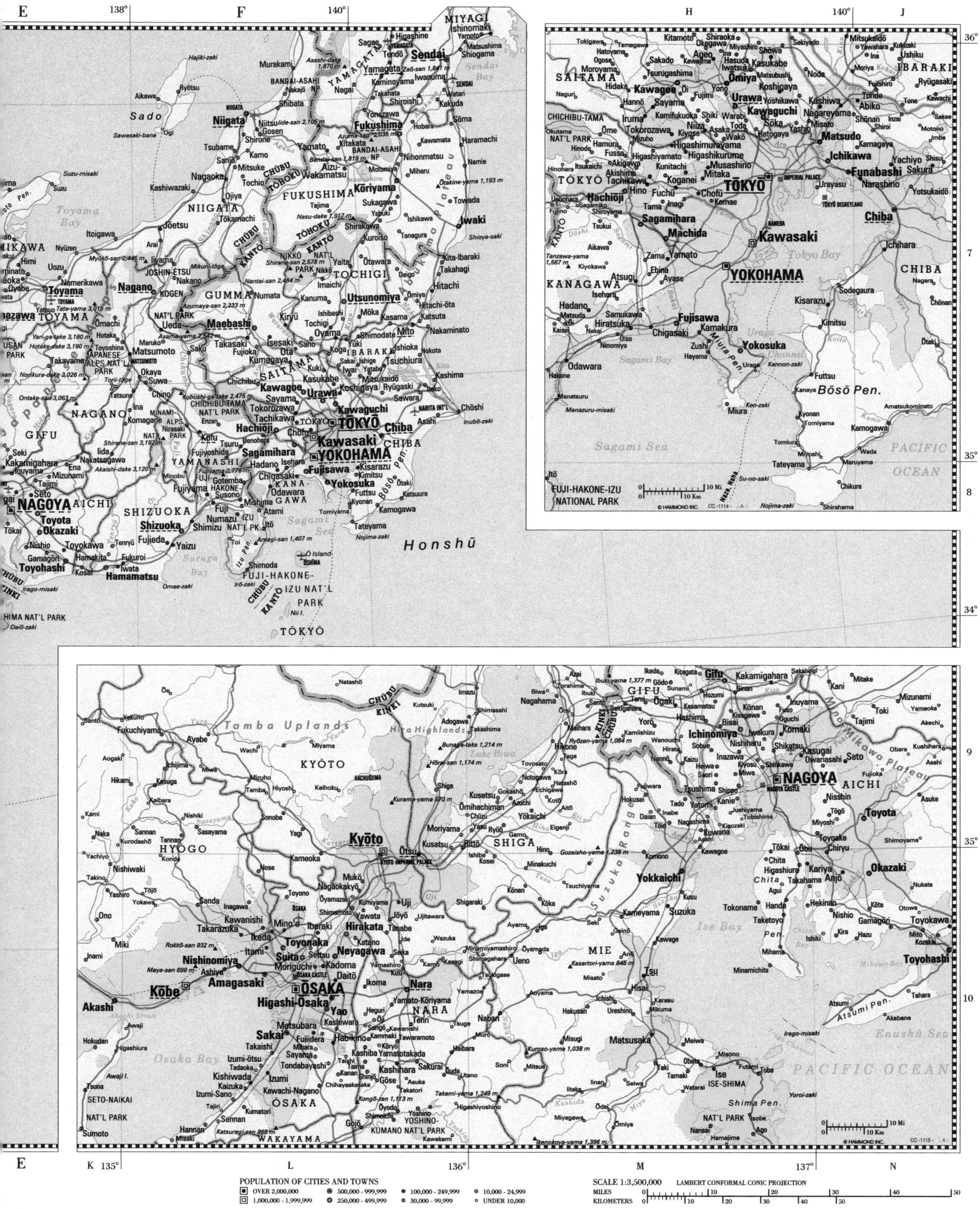

POPULATION OF CITIES AND TOWNS

▣ OVER 2,000,000	◉ 500,000 - 999,999	● 100,000 - 249,999	⊙ 10,000 - 24,999
◻ 1,000,000 - 1,999,999	◉ 250,000 - 499,999	● 30,000 - 99,999	○ UNDER 10,000

SCALE 1:3,500,000 LAMBERT CONFORMAL CONIC PROJECTION

MILES 0 10 20 30 40 50

KILOMETERS 0 10 20 30 40 50

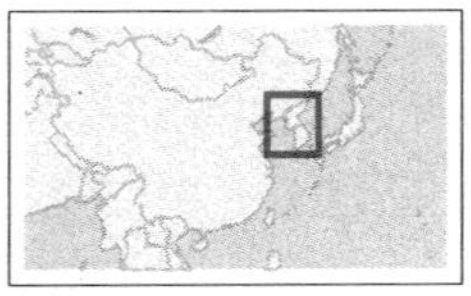

Korea

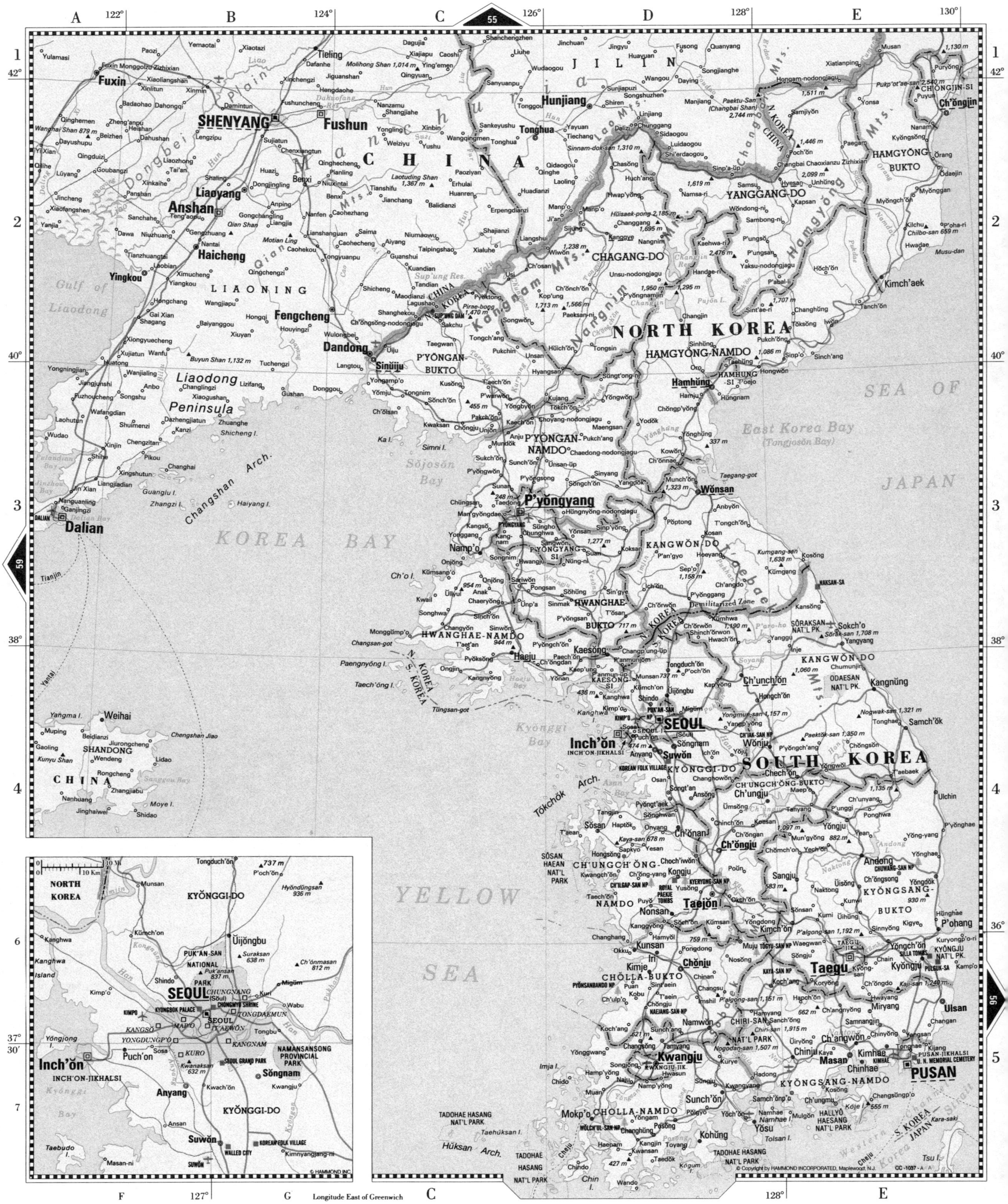

SCALE 1:3,500,000 LAMBERT CONFORMAL CONIC PROJECTION

MILES 0 50 100 150

KILOMETERS 0 50 100 150

Longitude East of Greenwich

POPULATION OF CITIES AND TOWNS

- OVER 2,000,000
- 1,000,000 - 1,999,999
- 500,000 - 999,999
- 250,000 - 499,999
- 100,000 - 249,999
- 30,000 - 99,999
- 10,000 - 29,999
- UNDER 10,000

Northeastern China

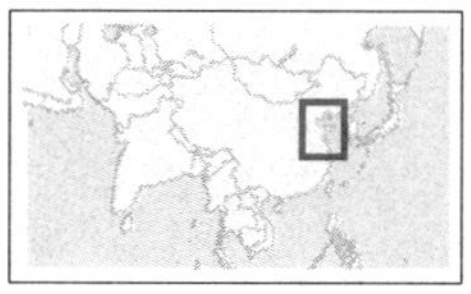

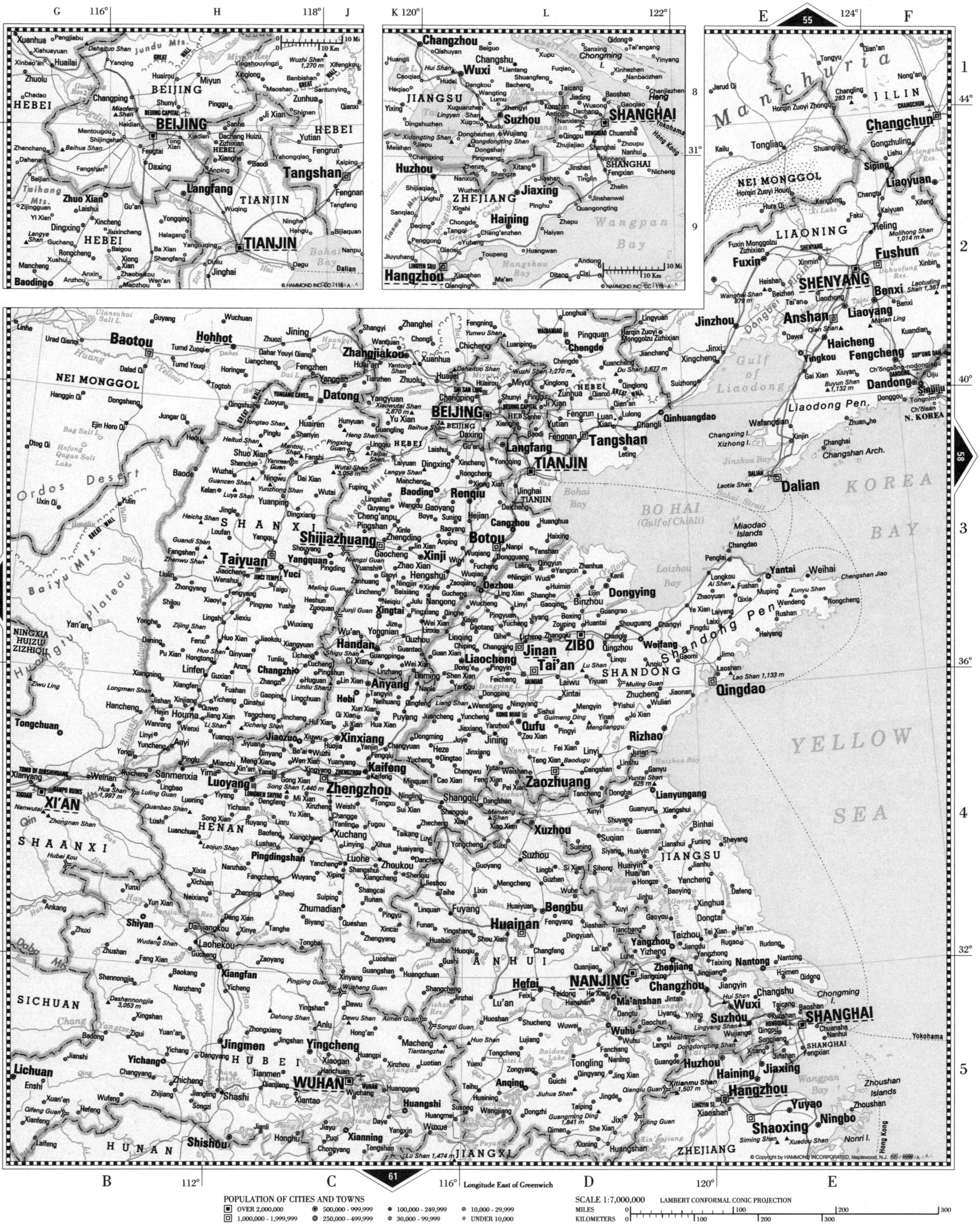

POPULATION OF CITIES AND TOWNS
- OVER 2,000,000
- 1,000,000 - 1,999,999
- 500,000 - 999,999
- 250,000 - 499,999
- 100,000 - 249,999
- 30,000 - 99,999
- 10,000 - 29,999
- UNDER 10,000

Longitude East of Greenwich

SCALE 1:7,000,000 LAMBERT CONFORMAL CONIC PROJECTION

MILES 0 100 200 300

KILOMETERS 0 100 200 300

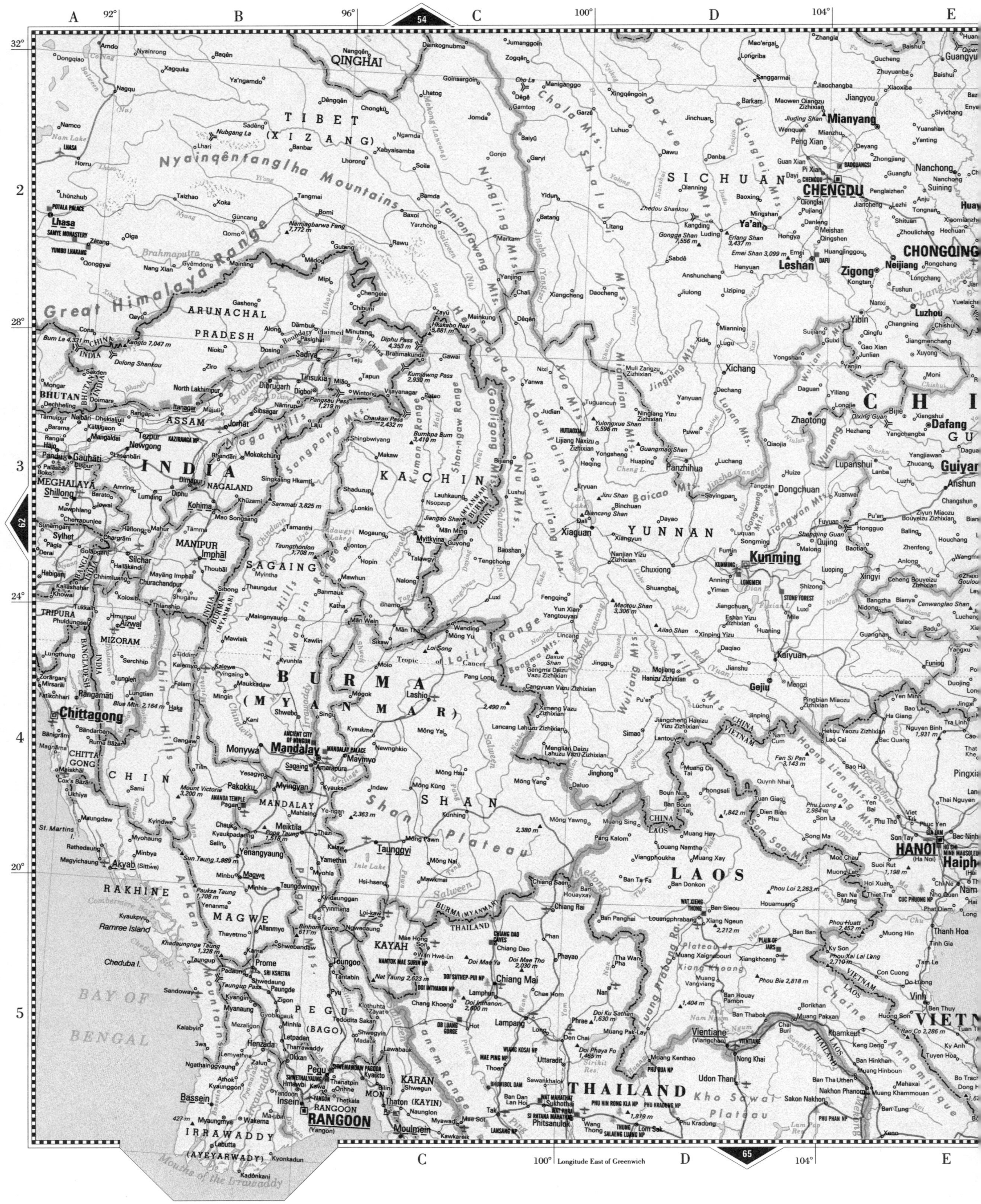

QINGHAI
TIBET (XIZANG)
SICHUAN
YUNNAN
CHI
KACHIN
BURMA (MYANMAR)
SHAN Plateau
SAGAING
MANDALAY
MAGWE
RAKHINE
PEGU (BAGO)
IRRAWADDY (AYEYARWADY)
KAYAH
KARAN
MON
CHIN
INDIA
ARUNACHAL PRADESH
ASSAM
NAGALAND
MANIPUR
MIZORAM
MEGHALAYA
TRIPURA
BHUTAN
BANGLADESH
CHITTAGONG
LAOS
THAILAND
VIETN
BAY OF BENGAL
Great Himalaya Range
Nyainqêntanglha Mountains
Hengduan Mountains
Lhasa
Chengdu
Chongqing
Kunming
Mandalay
Rangoon (Yangon)
Chittagong
Hanoi
Vientiane (Viangchan)
Chiang Mai
Tropic of Cancer
Longitude East of Greenwich

Southeastern China, Burma

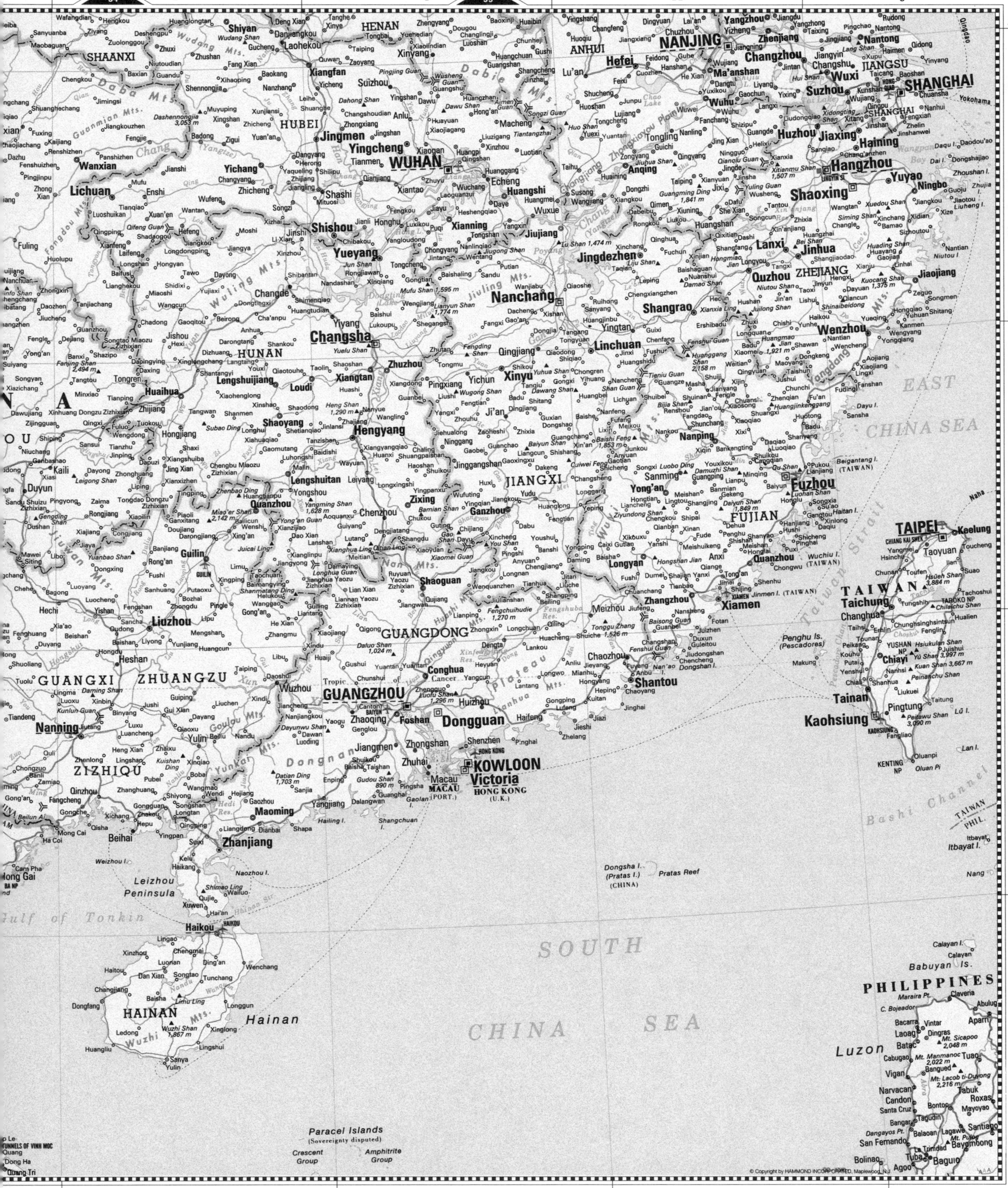

108° Longitude East of Greenwich 112° 116° 120°

POPULATION OF CITIES AND TOWNS

OVER 2,000,000	500,000 - 999,999	100,000 - 249,999	10,000 - 29,999
1,000,000 - 1,999,999	250,000 - 499,999	30,000 - 99,999	UNDER 10,000

SCALE 1:7,000,000 LAMBERT CONFORMAL CONIC PROJECTION

MILES 0 100 200 300

KILOMETERS 0 100 200 300

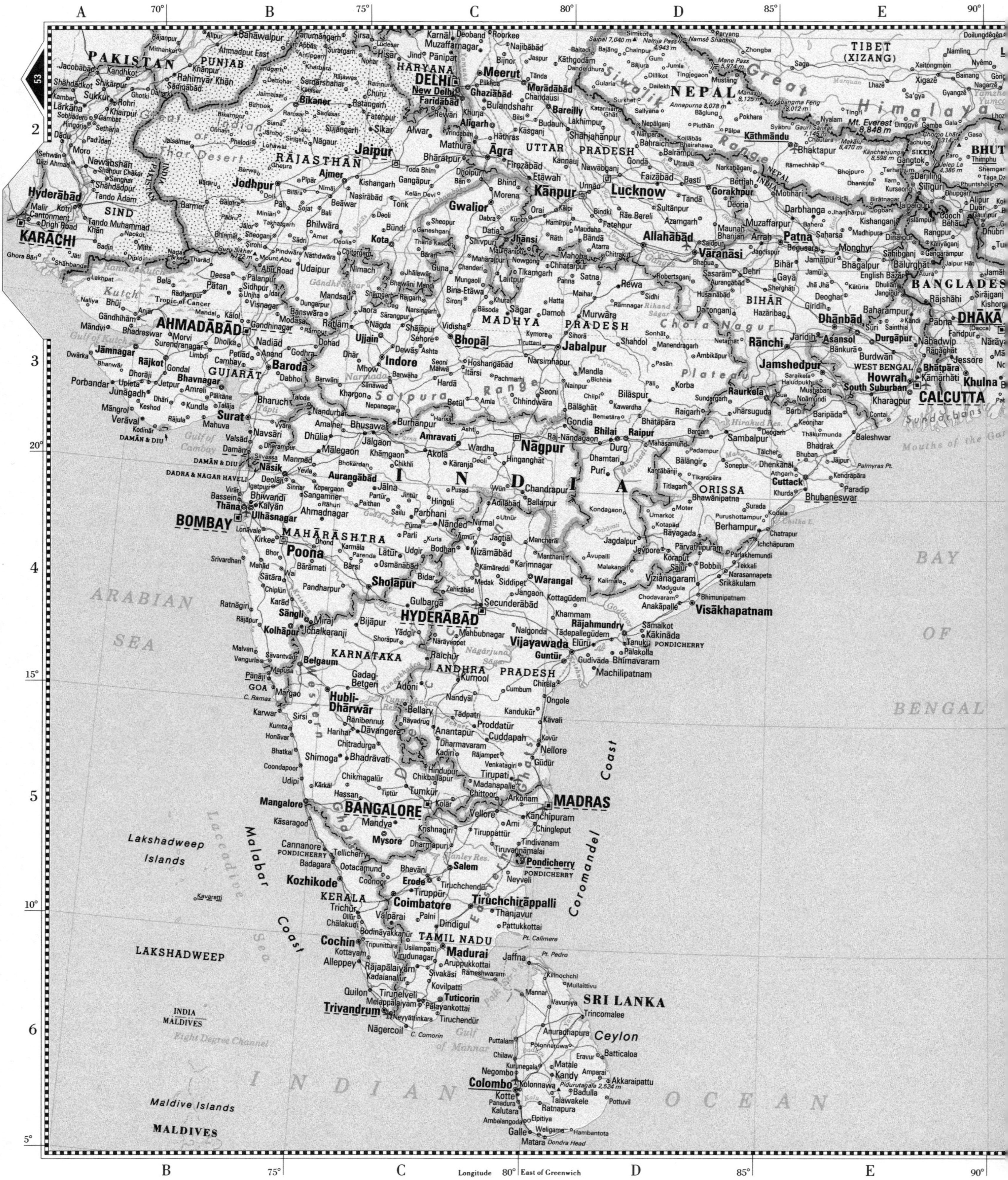
53
PAKISTAN
PUNJAB
SIND
INDIA
NEPAL
TIBET
(XIZANG)
SIKKIM
BHUT
BANGLADES
HARYANA
UTTAR PRADESH
RĀJASTHĀN
GUJARĀT
MADHYA PRADESH
MAHĀRĀSHTRA
BIHĀR
WEST BENGAL
ORISSA
ANDHRA PRADESH
KARNATAKA
KERALA
TAMIL NADU
GOA
DAMĀN & DIU
DADRA & NAGAR HAVELI
PONDICHERRY
LAKSHADWEEP
MALDIVES
SRI LANKA
Ceylon
KARĀCHI
Hyderābād
DELHI
New Delhi
Lahore
Kāthmāndu
Lucknow
Kānpur
Āgra
Jaipur
Allahābād
Vārānasi
Patna
AHMADĀBĀD
Baroda
Surat
Bhopāl
Indore
Jabalpur
Nāgpur
Rānchi
Jamshedpur
CALCUTTA
Howrah
DHĀKA
Khulna
BOMBAY
Poona
Sholāpur
HYDERĀBĀD
Secunderābād
Visākhapatnam
Vijayawada
MADRAS
BANGALORE
Mysore
Salem
Coimbatore
Madurai
Cochin
Trivandrum
Colombo
Jaffna
Great Indian or Thar Desert
Great Himalaya Range
Siwalik Range
Mt. Everest 8,848 m
Gulf of Kutch
Gulf of Cambay
ARABIAN SEA
BAY OF BENGAL
INDIAN OCEAN
Laccadive Sea
Malabar Coast
Coromandel Coast
Western Ghats
Eastern Ghats
Lakshadweep Islands
Maldive Islands
Eight Degree Channel
Gulf of Mannar
Palk Strait
C. Comorin
Mouths of the Ganges
Sundarbans
Chota Nagpur Plateau
Satpura Range
Tropic of Cancer
A
B
C
D
E
2
3
4
5
6
70°
75°
80°
85°
90°
20°
15°
10°
5°
Longitude 80° East of Greenwich

Southern Asia

Longitude 100° East of Greenwich

POPULATION OF CITIES AND TOWNS
OVER 2,000,000 · 1,000,000 - 1,999,999 · 500,000 - 999,999 · 250,000 - 499,999 · 100,000 - 249,999 · 30,000 - 99,999 · 10,000 - 29,999 · UNDER 10,000

SCALE 1:10,500,000 LAMBERT CONFORMAL CONIC PROJECTION
MILES 0 150 300 450
KILOMETERS 0 150 300 450

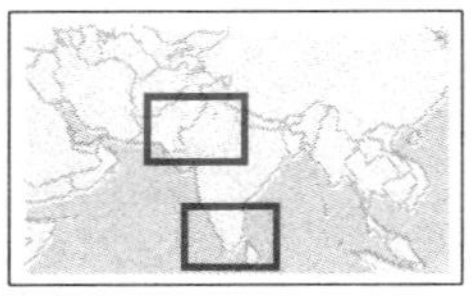

Punjab Plain, Southern India

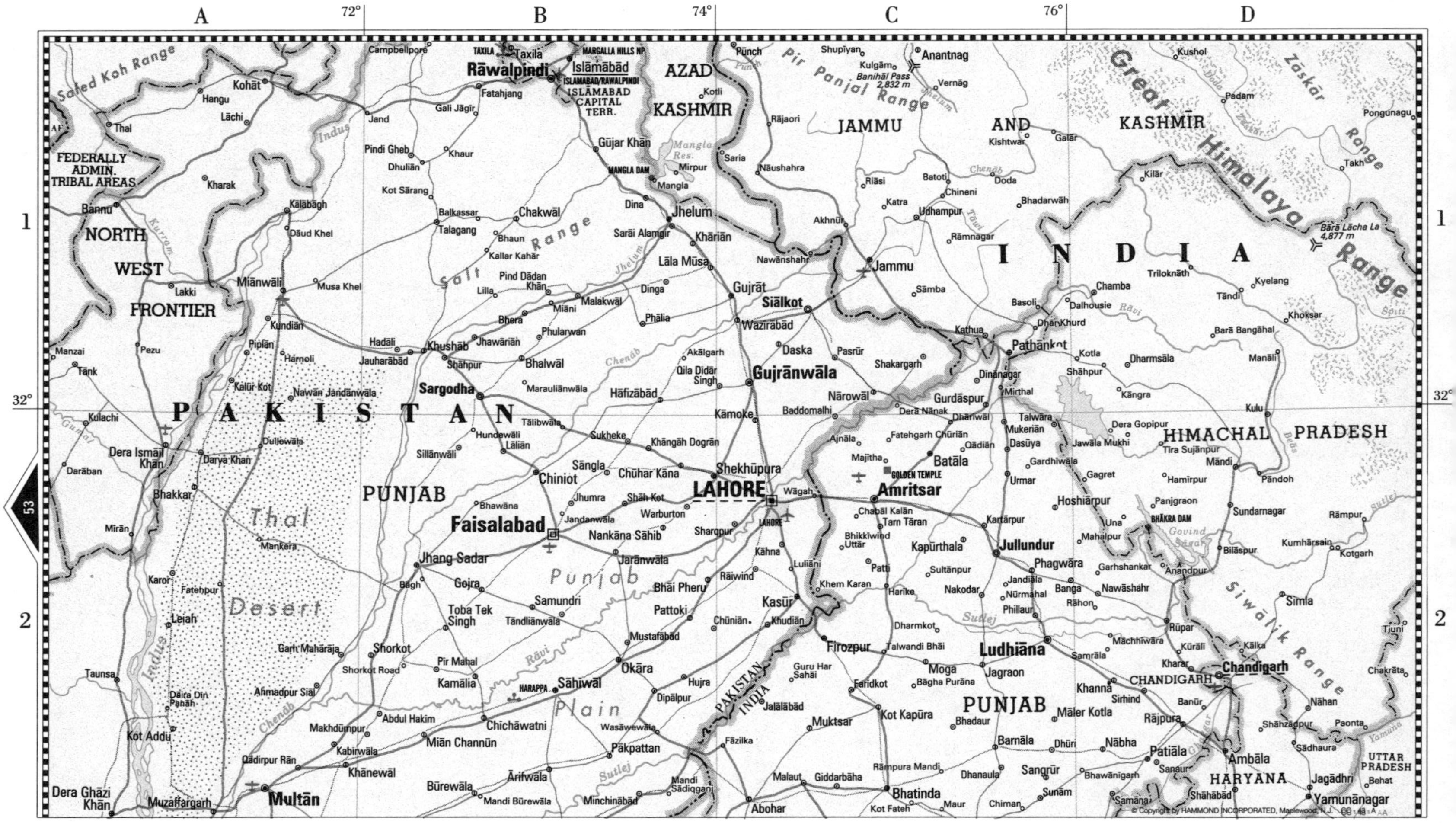

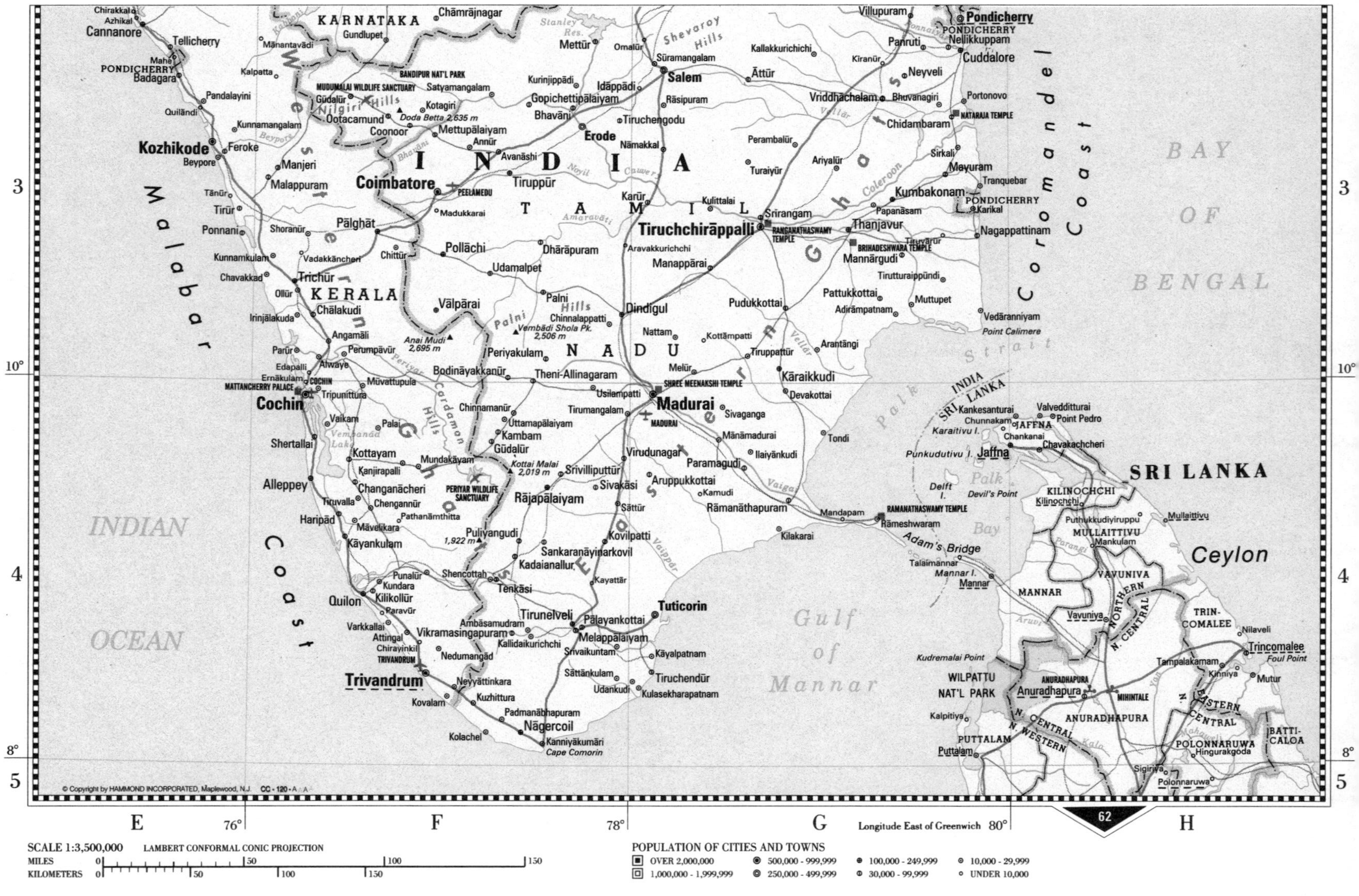

SCALE 1:3,500,000 LAMBERT CONFORMAL CONIC PROJECTION

MILES 0 50 100 150

KILOMETERS 0 50 100 150

Longitude East of Greenwich

POPULATION OF CITIES AND TOWNS

- OVER 2,000,000
- 1,000,000 - 1,999,999
- 500,000 - 999,999
- 250,000 - 499,999
- 100,000 - 249,999
- 30,000 - 99,999
- 10,000 - 29,999
- UNDER 10,000

Eastern Burma, Thailand, Indochina

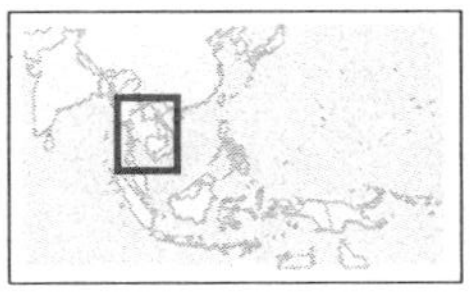

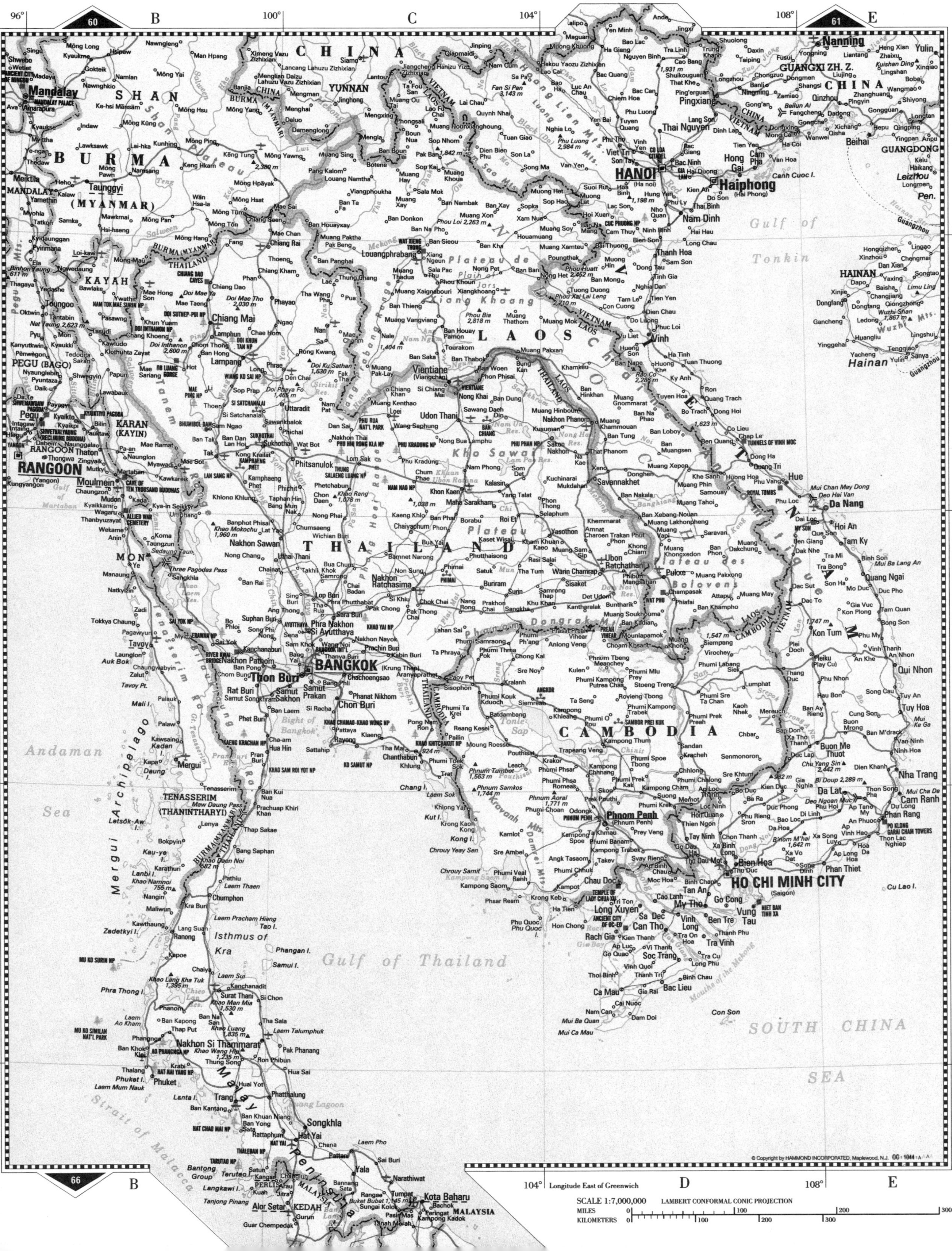

104° Longitude East of Greenwich

SCALE 1:7,000,000 LAMBERT CONFORMAL CONIC PROJECTION

MILES 0 100 200 300

KILOMETERS 0 100 200 300

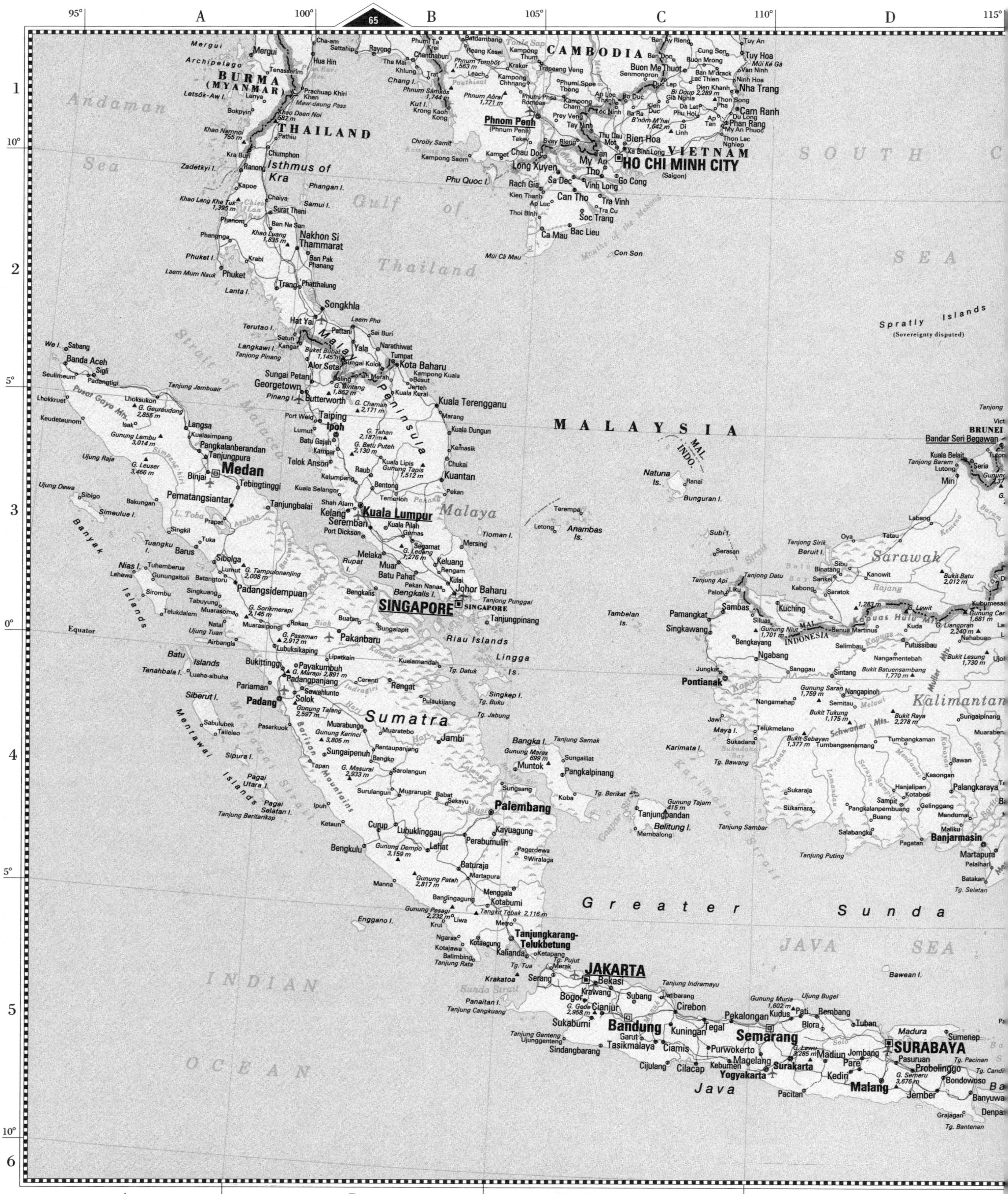

SCALE 1:10,500,000 LAMBERT CONFORMAL CONIC PROJECTION

MILES 0 150 300 450

KILOMETERS 0 150 300 450

Longitude East of Greenwich

POPULATION OF CITIES AND TOWNS

- OVER 2,000,000
- 1,000,000 - 1,999,999
- 500,000 - 999,999
- 250,000 - 499,999
- 100,000 - 249,999
- 30,000 - 99,999
- 10,000 - 29,999
- UNDER 10,000

Southeastern Asia

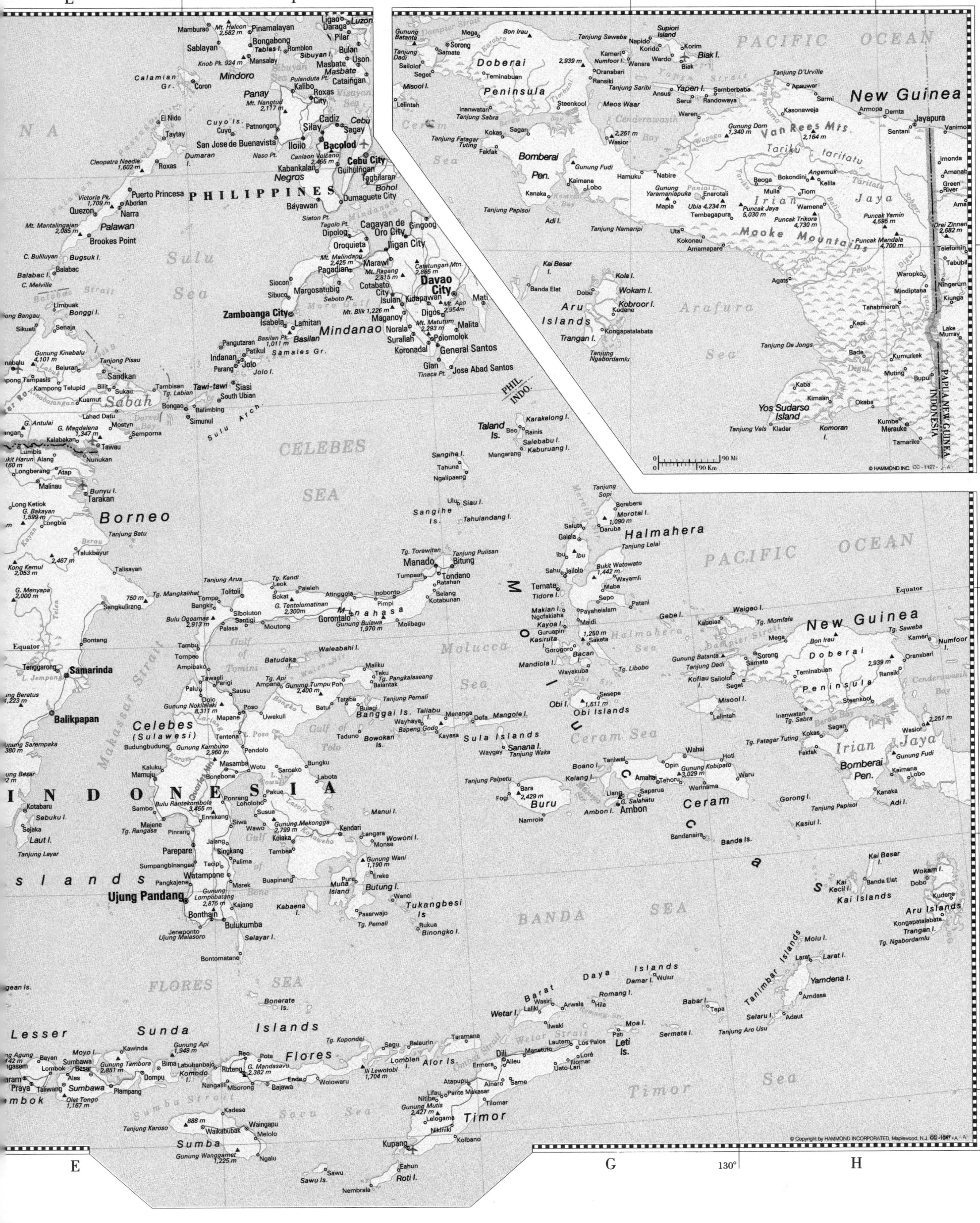

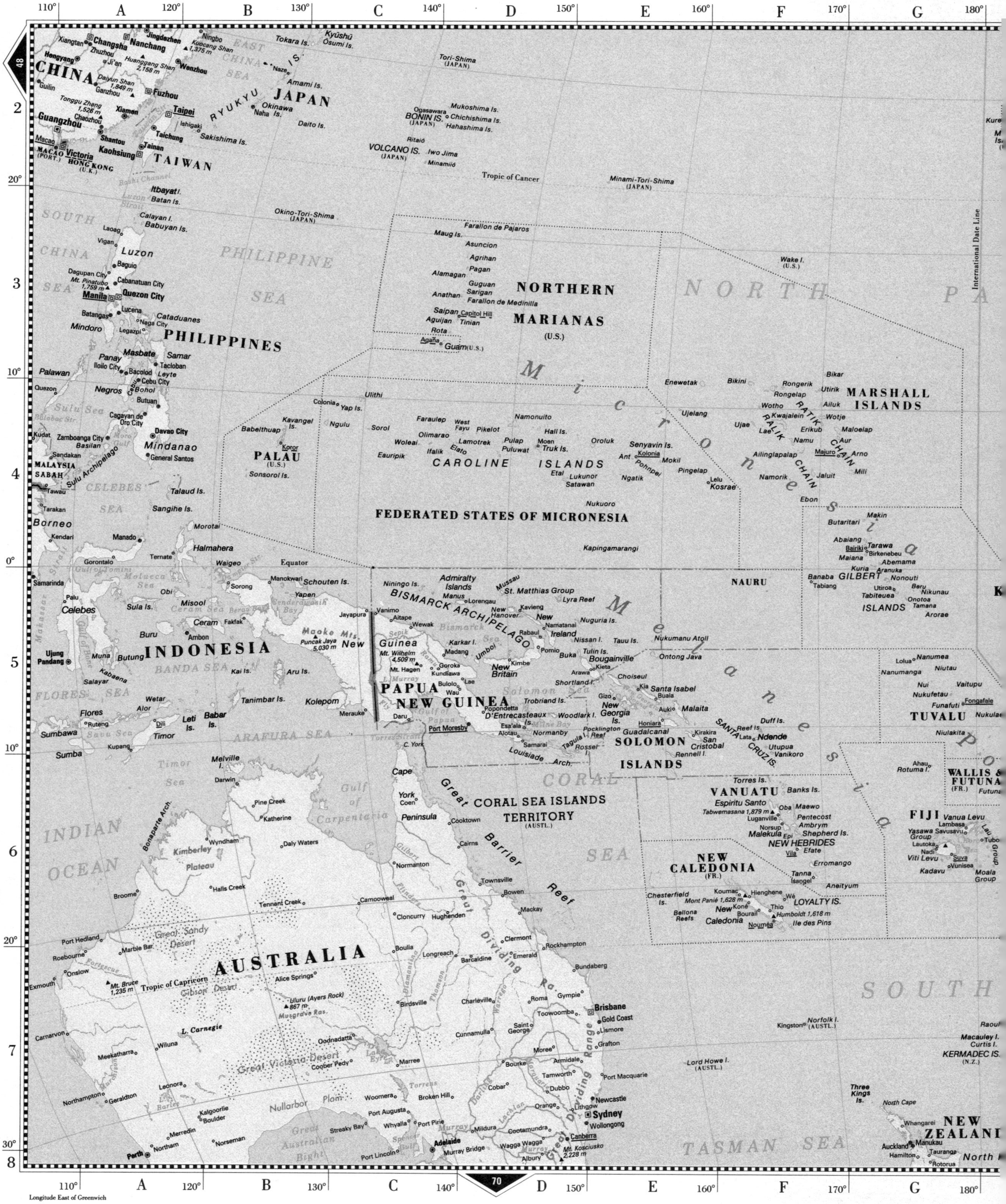
CHINA
Changsha
Nanchang
Jingdezhen
Hengyang
Guilin
Fuzhou
Wenzhou
Xiamen
Guangzhou
Shantou
Kaohsiung
Tainan
Taichung
Taipei
TAIWAN
MACAO (PORT.)
Victoria
HONG KONG (U.K.)
JAPAN
RYUKYU IS.
Okinawa
Naha
Amami Is.
Tokara Is.
Kyūshū
Ōsumi Is.
Daito Is.
Tori-Shima (JAPAN)
BONIN IS. (JAPAN)
Mukoshima Is.
Chichishima Is.
Hahashima Is.
VOLCANO IS. (JAPAN)
Iwo Jima
Minamiiō
Tropic of Cancer
Minami-Tori-Shima (JAPAN)
Okino-Tori-Shima (JAPAN)
International Date Line
SOUTH CHINA SEA
PHILIPPINE SEA
PHILIPPINES
Luzon
Manila
Quezon City
Mindoro
Palawan
Negros
Mindanao
Davao City
NORTHERN MARIANAS (U.S.)
Saipan
Tinian
Rota
Guam (U.S.)
Agaña
Wake I. (U.S.)
NORTH PACIFIC
Micronesia
MARSHALL ISLANDS
RATAK CHAIN
RALIK CHAIN
Majuro
Bikini
Enewetak
CAROLINE ISLANDS
PALAU (U.S.)
Koror
FEDERATED STATES OF MICRONESIA
Pohnpei
Kolonia
Kosrae
NAURU
GILBERT ISLANDS
Tarawa
Bairiki
Equator
INDONESIA
Celebes
Borneo
Halmahera
Ceram
Buru
Timor
Flores
Sumba
Sumbawa
Ujung Pandang
BANDA SEA
FLORES SEA
CELEBES SEA
ARAFURA SEA
Timor Sea
New Guinea
Jayapura
PAPUA NEW GUINEA
Port Moresby
BISMARCK ARCHIPELAGO
New Britain
New Ireland
Melanesia
SOLOMON ISLANDS
Honiara
Guadalcanal
TUVALU
VANUATU
Vila
NEW CALEDONIA (FR.)
Nouméa
FIJI
Suva
WALLIS & FUTUNA (FR.)
Coral Sea
GREAT CORAL SEA ISLANDS TERRITORY (AUSTL.)
Great Barrier Reef
INDIAN OCEAN
AUSTRALIA
Darwin
Cairns
Townsville
Brisbane
Sydney
Canberra
Newcastle
Wollongong
Adelaide
Perth
Alice Springs
Uluru (Ayers Rock) 867 m
Great Sandy Desert
Gibson Desert
Great Victoria Desert
Nullarbor Plain
Great Dividing Range
Gulf of Carpentaria
Great Australian Bight
Tropic of Capricorn
Mt. Kosciusko 2,228 m
TASMAN SEA
Norfolk I. (AUSTL.)
Lord Howe I. (AUSTL.)
KERMADEC IS. (N.Z.)
NEW ZEALAND
Auckland
Longitude East of Greenwich

Central Pacific Ocean

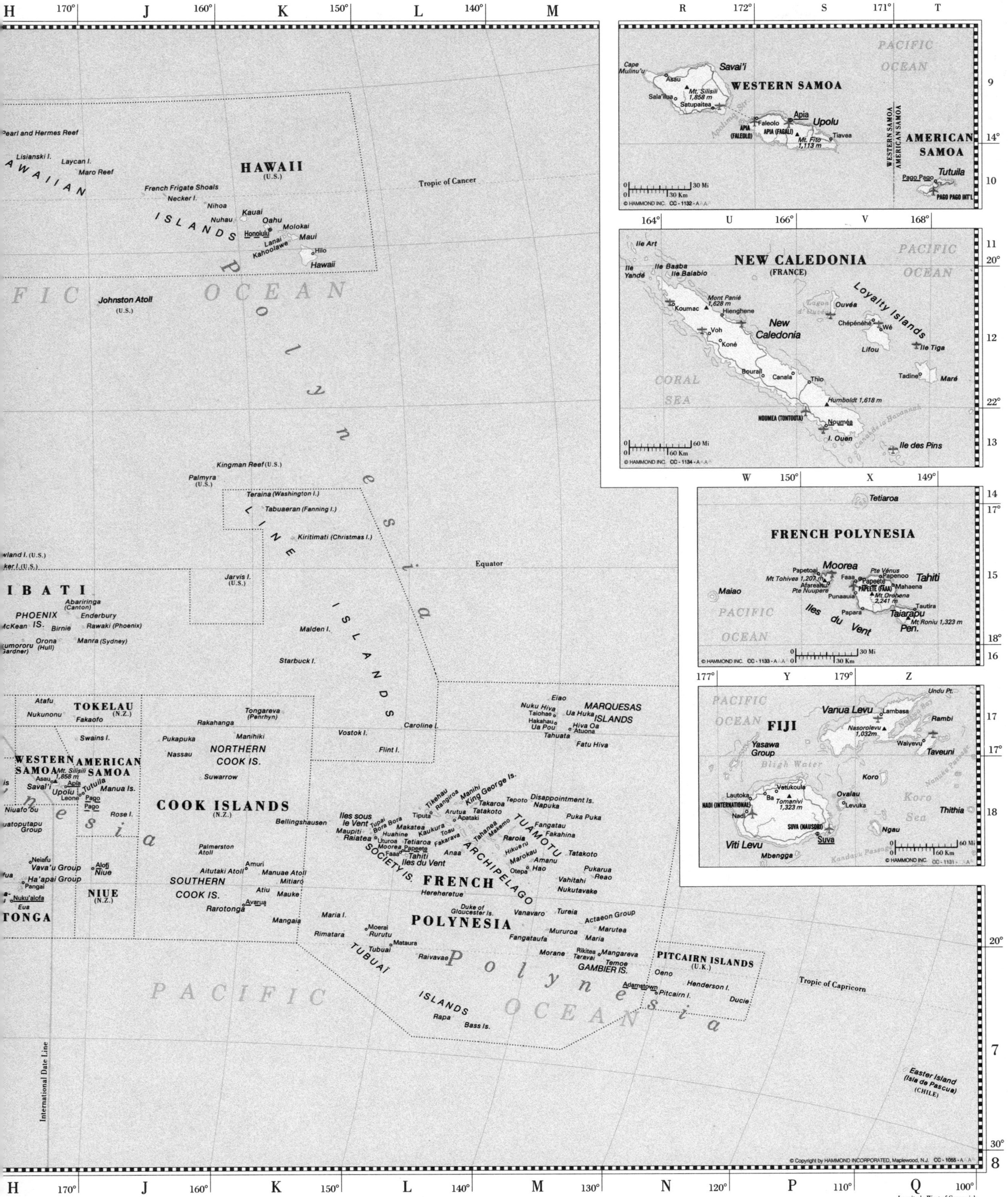

SCALE 1:31,500,000 LAMBERT AZIMUTHAL EQUAL-AREA PROJECTION

MILES 0 400 800 1200

KILOMETERS 0 400 800 1200

Longitude West of Greenwich

POPULATION OF CITIES AND TOWNS

- OVER 3,000,000
- 1,000,000 - 2,999,999
- 500,000 - 999,999
- 100,000 - 499,999
- UNDER 100,000

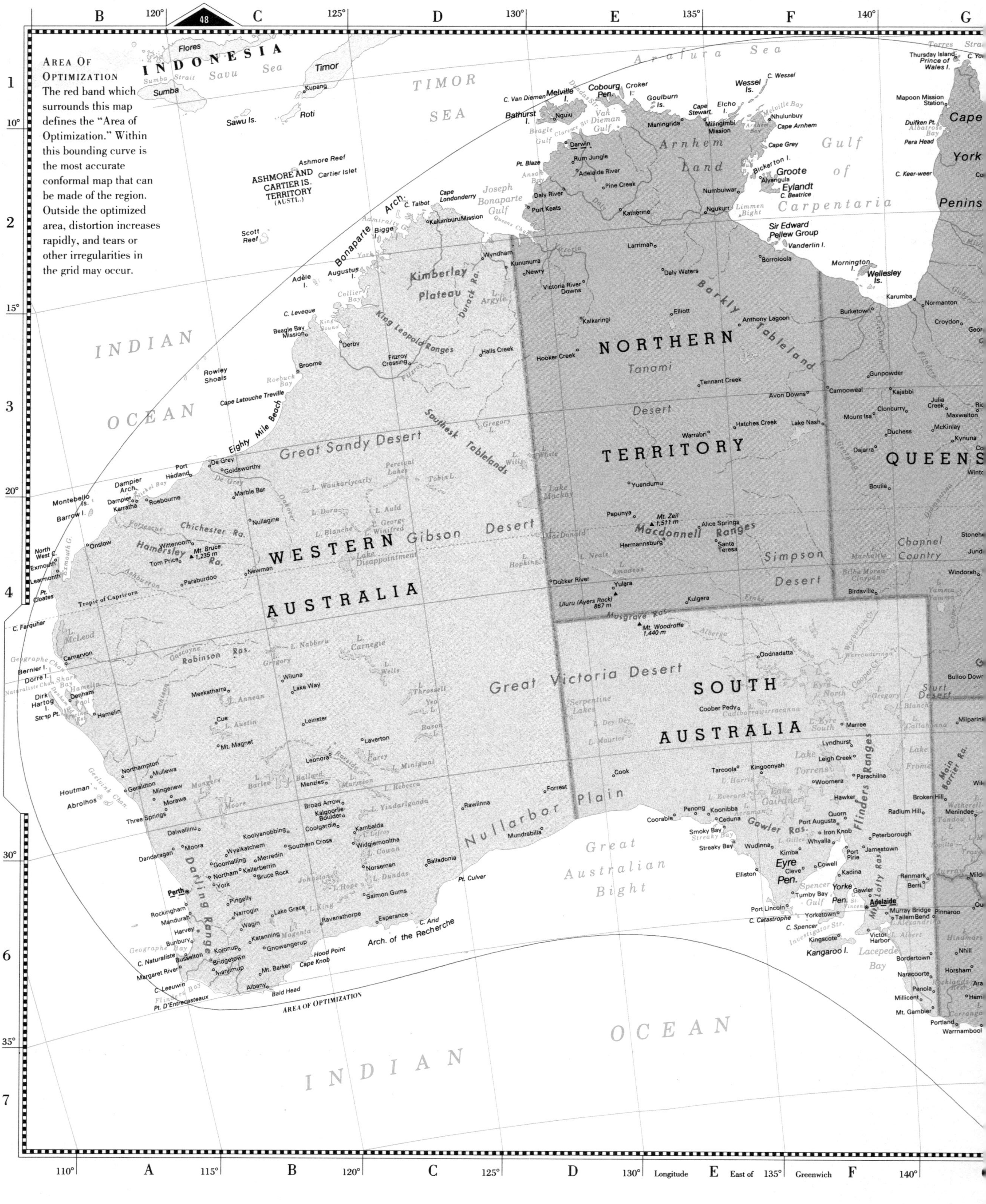
48
Area Of Optimization
The red band which surrounds this map defines the "Area of Optimization." Within this bounding curve is the most accurate conformal map that can be made of the region. Outside the optimized area, distortion increases rapidly, and tears or other irregularities in the grid may occur.
INDONESIA
Flores
Sumba
Timor
Savu Sea
TIMOR SEA
Arafura Sea
Gulf of Carpentaria
ASHMORE AND CARTIER IS. TERRITORY (AUSTL.)
INDIAN OCEAN
WESTERN AUSTRALIA
NORTHERN TERRITORY
SOUTH AUSTRALIA
QUEENS
Great Sandy Desert
Gibson Desert
Great Victoria Desert
Nullarbor Plain
Simpson Desert
Tanami Desert
Kimberley Plateau
Barkly Tableland
Macdonnell Ranges
Darling Range
Flinders Ranges
Great Australian Bight
Perth
Darwin
Adelaide
Alice Springs
Uluru (Ayers Rock) 867 m
Tropic of Capricorn
AREA OF OPTIMIZATION
Longitude East of Greenwich

Australia; New Zealand

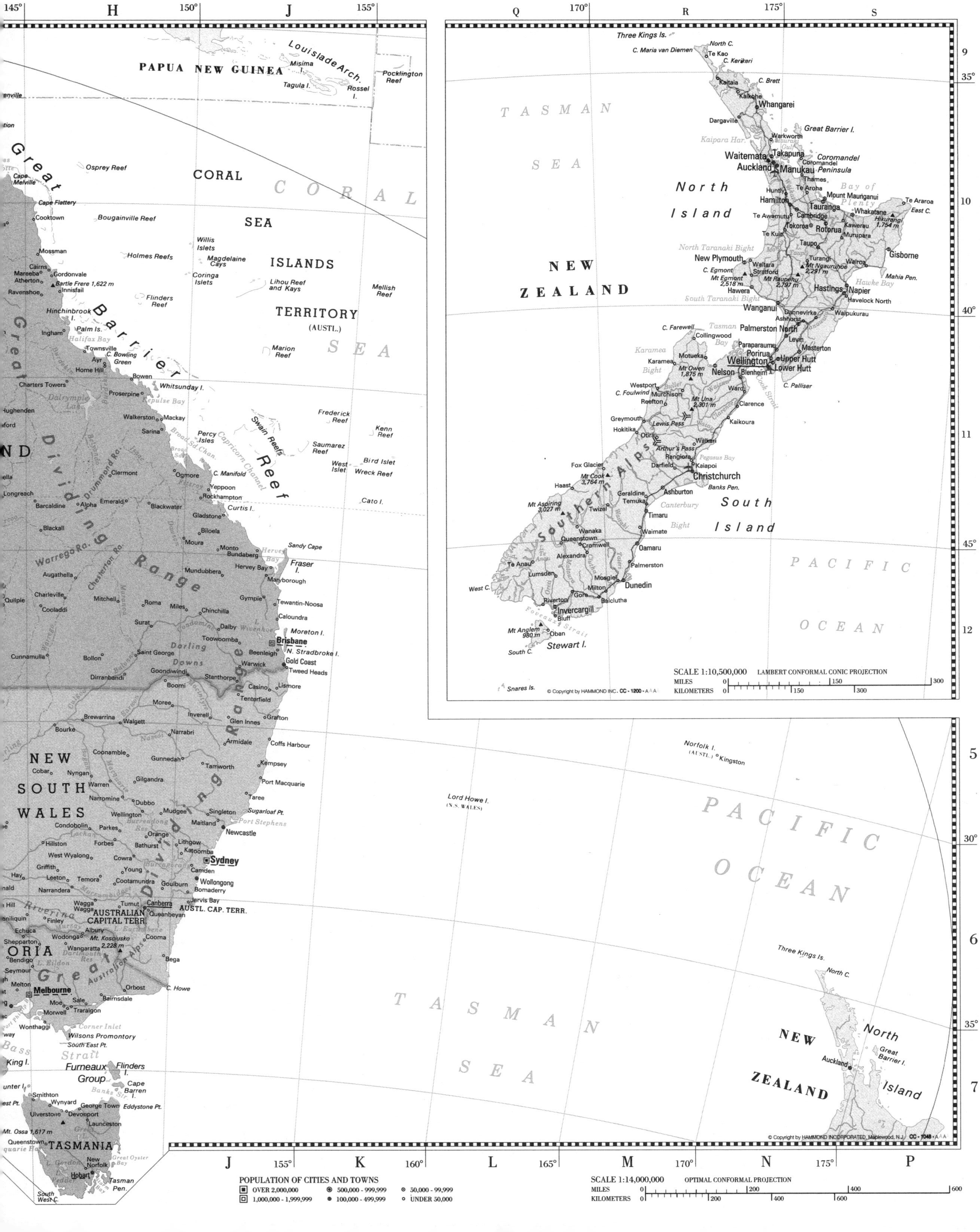

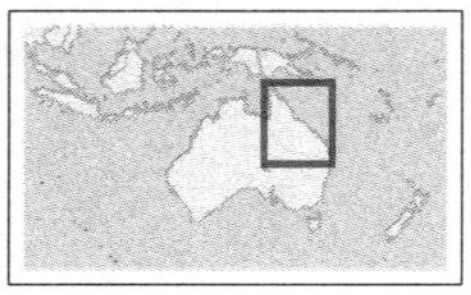

Northeastern Australia

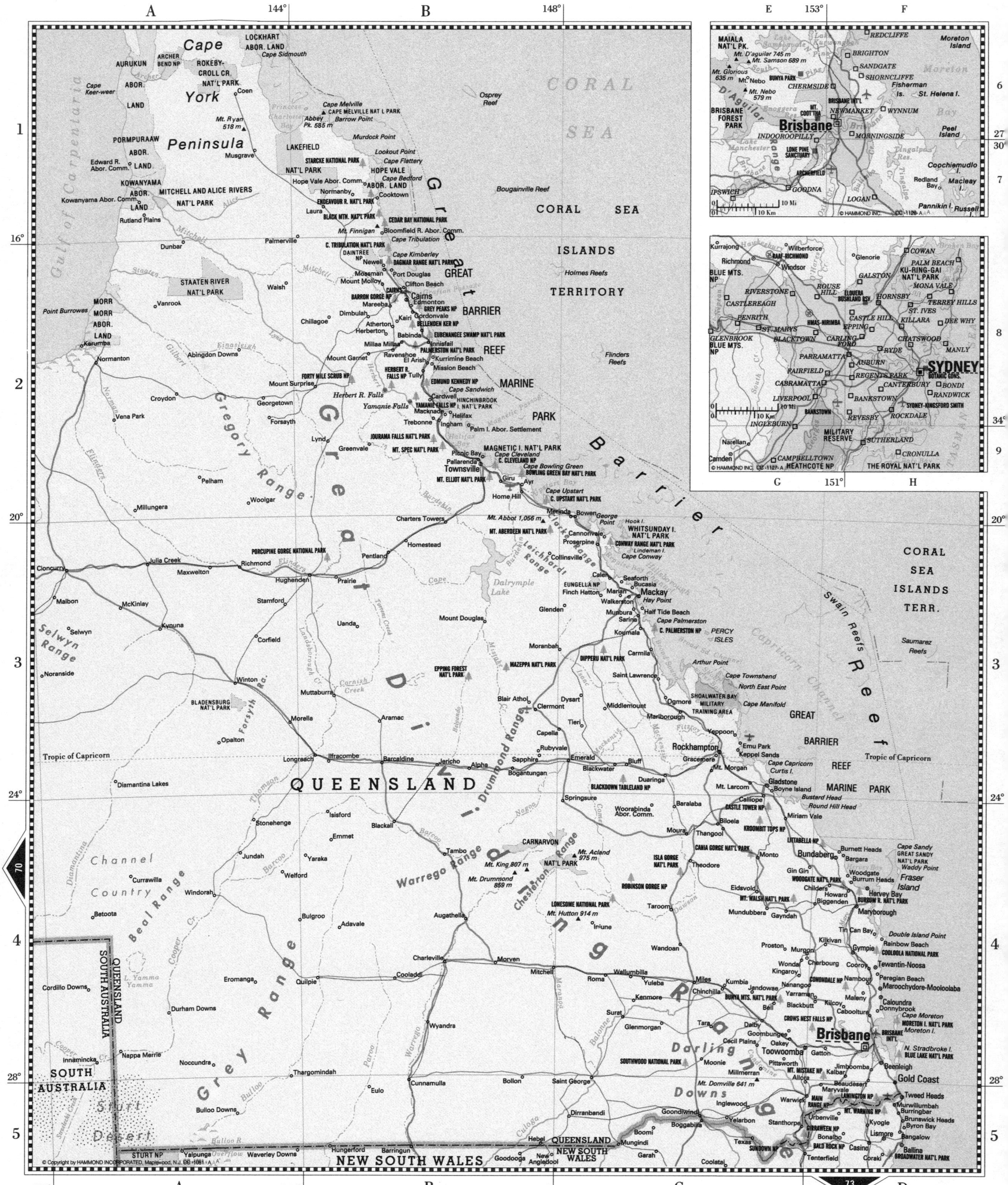

SCALE 1:7,000,000 LAMBERT CONFORMAL CONIC PROJECTION

MILES 0 100 200 300

KILOMETERS 0 100 200 300

Longitude East of Greenwich

POPULATION OF CITIES AND TOWNS

- OVER 2,000,000
- 1,000,000 - 1,999,999
- 500,000 - 999,999
- 250,000 - 499,999
- 100,000 - 249,999
- 30,000 - 99,999
- 10,000 - 29,999
- UNDER 10,000

70
73

Southeastern Australia

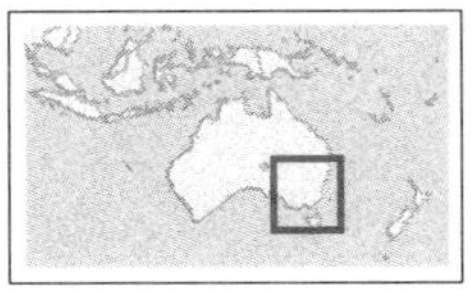

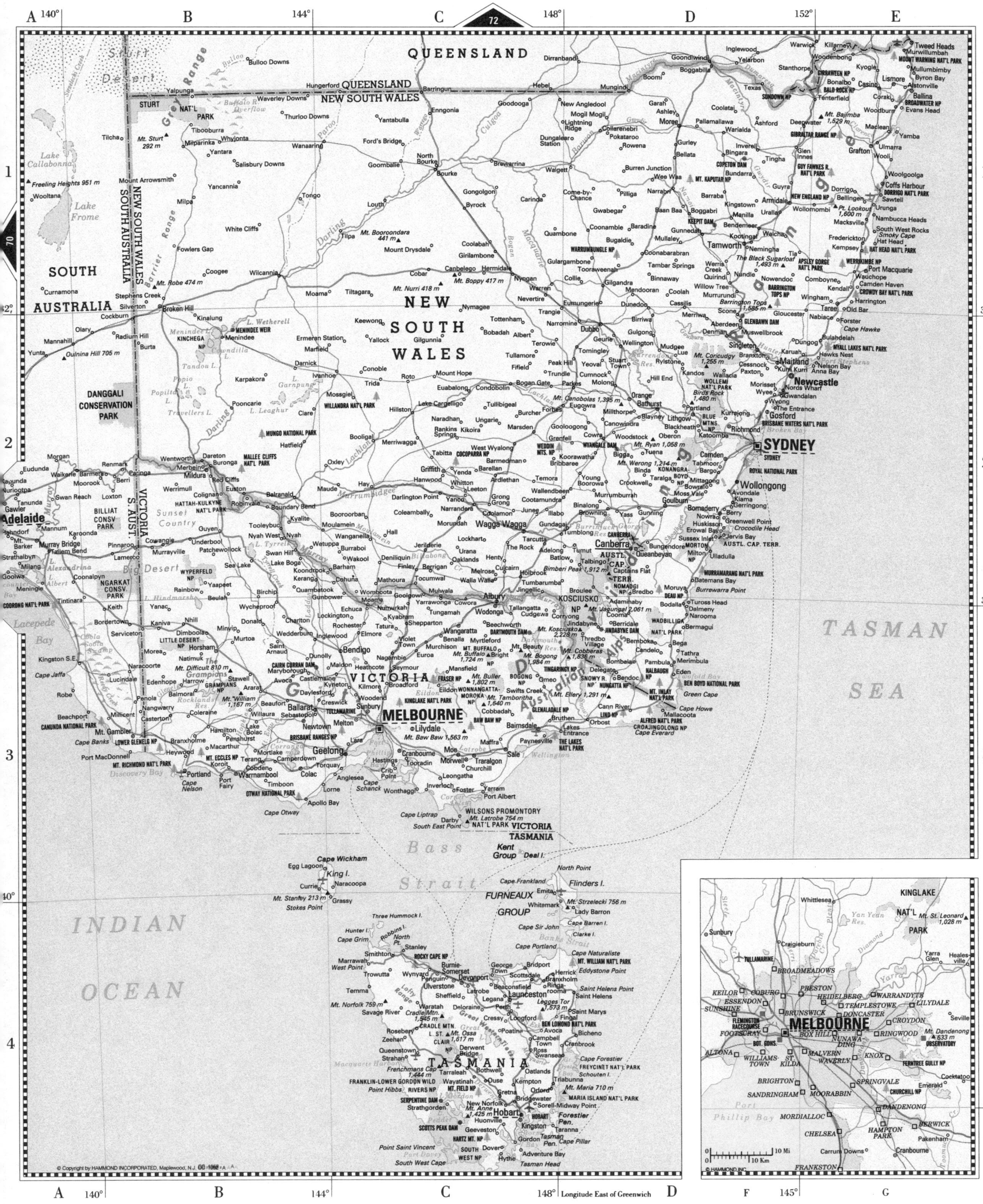

POPULATION OF CITIES AND TOWNS

- OVER 2,000,000
- 1,000,000 - 1,999,999
- 500,000 - 999,999
- 250,000 - 499,999
- 100,000 - 249,999
- 30,000 - 99,999
- 10,000 - 29,999
- UNDER 10,000

SCALE 1:7,000,000

LAMBERT CONFORMAL CONIC PROJECTION

MILES 0 100 200 300

KILOMETERS 0 100 200 300

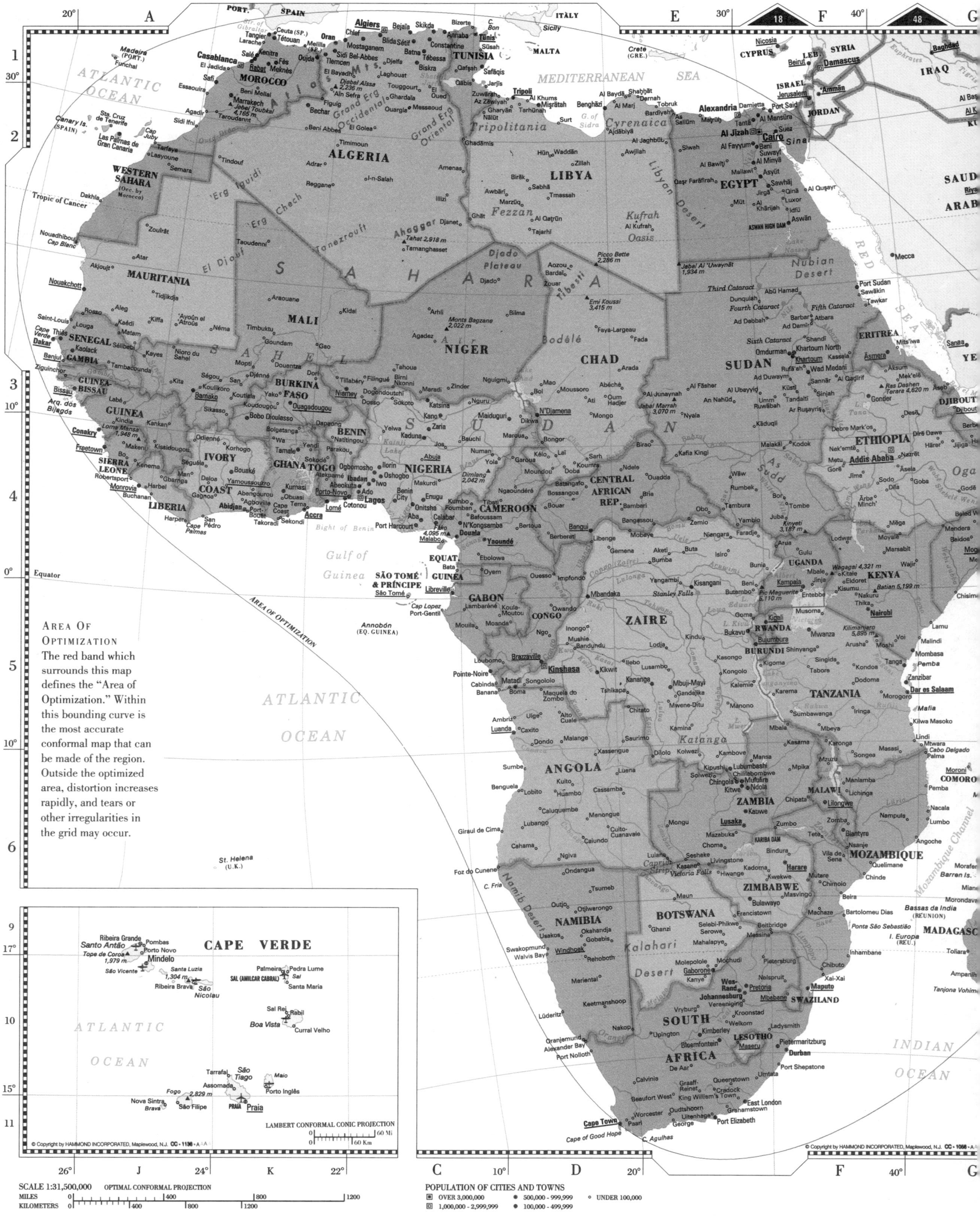

SCALE 1:31,500,000 OPTIMAL CONFORMAL PROJECTION

MILES 0 400 800 1200
KILOMETERS 0 400 800 1200

POPULATION OF CITIES AND TOWNS

- OVER 3,000,000
- 1,000,000 - 2,999,999
- 500,000 - 999,999
- 100,000 - 499,999
- UNDER 100,000

Africa

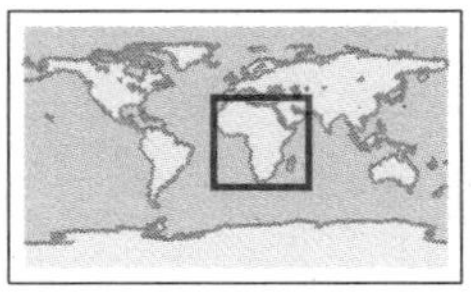

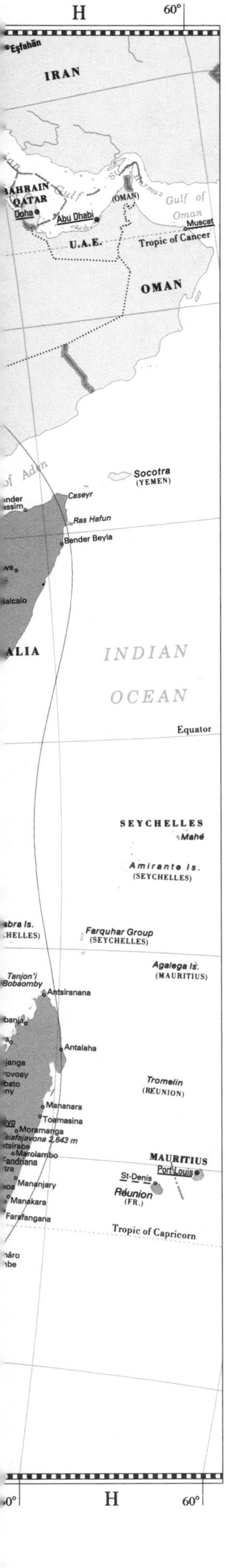
IRAN
BAHRAIN
QATAR
U.A.E.
OMAN
Tropic of Cancer
Muscat
Socotra (YEMEN)
INDIAN
OCEAN
Equator
SEYCHELLES
Mahé
Amirante Is. (SEYCHELLES)
Farquhar Group (SEYCHELLES)
Agalega Is. (MAURITIUS)
Tromelin (REUNION)
MAURITIUS
Port Louis
St-Denis
Réunion (FR.)
Tropic of Capricorn

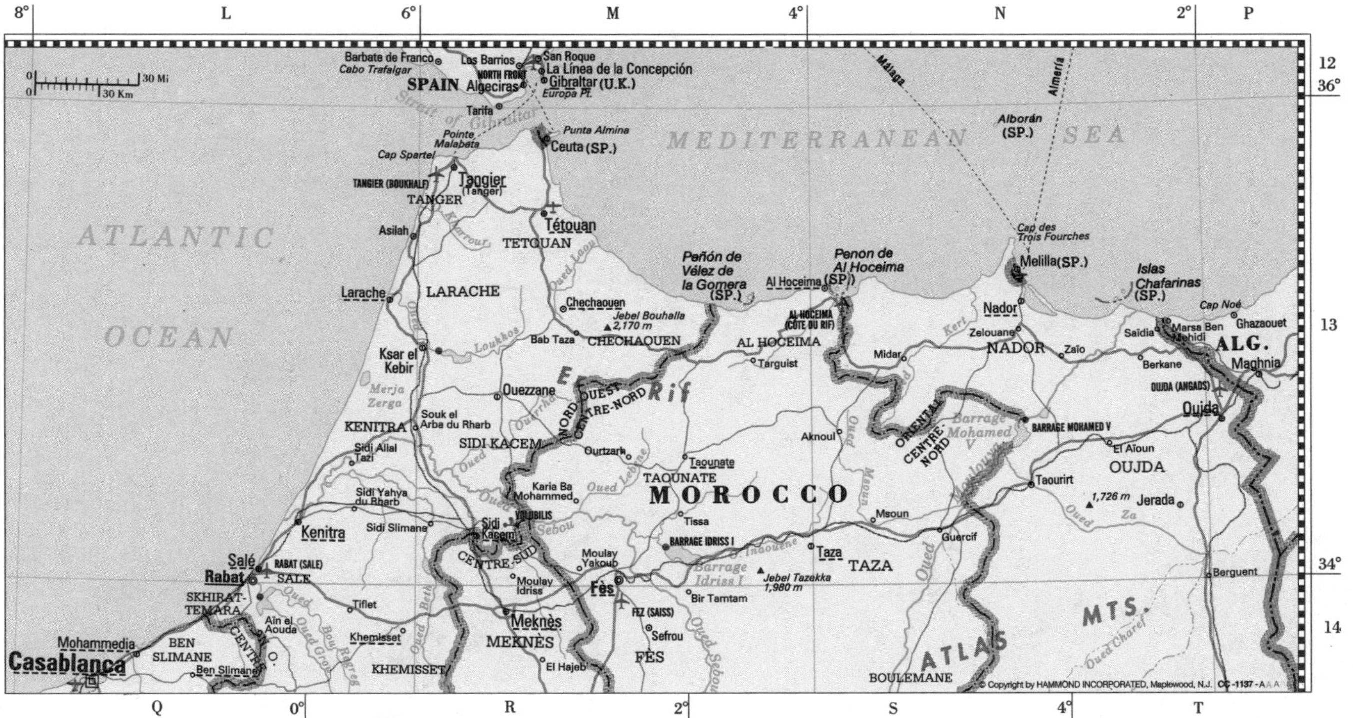
SPAIN
Gibraltar (U.K.)
Ceuta (SP.)
MEDITERRANEAN SEA
Alborán (SP.)
ATLANTIC
OCEAN
Tangier
TETOUAN
LARACHE
CHECHAOUEN
AL HOCEIMA
Melilla (SP.)
Islas Chafarinas (SP.)
NADOR
ALG.
MOROCCO
Kenitra
Rabat
Casablanca
Meknès
Fès
TAZA
OUJDA
ATLAS MTS.
© Copyright by HAMMOND INCORPORATED, Maplewood, N.J. CC-1137-A A A

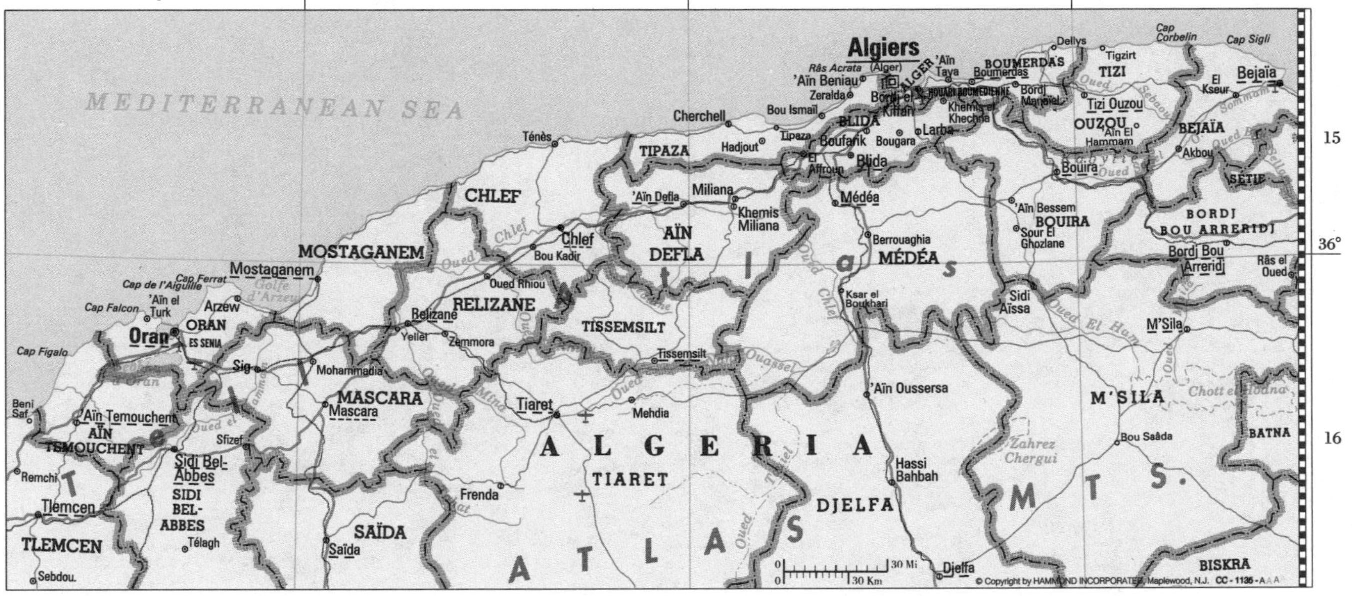
MEDITERRANEAN SEA
Algiers
Oran
Mostaganem
CHLEF
TIPAZA
BLIDA
MÉDÉA
BOUIRA
BEJAÏA
SETIF
TIARET
ALGERIA
ATLAS MTS.
DJELFA
M'SILA
TLEMCEN
MASCARA
SAÏDA
© Copyright by HAMMOND INCORPORATED, Maplewood, N.J. CC-1136-A A A

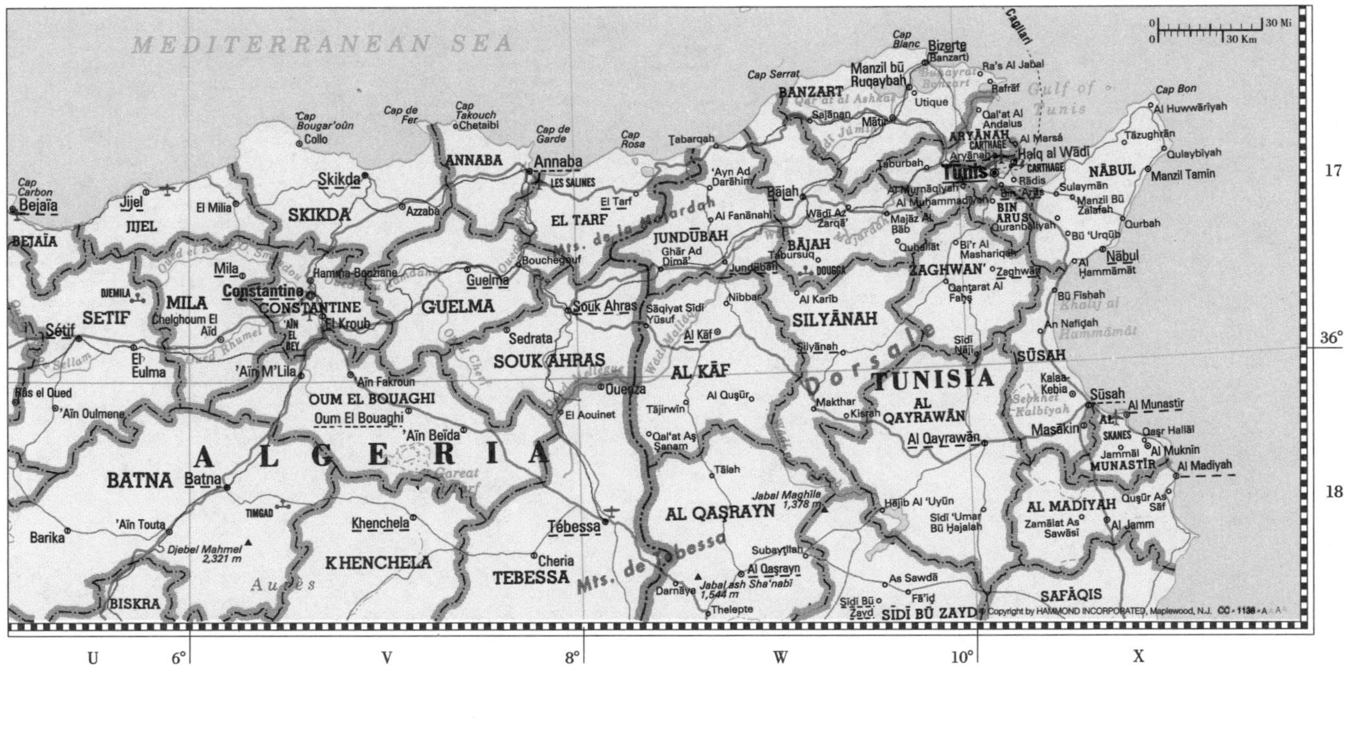
MEDITERRANEAN SEA
Bizerte
Tunis
Gulf of Tunis
ANNABA
SKIKDA
Constantine
GUELMA
SOUK AHRAS
TEBESSA
ALGERIA
BATNA
KHENCHELA
TUNISIA
AL QAYRAWAN
SŪSAH
SAFAQIS
© Copyright by HAMMOND INCORPORATED, Maplewood, N.J. CC-1136-A A A

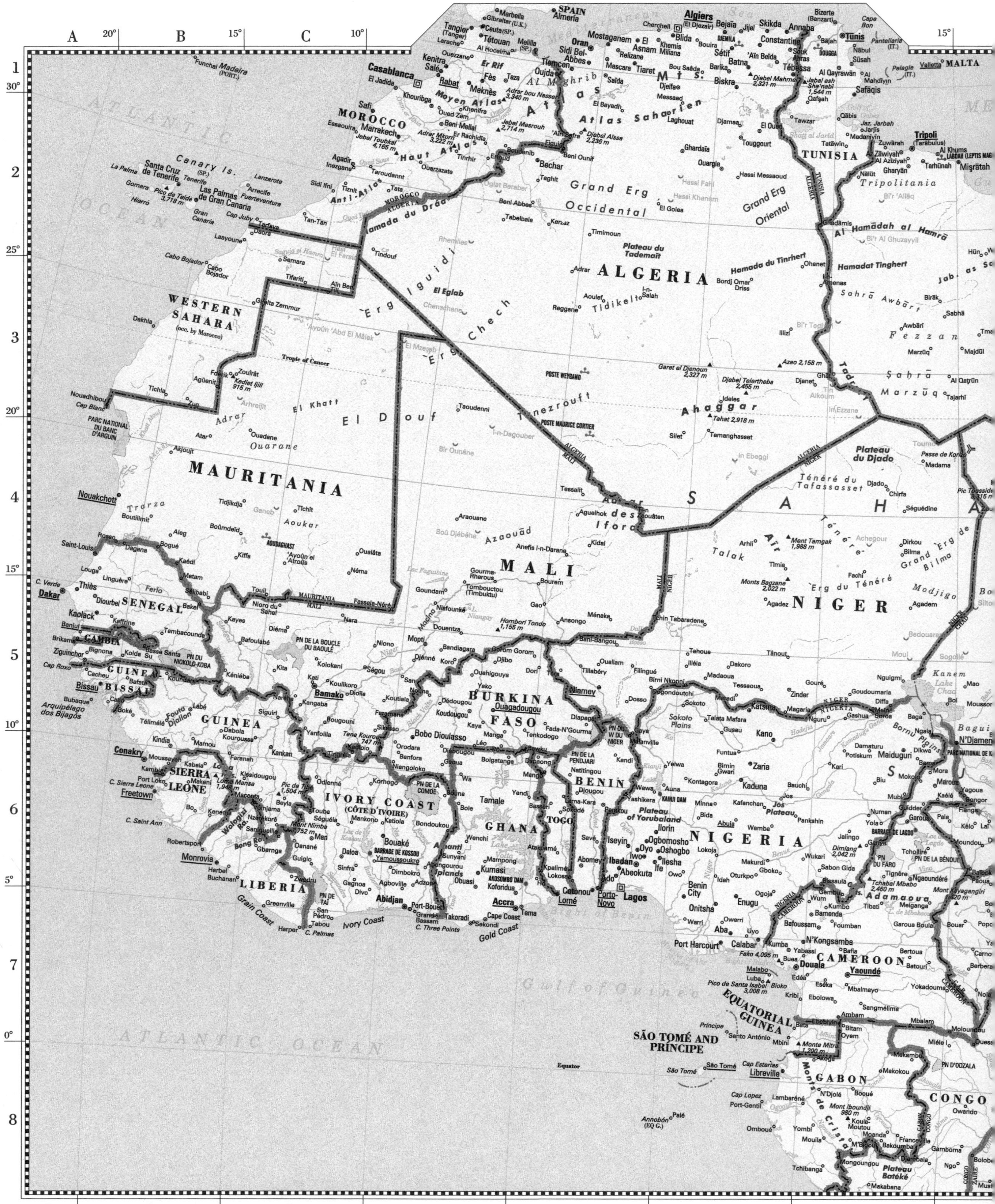

ALGERIA
MOROCCO
TUNISIA
WESTERN SAHARA
(occ. by Morocco)
MAURITANIA
MALI
NIGER
SENEGAL
GAMBIA
GUINEA-BISSAU
GUINEA
SIERRA LEONE
LIBERIA
IVORY COAST
(CÔTE D'IVOIRE)
BURKINA FASO
GHANA
TOGO
BENIN
NIGERIA
CAMEROON
EQUATORIAL GUINEA
SÃO TOMÉ AND PRÍNCIPE
GABON
CONGO
SPAIN
MALTA
ATLANTIC OCEAN
Gulf of Guinea
Canary Is.
Madeira
Tropic of Cancer
Equator
Algiers
Tunis
Tripoli
Casablanca
Rabat
Dakar
Nouakchott
Bamako
Niamey
Ouagadougou
Conakry
Freetown
Monrovia
Abidjan
Accra
Lomé
Porto-Novo
Lagos
Yaoundé
Libreville
Longitude West of Greenwich
Longitude East of Greenwich

Northern Africa

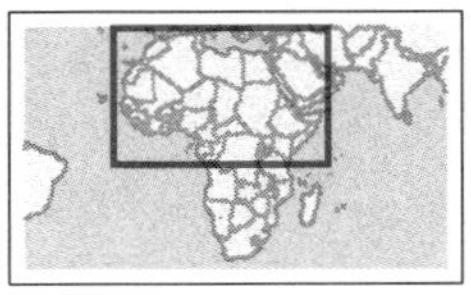

POPULATION OF CITIES AND TOWNS
- ▣ OVER 2,000,000
- ◻ 1,000,000 - 1,999,999
- ◉ 500,000 - 999,999
- ● 100,000 - 499,999
- ◎ 50,000 - 99,999
- ○ UNDER 50,000

SCALE 1:17,500,000 POLYCONIC PROJECTION

MILES 0 250 500 750

KILOMETERS 0 250 500 750

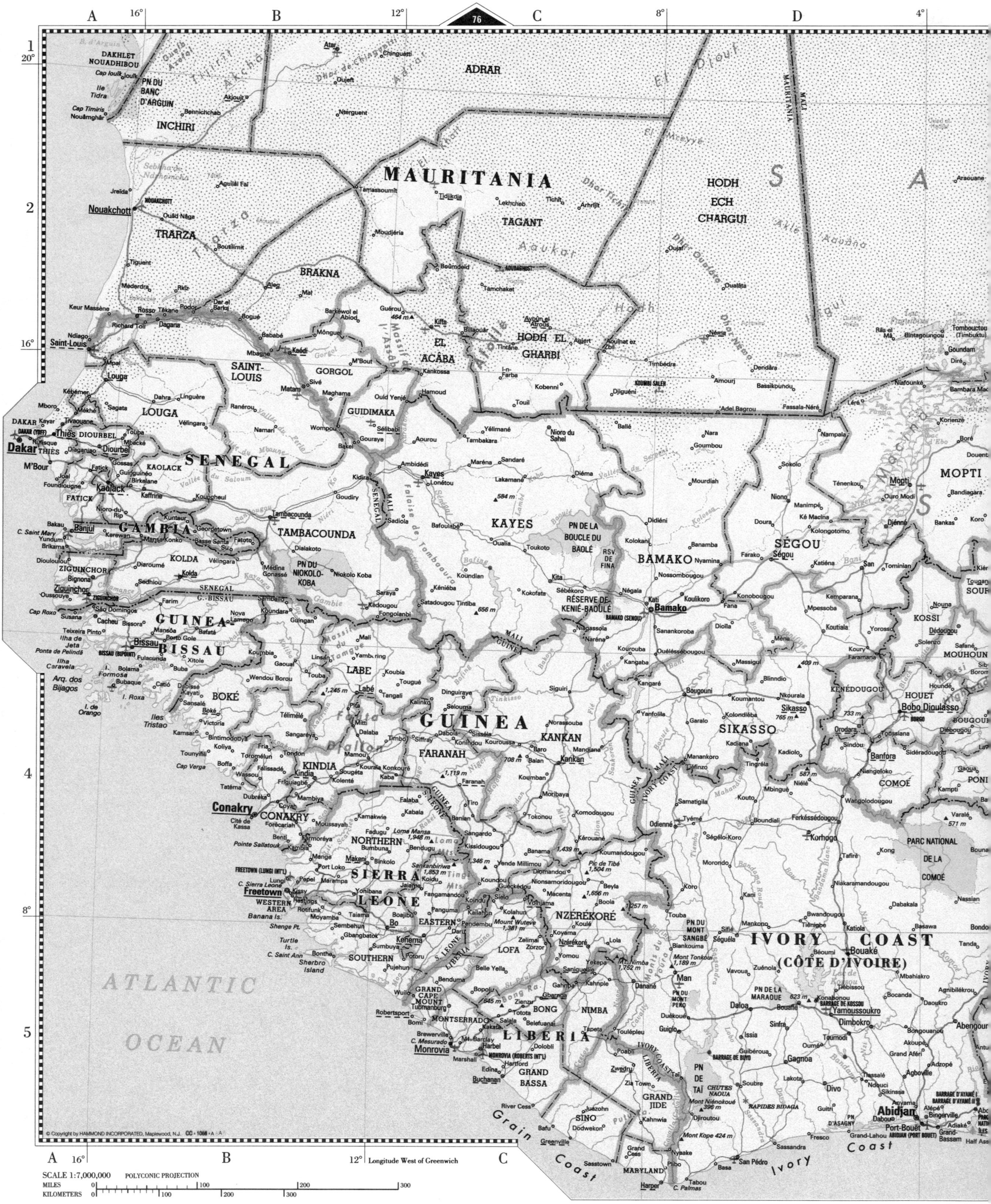

SCALE 1:7,000,000 POLYCONIC PROJECTION

MILES 0 100 200 300

KILOMETERS 0 100 200 300

West Africa

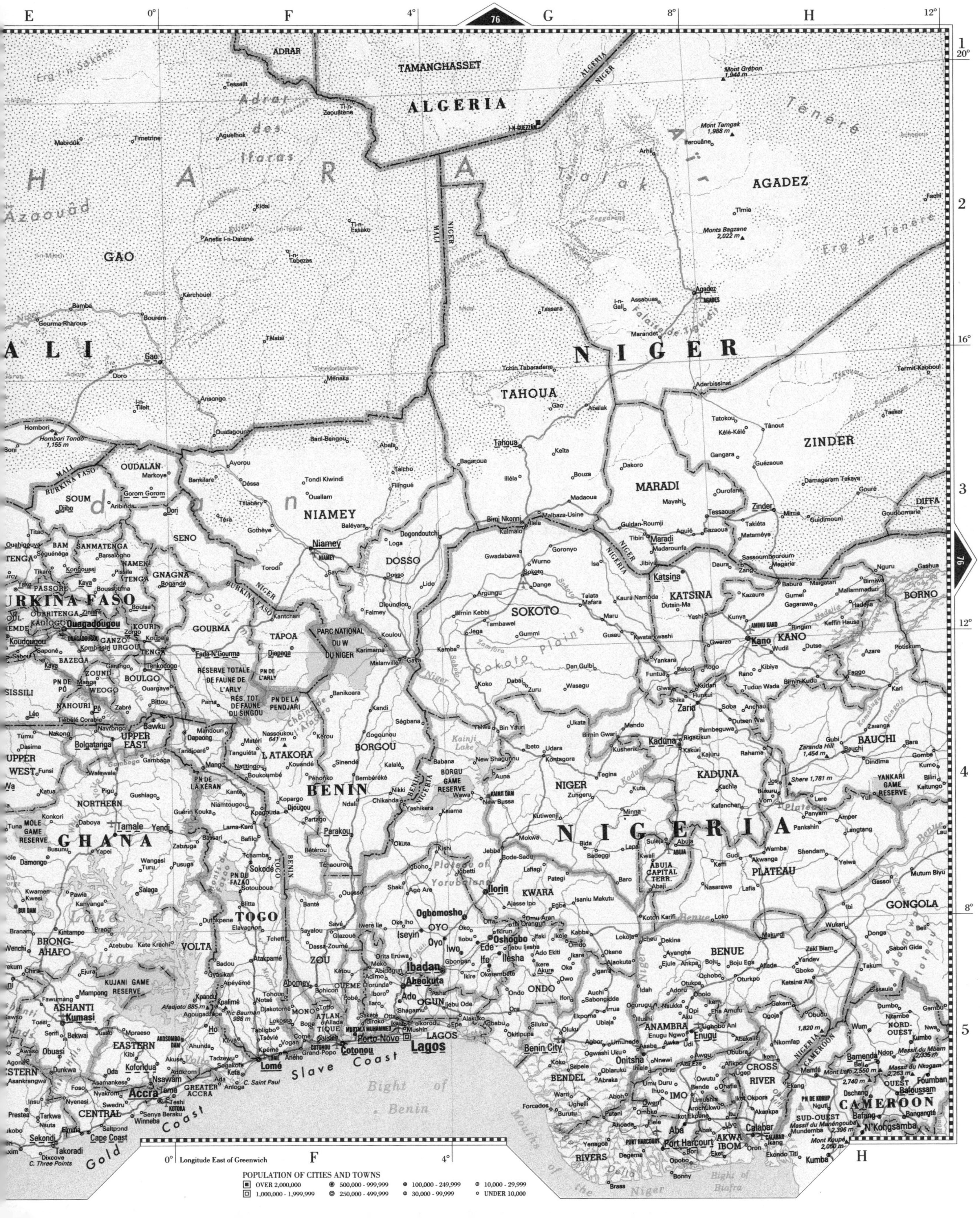

POPULATION OF CITIES AND TOWNS

OVER 2,000,000	500,000 - 999,999	100,000 - 249,999	10,000 - 29,999
1,000,000 - 1,999,999	250,000 - 499,999	30,000 - 99,999	UNDER 10,000

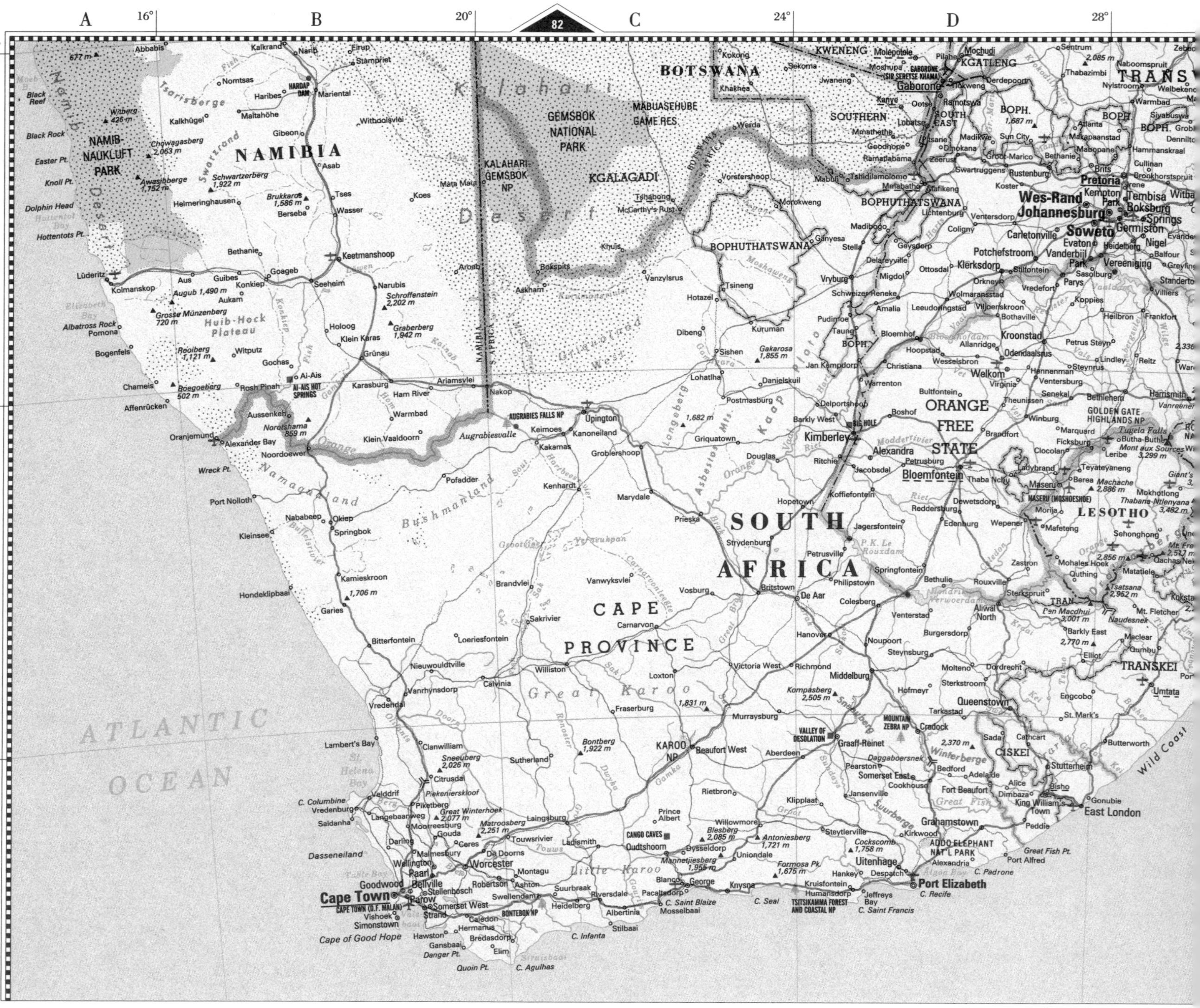
82
A
B
C
D
16°
20°
24°
28°
2
3
4
NAMIBIA
BOTSWANA
SOUTH AFRICA
CAPE PROVINCE
ORANGE FREE STATE
LESOTHO
TRANSKEI
CISKEI
BOPHUTHATSWANA
SOUTHERN
KGALAGADI
KWENENG
KGATLENG
GEMSBOK NATIONAL PARK
MABUASEHUBE GAME RES.
KALAHARI-GEMSBOK NP
NAMIB-NAUKLUFT PARK
ATLANTIC OCEAN
Kalahari Desert
Namib Desert
Great Karoo
Little Karoo
Bushmanland
Namaqualand
Huib-Hock Plateau
Orange
Gaborone
Pretoria
Wes-Rand
Johannesburg
Soweto
Kimberley
Bloemfontein
Cape Town
Port Elizabeth
East London
Lüderitz
Keetmanshoop
Upington
Beaufort West
Worcester
Paarl
Stellenbosch
George
Knysna
Oudtshoorn
Graaff-Reinet
Grahamstown
Queenstown
Umtata
Maseru
Welkom
Kroonstad
Potchefstroom
Klerksdorp
Vereeniging
Mafikeng
Wild Coast
Cape of Good Hope
C. Agulhas
AUGRABIES FALLS NP
KAROO NP
CANGO CAVES
VALLEY OF DESOLATION
ADDO ELEPHANT NAT'L PARK
TSITSIKAMMA FOREST AND COASTAL NP
BONTEBOK NP
MOUNTAIN ZEBRA NP
GOLDEN GATE HIGHLANDS NP

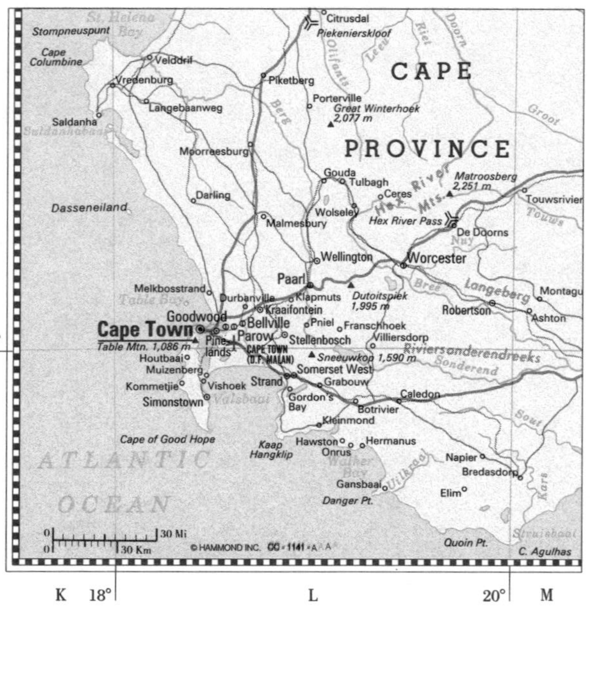
CAPE PROVINCE
ATLANTIC OCEAN
Cape Town
Table Mtn. 1,086 m
Stellenbosch
Paarl
Worcester
Wellington
Somerset West
Strand
Simonstown
Cape of Good Hope
Hermanus
Saldanha
Vredenburg
Dasseneiland
Piketberg
Citrusdal
Hex River Pass
C. Agulhas
Quoin Pt.
Danger Pt.
10
11
34°
K
L
M
18°
20°
0 30 Mi
0 30 Km
© HAMMOND INC.

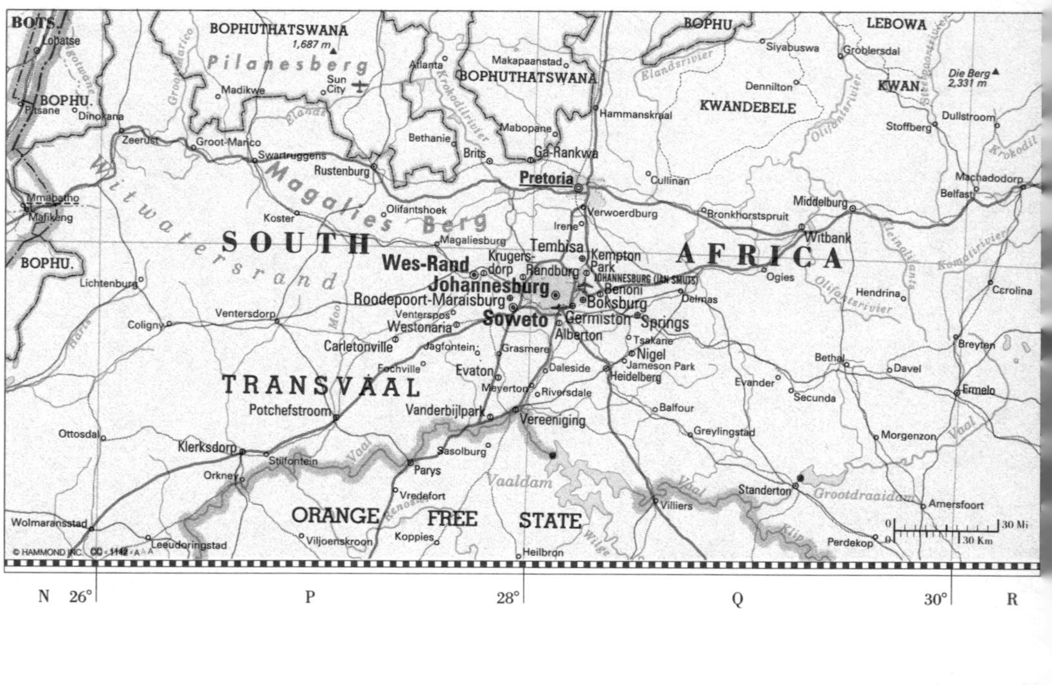
SOUTH AFRICA
TRANSVAAL
ORANGE FREE STATE
BOPHUTHATSWANA
KWANDEBELE
LEBOWA
KWAN.
BOTS.
BOPHU.
Pretoria
Wes-Rand
Johannesburg
Soweto
Roodepoort-Maraisburg
Germiston
Springs
Boksburg
Benoni
Kempton Park
Vereeniging
Vanderbijlpark
Potchefstroom
Klerksdorp
Rustenburg
Witbank
Middelburg
Standerton
Heidelberg
Mmabatho
Mafikeng
Pilanesberg
Magaliesberg
Witwatersrand
Vaal
Vaaldam
N
P
Q
R
26°
28°
30°
0 30 Mi
0 30 Km
© HAMMOND INC.

South Africa

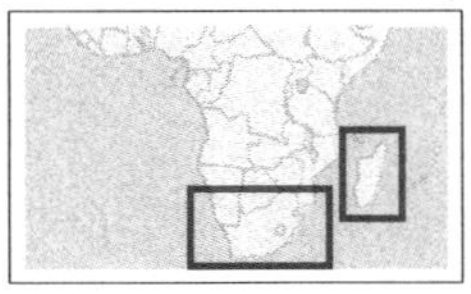

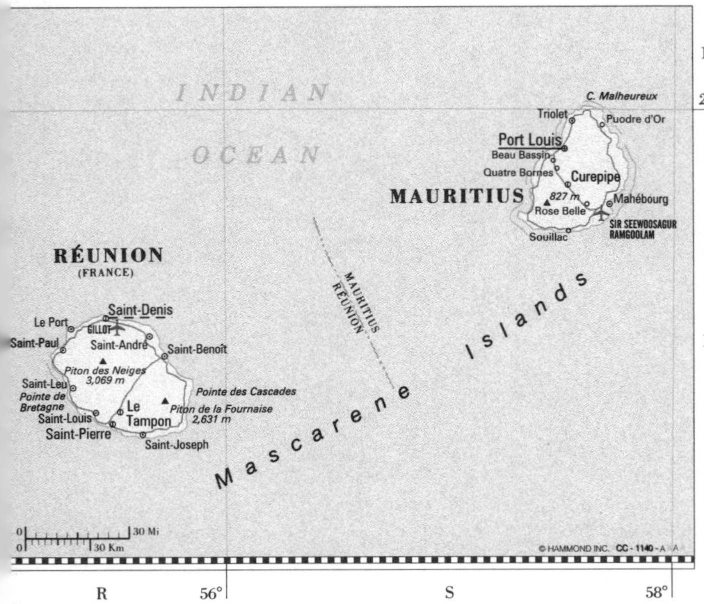

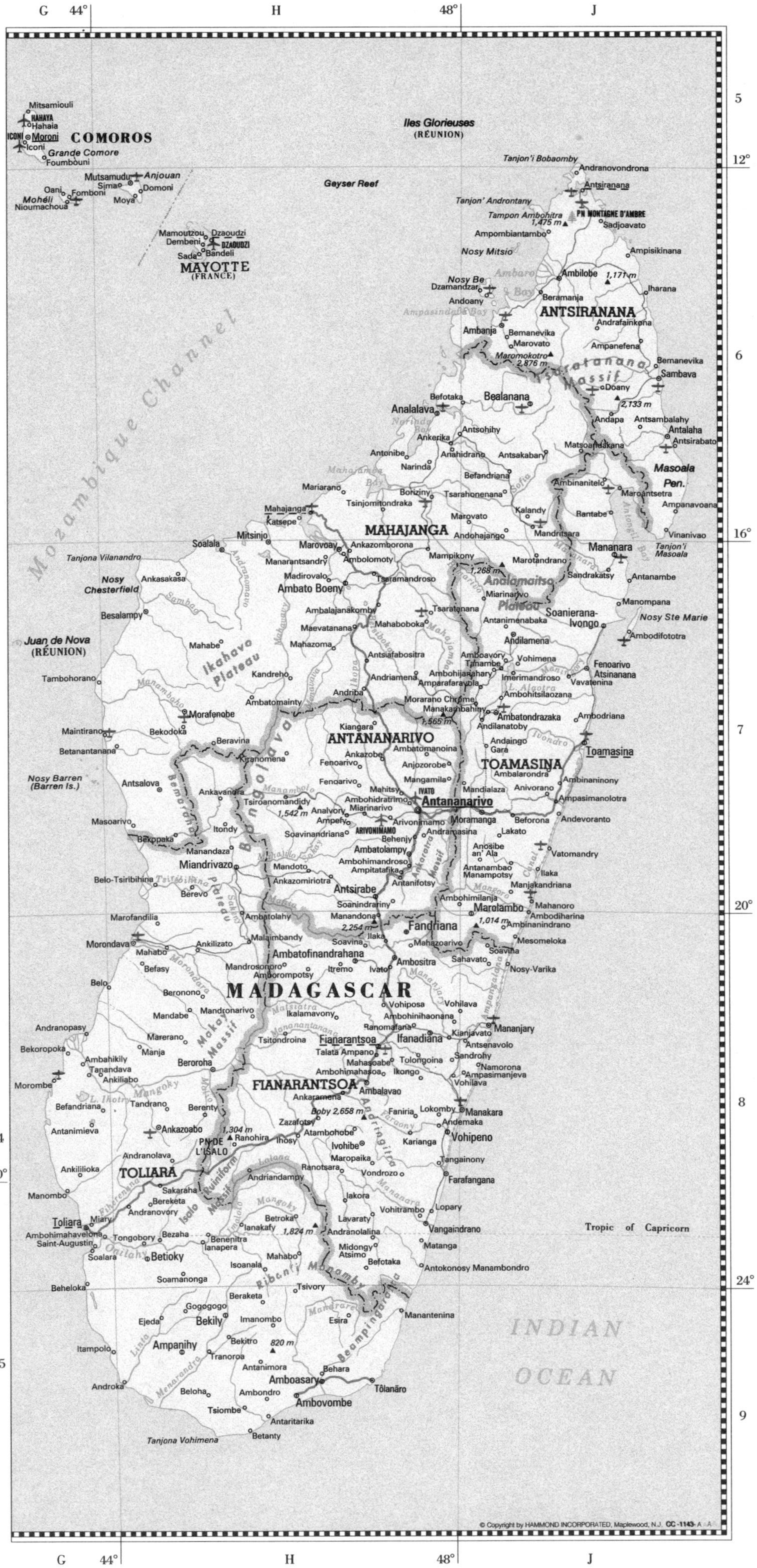

POPULATION OF CITIES AND TOWNS

OVER 2,000,000	500,000 - 999,999	100,000 - 249,999	10,000 - 29,999
1,000,000 - 1,999,999	250,000 - 499,999	30,000 - 99,999	UNDER 10,000

SCALE 1:7,000,000 LAMBERT CONFORMAL CONIC PROJECTION

MILES 0 100 200 300

KILOMETERS 0 100 200 300

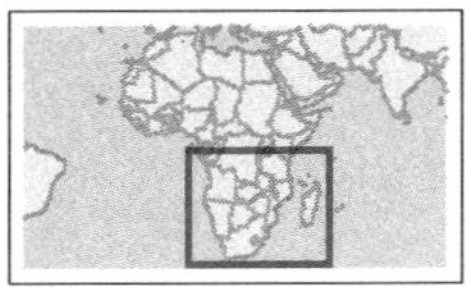

Southern Africa

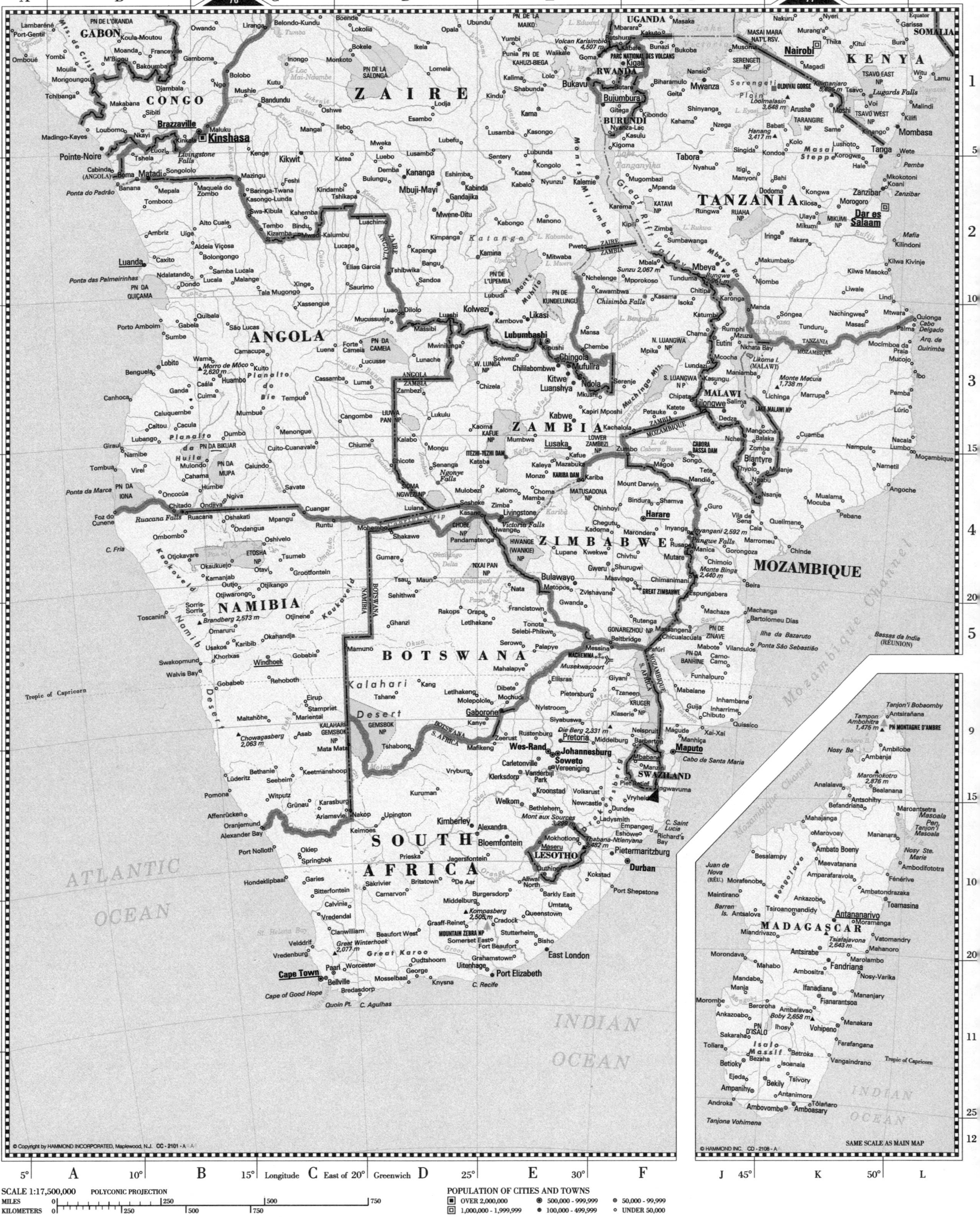

SCALE 1:17,500,000 POLYCONIC PROJECTION

MILES 0 250 500 750

KILOMETERS 0 250 500 750

Longitude East of 20° Greenwich

POPULATION OF CITIES AND TOWNS

- OVER 2,000,000
- 1,000,000 - 1,999,999
- 500,000 - 999,999
- 100,000 - 499,999
- 50,000 - 99,999
- UNDER 50,000

Antarctica

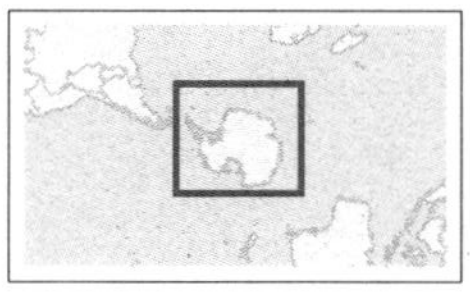

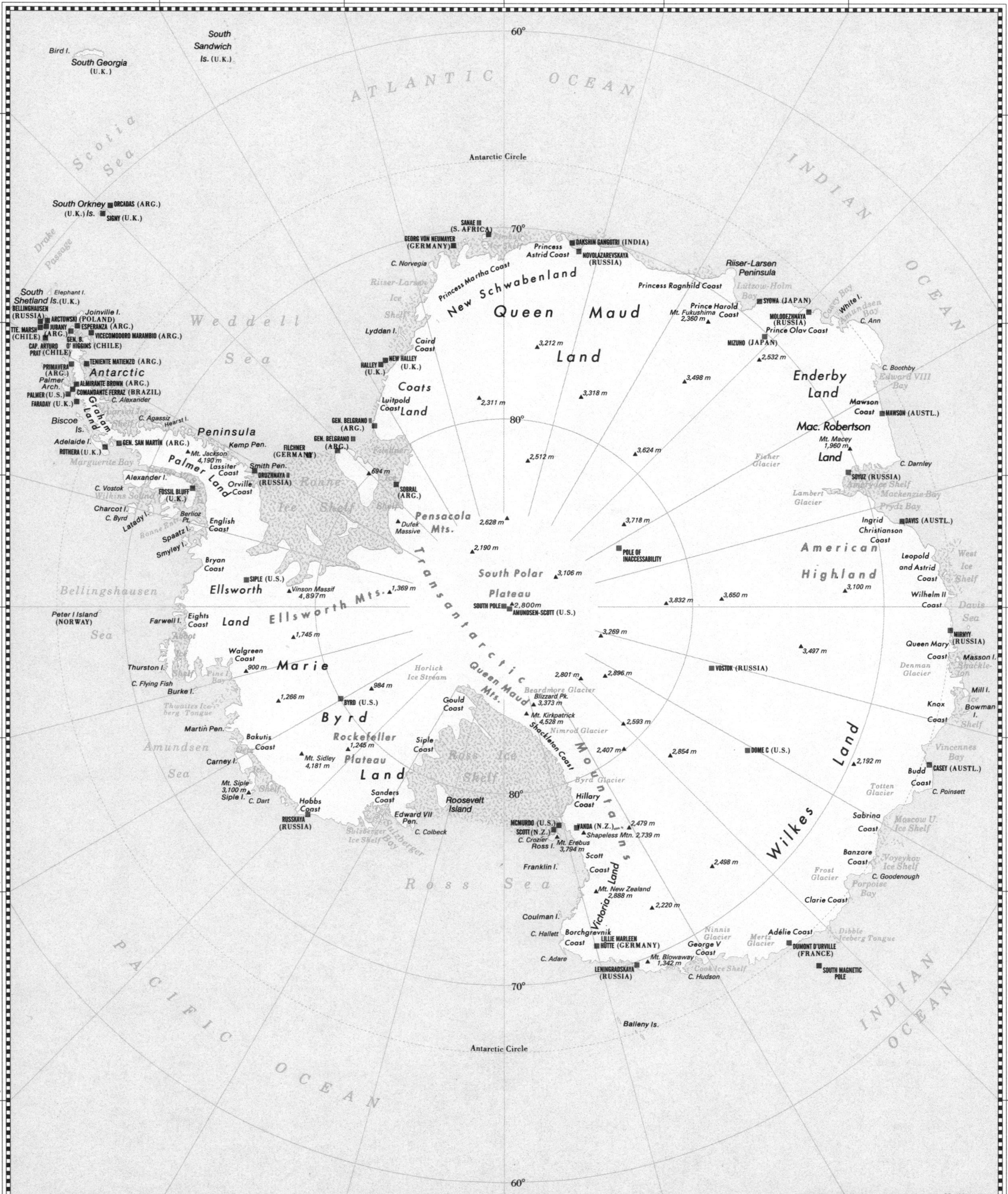

SCALE 1:28,000,000 POLAR STEREOGRAPHIC PROJECTION
MILES 0 300 600 900 1200
KILOMETERS 0 300 600 900 1200

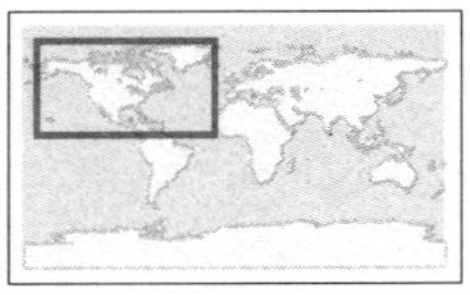

North America

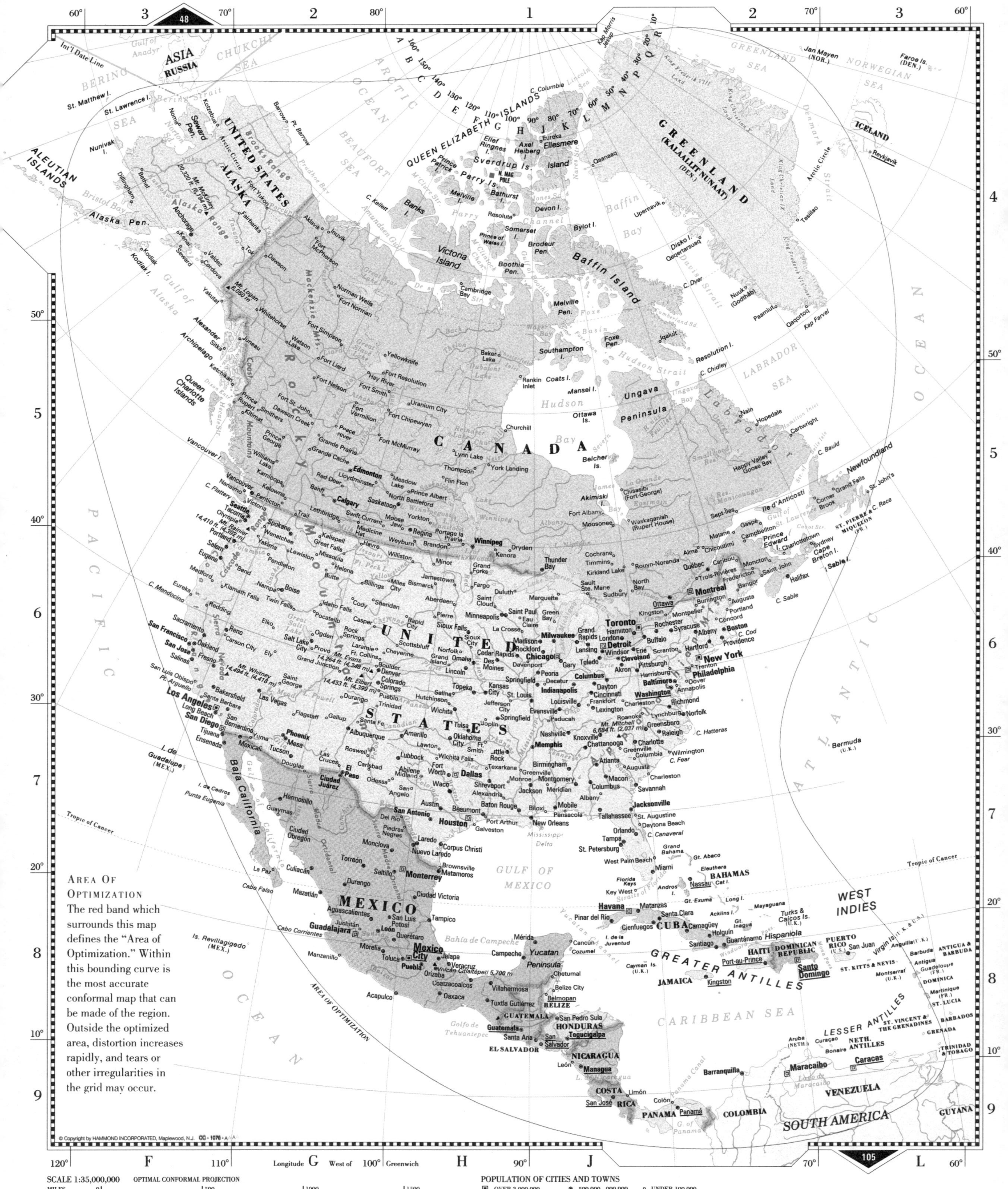

AREA OF OPTIMIZATION
The red band which surrounds this map defines the "Area of Optimization." Within this bounding curve is the most accurate conformal map that can be made of the region. Outside the optimized area, distortion increases rapidly, and tears or other irregularities in the grid may occur.

SCALE 1:35,000,000 OPTIMAL CONFORMAL PROJECTION
MILES 0 500 1000 1500
KILOMETERS 0 500 1000 1500

Longitude West of Greenwich

POPULATION OF CITIES AND TOWNS
- OVER 3,000,000
- 1,000,000 - 2,999,999
- 500,000 - 999,999
- 100,000 - 499,999
- UNDER 100,000

Alaska

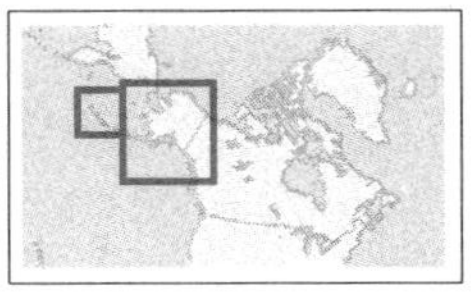

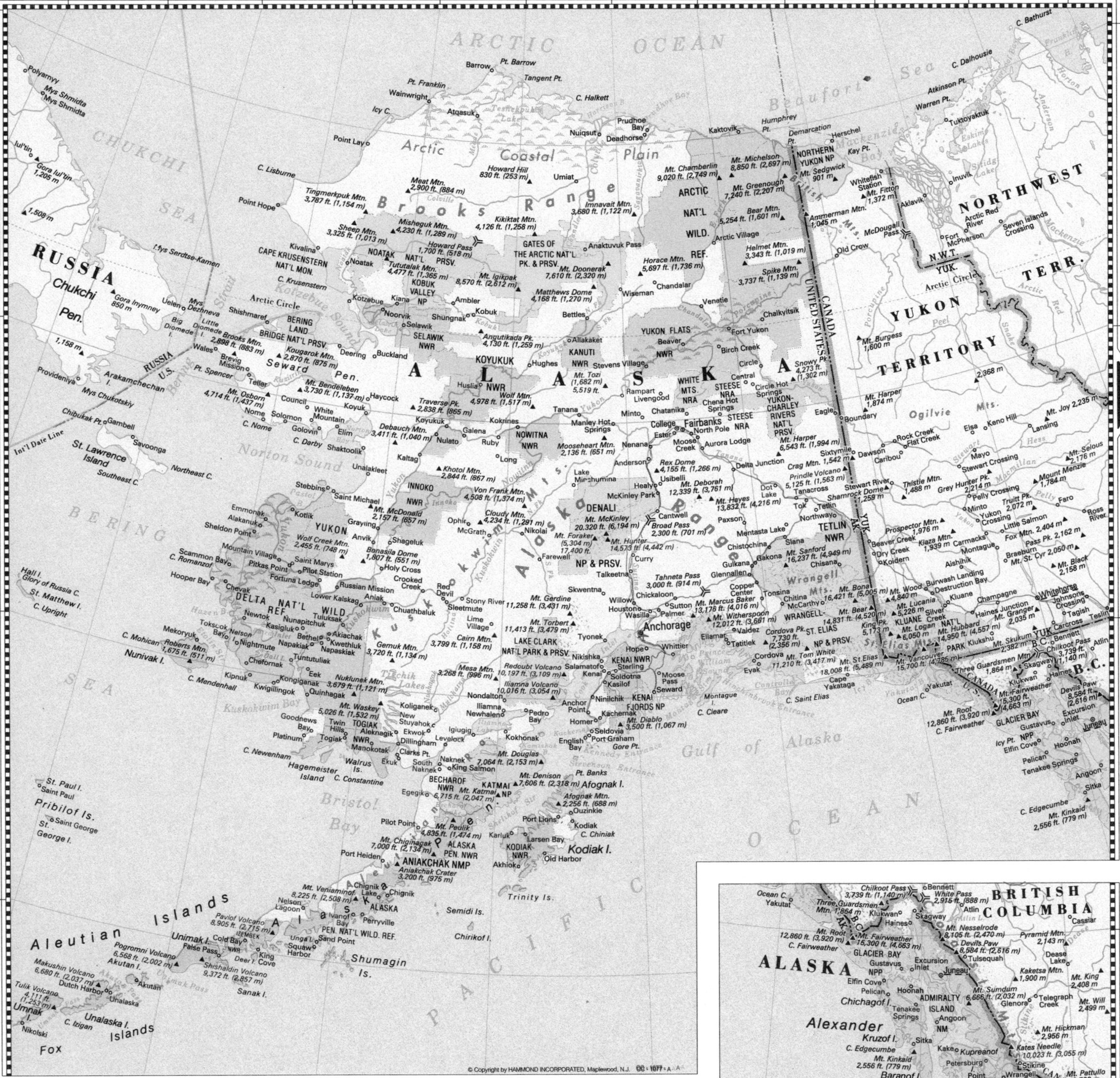

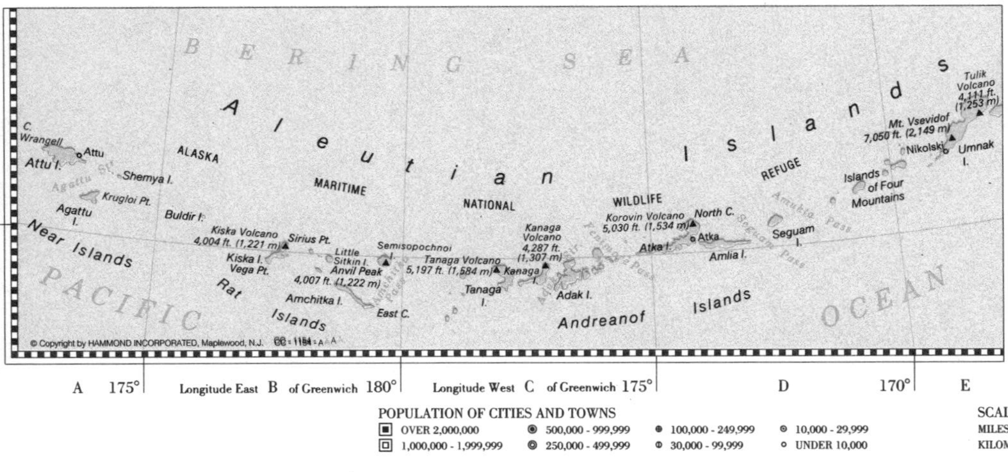

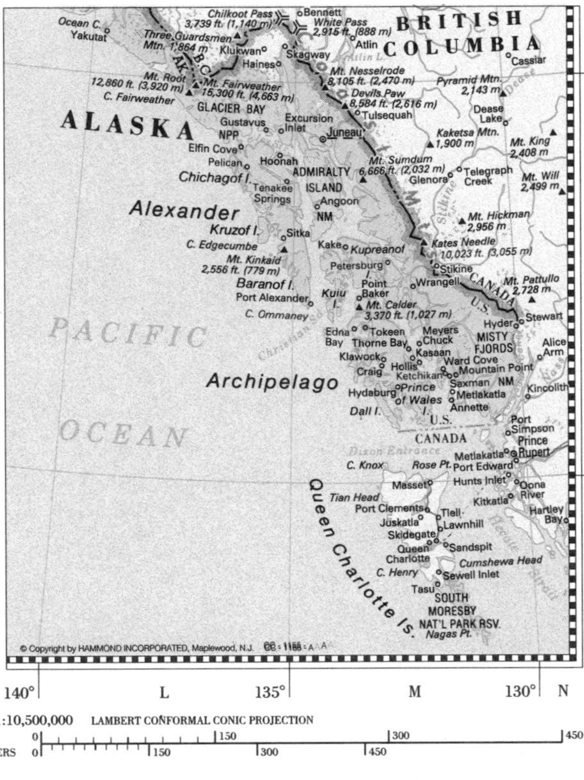

Longitude East of Greenwich | Longitude West of Greenwich

POPULATION OF CITIES AND TOWNS

- OVER 2,000,000
- 1,000,000 - 1,999,999
- 500,000 - 999,999
- 250,000 - 499,999
- 100,000 - 249,999
- 30,000 - 99,999
- 10,000 - 29,999
- UNDER 10,000

SCALE 1:10,500,000 LAMBERT CONFORMAL CONIC PROJECTION

MILES 0 150 300 450

KILOMETERS 0 150 300 450

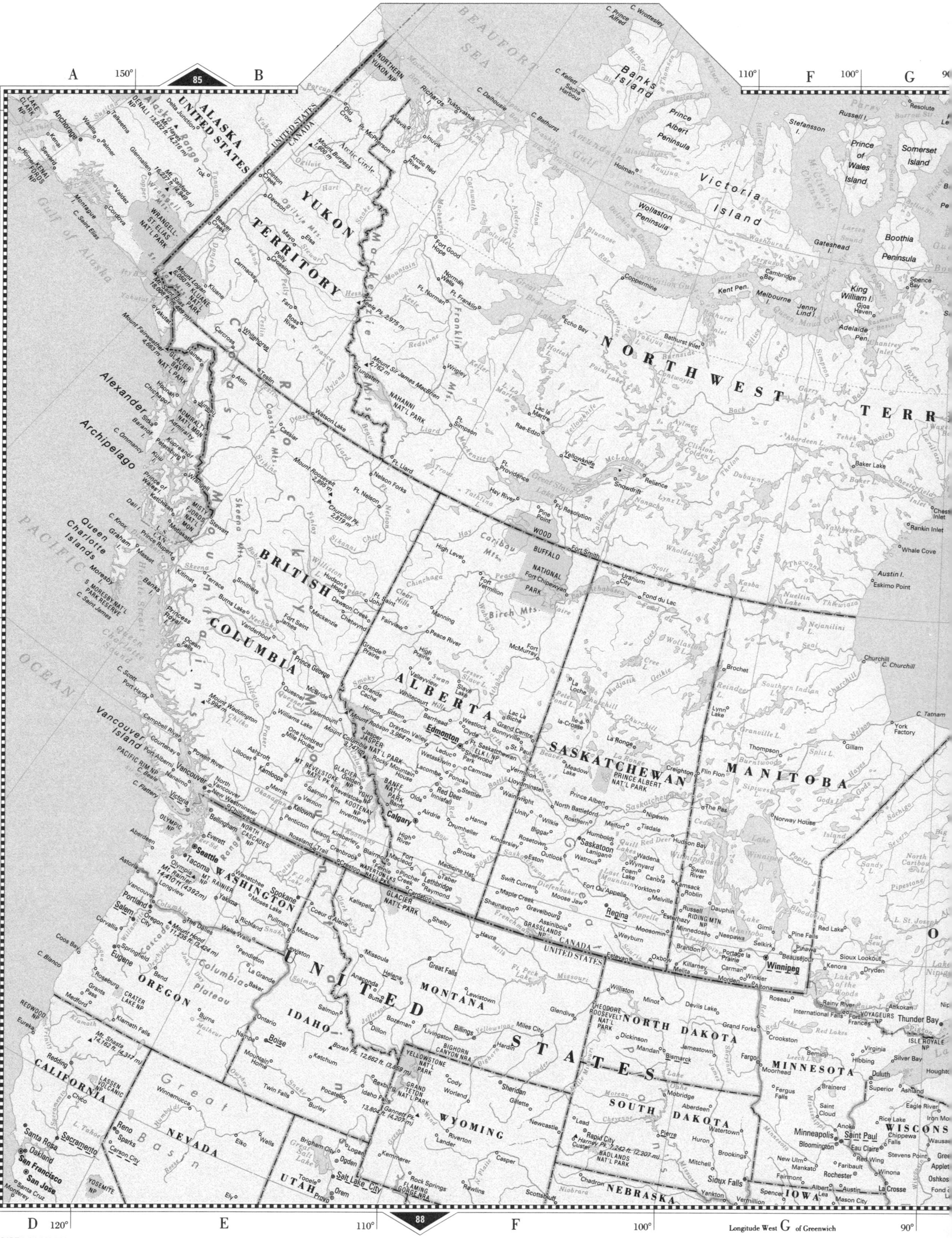

SCALE 1:14,000,000 LAMBERT CONFORMAL CONIC PROJECTION

MILES 0 200 400 600

KILOMETERS 0 200 400 600

POPULATION OF CITIES AND TOWNS

- OVER 2,000,000
- 1,000,000 - 1,999,999
- 500,000 - 999,999
- 100,000 - 499,999
- 50,000 - 99,999
- UNDER 50,000

Canada

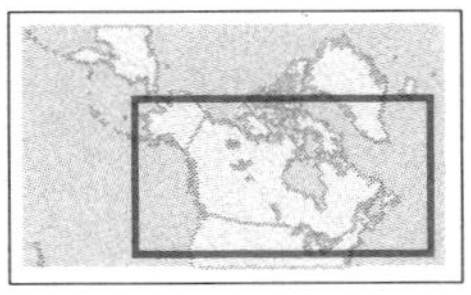

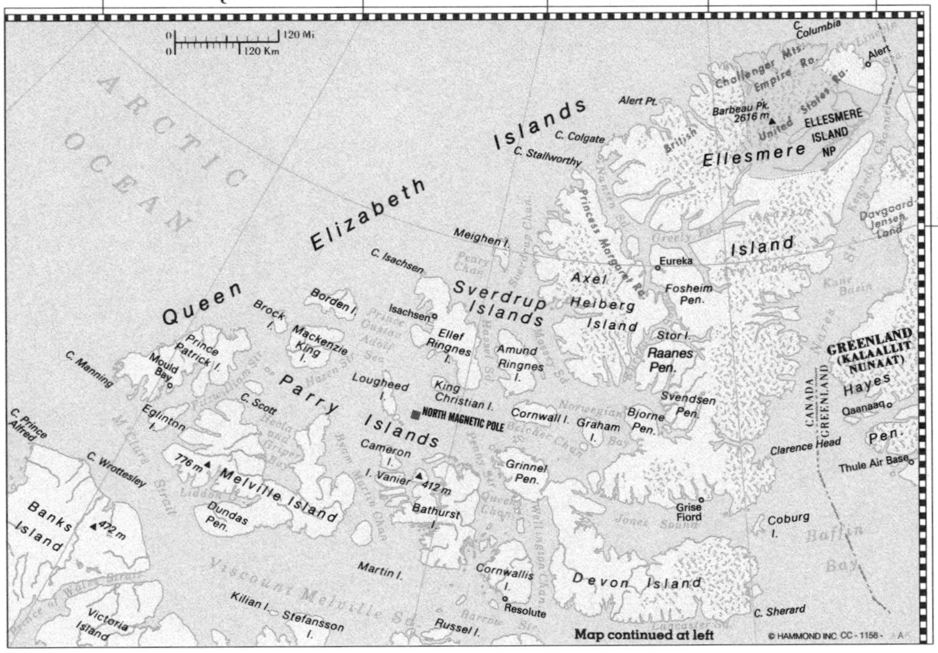

ARCTIC OCEAN
Queen Elizabeth Islands
Ellesmere Island
Ellesmere Island NP
Axel Heiberg Island
Sverdrup Islands
Parry Islands
Melville Island
Devon Island
Banks Island
Victoria Island
Prince Patrick I.
Mackenzie King I.
Borden I.
Ellef Ringnes I.
Amund Ringnes I.
Cornwallis I.
Bathurst I.
Cornwall I.
Lougheed I.
King Christian I.
NORTH MAGNETIC POLE
Eureka
Alert
Grise Fiord
Resolute
Thule Air Base
Qaanaaq
GREENLAND (KALAALLIT NUNAAT)
CANADA
GREENLAND
Viscount Melville Sd.
Map continued at left
© HAMMOND INC CC - 1156

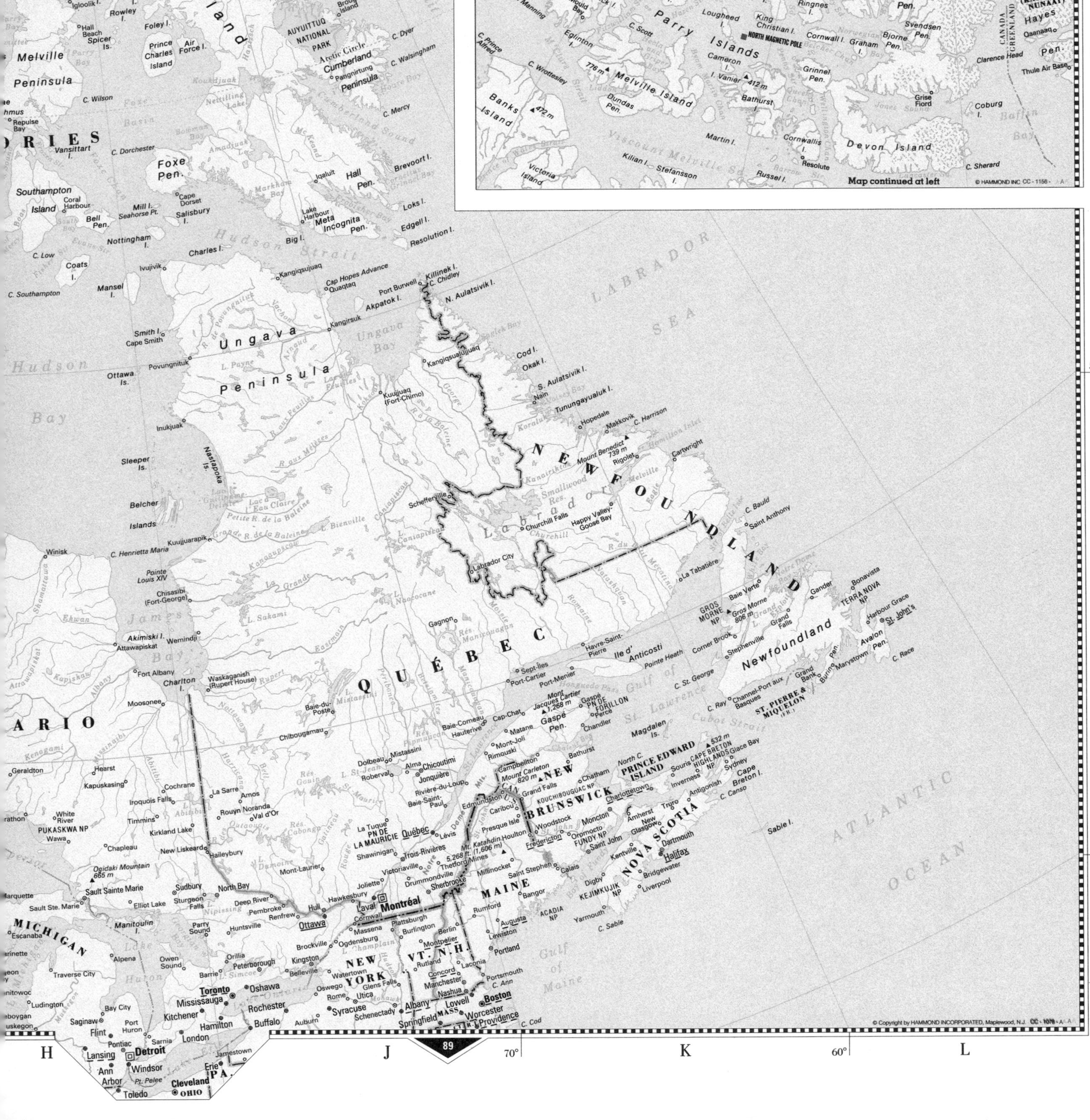

Map continued at right
Baffin Island
Baffin Bay
Davis Strait
GREENLAND (KALAALLIT NUNAAT) (DEN.)
Bylot Island
Melville Peninsula
Southampton Island
Foxe Pen.
Hudson Strait
Hudson Bay
James Bay
Ungava Peninsula
Ungava Bay
LABRADOR SEA
NEWFOUNDLAND
Labrador
QUÉBEC
ONTARIO
Newfoundland
NEW BRUNSWICK
NOVA SCOTIA
PRINCE EDWARD ISLAND
ST. PIERRE & MIQUELON (FR.)
Gulf of St. Lawrence
Cabot Strait
Gulf of Maine
ATLANTIC OCEAN
MAINE
NEW YORK
VT.
N.H.
MASS.
MICHIGAN
Iqaluit
Kuujjuaq (Fort-Chimo)
Schefferville
Labrador City
Churchill Falls
Happy Valley-Goose Bay
Sept-Îles
Gaspé
Québec
Montréal
Ottawa
Toronto
Fredericton
Saint John
Charlottetown
Halifax
St. John's
Corner Brook
Gander
Sydney
Boston
Sable I.
89
© Copyright by HAMMOND INCORPORATED, Maplewood, N.J.

PACIFIC OCEAN
BRITISH COLUMBIA
ALBERTA
SASKATCHEWAN
CANADA
UNITED STATES
WASHINGTON
OREGON
IDAHO
MONTANA
NORTH DAKOTA
SOUTH DAKOTA
WYOMING
NEBRASKA
NEVADA
UTAH
COLORADO
CALIFORNIA
ARIZONA
NEW MEXICO
MEXICO
SONORA
CHIHUAHUA
COAHUILA
NUEVO LEON
ZACATECAS
SAN LUIS POTOSI
JALISCO
GUANAJUATO
Vancouver Island
Seattle
Portland
San Francisco
Los Angeles
San Diego
Las Vegas
Phoenix
Salt Lake City
Denver
Albuquerque
El Paso
Ciudad Juárez
Calgary
Regina
HAWAII
Kauai
Niihau
Oahu
Honolulu
Molokai
Lanai
Maui
Kahoolawe
Hawaii
Kauai Channel
Kaiwi Channel
Alenuihaha Channel
HONOLULU
© Copyright by HAMMOND INCORPORATED, Maplewood, N.J. CC-1157
86
100
Longitude W

United States

POPULATION OF CITIES AND TOWNS

▣ OVER 2,000,000	◉ 500,000 - 999,999
◻ 1,000,000 - 1,999,999	● 100,000 - 499,999
◎ 50,000 - 99,999	○ UNDER 50,000

SCALE 1:14,000,000 LAMBERT CONFORMAL CONIC PROJECTION

MILES 0 200 400 600

KILOMETERS 0 200 400 600

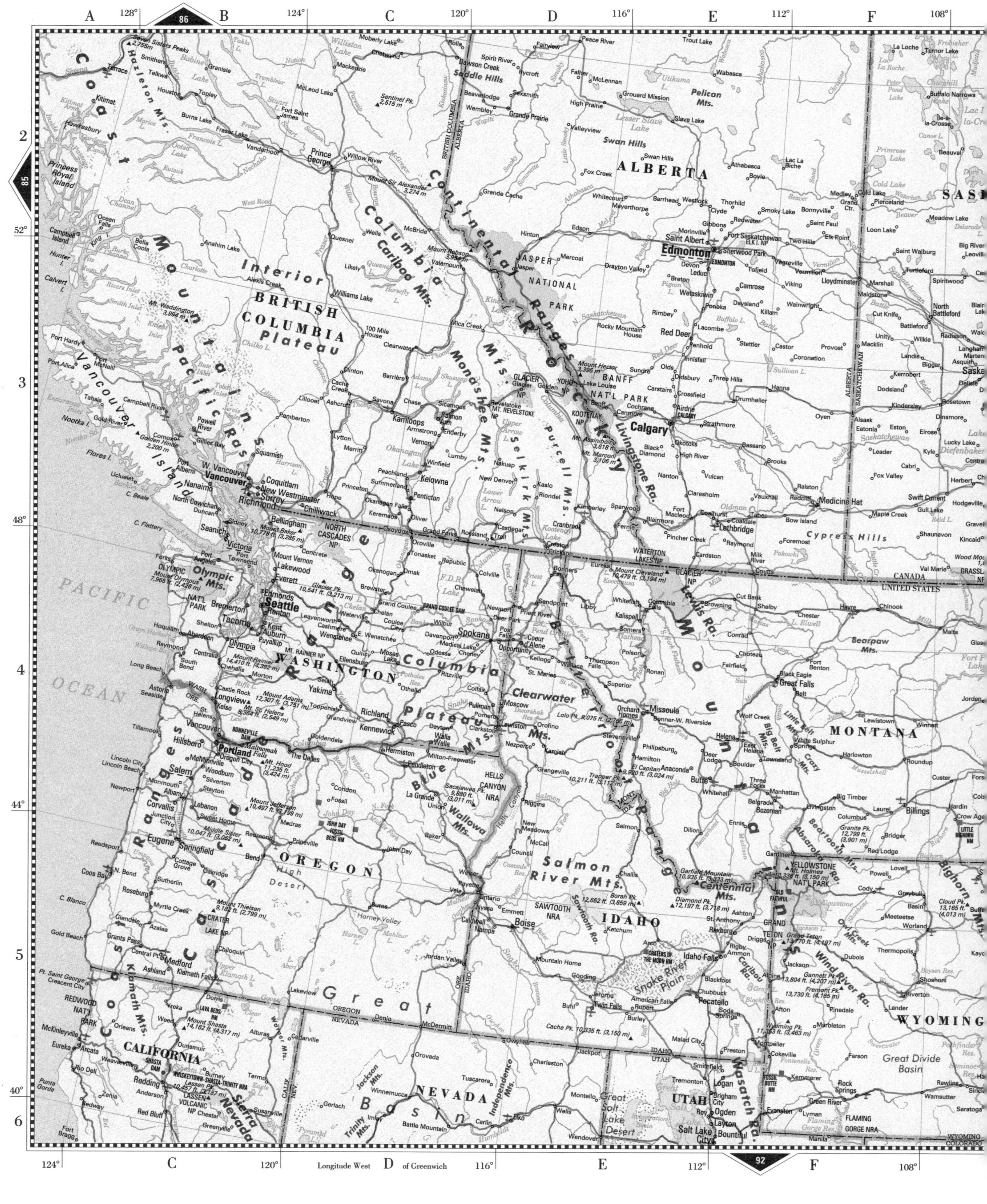

A
B
C
D
E
F
128°
124°
120°
116°
112°
108°
52°
48°
44°
40°
2
3
4
5
6
86
85
92
ALBERTA
BRITISH COLUMBIA
Interior
BRITISH COLUMBIA Plateau
WASHINGTON
OREGON
IDAHO
MONTANA
WYOMING
NEVADA
UTAH
CALIFORNIA
CANADA
UNITED STATES
PACIFIC
OCEAN
Coast Mountains
Rocky Mountains
Continental Ranges
Cascade Range
Coast Ranges
Great Basin
Columbia Plateau
Columbia Mts.
Cariboo Mts.
Monashee Mts.
Selkirk Mts.
Purcell Mts.
Pacific Ras.
Vancouver Island
Hazleton Mts.
Livingstone Ra.
Lewis Ra.
Bitterroot Range
Clearwater Mts.
Blue Mts.
Wallowa Mts.
Salmon River Mts.
Sawtooth Ra.
Centennial Mts.
Beartooth Mts.
Absaroka Ra.
Bighorn Mts.
Wind River Ra.
Wasatch Ra.
Klamath Mts.
Sierra Nevada
Olympic Mts.
Snake River Plain
Great Divide Basin
Great Salt Lake Desert
Cypress Hills
Swan Hills
Pelican Mts.
Saddle Hills
Bearpaw Mts.
Big Belt Mts.
Little Belt Mts.
Crazy Mts.
Owl Creek Mts.
Independence Mts.
Jackson Mts.
Trinity Mts.
Warner Mts.
JASPER NATIONAL PARK
BANFF NAT'L PARK
GLACIER NP
YOHO NP
KOOTENAY NP
MT. REVELSTOKE NP
WATERTON LAKES NP
NORTH CASCADES NP
OLYMPIC NAT'L PARK
MT. RAINIER NP
HELLS CANYON NRA
SAWTOOTH NRA
YELLOWSTONE NAT'L PARK
GRAND TETON NP
CRATER LAKE NP
LASSEN VOLCANIC NP
REDWOOD NAT'L PARK
FLAMING GORGE NRA
Seattle
Portland
Vancouver
Victoria
Spokane
Calgary
Edmonton
Boise
Salt Lake City
Missoula
Great Falls
Billings
Butte
Helena
Medicine Hat
Lethbridge
Red Deer
Kamloops
Kelowna
Prince George
Tacoma
Olympia
Salem
Eugene
Medford
Redding
Pocatello
Idaho Falls
Ogden
Logan
Yakima
Richland
Kennewick
Pasco
Bellingham
Everett
Lewiston
Longitude West of Greenwich

Southwestern Canada, Northwestern United States

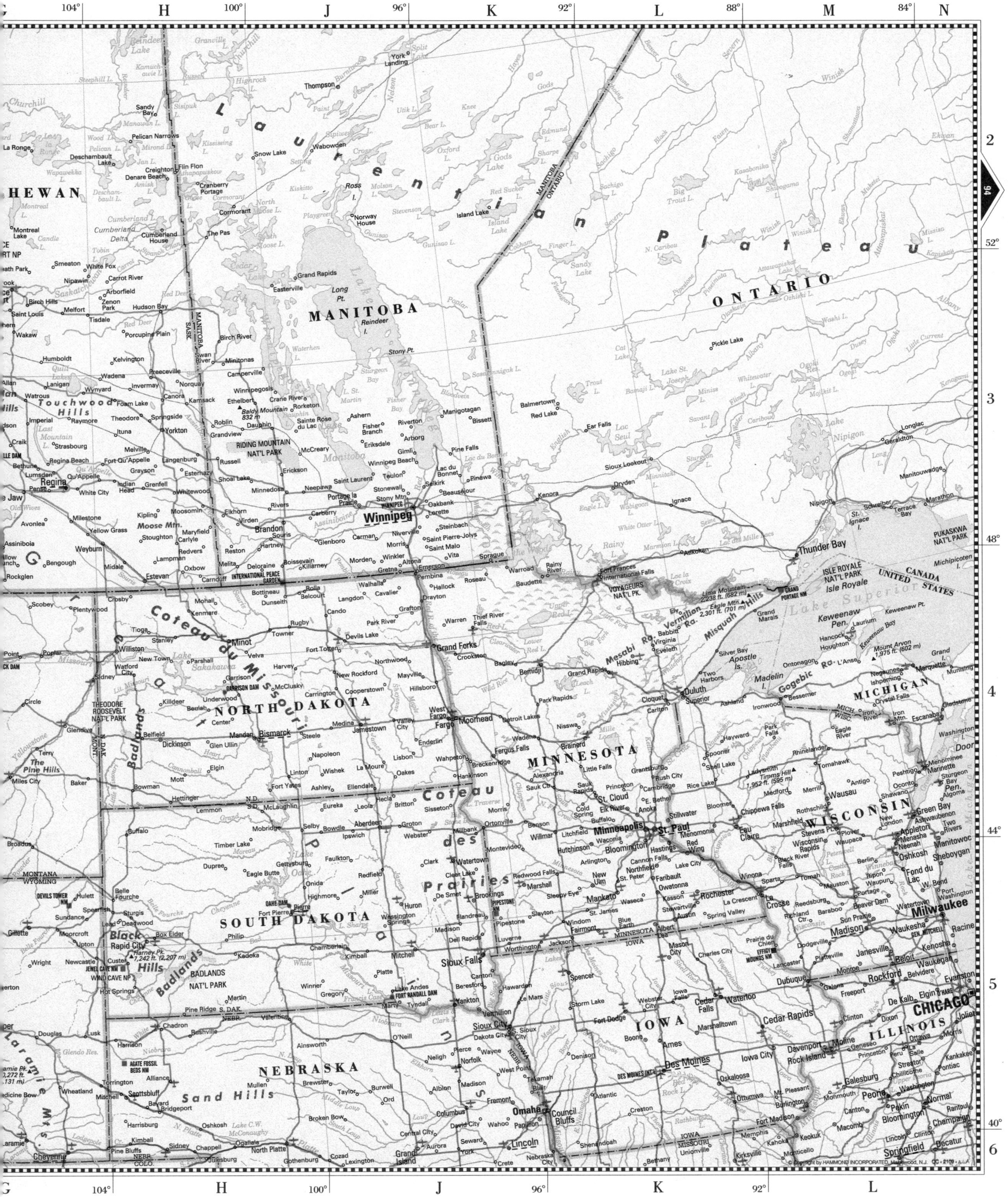

POPULATION OF CITIES AND TOWNS

- OVER 2,000,000
- 1,000,000 - 1,999,999
- 500,000 - 999,999
- 250,000 - 499,999
- 100,000 - 249,999
- 30,000 - 99,999
- 10,000 - 29,999
- UNDER 10,000

SCALE 1:7,000,000 LAMBERT CONFORMAL CONIC PROJECTION

MILES 0 100 200 300

KILOMETERS 0 100 200 300

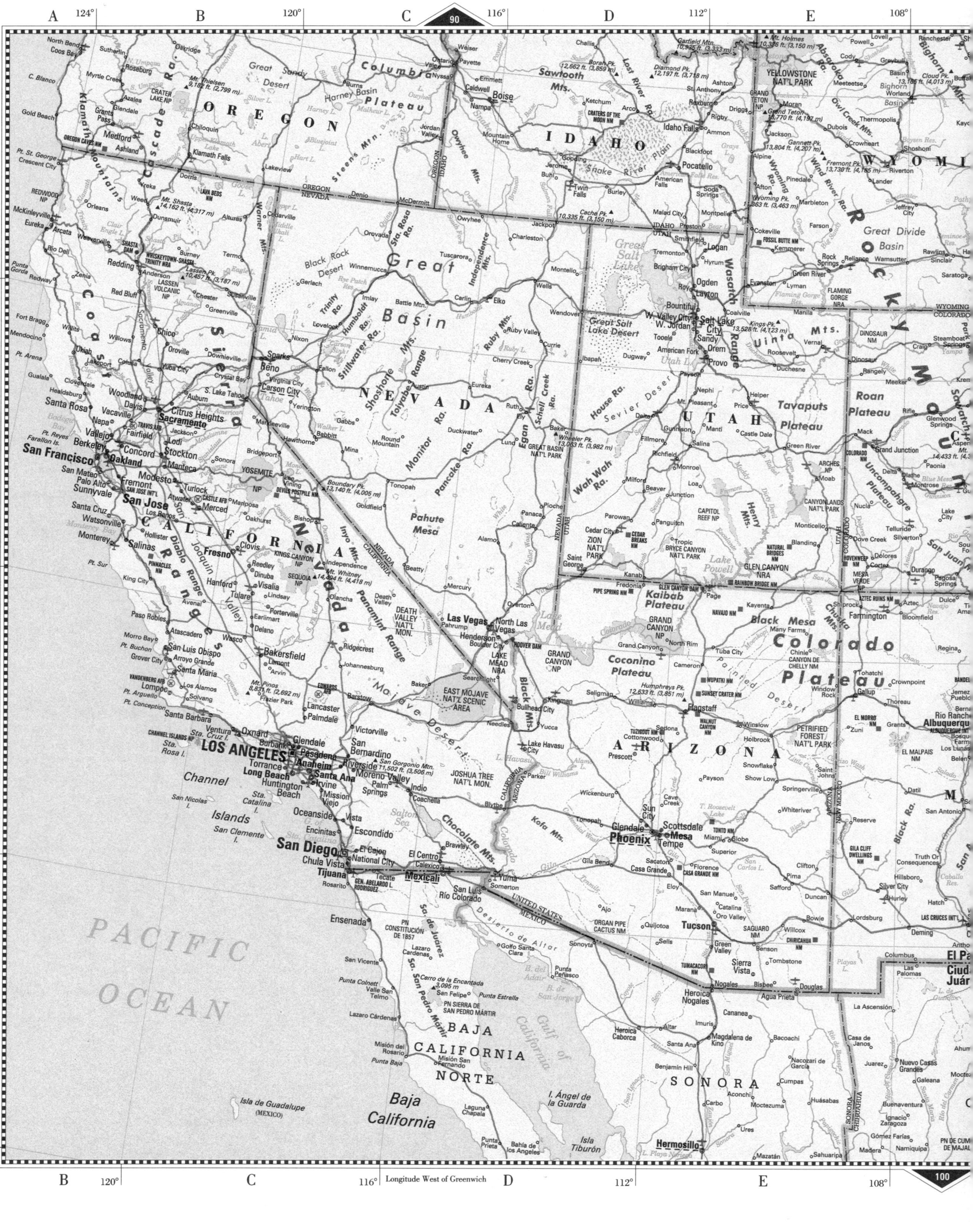
90
100
Longitude West of Greenwich
OREGON
IDAHO
NEVADA
UTAH
ARIZONA
CALIFORNIA
WYOMI
Rocky Mountains
Great Basin
Sierra Nevada
Coast Ranges
Cascade Ra.
Klamath Mountains
Columbia Plateau
Colorado Plateau
Great Sandy Desert
Mojave Desert
PACIFIC OCEAN
Gulf of California
BAJA CALIFORNIA NORTE
SONORA
Baja California
San Francisco
Oakland
San Jose
Sacramento
Fresno
Bakersfield
LOS ANGELES
Long Beach
Anaheim
Santa Ana
San Diego
Tijuana
Mexicali
Las Vegas
Reno
Carson City
Boise
Salt Lake City
Provo
Ogden
Phoenix
Tucson
Mesa
Flagstaff
Hermosillo
Ensenada
YELLOWSTONE NAT'L PARK
YOSEMITE NP
GRAND CANYON NP
ZION NAT'L PARK
DEATH VALLEY NAT'L MON.
JOSHUA TREE NAT'L MON.
EAST MOJAVE NAT'L SCENIC AREA
PETRIFIED FOREST NAT'L PARK
Great Salt Lake
Lake Powell
Lake Mead
Channel Islands
Isla de Guadalupe (MEXICO)
Isla Tiburón
UNITED STATES
MEXICO

Southwestern United States

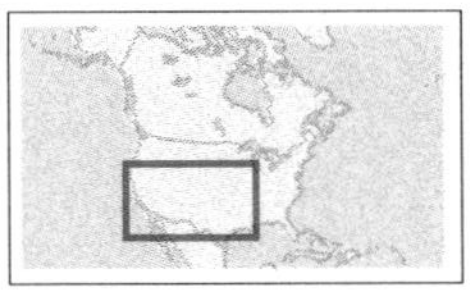

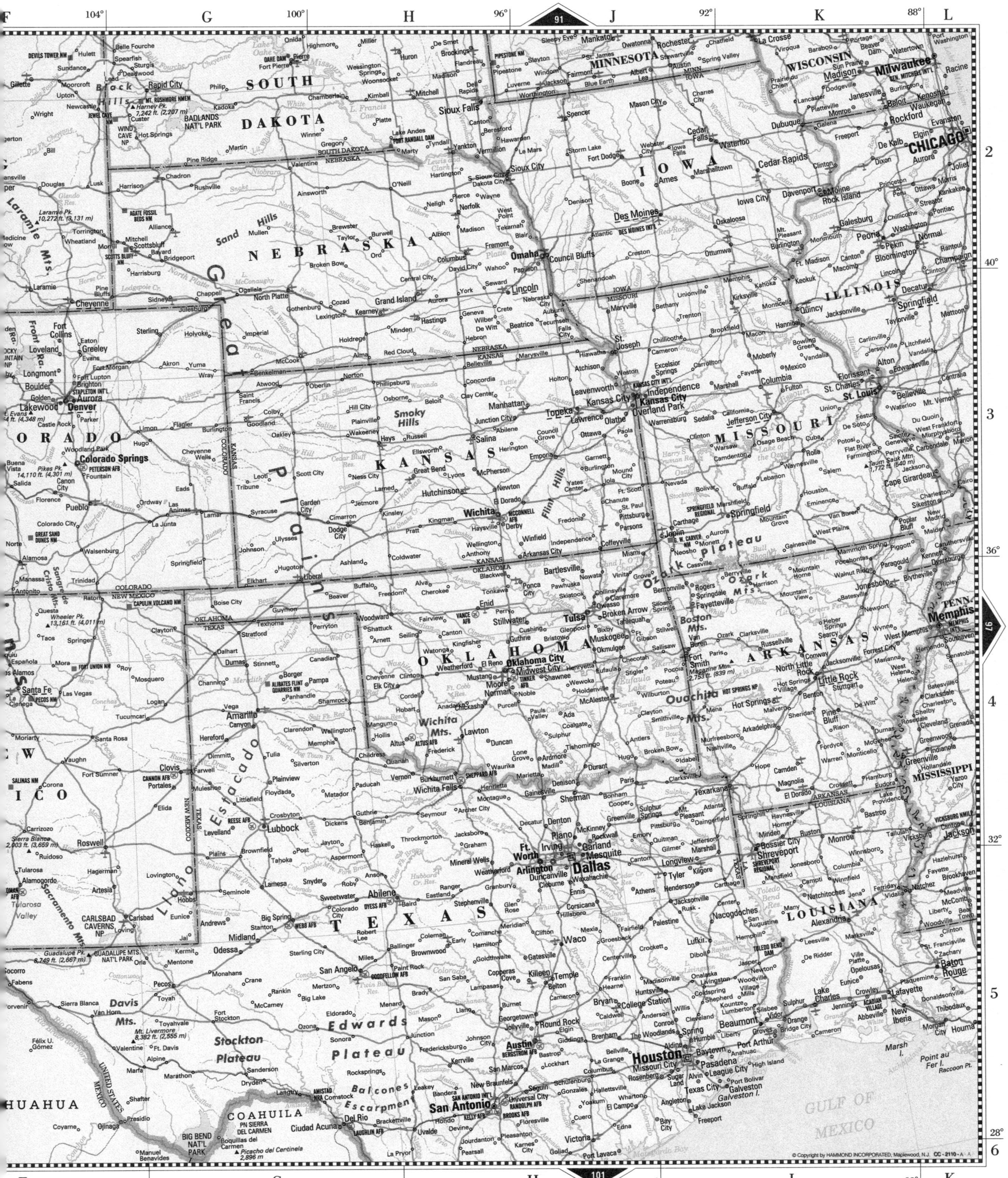

POPULATION OF CITIES AND TOWNS

OVER 2,000,000	500,000 - 999,999	100,000 - 249,999	10,000 - 29,999	
1,000,000 - 1,999,999	250,000 - 499,999	30,000 - 99,999	UNDER 10,000	

SCALE 1:7,000,000 LAMBERT CONFORMAL CONIC PROJECTION

MILES 0 100 200 300

KILOMETERS 0 100 200 300

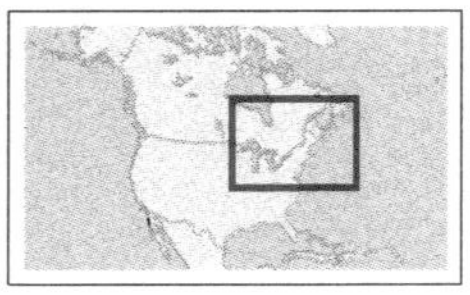

Southeastern Canada, Northeastern United States

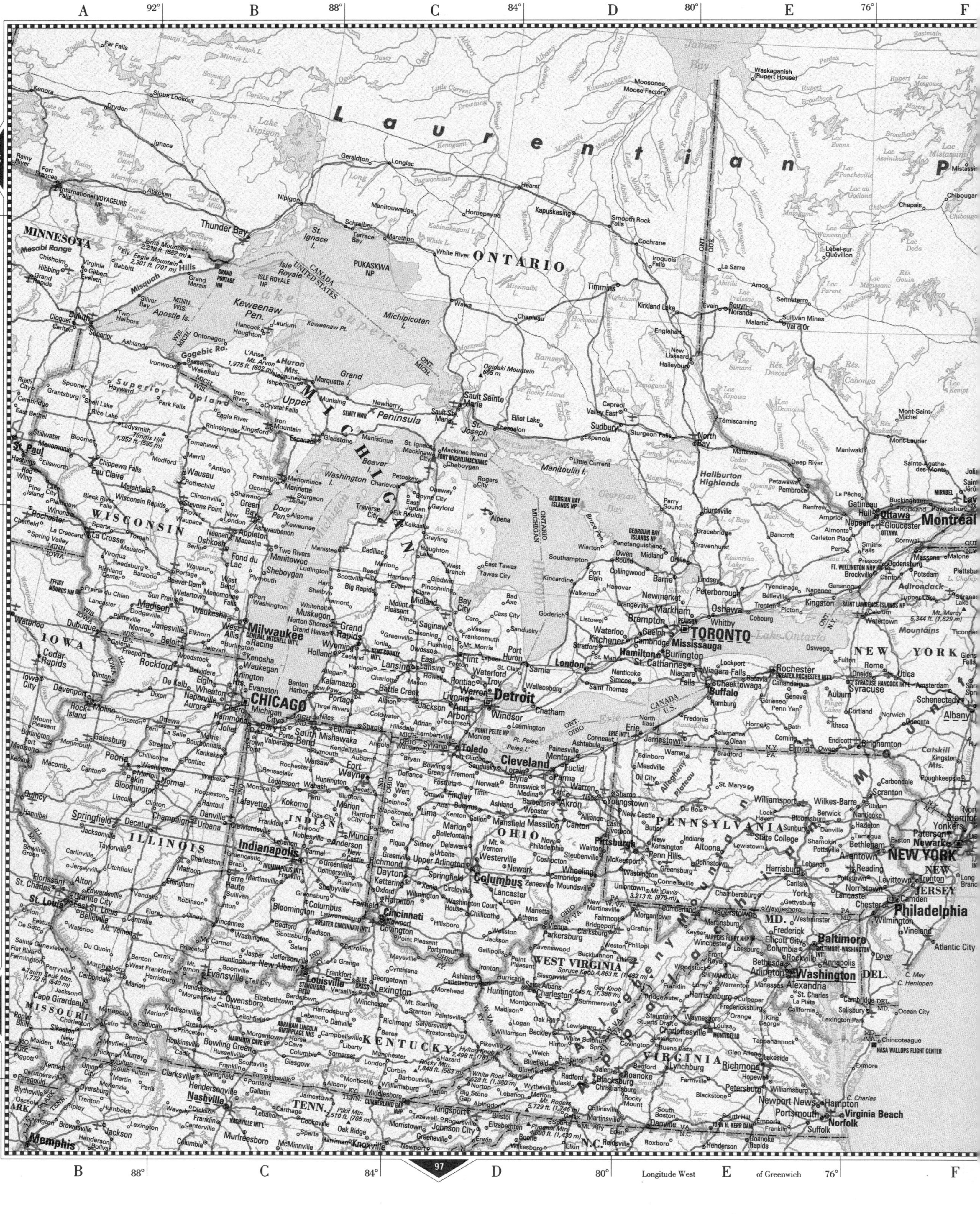

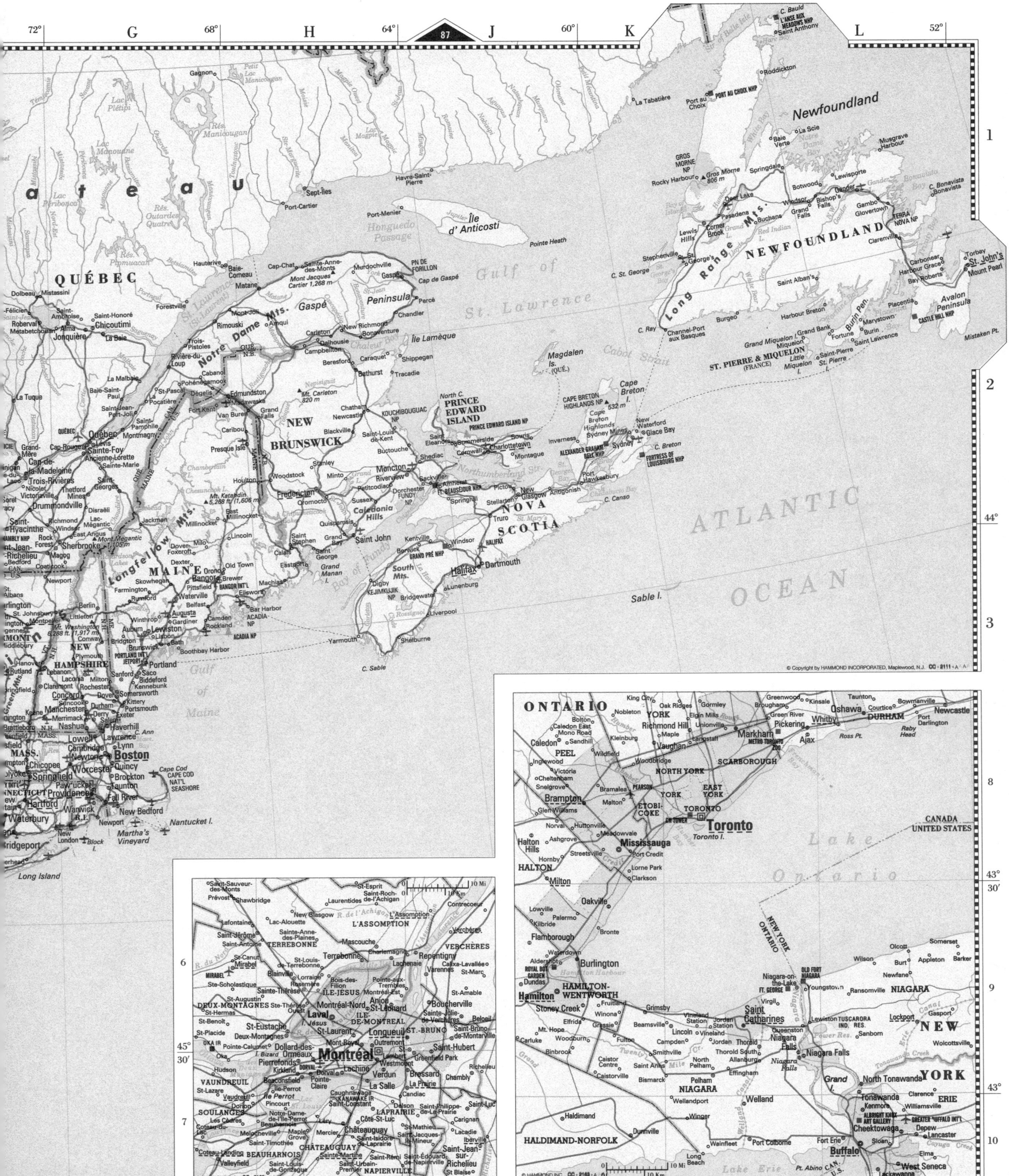

POPULATION OF CITIES AND TOWNS

▣ OVER 2,000,000	◉ 500,000 - 999,999	● 100,000 - 249,999	◎ 10,000 - 29,999
◻ 1,000,000 - 1,999,999	◎ 250,000 - 499,999	• 30,000 - 99,999	○ UNDER 10,000

SCALE 1:7,000,000 LAMBERT CONFORMAL CONIC PROJECTION

MILES 0 100 200 300

KILOMETERS 0 100 200 300

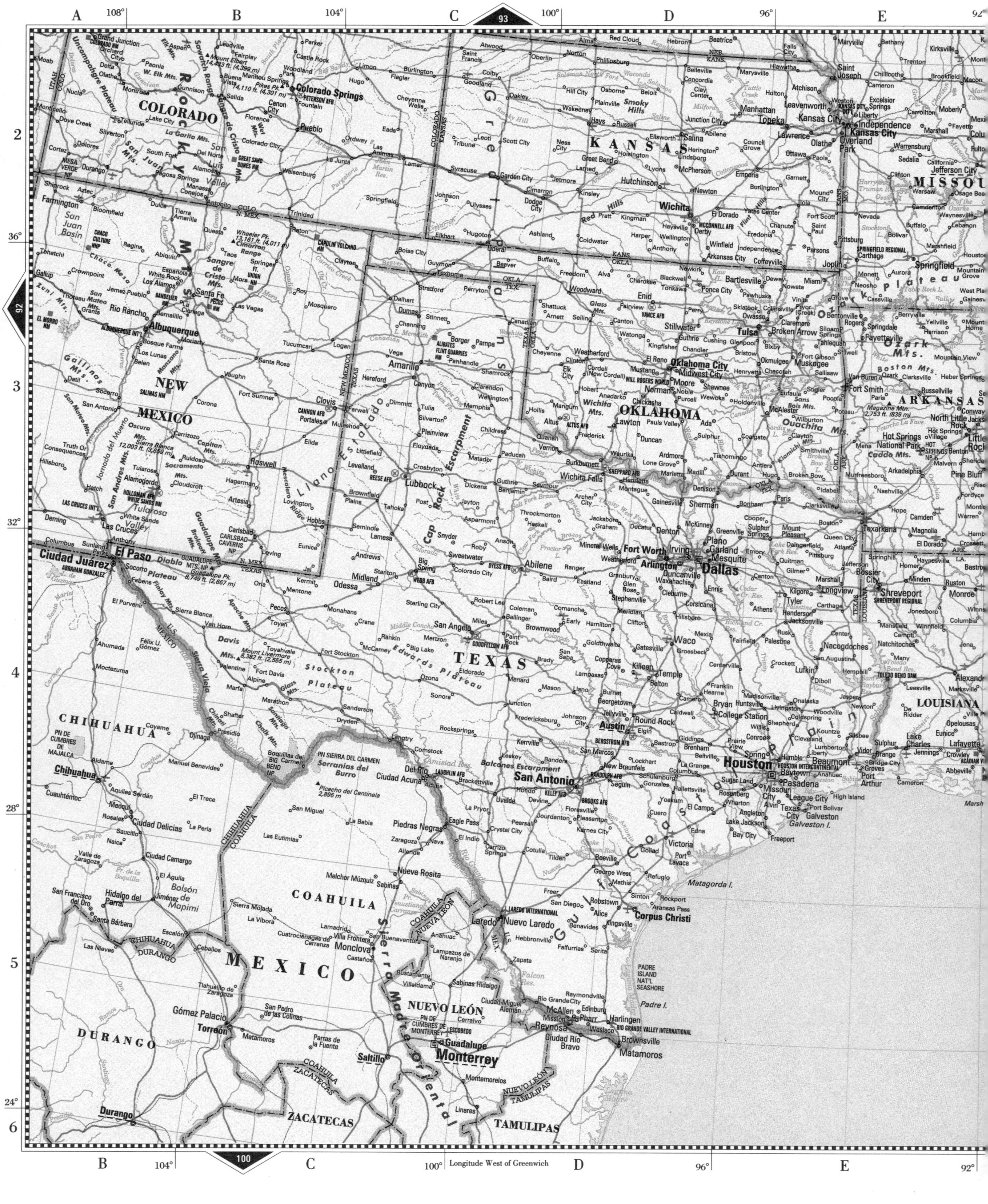

COLORADO
KANSAS
OKLAHOMA
ARKANSAS
NEW MEXICO
TEXAS
LOUISIANA
MEXICO
CHIHUAHUA
COAHUILA
NUEVO LEÓN
DURANGO
ZACATECAS
TAMULIPAS
Great Plains
Rocky Mts.
Llano Estacado
Edwards Plateau
Gulf Coastal Plain
Sierra Madre Oriental
Denver
Colorado Springs
Pueblo
Albuquerque
Santa Fe
El Paso
Ciudad Juárez
Wichita
Kansas City
Oklahoma City
Tulsa
Amarillo
Lubbock
Fort Worth
Dallas
Austin
San Antonio
Houston
Corpus Christi
Shreveport
Chihuahua
Monterrey
Torreón
Saltillo
Durango
Longitude West of Greenwich

Southeastern United States

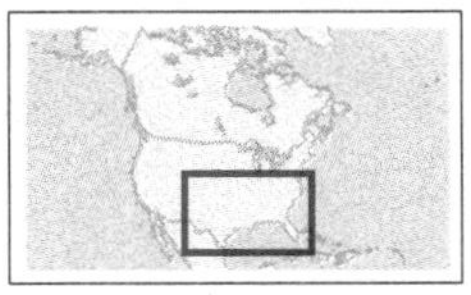

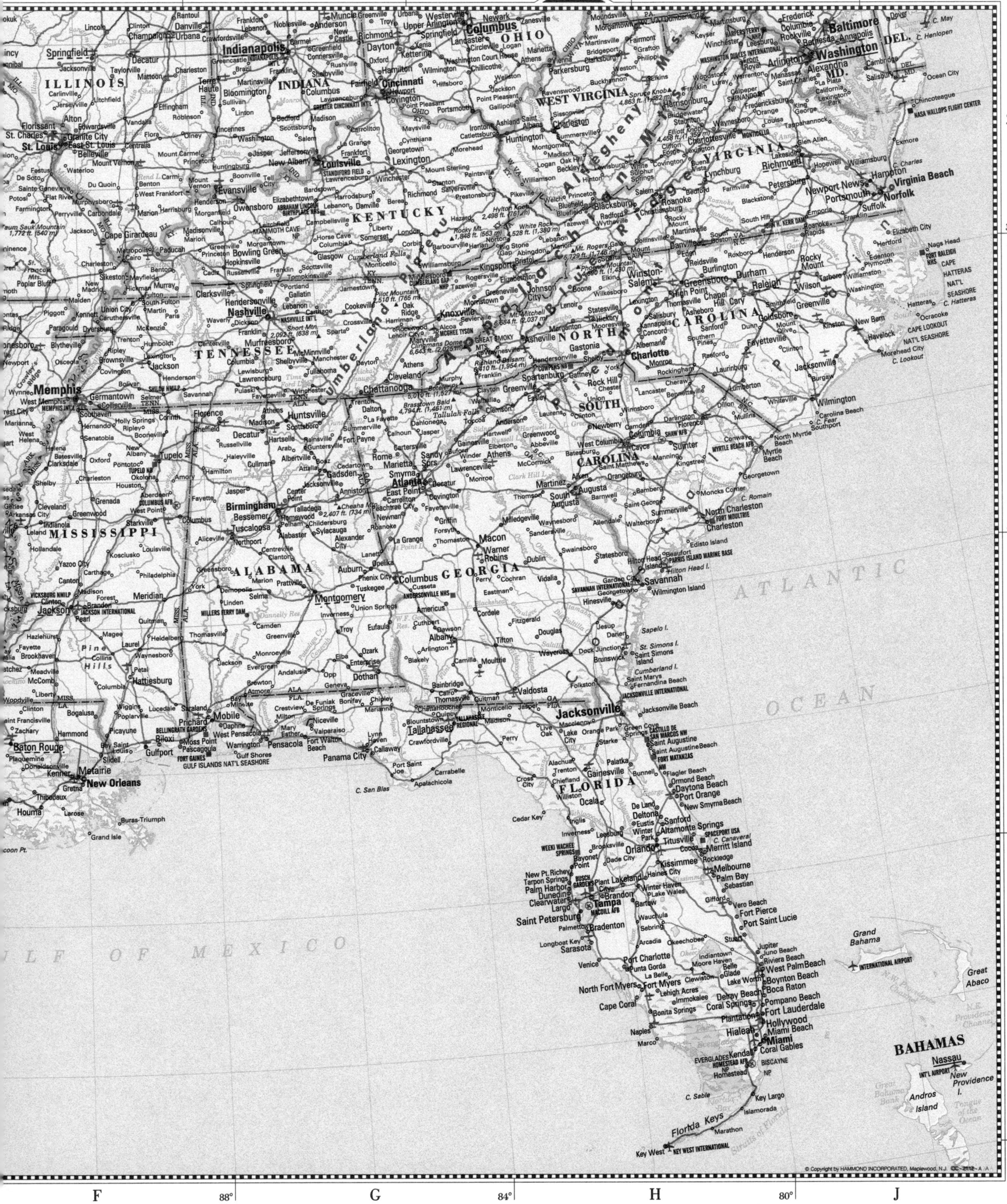

F | 88° | G | 84° | H | 80° | J

POPULATION OF CITIES AND TOWNS

- ▣ OVER 2,000,000
- ◻ 1,000,000 - 1,999,999
- ◉ 500,000 - 999,999
- ◎ 250,000 - 499,999
- ● 100,000 - 249,999
- ⊕ 30,000 - 99,999
- ⊙ 10,000 - 29,999
- ○ UNDER 10,000

SCALE 1:7,000,000 LAMBERT CONFORMAL CONIC PROJECTION

MILES 0 100 200 300

KILOMETERS 0 100 200 300

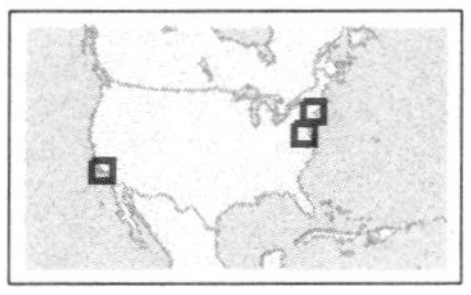

Los Angeles, New York, Philadelphia, Washington

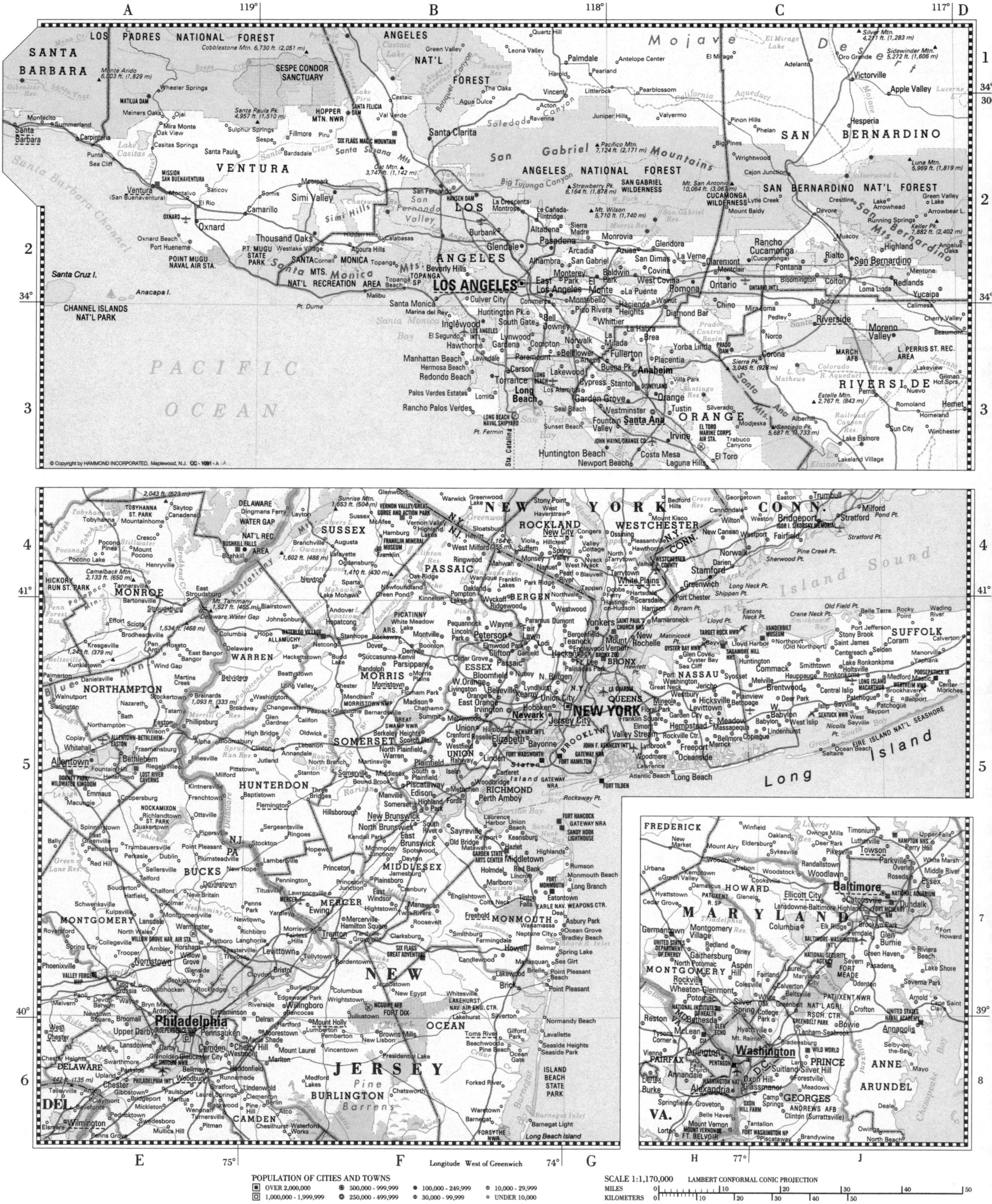

Longitude West of Greenwich

POPULATION OF CITIES AND TOWNS

OVER 2,000,000	500,000 - 999,999	100,000 - 249,999	10,000 - 29,999
1,000,000 - 1,999,999	250,000 - 499,999	30,000 - 99,999	UNDER 10,000

SCALE 1:1,170,000 LAMBERT CONFORMAL CONIC PROJECTION

MILES 0 10 20 30 40 50

KILOMETERS 0 10 20 30 40 50

Seattle, San Francisco, Detroit, Chicago

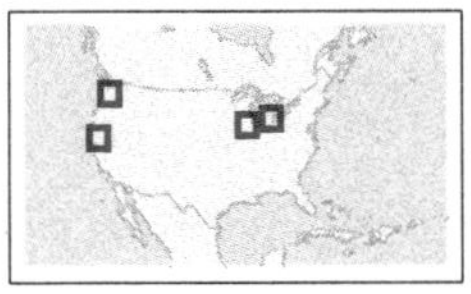

Longitude West of Greenwich

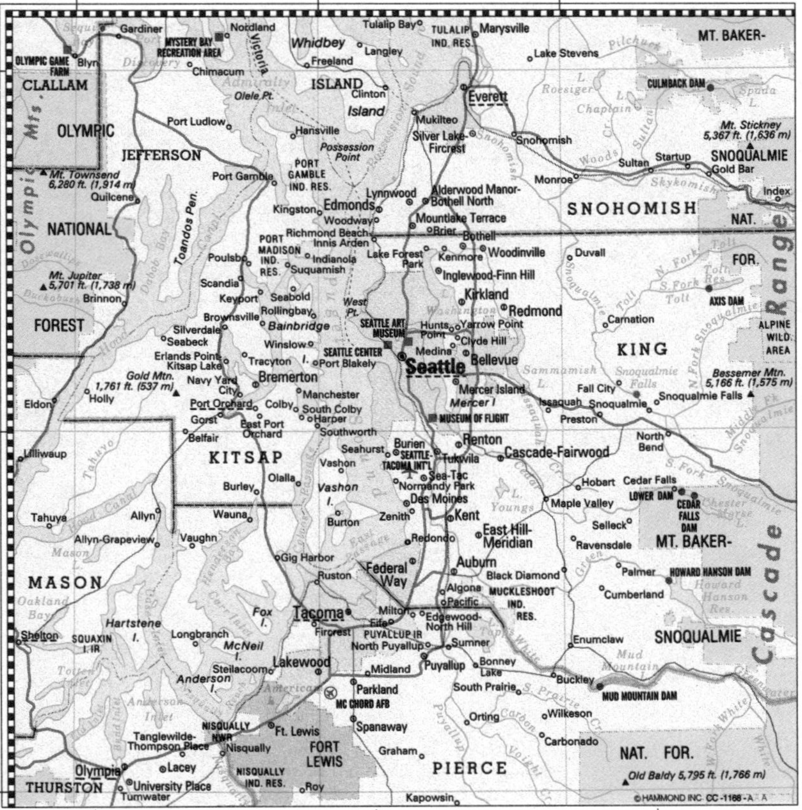

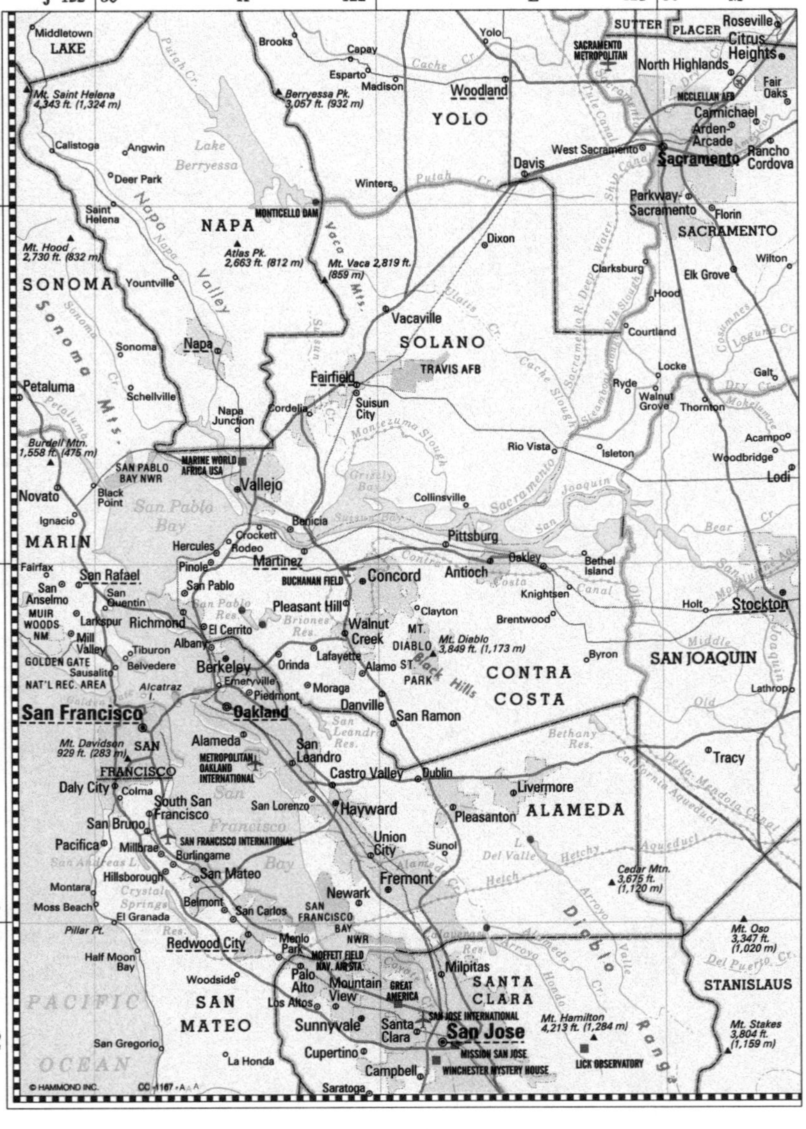

SCALE 1:1,170,000 LAMBERT CONFORMAL CONIC PROJECTION

MILES 0 10 20 30 40 50

KILOMETERS 0 10 20 30 40 50

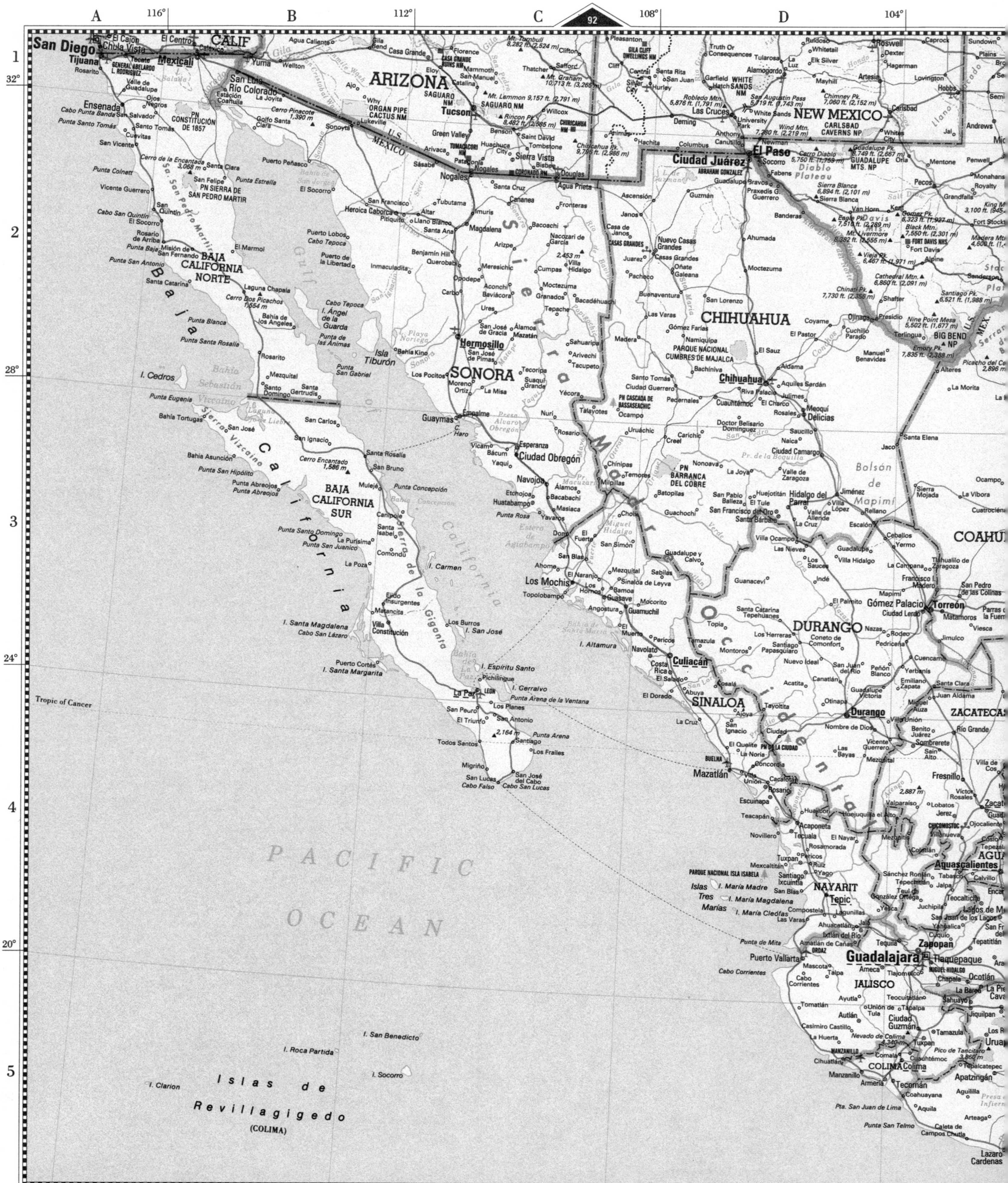
92
A
B
C
D
E
1
2
3
4
5
116°
112°
108°
104°
32°
28°
24°
20°
Longitude West of Greenwich
Tropic of Cancer
ARIZONA
NEW MEXICO
CALIF
U.S.
MEXICO
BAJA CALIFORNIA NORTE
BAJA CALIFORNIA SUR
SONORA
CHIHUAHUA
COAHUI
DURANGO
SINALOA
ZACATECAS
NAYARIT
JALISCO
COLIMA
AGUA
Baja California
Gulf of California
Sierra Madre Occidental
Bolsón de Mapimí
Diablo Plateau
PACIFIC OCEAN
Islas de Revillagigedo
(COLIMA)
I. Clarion
I. Roca Partida
I. San Benedicto
I. Socorro
Islas Tres Marías
PARQUE NACIONAL ISLA ISABELA
I. María Madre
I. María Magdalena
I. María Cleofas
I. Cedros
Isla Tiburón
I. Carmen
I. San José
I. Espíritu Santo
I. Cerralvo
I. Santa Magdalena
I. Santa Margarita
I. Altamura
San Diego
Tijuana
El Cajon
Chula Vista
Tecate
Mexicali
El Centro
Calexico
Yuma
San Luis Río Colorado
Ensenada
Rosarito
San Quintín
Tucson
Nogales
Hermosillo
Guaymas
Ciudad Obregón
Navojoa
Los Mochis
Culiacán
Mazatlán
Santa Rosalía
La Paz
San José del Cabo
Cabo San Lucas
El Paso
Ciudad Juárez
Las Cruces
Chihuahua
Delicias
Hidalgo del Parral
Torreón
Gómez Palacio
Durango
Tepic
Guadalajara
Zapopan
Tlaquepaque
Puerto Vallarta
Colima
Manzanillo
Aguascalientes
Fresnillo
Roswell
Carlsbad
Douglas
Agua Prieta
Cananea
Sierra Vista
Deming
Alamogordo
PARQUE NACIONAL CUMBRES DE MAJALCA
PN BARRANCA DEL COBRE
PN CASCADA DE BASASEACHIC
PN SIERRA DE SAN PEDRO MARTIR
PN CONSTITUCIÓN DE 1857
ORGAN PIPE CACTUS NM
SAGUARO NM
WHITE SANDS NM
CARLSBAD CAVERNS NP
GUADALUPE MTS. NP
BIG BEND NP
Cabo Corrientes
Punta de Mita
Punta Eugenia
Bahía Sebastián Vizcaíno
Cerro de la Encantada 3,068 m
Cerro Encantado 1,586 m
Mt. Graham 10,713 ft. (3,265 m)
Mt. Lemmon 9,157 ft. (2,791 m)
Guadalupe Pk. 8,749 ft. (2,667 m)
Nevado de Colima 4,340 m
Pico de Tancítaro 3,850 m

Northern and Central Mexico

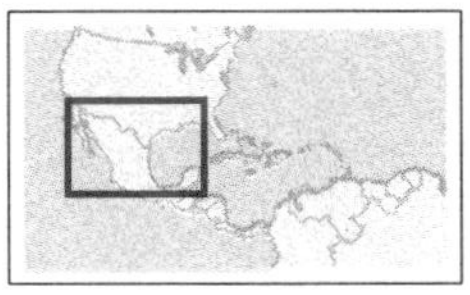

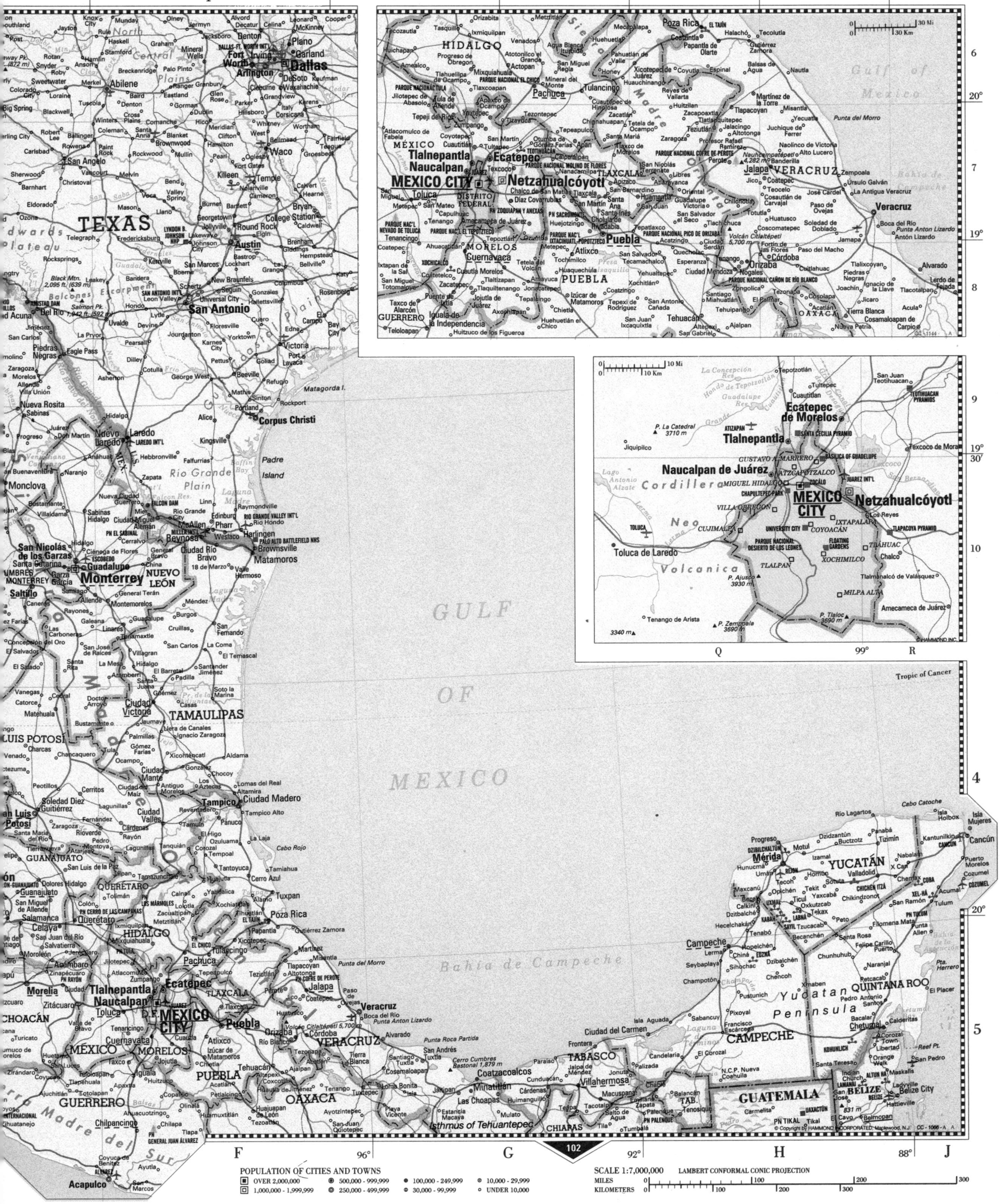

102

POPULATION OF CITIES AND TOWNS

OVER 2,000,000	500,000 - 999,999	100,000 - 249,999	10,000 - 29,999
1,000,000 - 1,999,999	250,000 - 499,999	30,000 - 99,999	UNDER 10,000

SCALE 1:7,000,000 LAMBERT CONFORMAL CONIC PROJECTION

MILES 0 100 200 300

KILOMETERS 0 100 200 300

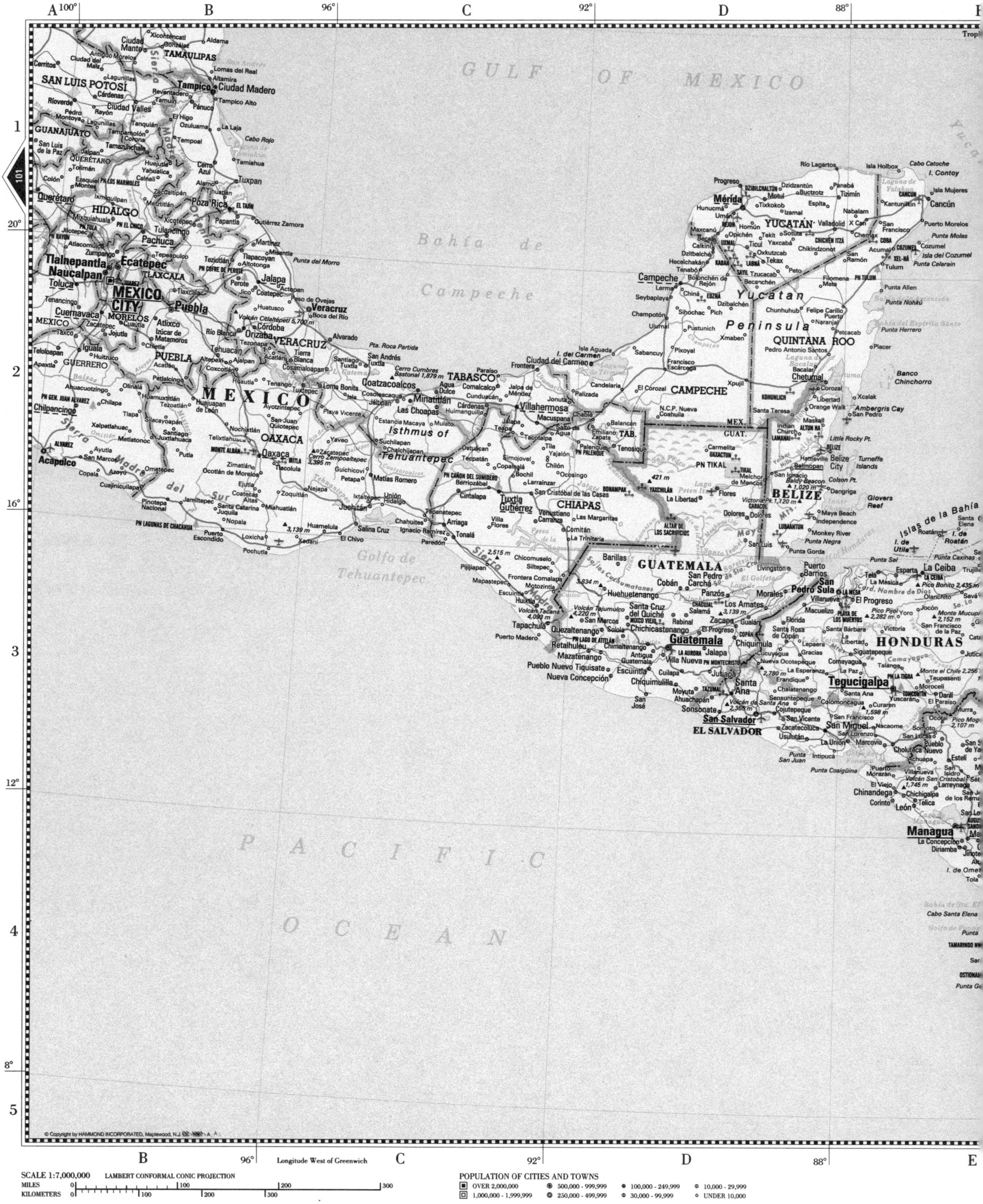

SCALE 1:7,000,000 LAMBERT CONFORMAL CONIC PROJECTION

MILES 0 100 200 300

KILOMETERS 0 100 200 300

POPULATION OF CITIES AND TOWNS

- OVER 2,000,000
- 1,000,000 - 1,999,999
- 500,000 - 999,999
- 250,000 - 499,999
- 100,000 - 249,999
- 30,000 - 99,999
- 10,000 - 29,999
- UNDER 10,000

Southern Mexico, Central America, Western Caribbean

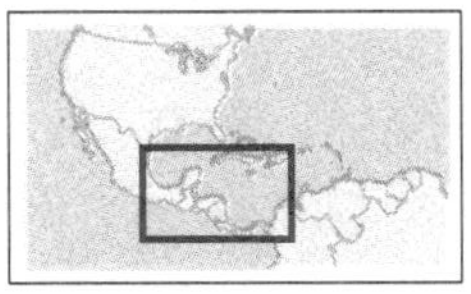

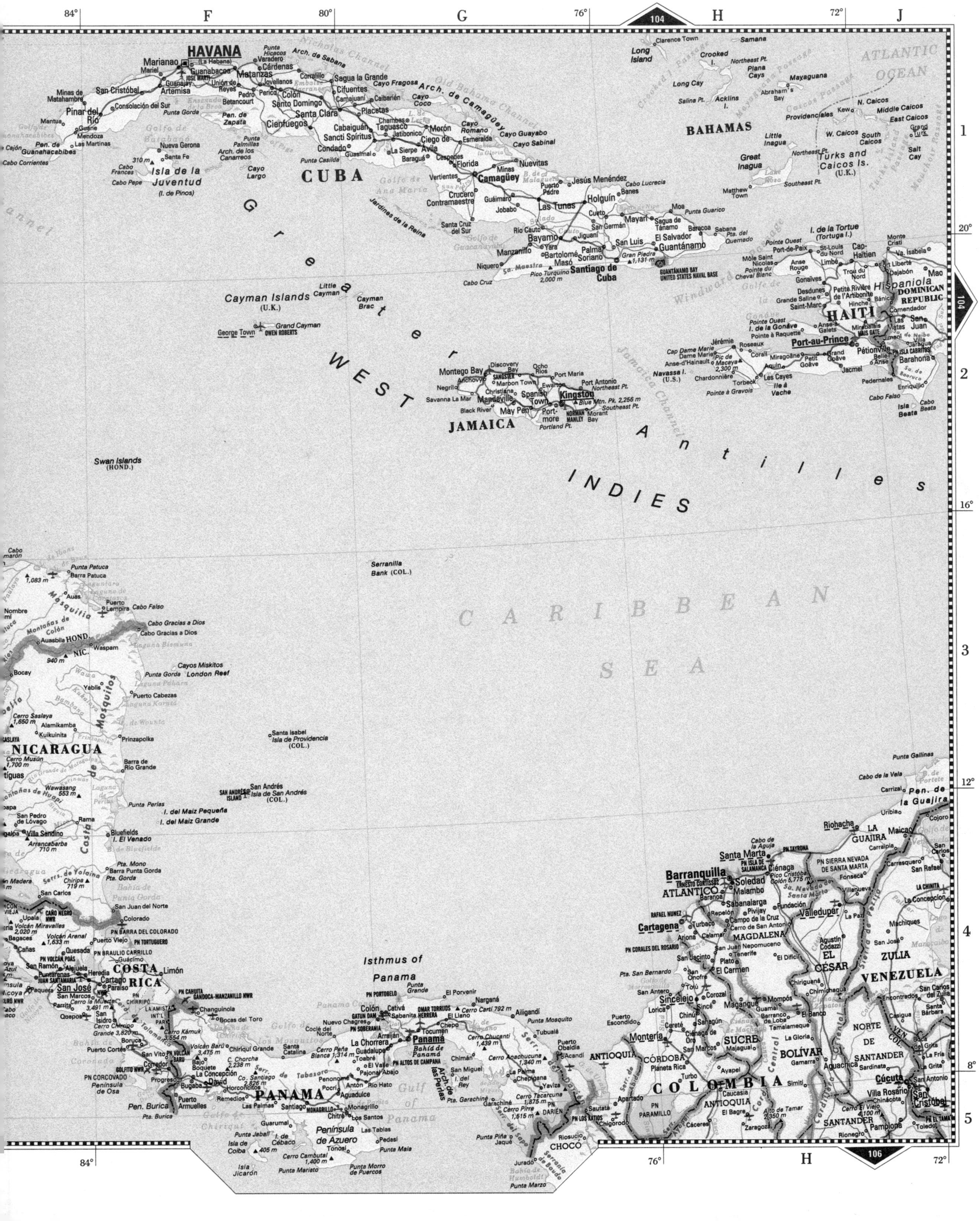

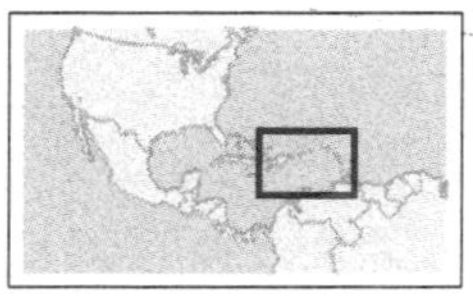

Eastern Caribbean, Bahamas

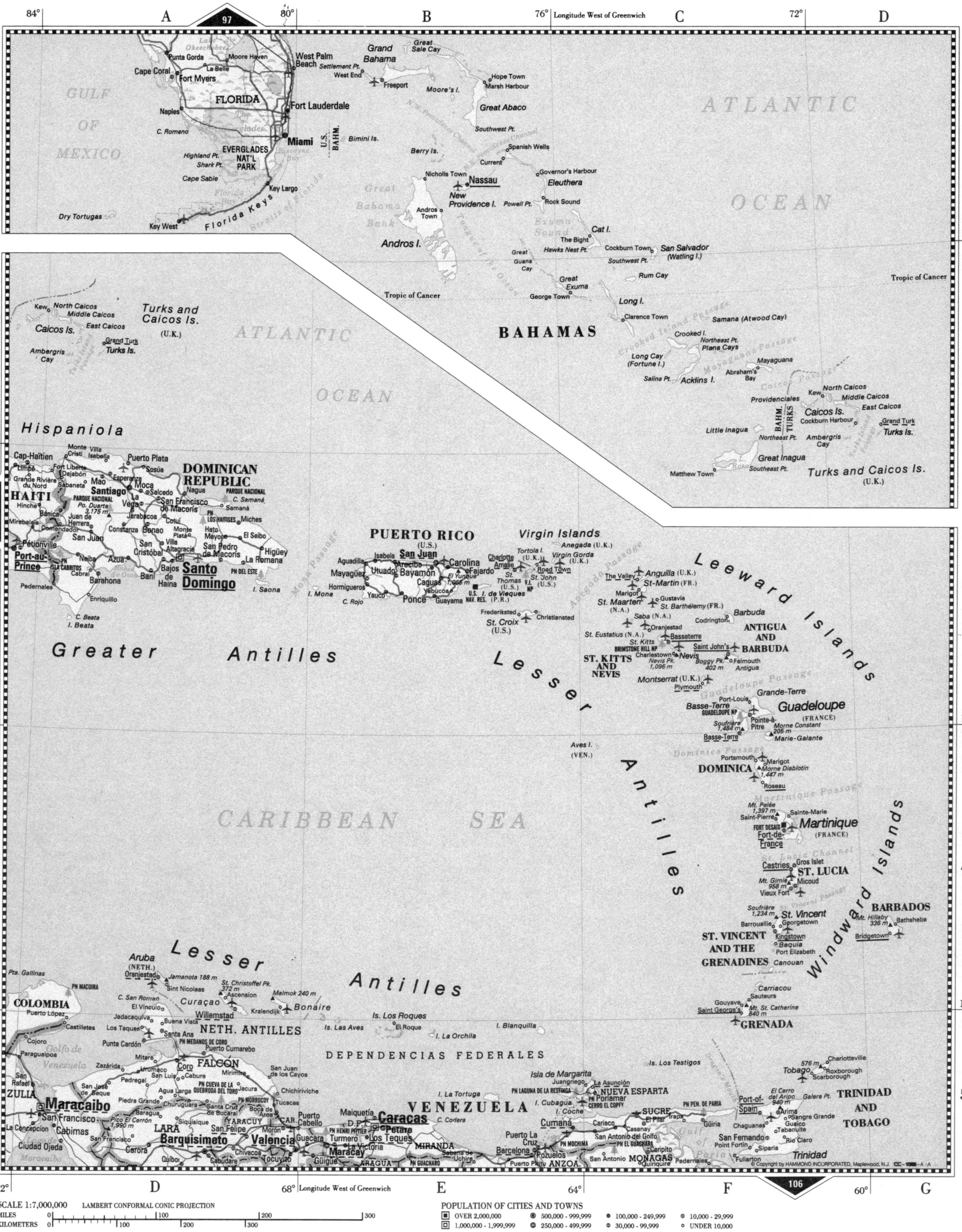

SCALE 1:7,000,000 LAMBERT CONFORMAL CONIC PROJECTION

MILES 0 100 200 300

KILOMETERS 0 100 200 300

POPULATION OF CITIES AND TOWNS

- OVER 2,000,000
- 1,000,000 - 1,999,999
- 500,000 - 999,999
- 250,000 - 499,999
- 100,000 - 249,999
- 30,000 - 99,999
- 10,000 - 29,999
- UNDER 10,000

South America

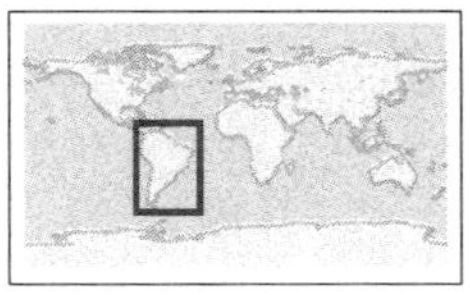

POPULATION OF CITIES AND TOWNS
- OVER 3,000,000
- 1,000,000 - 2,999,999
- 500,000 - 999,999
- 100,000 - 499,999
- UNDER 100,000

SCALE 1:28,000,000 OPTIMAL CONFORMAL PROJECTION

MILES 0 400 800 1200

KILOMETERS 0 400 800 1200

103
109
A
B
C
D
E
F
85°
80°
75°
70°
65°
60°
10°
5°
0°
5°
10°
15°
20°
1
2
3
4
5
6
7
8
Longitude
West of
Greenwich
Equator
Tropic of Capricorn
CARIBBEAN SEA
PACIFIC
OCEAN
NETH. ANTILLES
SAINT VINCENT AND THE GRENADINES
GRENADA
TRINIDAD AND TOBAGO
Kingstown
Saint George's
Port-of-Spain
Aruba (NETH.)
Oranjestad
Willemstad
Curaçao
Bonaire
Kralendijk
COSTA RICA
San José
NICARAGUA
PANAMA
Panamá
Isthmus of Panama
Pen. de Azuero
VENEZUELA
Caracas
Maracaibo
Barquisimeto
Valencia
Maracay
Ciudad Bolívar
Ciudad Guayana
Cumaná
Barcelona
Maturín
Delta del Orinoco
COLOMBIA
Bogotá
Medellín
Cali
Barranquilla
Cartagena
Bucaramanga
Cúcuta
Santa Marta
Llanos
ECUADOR
Quito
Guayaquil
Cuenca
Gulf of Guayaquil
PERU
Lima
Callao
Iquitos
Arequipa
Cusco
Trujillo
Chiclayo
Piura
Huancayo
Cordillera Occidental
Cordillera Central
Cordillera Oriental
Los Andes
La Montaña
Lago Titicaca
Altiplano
BOLIVIA
La Paz
Sucre
Santa Cruz
Cochabamba
Oruro
Potosí
Cordillera Real
Yungas
CHILE
Arica
Iquique
Atacama Desert
ARGENTINA
PARAGUAY
Gran Chaco
Chaco Boreal
BRAZIL
Manaus
Porto Velho
Rio Branco
Selvas
Amazon (Solimões)
Guiana Highlands
Serra Pacaraima
Serra dos Parecis
GUYANA
Georgetown
Isla del Coco (COSTA RICA)
I. de Malpelo (COLOMBIA)

Northern South America

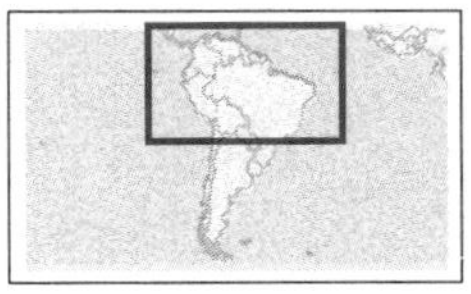

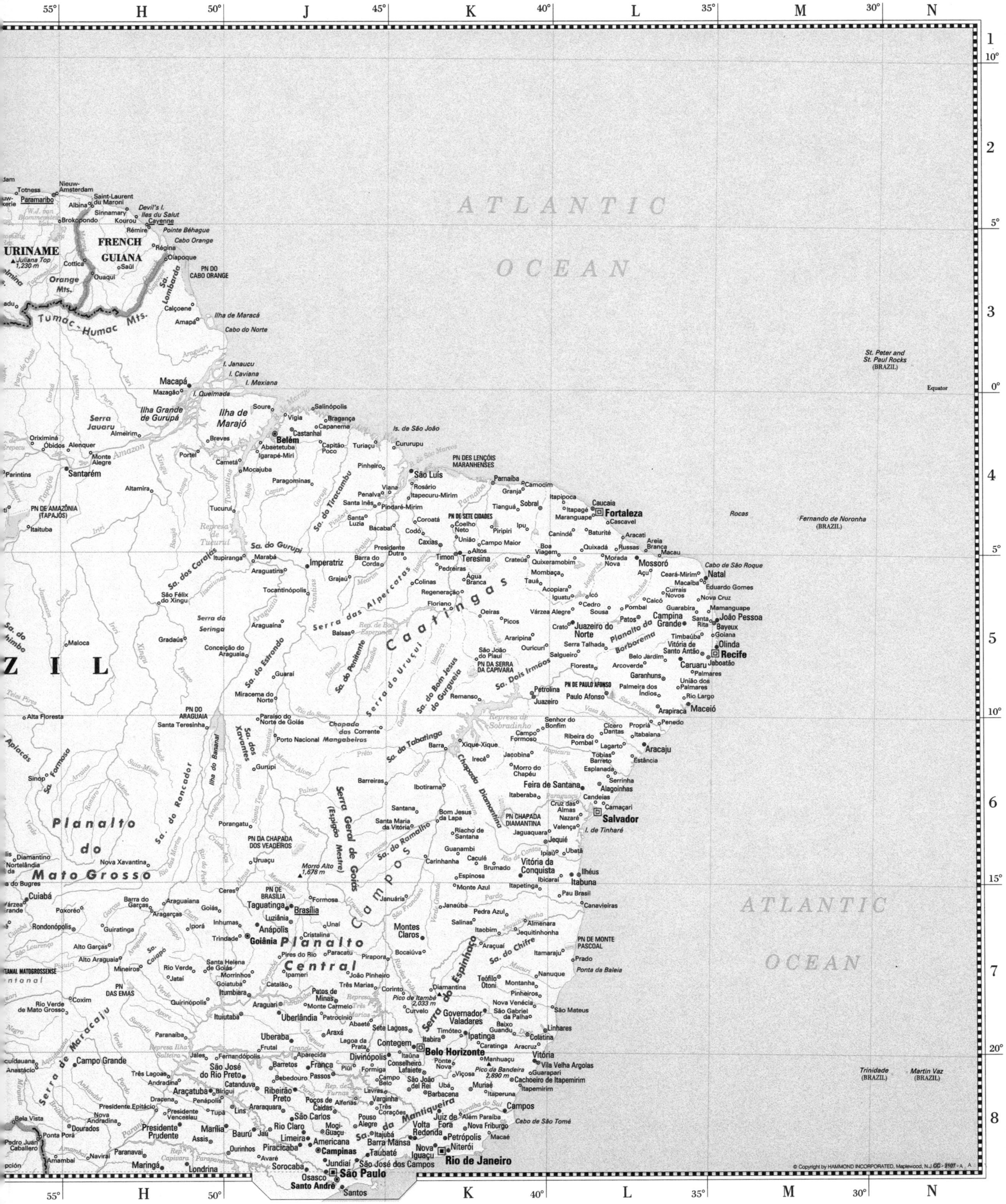

POPULATION OF CITIES AND TOWNS

■ OVER 2,000,000 ◉ 500,000 - 999,999 ◎ 50,000 - 99,999
▣ 1,000,000 - 1,999,999 ● 100,000 - 499,999 ○ UNDER 50,000

SCALE 1:15,000,000 LAMBERT CONFORMAL CONIC PROJECTION

MILES 0 200 400 600
KILOMETERS 0 200 400 600

Southeastern Brazil

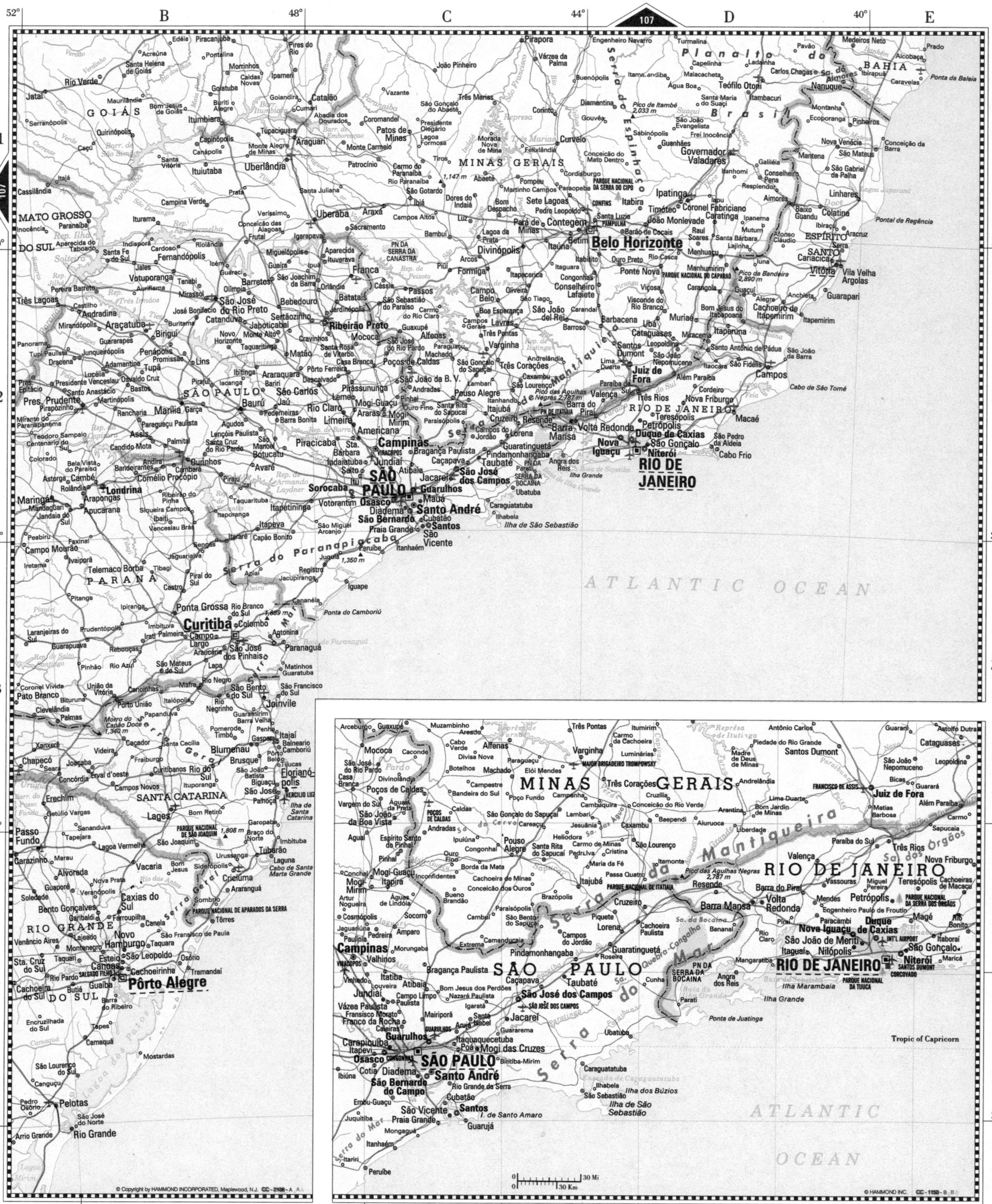

Longitude West of Greenwich

POPULATION OF CITIES AND TOWNS
- OVER 2,000,000
- 1,000,000 - 1,999,999
- 500,000 - 999,999
- 250,000 - 499,999
- 100,000 - 249,999
- 30,000 - 99,999
- 10,000 - 29,999
- UNDER 10,000

SCALE 1:7,000,000
LAMBERT CONFORMAL CONIC PROJECTION
MILES 0 100 200 300
KILOMETERS 0 100 200 300

Southern South America

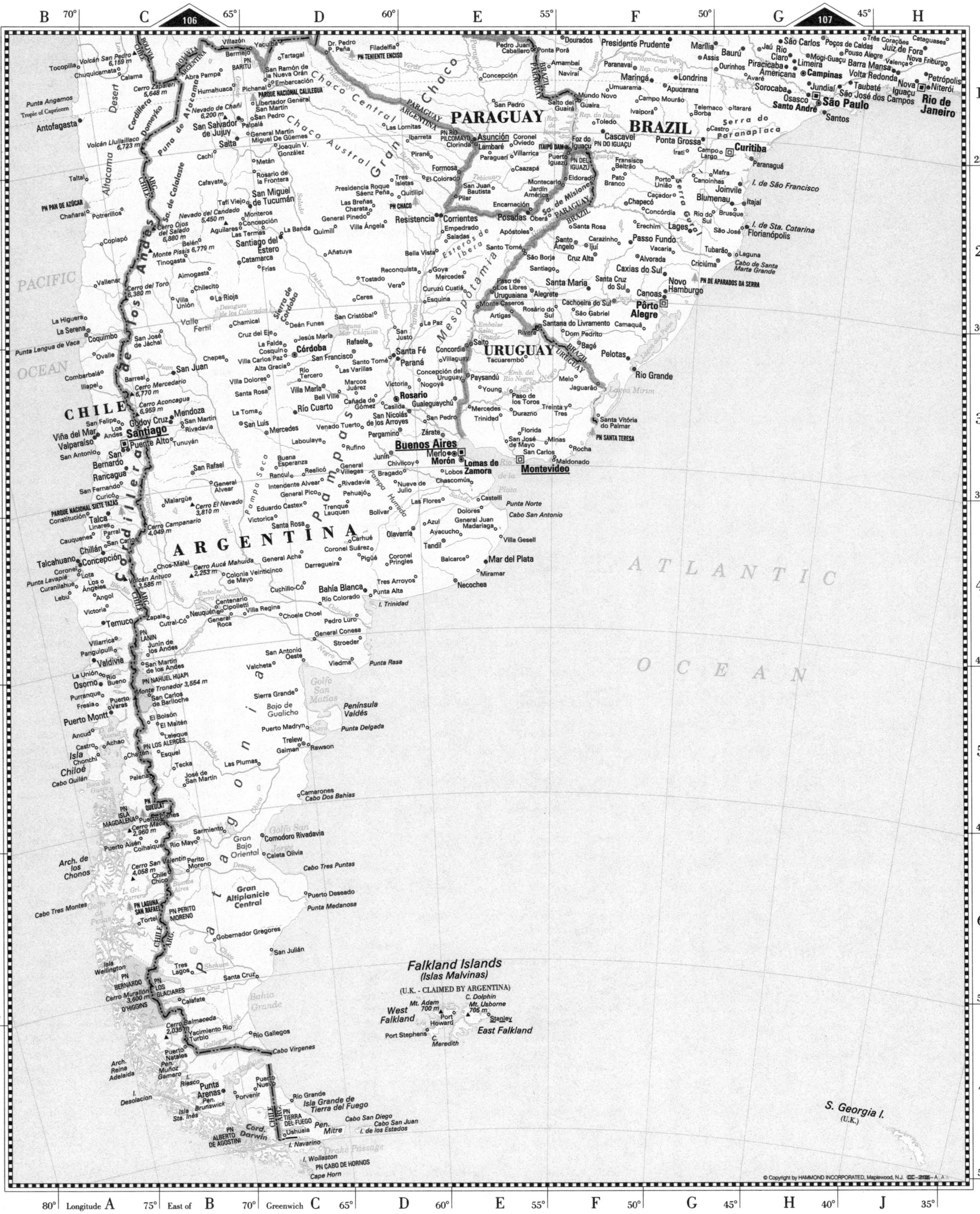

POPULATION OF CITIES AND TOWNS

OVER 2,000,000	500,000 - 999,999
1,000,000 - 1,999,999	100,000 - 499,999
50,000 - 99,999	UNDER 50,000

SCALE 1:15,000,000 LAMBERT CONFORMAL CONIC PROJECTION

MILES 0 200 400 600

KILOMETERS 0 200 400 600

Index of the World

This index lists places and geographic features found in the atlas. Every name is followed by the country or area to which it belongs. Except for cities, towns, countries and cultural areas, all entries include a reference to feature type, such as province, river, island, peak, and so on. The page number and alpha-numeric code appear in blue to the left of each listing. The page number directs you to the largest scale map on which the name can be found. The code refers to the grid squares formed by the horizontal and vertical lines of latitude and longitude on each map. Following the letters from left to right, and the numbers from top to bottom, helps you to locate quickly the square containing the place or feature. Inset maps have their own alpha-numeric codes. Names that are accompanied by a point symbol are indexed to the symbol's location on the map. Other names are indexed to the initial letter of the name. The primary abbreviations used in this index are listed below.

Index Abbreviations

A	**A.F.B.**	Air Force Base
	Afghan.	Afghanistan
	Ala.	Alabama
	Alg.	Algeria
	Alta.	Alberta
	Ant. & Barb.	Antigua and Barbuda
	Antarc.	Antarctica
	arch.	archipelago
	Arg.	Argentina
	Ariz.	Arizona
	Ark.	Arkansas
	Austr.	Australia
	aut.	autonomous
B	**Bah.**	Bahamas
	Bang.	Bangladesh
	Belg.	Belgium
	Bol.	Bolivia
	Bosn.	Bosnia and Hercegovina
	Bots.	Botswana
	Braz.	Brazil
	Br., Brit.	British
	Br. Col.	British Columbia
	Bulg.	Bulgaria
	Burk. Faso	Burkina Faso
C	**Calif.**	California
	Camb.	Cambodia
	Can.	Canada
	cap.	capital
	Cent. Afr. Rep.	Central African Republic
	chan.	channel
	Chan. Is.	Channel Islands
	Col.	Colombia
	Colo.	Colorado
	Conn.	Connecticut
	C. Rica	Costa Rica
	Czech Rep.	Czech Republic
D	**DC**	District of Columbia
	Del.	Delaware
	Dem.	Democratic
	Den.	Denmark
	depr.	depression
	des.	desert
	dist.	district
	Dom. Rep.	Dominican Republic
E	**E.**	East, Eastern
	Ecua.	Ecuador
	El Sal.	El Salvador
	Eng.	England
	Equat. Guin.	Equatorial Guinea
	est.	estuary
	Eth.	Ethiopia
F	**Fed.**	Federal, Federated
	Fin.	Finland
	Fla.	Florida
	for.	forest
	Fr.	France, French
	Fr. Pol.	French Polynesia
	Ft.	Fort
G	**Ga.**	Georgia
	Ger.	Germany
	Greenl.	Greenland
	Gt.	Great
	Guad.	Guadeloupe
	Guat.	Guatemala
	Guy.	Guyana
H	**har., harb.**	harbor
	Hon.	Honduras
	Hun.	Hungary
I	**Ill.**	Illinois
	Ind.	Indiana
	Indon.	Indonesia
	Int'l	International
	Ire.	Ireland
	isl., isls.	isle, island, islands
	Isr.	Israel
	isth.	isthmus
	Iv. Coast	Ivory Coast
J	**Jam.**	Jamaica
K	**Kans.**	Kansas
	Ky.	Kentucky
L	**La.**	Louisiana
	Leb.	Lebanon
	Lux.	Luxembourg
M	**Madag.**	Madagascar
	Man.	Manitoba
	Mass.	Massachusetts
	Maur.	Mauritania
	Md.	Maryland
	Mex.	Mexico
	Mich.	Michigan
	Minn.	Minnesota
	Miss.	Mississippi
	Mo.	Missouri
	Mong.	Mongolia
	Mont.	Montana
	Mor.	Morocco
	Moz.	Mozambique
	mt.	mount
	mtn., mts.	mountain, mountains
N	**N., No.**	North, Northern
	N. Amer.	North America
	Nat'l Pk.	National Park
	N. Br.	New Brunswick
	N.C.	North Carolina
	N. Dak.	North Dakota
	Nebr.	Nebraska
	Neth.	Netherlands
	Neth. Ant.	Netherlands Antilles
	Nev.	Nevada
	Newf.	Newfoundland
	N.H.	New Hampshire
	Nic.	Nicaragua
	N. Ire.	Northern Ireland
	N.J.	New Jersey
	N. Korea	North Korea
	N. Mex.	New Mexico
	Nor.	Norway
	N.S.	Nova Scotia
	N.W.T.	Northwest Territories
	N.Y.	New York
	N.Z.	New Zealand
O	**Okla.**	Oklahoma
	Ont.	Ontario
	Oreg.	Oregon
P	**Pa.**	Pennsylvania
	Pak.	Pakistan
	Pan.	Panama
	Papua N.G.	Papua New Guinea
	Par.	Paraguay
	P.E.I.	Prince Edward Island
	pen.	peninsula
	Phil.	Philippines
	pk.	park
	plat.	plateau
	Pol.	Poland
	Port.	Portugal, Portuguese
	P. Rico	Puerto Rico
	prom.	promontory
	prov.	province, provincial
	pt., pte.	point, pointe
Q	**Que.**	Québec
R	**reg.**	region
	Rep.	Republic
	res.	reservoir
	R.I.	Rhode Island
	riv.	river
	Rom.	Romania
S	**S., So.**	South, Southern
	sa.	serra, sierra
	S. Africa	South Africa
	S. Amer.	South America
	São T. & Pr.	São Tomé and Príncipe
	Sask.	Saskatchewan
	S.C.	South Carolina
	Scot.	Scotland
	S. Dak.	South Dakota
	Sen.	Senegal
	Sing.	Singapore
	S. Korea	South Korea
	S. Leone	Sierra Leone
	Sol. Is.	Solomon Islands
	Sp.	Spain, Spanish
	St., Ste.	Saint, Sainte
	str.	strait
	St. Vinc. & Grens.	Saint Vincent and the Grenadines
	Switz.	Switzerland
T	**Tanz.**	Tanzania
	Tenn.	Tennessee
	Terr.	Territory
	Thai.	Thailand
	Trin. & Tob.	Trinidad and Tobago
	Tun.	Tunisia
U	**U. A. E.**	United Arab Emirates
	U. K.	United Kingdom
	Ukr.	Ukraine
	Urug.	Uruguay
	U. S.	United States
V	**Va.**	Virginia
	Ven., Venez.	Venezuela
	V.I. (Br.)	Virgin Islands (British)
	V.I. (U.S.)	Virgin Islands (U.S.)
	Viet.	Vietnam
	vol.	volcano
	Vt.	Vermont
W	**W.**	West, Western
	Wash.	Washington
	W. Indies	West Indies
	Wis.	Wisconsin
	W. Samoa	Western Samoa
	W. Va.	West Virginia
	Wyo.	Wyoming
Y	**Yugo.**	Yugoslavia
Z	**Zim.**	Zimbabwe

A

31/F2 Aachen, Ger.
36/E2 Aare (riv.), Switz.
79/G5 Aba, Nigeria
51/G4 Abadan, Iran
46/K4 Abakan, Russia
79/F5 Abeokuta, Nigeria
21/D2 Aberdeen, Scot.
91/J4 Aberdeen, S. Dak.
90/B4 Aberdeen, Wash.
78/D5 Abidjan, Iv. Coast
93/H3 Abilene, Kans.
93/H4 Abilene, Texas
94/D1 Abitibi (riv.), Ont.
94/C4 Abraham Lincoln Birthplace Nat'l Hist. Site, Ky.
38/C1 Abruzzi (reg.), Italy
53/F4 Abu Dhabi (cap.), U.A.E.
79/G4 Abuja (cap.), Nigeria
95/G2 Acadia Nat'l Pk., Maine
101/E5 Acapulco, Mex.
79/E5 Accra (cap.), Ghana
46/K4 Achinsk, Russia
109/C3 Aconcagua (mt.), Arg.
93/H4 Ada, Okla.
69/M7 Adamstown (cap.), Pitcairn
49/D1 Adana, Turkey
52/D3 Ad Dahnā (des.), Saudi Arabia
52/F3 Ad Dammān, Saudi Arabia
77/N6 Addis Ababa (cap.), Eth.
99/Q16 Addison, Ill.
73/A2 Adelaide, Austr.
77/Q5 Aden (gulf), Afr., Asia
52/D6 Aden, Yemen
33/J4 Adige (riv.), Italy
94/F2 Adirondack (mts.), N.Y.
68/D5 Admiralty (isls.), Papua N.G.
94/C3 Adrian, Mich.
18/E4 Adriatic (sea), Europe
39/J3 Aegean (sea)
53/H2 Afghanistan
74/* Africa
76/D1 Agadir, Morocco
68/D3 Agana (cap.), Guam
93/G2 Agate Fossil Beds Nat'l Mon., Nebr.
57/H7 Ageo, Japan
62/C2 Agra, India
100/E4 Aguascalientes, Mex.
76/F3 Ahaggar (mts.), Alg.
62/B3 Ahmadabad, India
51/G4 Ahvaz, Iran
88/W13 Aiea, Hawaii
97/H3 Aiken, S.C.
32/F5 Aix-en-Provence, France
38/A2 Ajaccio, France
62/B2 Ajmer, India
56/D3 Akashi, Japan
55/M4 Akita, Japan
49/D3 Akko, Isr.
62/C3 Akola, India
94/D3 Akron, Ohio
45/L2 Aktyubinsk, Kazakhstan
97/G4 Alabama (riv.), Ala.
97/G3 Alabama (state), U.S.
99/K11 Alameda, Calif.
93/F4 Alamogordo, N. Mex.
93/F3 Alamosa, Colo.
20/G3 Aland (isls.), Fin.
85/J4 Alaska (gulf), Alaska
85/F4 Alaska (pen.), Alaska
85/H3 Alaska (range), Alaska
85/* Alaska (state), U.S.
34/E3 Albacete, Spain
39/F2 Albania
97/G4 Albany, Ga.
94/F3 Albany (cap.), N.Y.
90/C4 Albany, Oreg.
87/H3 Albany (riv.), Ont.
51/F4 Al Başrah, Iraq
77/N7 Albert (lake), Africa
91/K5 Albert Lea, Minn.
86/E3 Alberta (prov.), Can.
20/D4 Alborg, Den.
92/F4 Albuquerque, N. Mex.
32/B2 Alderney (isl.), Chan. Is.
88/T10 Alenuihaha (chan.), Hawaii
49/E1 Aleppo, Syria
85/E5 Aleutian (isls.), Alaska
85/L4 Alexander (arch.), Alaska
49/A4 Alexandria, Egypt
96/E4 Alexandria, La.
94/E4 Alexandria, Va.
49/B4 Al Fayyum, Egypt
53/G3 Al Fujayrah, U.A.E.
76/F2 Algeria
75/S15 Algiers (cap.), Alg.
98/B2 Alhambra, Calif.
52/D6 Al Ḩudaydah, Yemen
52/E3 Al Hufūf, Saudi Arabia
35/E3 Alicante, Spain
62/C2 Aligarh, India
49/B4 Al Jīzah, Egypt
76/H1 Al Khums, Libya
51/F4 Al Kuwait (cap.), Kuwait
62/D2 Allahabad, India
94/D4 Allegheny (mts.), U.S.
99/F7 Allen Park, Mich.
94/F3 Allentown, Pa.
64/F4 Allepey, India
94/D3 Alliance, Ohio
46/H5 Alma-Ata (cap.), Kazakhstan
50/B4 Al Mahallah al Kubrá, Egypt
49/B4 Al Manşūra, Egypt
34/D4 Almeria, Spain
52/B4 Al Minyā, Egypt
52/B4 Al Minyā, Egypt
33/G4 Alps (mts.), Europe
36/D2 Alsace (reg.), Fr.
98/B2 Altadena, Calif.
46/J5 Altai (mts.), Asia
94/B4 Alton, Ill.
94/E3 Altoona, Pa.
54/C4 Altun (mts.), China
93/H4 Altus, Okla.
57/L10 Amagasaki, Japan
93/G4 Amarillo, Texas
107/H4 Amazon (riv.), S. Amer.
67/G4 Ambon, Indon.
92/E2 American Fork, Utah
69/J6 American Samoa
97/G3 Americus, Ga.
93/J2 Ames, Iowa
95/H2 Amherst, N.S.
30/B4 Amiens, France
93/G5 Amistad Nat'l Rec. Area, Texas
49/D4 Amman (cap.), Jordan
61/H3 Amoy (Xiamen), China
62/C3 Amravati, India
64/C2 Amritsar, India
28/B4 Amsterdam (cap.), Neth.
94/F3 Amsterdam, N.Y.
48/F5 Amudar'ya (riv.), Asia
83/S Amundsen (sea), Antarc.
86/D1 Amundsen (gulf), N.W.T.
55/M1 Amur (riv.), Asia
90/E4 Anaconda, Mont.
47/T3 Anadyr', Russia
47/R3 Anadyr (gulf), Russia
98/C3 Anaheim, Calif.
50/B2 Anatolia (reg.), Turkey
85/J3 Anchorage, Alaska
33/K5 Ancona, Italy
34/C4 Andalusia (reg.), Spain
63/F5 Andaman (sea), Asia
63/F5 Andaman (isls.), India
94/C3 Anderson, Ind.
97/H3 Anderson, S.C.
105/B3 Andes (mts.), S. Amer.
46/H5 Andizhan, Uzbekistan
35/F1 Andorra
35/F1 Andorra la Vella (cap.), Andorra
98/K8 Andrews A.F.B., Md.
104/B1 Andros (isl.), Bah.
54/E1 Angara (riv.), Russia
54/E1 Angarsk, Russia
106/F2 Angel (falls), Ven.
32/C3 Angers, France
65/C3 Angkor (ruins), Camb.
82/C3 Angola
104/F3 Anguilla (isl.)
50/C2 Ankara (cap.), Turkey
75/V17 Annaba, Alg.
50/D4 An Nafūd (des.), Saudi Arabia
51/F4 An Najaf, Iraq
63/J4 Annamitique (mts.), Laos, Viet.
98/J8 Annandale, Va.
94/E4 Annapolis (cap.), Md.
62/D2 Annapurna (mt.), Nepal
99/E7 Ann Arbor, Mich.
95/G3 Ann (cape), Mass.
97/G3 Anniston, Ala.
D5/D5 Anqing, China
58/B2 Anshan, China
49/E1 Antakya (Antioch), Turkey
50/B2 Antalya, Turkey
81/H7 Antananarivo (cap.), Madag.
83/* Antarctica
83/V Antarctic (pen.), Antarc.
33/G5 Antibes, France
95/J1 Anticosti (isl.), Que.
104/F3 Antigua and Barbuda
49/E1 Antioch (Antayka), Turkey
99/L10 Antioch, Calif.
109/B1 Antofagasta, Chile
81/J6 Antsiranana (Diégo-Suarez), Madag.
30/D1 Antwerp, Belg.
59/C3 Anyang, China
55/N3 Aomori, Japan
26/C2 Apeldoorn, Neth.
38/C1 Apennines (mts.), Italy
69/S9 Apia (cap.), W. Samoa
89/K4 Appalachian (mts.), U.S.
94/B2 Appleton, Wis.
50/C4 Aqaba (gulf), Asia
52/D4 Arabian (pen.), Asia
53/H5 Arabian (sea), Asia
52/B3 Arabian (des.), Egypt
107/L6 Aracaju, Braz.
40/E2 Arad, Rom.
68/C5 Arafura (sea)
35/E2 Aragón (reg.), Spain
107/J5 Araguaia (riv.), Braz.
51/G3 Arāk, Iran
46/G5 Aral (sea), Asia
21/H7 Aran (isls.), Ire.
51/F2 Ararat (mt.), Turkey
98/B2 Arcadia, Calif.
42/J2 Archangel, Russia
92/E3 Arches Nat'l Pk., Utah
16/A1 Arctic (ocean)
51/G2 Ardabil, Iran
31/E4 Ardennes (for.), Belg.
93/H4 Ardmore, Okla.
104/E3 Arecibo, P. Rico
106/D7 Arequipa, Peru
30/B6 Argenteuil, France
109/C4 Argentina
99/Q16 Argonne Nat'l Lab., Ill.
39/H4 Argos, Greece
20/D4 Arhus, Den.
106/D7 Arica, Chile
92/D4 Arizona (state), U.S.
93/J4 Arkadelphia, Ark.
97/E3 Arkansas (riv.), U.S.
97/E3 Arkansas (state), U.S.
32/F5 Arles, France
96/D3 Arlington, Texas
94/E4 Arlington, Va.
99/Q15 Arlington Heights, Ill.
22/B3 Armagh, N. Ire.
45/G3 Armavir, Russia
45/H4 Armenia
28/C5 Arnhem, Neth.
70/E2 Arnhem Land (reg.), Austr.
33/J5 Arno (riv.), Italy
21/C3 Arran (isl.), Scot.
104/D4 Aruba (isl.)
55/N3 Asahikawa, Japan
62/E3 Asansol, India
98/G5 Asbury Park, N.J.
16/J6 Ascension (isl.), St. Helena
78/E5 Ashanti (reg.), Ghana
97/H3 Asheville, N.C.
51/J2 Ashkhabad (cap.), Turkmenistan
97/H2 Ashland, Ky.
90/C5 Ashland, Oreg.
70/C2 Ashmore and Cartier Is. (terr.), Austr.
53/G3 Ash Shāriqah, U.A.E.
94/D3 Ashtabula, Ohio
48/* Asia
52/C5 Asmera (cap.), Eritrea
92/F3 Aspen, Colo.
98/J7 Aspen Hill, Md.
52/E3 As Sālimīyah, Kuwait
63/F2 Assam (state), India
90/C4 Astoria, Oreg.
45/J3 Astrakhan', Russia
34/B1 Asturias (reg.), Spain
109/E2 Asunción (cap.), Par.
52/B4 Aswān, Egypt
52/B3 Asyūt, Egypt
106/E7 Atacama (des.), Chile
93/J3 Atchison, Kans.
86/F3 Athabasca (lake), Can.
97/H3 Athens, Ga.
39/H4 Athens (cap.), Greece
94/D4 Athens, Ohio
39/J2 Athos (mt.), Greece
85/C5 Atka (isl.), Alaska
97/G3 Atlanta (cap.), Ga.
16/G3 Atlantic (ocean)
94/F4 Atlantic City, N.J.
76/E1 Atlas (mts.), Africa
57/H7 Atsugi, Japan
52/D4 Aţ Ţā'if, Saudi Arabia
85/A5 Attu (isl.), Alaska
97/G3 Auburn, Ala.
95/G2 Auburn, Maine
94/E3 Auburn, N.Y.
99/C3 Auburn, Wash.
71/R10 Auckland, N.Z.
37/G1 Augsburg, Ger.
97/H3 Augusta, Ga.
95/G2 Augusta (cap.), Maine
62/C4 Aurangabad, India
93/F3 Aurora, Colo.
99/P16 Aurora, Ill.
27/K3 Auschwitz (Oświęcim), Poland
96/D4 Austin (cap.), Texas
70/* Australia
73/C3 Australian Alps (mts.), Austr.
73/D3 Australian Cap. Terr., Austr.
33/L3 Austria
95/L2 Avalon (pen.), Newf.
32/F5 Avignon, France
25/E2 Avon (riv.), Eng.
70/E5 Ayers Rock (mt.), Austr.
45/H4 Azerbaijan
35/R12 Azores (isls.), Port.
44/E3 Azov (sea), Europe
92/E3 Aztec Ruins Nat'l Mon., N. Mex.
98/C2 Azusa, Calif.
49/B4 Az Zagāzig, Egypt

B

77/P5 Bab el Mandeb (str.)
41/H2 Bacău, Rom.
67/F1 Bacolod, Phil.
35/L7 Badalona, Spain
26/E4 Baden-Baden, Ger.
91/H5 Badlands Nat'l Pk., S. Dak.
87/K1 Baffin (bay), N. Amer.
87/H1 Baffin (isl.), N.W.T.
52/D2 Baghdad (cap.), Iraq
104/B2 Bahamas
53/K3 Bahawalpur, Pak.
109/D4 Bahia Blanca, Arg.
52/F4 Bahrain
55/J2 Baicheng, China
68/G4 Bairiki (cap.), Kiribati
100/B2 Baja California (pen.), Mex.
92/C4 Bakersfield, Calif.
51/F3 Bakhtarān, Iran
45/J4 Baku (cap.), Azerbaijan
45/H1 Balakovo, Russia
98/C2 Baldwin Park, Calif.
35/F3 Balearic (isls.), Spain
66/D5 Bali (isl.), Indon.
67/E4 Balikpapan, Indon.
41/F4 Balkan (mts.), Bulg.
46/H5 Balkhash (lake), Kazakhstan
18/E3 Baltic (sea), Europe
94/E4 Baltimore, Md.
53/H3 Baluchistan (reg.), Pak.
78/D3 Bamako (cap.), Mali
68/F5 Banaba (isl.), Kiribati
66/D3 Bandar Seri Begawan (cap.), Brunei
67/G5 Banda (sea), Indon.
92/F4 Bandelier Nat'l Mon., N. Mex.
66/C5 Bandung, Indon.
90/E2 Banff Nat'l Pk., Alta.
62/C5 Bangalore, India
65/C3 Bangkok (cap.), Thai.
62/E3 Bangladesh
95/G2 Bangor, Maine
77/J7 Bangui (cap.), Cent. Afr. Rep.
40/C3 Banja Luka, Bosn.
66/D4 Banjarmasin, Indon.
78/A3 Banjul (cap.), Gambia
86/D1 Banks (isl.), N.W.T.
59/C3 Baoding, China
54/F5 Baoji, China
59/B2 Baotou, China
44/C1 Baranovichi, Belarus
104/G4 Barbados
94/D3 Barberton, Ohio
35/G2 Barcelona, Spain
106/F1 Barcelona, Ven.
62/C2 Bareilly, India
46/D2 Barents (sea), Europe
95/G2 Bar Harbor, Maine
38/E2 Bari, Italy
97/G2 Barkley (lake), Ky., Tenn.
46/J4 Barnaul, Russia
62/B3 Baroda, India
106/E1 Barquisimeto, Ven.
106/D1 Barranquilla, Col.
94/E2 Barrie, Ont.
85/G1 Barrow (pt.), Alaska
92/C4 Barstow, Calif.
93/H3 Bartlesville, Okla.
73/C3 Bass (str.), Austr.
36/D2 Basel, Switz.
60/B5 Bassein, Burma
104/F3 Basse-Terre (cap.), Guad.
104/F3 Basseterre (cap.), St. Kitts & Nevis
96/F3 Bastrop, La.
76/H8 Batéké (plat.), Congo
24/D4 Bath, Eng.
95/H2 Bathurst, N. Br.
87/R7 Bathurst (isl.), N.W.T.
75/V18 Batna, Alg.
97/F4 Baton Rouge (cap.), La.
94/C3 Battle Creek, Mich.
45/G4 Batumi, Georgia
49/F7 Bat Yam, Isr.
26/F4 Bavaria (state), Ger.
37/G3 Bavarian Alps (mts.), Austria, Ger.
104/E3 Bayamón, P. Rico
54/D5 Bayan Har (mts.), China
94/D3 Bay City, Mich.
32/C2 Bayeux, France
47/L4 Baykal (lake), Russia
46/G5 Baykonyr, Kazakhstan
98/F5 Bayonne, N.J.
26/F4 Bayreuth, Ger.
96/E4 Baytown, Texas
92/E2 Bear (lake), U.S.
90/F3 Bearpaw (mts.), Mont.
93/H2 Beatrice, Nebr.
86/C1 Beaufort (sea), N. Amer.
97/H3 Beaufort, S.C.
96/E4 Beaumont, Texas
94/D4 Beckley, W. Va.
49/D4 Beersheba, Isr.
61/F4 Beihai, China
59/D3 Beijing (Peking) (cap.), China
59/E2 Beipiao, China
49/D3 Beirut (cap.), Leb.
76/G1 Bejaïa, Alg.
46/C4 Belarus
107/J4 Belém, Braz.
95/G2 Belfast, Maine
22/C2 Belfast (cap.), N. Ire.
62/B4 Belgaum, India
26/C3 Belgium
44/F2 Belgorod, Russia
40/E3 Belgrade (cap.), Yugo.
102/D2 Belize
102/D2 Belize City, Belize
62/C4 Bellary, India
94/B4 Belleville, Ill.
98/F5 Belleville, N.J.
94/E2 Belleville, Ont.
99/C2 Bellevue, Wash.
98/B3 Bellflower, Calif.
90/C3 Bellingham, Wash.
83/U Bellingshausen (sea), Antarc.
102/D2 Belmopan (cap.), Belize
108/D2 Belo Horizonte, Braz.
94/B3 Beloit, Wis.
98/K7 Beltsville, Md.
41/H2 Bel'tsy, Moldova
91/K4 Bemidji, Minn.
62/D2 Benares (Varanasi), India
90/C4 Bend, Oreg.
62/E4 Bengal (bay), Asia
59/D4 Bengbu, China
77/K1 Benghazi, Libya
82/B3 Benguela, Angola
79/F4 Benin
76/G6 Benin City, Nigeria
95/F3 Bennington, Vt.
93/J4 Benton, Ark.
94/C3 Benton Harbor, Mich.
76/G6 Benue (riv.), Nigeria
58/B2 Benxi, China
56/B4 Beppu, Japan
33/K3 Berchtesgaden, Ger.
94/C4 Berea, Ky.
43/N4 Berezniki, Russia
33/H4 Bergamo, Italy
20/C3 Bergen, Nor.
47/T4 Bering (sea)
85/E3 Bering (str.)
99/K11 Berkeley, Calif.
27/G2 Berlin (cap.), Ger.
95/G2 Berlin, N.H.
84/L6 Bermuda
36/D4 Bern (cap.), Switz.
36/D5 Bernese Alps (range), Switz.
99/Q16 Berwyn, Ill.
36/C3 Besançon, France
97/G3 Bessemer, Ala.
98/J8 Bethesda, Md.
94/F3 Bethlehem, Pa.
49/D4 Bethlehem, West Bank
98/B2 Beverly Hills, Calif.
62/E2 Bhagalpur, India
62/B3 Bhavnagar, India
62/C3 Bhopal, India
62/E2 Bhutan
27/M2 Bialystok, Pol.
32/C5 Biarritz, France
95/G3 Biddeford, Maine
29/F4 Bielefeld, Ger.
27/K4 Bielsko-Biala, Poland
63/J5 Bien Hoa, Viet.
96/C4 Big Bend Nat'l Pk., Texas
90/F4 Bighorn (mts.), Wyo.
90/G4 Bighorn (riv.), U.S.
96/C3 Big Spring, Texas
62/B2 Bikaner, India
68/F3 Bikini (atoll), Marshall Is.
34/D1 Bilbao, Spain
90/F4 Billings, Mont.
97/F4 Biloxi, Miss.
104/B1 Biminis, The (isls.), Bah.
94/F3 Binghamton, N.Y.
86/E3 Birch (mts.), Alb.
23/E5 Birkenhead, Eng.
97/G3 Birmingham, Ala.
25/E2 Birmingham, Eng.
99/F6 Birmingham, Mich.
92/E5 Bisbee, Ariz.
32/B4 Biscay (bay), Europe
97/H5 Biscayne Nat'l Pk., Fla.
46/H5 Bishkek (cap.), Kyrgyzstan
80/D4 Bisho, S. Africa
91/H4 Bismarck (cap.), N. Dak.
68/D5 Bismarck (arch.), Papua N.G.
78/B4 Bissau (cap.), Guinea-Bissau
90/E4 Bitterroot (range), U.S.
46/J4 Biysk, Russia
75/W17 Bizerte, Tun.
44/D4 Black (sea)
90/E5 Blackfoot, Idaho
36/D2 Black (for.), Ger.
91/H5 Black Hills (mts.), U.S.
23/E4 Blackpool, Eng.
97/H2 Blacksburg, Va.
98/K8 Bladensburg, Md.
55/K1 Blagoveshchensk, Russia
36/C6 Blanc (mt.), Europe
82/G4 Blantyre, Malawi
75/S15 Blida, Alg.
95/G3 Block (isl.), R.I.
80/D3 Bloemfontein, S. Africa
98/F5 Bloomfield, N.J.
94/B3 Bloomington, Ill.
94/C4 Bloomington, Ind.
91/K4 Bloomington, Minn.
90/D4 Blue (mts.), Oreg.
97/H2 Bluefield, W. Va.
77/M5 Blue Nile (riv.), Africa

97/H2 **Blue Ridge** (mts.), U.S.
93/K4 **Blytheville**, Ark.
78/D4 **Bobo-Dioulasso**, Burk. Faso
44/D1 **Bobruysk**, Belarus
97/H5 **Boca Raton**, Fla.
29/E6 **Bochum**, Ger.
97/F4 **Bogalusa**, La.
66/C5 **Bogor**, Indon.
106/D3 **Bogotá** (cap.), Col.
59/D3 **Bo Hai** (gulf), China
27/G4 **Bohemia** (reg.), Czech Rep.
90/D5 **Boise** (cap.), Idaho
106/D2 **Bolívar** (mt.), Ven.
106/F7 **Bolivia**
33/J4 **Bologna**, Italy
23/F4 **Bolton**, Eng.
37/H5 **Bolzano**, Italy
62/B4 **Bombay**, India
104/D4 **Bonaire** (isl.), Neth. Ant.
75/X17 **Bon** (cape), Tun.
68/D2 **Bonin** (isls.), Japan
31/G2 **Bonn**, Ger.
90/C4 **Bonneville** (dam), U.S.
93/J2 **Boone**, Iowa
69/K6 **Bora Bora** (isl.), Fr. Poly.
90/E4 **Borah** (peak), Idaho
32/C4 **Bordeaux**, France
96/C3 **Borger**, Texas
46/C4 **Borisov**, Belarus
67/E3 **Borneo** (isl.), Asia
20/E5 **Bornholm** (isl.), Den.
40/C3 **Bosnia and Hercegovina**
41/J5 **Bosporus** (str.), Turkey
92/E3 **Bossier City**, La.
95/G3 **Boston** (cap.), Mass.
20/F3 **Bothnia** (gulf), Europe
59/D3 **Botou**, China
82/D5 **Botswana**
78/D5 **Bouaké**, Iv. Coast
68/E5 **Bougainville** (isl.), Papua N.G.
93/F2 **Boulder**, Colo.
92/D4 **Boulder City**, Nev.
30/A2 **Boulogne-sur-Mer**, France
92/E2 **Bountiful**, Utah
32/E3 **Bourges**, France
25/E5 **Bournemouth**, Eng.
98/J8 **Bowie**, Md.
97/G2 **Bowling Green**, Ky.
94/D3 **Bowling Green**, Ohio
97/H5 **Boynton Beach**, Fla.
90/F4 **Bozeman**, Mont.
97/H5 **Bradenton**, Fla.
23/G4 **Bradford**, Eng.
34/A2 **Braga**, Port.
63/F2 **Brahmaputra** (riv.), Asia
41/H2 **Brăila**, Rom.
26/G2 **Brandenburg** (state), Ger.
94/D3 **Brantford**, Ont.
107/J7 **Brasília** (cap.), Braz.
41/G3 **Braşov**, Rom.
27/J4 **Bratislava** (cap.), Slovakia
47/L4 **Bratsk**, Russia
95/F3 **Brattleboro**, Vt.
29/H4 **Braunschweig**, Ger.
105/D3 **Brazil**
96/D4 **Brazos** (riv.), Texas
82/C1 **Brazzaville** (cap.), Congo
28/B5 **Breda**, Neth.
29/F2 **Bremen**, Ger.
29/F1 **Bremerhaven**, Ger.
99/B2 **Bremerton**, Wash.
37/H4 **Brenner** (pass), Europe
33/J4 **Brescia**, Italy
27/M2 **Brest**, Belarus
32/A2 **Brest**, France
98/F5 **Brick**, N.J.
95/F3 **Bridgeport**, Conn.
104/G4 **Bridgetown** (cap.), Barbados
92/D2 **Brigham City**, Utah
25/F5 **Brighton**, Eng.
39/E2 **Brindisi**, Italy
72/D4 **Brisbane**, Austr.
85/F4 **Bristol** (bay), Alaska
24/D4 **Bristol**, Eng.
97/H2 **Bristol**, Tenn.
24/B4 **Bristol** (chan.), U.K.
97/H2 **Bristol**, Va.
86/D3 **British Columbia** (prov.), Can.
48/G10 **British Indian Ocean Terr.**
27/J4 **Brno**, Czech Rep.
95/G3 **Brockton**, Mass.
93/J3 **Broken Arrow**, Okla.
73/B1 **Broken Hill**, Austr.
98/G5 **Bronx** (borough), N.Y.
99/P13 **Brookfield**, Wis.
91/J4 **Brookings**, S. Dak.
98/G5 **Brooklyn** (borough), N.Y.
85/F2 **Brooks** (range), Alaska
96/D5 **Brownsville**, Texas
96/D4 **Brownwood**, Texas
30/C1 **Brugge**, Belg.
66/D2 **Brunei**
97/H4 **Brunswick**, Ga.
95/G3 **Brunswick**, Maine
30/D2 **Brussels** (cap.), Belg.
44/E1 **Bryansk**, Russia
96/D4 **Bryan**, Texas
92/D3 **Bryce Canyon Nat'l Pk.**, Utah
106/D2 **Bucaramanga**, Col.
41/H3 **Bucharest** (cap.), Rom.
40/D2 **Budapest** (cap.), Hung.
98/C3 **Buena Park**, Calif.
106/C3 **Buenaventura**, Col.
109/E3 **Buenos Aires** (cap.), Arg.
94/E3 **Buffalo**, N.Y.
44/B1 **Bug** (riv.), Europe
82/E1 **Bujumbura** (cap.), Burundi
82/E1 **Bukavu**, Zaire
46/G6 **Bukhara**, Uzbekistan
82/E5 **Bulawayo**, Zim.
41/E4 **Bulgaria**
98/B2 **Burbank**, Calif.
62/E3 **Burdwan**, India
41/H4 **Burgas**, Bulg.
34/D1 **Burgos**, Spain
79/E3 **Burkina Faso**
99/K11 **Burlingame**, Calif.
93/K2 **Burlington**, Iowa
97/J2 **Burlington**, N.C.
98/F5 **Burlington**, N.J.
94/E3 **Burlington**, Ont.
95/F2 **Burlington**, Vt.
63/G3 **Burma**
41/J5 **Bursa**, Turkey
82/E1 **Burundi**
94/E3 **Butler**, Pa.
48/M9 **Butuan**, Phil.
27/J2 **Bydgoszcz**, Pol.
27/K3 **Bytom**, Pol.

C

82/B2 **Cabinda**, Angola
94/E2 **Cabonga** (res.), Que.
82/F4 **Cabora Bassa** (lake), Moz.
95/J2 **Cabot** (str.), Can.
34/B4 **Cádiz**, Spain
34/B4 **Cádiz** (gulf), Sp.
32/C2 **Caen**, France
67/F2 **Cagayan de Oro**, Phil.
38/A3 **Cagliari**, Italy
104/C2 **Caicos** (isls.), Turks & Caicos Is.
72/B2 **Cairns**, Austr.
49/B4 **Cairo** (cap.), Egypt
94/B4 **Cairo**, Ill.
38/E3 **Calabria** (reg.), Italy
30/A2 **Calais**, France
95/H2 **Calais**, Maine
62/E3 **Calcutta**, India
90/D5 **Caldwell**, Idaho
90/E3 **Calgary**, Alta.
106/C3 **Cali**, Col.
64/E3 **Calicut** (Kozhikode), India
92/B3 **California** (state), U.S.
106/C6 **Callao**, Peru
99/Q16 **Calumet City**, Ill.
103/G1 **Camagüey**, Cuba
65/D3 **Cambodia**
21/D4 **Cambrian** (mts.), Wales
25/G2 **Cambridge**, Eng.
94/E4 **Cambridge**, Md.
95/G3 **Cambridge**, Mass.
93/J4 **Camden**, Ark.
98/E6 **Camden**, N.J.
97/H3 **Camden**, S.C.
76/H7 **Cameroon**
38/D2 **Campania** (reg.), Italy
101/G4 **Campeche** (bay), Mex.
107/L5 **Campina Grande**, Braz.
108/C2 **Campinas**, Braz.
107/H8 **Campo Grande**, Braz.
108/D2 **Campos**, Braz.
65/E4 **Cam Ranh**, Viet.
86/* **Canada**
93/G3 **Canadian** (riv.), U.S.
35/X16 **Canary** (isls.), Spain
73/D2 **Canberra** (cap.), Austr.
101/J4 **Cancún**, Mex.
33/G5 **Cannes**, France
25/H4 **Canterbury**, Eng.
65/D4 **Can Tho**, Viet.
61/G4 **Canton** (Guangzhou), China
69/H5 **Canton** (isl.), Kiribati
94/D3 **Canton**, Ohio
92/E3 **Canyon de Chelly Nat'l Mon.**, Ariz.
92/E3 **Canyonlands Nat'l Pk.**, Utah
95/J2 **Cape Breton** (isl.), N.S.
95/G3 **Cape Cod Nat'l Seashore**, Mass.
97/H5 **Cape Coral**, Fla.
97/F2 **Cape Girardeau**, Mo.
97/K3 **Cape Hatteras Nat'l Seashore**, N.C.
97/J3 **Cape Lookout Nat'l Seashore**, N.C.
80/B4 **Cape Town** (cap.), S. Africa
74/J9 **Cape Verde**
70/G2 **Cape York** (pen.), Austr.
92/E3 **Capitol Reef Nat'l Pk.**, Utah
38/D2 **Capri** (isl.), Italy
93/G3 **Capulin Volcano Nat'l Mon.**, N. Mex.
106/D4 **Caquetá** (riv.), Col.
106/E1 **Caracas** (cap.), Ven.
94/B4 **Carbondale**, Ill.
32/E5 **Carcassonne**, France
24/C4 **Cardiff** (cap.), Wales
84/J8 **Caribbean** (sea)
90/C2 **Cariboo** (mts.), Br. Col.
86/E3 **Caribou** (mts.), Alb.
95/G2 **Caribou**, Maine
94/E3 **Carlisle**, Pa.
93/F4 **Carlsbad**, N. Mex.
93/F4 **Carlsbad Caverns Nat'l Pk.**, N. Mex.
49/D3 **Carmel** (Har Karmel) (mt.), Isr.
99/M9 **Carmichael**, Calif.
68/D4 **Caroline** (isls.), Micronesia
18/F4 **Carpathians** (mts.), Europe
70/F2 **Carpentaria** (gulf), Austr.
98/A2 **Carpinteria**, Calif.
33/J4 **Carrara**, Italy
88/E4 **Carrizo** (mts.), Ariz.
98/B3 **Carson**, Calif.
92/C3 **Carson** (sink), Nev.
92/C3 **Carson City** (cap.), Nev.
106/C1 **Cartagena**, Col.
34/E4 **Cartagena**, Spain
75/L14 **Casablanca**, Mor.
92/E4 **Casa Grande**, Ariz.
92/E4 **Casa Grande Ruins Nat'l Mon.**, Ariz.
90/C5 **Cascade** (range), U.S.
90/G5 **Casper**, Wyo.
46/F6 **Caspian** (sea)
34/C3 **Castile-La Mancha** (reg.), Spain
104/F4 **Castries** (cap.), St.Lucia
99/K11 **Castro Valley**, Calif.
35/F2 **Catalonia** (reg.), Spain
38/D4 **Catania**, Italy
50/C4 **Catherine** (mt.), Egypt
98/K7 **Catonsville**, Md.
95/F3 **Catskill** (mts.), N.Y.
44/G4 **Caucasus** (mts.), Europe
62/D2 **Cawnpore** (Kanpur), India
107/H3 **Cayenne** (cap.), Fr. Guiana
103/J8 **Cayman Islands**
67/F1 **Cebu**, Phil.
92/D3 **Cedar Breaks Nat'l Mon.**, Utah
92/D3 **Cedar City**, Utah
93/J2 **Cedar Falls**, Iowa
93/K2 **Cedar Rapids**, Iowa
67/F3 **Celebes** (sea), Asia
67/E4 **Celebes** (isl.), Indon.
21/A5 **Celtic** (sea), Eur.
77/J6 **Central African Republic**
102/* **Central America**
94/B4 **Centralia**, Ill.
90/C4 **Centralia**, Wash.
67/G4 **Ceram** (isl.), Indon.
101/E4 **Cerritos**, Calif.
62/D6 **Ceylon** (isl.)
105/C5 **Chaco, Gran** (reg.), S. Amer.
77/J4 **Chad**
76/H5 **Chad** (lake), Africa
48/G10 **Chagos** (arch.), Br. Ind. Oc. Terr.
94/E4 **Chambersburg**, Pa.
30/C5 **Champagne** (reg.), Fr.
94/B3 **Champaign**, Ill.
94/F2 **Champlain** (lake), N. Amer.
64/D2 **Chandigarh**, India
59/F2 **Changchun**, China
61/J3 **Changhua**, Taiwan
59/D5 **Chang Jiang** (Yangtze) (riv.), China
61/G2 **Changsha**, Taiwan
59/D5 **Changzhou**, China
92/C4 **Channel** (isls.), Calif.
32/B2 **Channel Islands**, U.K.
98/A2 **Channel Is. Nat'l Pk.**, Calif.
97/J3 **Chapel Hill**, N.C.
46/G6 **Chardzhou**, Turkmenistan
76/J5 **Chari** (riv.), Africa
26/C3 **Charleroi**, Belg.
97/J3 **Charleston**, S.C.
94/D4 **Charleston** (cap.), W. Va.
97/H3 **Charlotte**, N.C.
104/E3 **Charlotte Amalie** (cap.), V.I. (U.S.)
97/J2 **Charlottesville**, Va.
95/J2 **Charlottetown** (cap.), P.E.I.
32/D2 **Chartres**, France
95/H2 **Chatham**, N.Br.
97/G4 **Chattahoochee**, Fla.
97/G4 **Chattahoochee** (riv.), U.S.
97/G3 **Chattanooga**, Tenn.
43/K4 **Cheboksary**, Russia
94/C2 **Cheboygan**, Mich.
76/E2 **Chech, Erg** (des.), Alg.
94/E3 **Cheektowaga**, N.Y.
59/E3 **Chefoo** (Yantai), China
90/C4 **Chehalis**, Wash.
55/K5 **Cheju**, S. Korea
55/K5 **Cheju** (isl.), S. Korea
90/C4 **Chelan** (lake), Wash.
43/P5 **Chelyabinsk**, Russia
47/L2 **Chelyuskina** (cape), Russia
26/G3 **Chemnitz**, Ger.
59/D2 **Chengde**, China
60/E2 **Chengdu** (Chengtu), China
44/C2 **Chenovtsy**, Ukraine
32/C2 **Cherbourg**, France
42/H4 **Cherepovets**, Russia
44/E2 **Cherkassy**, Ukraine
44/D2 **Chernigov**, Ukraine
98/E6 **Cherry Hill**, N.J.
94/E4 **Chesapeake** (bay), U.S.
23/F5 **Chester**, Eng.
98/E6 **Chester**, Pa.
93/F2 **Cheyenne** (riv.), U.S.
93/F2 **Cheyenne** (cap.), Wyo.
61/J4 **Chiayi**, Taiwan
57/G3 **Chiba**, Japan
99/Q16 **Chicago**, Ill.
99/Q16 **Chicago Heights**, Ill.
85/L4 **Chichagof** (isl.), Alaska
101/H4 **Chichén-Itzá** (ruins), Mex.
93/H4 **Chickasha**, Okla.
106/C5 **Chiclayo**, Peru
92/B3 **Chico**, Calif.
94/F3 **Chicopee**, Mass.
95/G1 **Chicoutimi**, Que.
55/H3 **Chifeng**, China
105/B6 **Chile**
94/D4 **Chillicothe**, Ohio
106/C4 **Chimborazo** (mt.), Ecua.
106/C5 **Chimbote**, Peru
46/G5 **Chimkent**, Kazakhstan
48/J6 **China, People's Rep. of**
61/J3 **China, Rep. of** (Taiwan)
58/E5 **Chinju**, S. Korea
98/C2 **Chino**, Calif.
46/G5 **Chirchik**, Uzbekistan
92/E4 **Chiricahua Nat'l Mon.**, Ariz.
54/G1 **Chita**, Russia
63/F3 **Chittagong**, Bang.
75/R15 **Chlef**, Alg.
57/F3 **Chofu**, Japan
58/E2 **Chŏngjin**, N. Korea
58/D5 **Chongju**, S. Korea
60/E2 **Chongqing** (Chungking), China
58/D5 **Chŏnju**, S. Korea
27/K3 **Chorzów**, Poland
62/D3 **Chota Nagur** (plat.), India
71/R11 **Christchurch**, N.Z.
47/U3 **Chukchi** (pen.), Russia
47/U3 **Chukchi** (sea), Russia
92/C4 **Chula Vista**, Calif.
58/D4 **Ch'unch'ŏn**, S. Korea
86/G3 **Churchill**, Man.
86/G3 **Churchill** (riv.), Man., Sask.
87/K3 **Churchill Falls**, Newf.
99/Q16 **Cicero**, Ill.
93/G3 **Cimarron** (riv.), U.S.
94/C4 **Cincinnati**, Ohio
66/C5 **Cirebon**, Indon.
101/M7 **Citlaltépetl** (mt.), Mex.
99/M9 **Citrus Heights**, Calif.
106/F2 **Ciudad Bolívar**, Ven.
106/F2 **Ciudad Guayana**, Venez.
101/F4 **Ciudad Madero**, Mex.
100/C3 **Ciudad Obregón**, Mex.
98/C2 **Claremont**, Calif.
95/F3 **Claremont**, N.H.
93/J3 **Claremore**, Okla.
94/D4 **Clarksburg**, W. Va.
97/F3 **Clarksdale**, Miss.
97/G2 **Clarksville**, Tenn.
97/H5 **Clearwater**, Fla.
90/D4 **Clearwater** (mts.), Idaho
32/E4 **Clermont-Ferrand**, France
95/D3 **Cleveland**, Ohio
97/G3 **Cleveland**, Tenn.
98/F5 **Clifton**, N.J.
93/K2 **Clinton**, Iowa
99/G6 **Clinton**, Mich.
92/C3 **Clovis**, Calif.
93/G4 **Clovis**, N. Mex.
41/F2 **Cluj-Napoca**, Rom.
90/A2 **Coast** (mts.), Can.
88/B4 **Coast** (ranges), U.S.
97/H4 **Coastal** (plain), U.S.
21/A5 **Cóbh**, Ire.
106/E7 **Cochabamaba**, Bol.
64/F4 **Cochin**, India
95/G3 **Cod** (cape), Mass.
90/F4 **Cody**, Wyo.
90/D4 **Coeur d'Alene**, Idaho
93/J3 **Coffeyville**, Kans.
64/F3 **Coimbatore**, India
34/A2 **Coimbra**, Port.
98/K8 **College Park**, Md.
96/D4 **College Station**, Texas
31/F2 **Cologne** (Köln), Ger.
106/D3 **Colombia**
62/C6 **Colombo** (cap.), Sri Lanka
103/G4 **Colón**, Pan.
96/D4 **Colorado** (riv.), Texas
92/E3 **Colorado** (plat.), U.S.
92/D4 **Colorado** (riv.), U.S.
92/F3 **Colorado** (state), U.S.
92/E3 **Colorado Nat'l Mon.**, Colo.
93/F3 **Colorado Springs**, Colo.
90/C2 **Columbia** (mts.), Br. Col.
98/K7 **Columbia**, Md.
93/J3 **Columbia**, Mo.
90/C4 **Columbia** (riv.), N. Amer.
90/D4 **Columbia** (plat.), Oreg., Wash.
97/H3 **Columbia** (cap.), S.C.
97/G3 **Columbia**, Tenn.
97/G3 **Columbus**, Ga.
94/C4 **Columbus**, Ind.
97/F3 **Columbus**, Miss.
94/D4 **Columbus** (cap.), Ohio
85/H2 **Colville** (riv.), Alaska
46/H6 **Communism** (peak), Tajikistan
37/F5 **Como** (lake), Italy
64/F4 **Comorin** (cape), India
81/G5 **Comoros**
30/B5 **Compiègne**, France
98/B3 **Compton**, Calif.
78/B4 **Conakry** (cap.), Guinea,
109/B4 **Concepción**, Chile
99/K11 **Concord**, Calif.
95/G3 **Concord** (cap.), N.H.
97/H3 **Concord**, N.C.
74/D5 **Congo**
74/D5 **Congo** (riv.), Africa
77/K7 **Congo** (basin), Zaire
74/E5 **Congo** (Zaire)
95/G2 **Connecticut** (riv.), U.S.
95/F3 **Connecticut** (state), U.S.
37/F2 **Constance** (lake), Europe
41/J3 **Constanta**, Rom.
75/V17 **Constantine**, Alg.
108/C1 **Contagem**, Braz.
90/C2 **Continental** (ranges), Alb., Br. Col.
93/J4 **Conway**, Ark.
85/H3 **Cook** (inlet), Alaska
71/R11 **Cook** (mt.), N.Z.
71/R11 **Cook** (str.), N.Z.
69/J6 **Cook Islands**
90/B5 **Coos Bay**, Oreg.
20/E5 **Copenhagen** (cap.), Den.
86/B2 **Copper** (riv.), Alaska
68/E6 **Coral** (sea)
97/H5 **Coral Gables**, Fla.
71/J3 **Coral Sea Is.** (terr.), Austr.
97/H5 **Coral Springs**, Fla.
109/D3 **Córdoba**, Arg.
34/C4 **Córdoba**, Spain
39/F3 **Corfu** (Kérkira), Greece
39/H4 **Corinth**, Greece
21/A5 **Cork**, Ire.
95/K1 **Corner Brook**, Newf.
94/E3 **Corning**, N.Y.
94/F2 **Cornwall**, Ont.
62/D5 **Coromandel** (coast), India
98/C3 **Corona**, Calif.
106/E1 **Coro**, Ven.
96/D5 **Corpus Christi**, Texas
38/A1 **Corsica** (isl.), France
96/D3 **Corsicana**, Texas
94/E3 **Cortland**, N.Y.
90/C4 **Corvallis**, Oreg.
94/D3 **Coshocton**, Ohio
35/G2 **Costa Brava** (reg.), Spain
98/C3 **Costa Mesa**, Calif.
103/F4 **Costa Rica**
32/F3 **Côte-d'Or** (mts.), France
32/C2 **Cotentin** (pen.), France
79/F5 **Cotonou**, Benin
93/J2 **Council Bluffs**, Iowa
25/E2 **Coventry**, Eng.
98/C2 **Covina**, Calif.
94/C4 **Covington**, Ky.
102/E1 **Cozumel** (isl.), Mex.
41/F3 **Craiova**, Rom.
90/E3 **Cranbrook**, Br. Col.
98/F5 **Cranford**, N.J.
90/C5 **Crater Lake Nat'l Pk.**, Oreg.
90/E5 **Craters of the Moon Nat'l Mon.**, Idaho
94/C3 **Crawfordsville**, Ind.
39/J5 **Crete** (isl.), Greece
39/J5 **Crete** (sea), Greece
44/E3 **Crimea** (pen.), Ukraine
76/H8 **Cristal** (mts.), Gabon
40/C3 **Croatia**
96/E4 **Crowley**, La.
82/B2 **Cuanza** (riv.), Angola
103/F1 **Cuba**
82/C4 **Cubango** (riv.), Angola
98/C2 **Cucamonga**, Calif.
106/D2 **Cucuta**, Col.
106/C4 **Cuenca**, Ecua.
101/F5 **Cuernavaca**, Mex.
108/G7 **Cuiabá**, Braz.
100/D3 **Culiacán**, Mex.
97/G3 **Cullman**, Ala.
98/B2 **Culver City**, Calif.
106/F1 **Cumaná**, Ven.
94/E4 **Cumberland**, Md.
97/G3 **Cumberland** (plat.), U.S.
97/G2 **Cumberland** (riv.), U.S.
23/E3 **Cumbrian** (mts.), Eng.
99/K12 **Cupertino**, Calif.
104/D4 **Curaçao** (isl.), Neth. Ant.
108/B3 **Curitiba**, Braz.
106/D6 **Cusco**, Peru
62/E3 **Cuttack**, India
39/J4 **Cyclades** (isls.), Greece
98/B3 **Cypress**, Calif.
49/C2 **Cyprus**
77/K1 **Cyrenaica** (reg.), Libya
27/H4 **Czech Republic**
27/K3 **Czestochowa**, Pol.

D

62/E4 **Dacca** (Dhaka) (cap.), Bang.
37/H1 **Dachau**, Ger.
60/E3 **Dafang**, China
55/J2 **Da Hinggang** (mts.), China
68/C2 **Daito** (isls.), Japan
78/A3 **Dakar** (cap.), Sen.

65/E4 **Da Lat**, Viet.
95/H1 **Dalhousie**, N.Br.
58/A3 **Dalian**, China
96/D3 **Dallas**, Texas
97/G3 **Dalton**, Ga.
99/K11 **Daly City**, Calif.
49/B4 **Damanhur**, Egypt
49/E3 **Damascus** (cap.), Syria
51/H3 **Damavand** (mt.), Iran
51/E4 **Damietta**, Egypt
65/E2 **Da Nang**, Viet.
58/C2 **Dandong**, China
18/F4 **Danube** (riv.), Europe
95/C3 **Danville**, Ill.
94/E4 **Danville**, Va.
55/K2 **Daqing**, China
98/E6 **Darby**, Pa.
41/H5 **Dardanelles** (str.), Turkey
82/G2 **Dar es Salaam** (cap.), Tanz.
98/G4 **Darien**, Conn.
103/G4 **Darién** (mts.), Pan.
62/E2 **Darjiling**, India
70/B6 **Darling** (range), Austr.
73/C1 **Darling** (riv.), Austr.
72/C4 **Darling Downs** (ridge), Austr.
26/E4 **Darmstadt**, Ger.
95/J2 **Dartmouth**, N.S.
70/E2 **Darwin**, Austr.
59/C2 **Datong**, China
67/G2 **Davao**, Phil.
93/K2 **Davenport**, Iowa
83/F **Davis** (sea), Antarc.
99/L9 **Davis**, Calif.
84/M3 **Davis** (str.), N. Amer.
90/C2 **Dawson Creek**, Br. Col.
85/L3 **Dawson**, Yukon
97/H4 **Daytona Beach**, Fla.
94/C4 **Dayton**, Ohio
49/D4 **Dead** (sea), Asia
99/F7 **Dearborn**, Mich.
99/F7 **Dearborn Heights**, Mich.
92/C3 **Death Valley Nat'l Mon.**, U.S.
40/E2 **Debrecen**, Hung.
97/G3 **Decatur**, Ala.
97/G3 **Decatur**, Ga.
94/B4 **Decatur**, Ill.
62/C5 **Deccan** (plat.), India
99/Q15 **Deerfield**, Ill.
94/C3 **Defiance**, Ohio
53/L2 **Dehra Dun**, India
94/B3 **De Kalb**, Ill.
97/H4 **De Land**, Fla.
94/D3 **Delaware**, Ohio
94/F4 **Delaware** (bay), U.S.
98/E5 **Delaware** (riv.), U.S.
94/F4 **Delaware** (state), U.S.
98/F4 **Delaware Water Gap Nat'l Rec. Area**, U.S.
62/C2 **Delhi**, India
97/H5 **Delray Beach**, Fla.
96/C4 **Del Rio**, Texas
85/H3 **Denali Nat'l Pk.**, Alaska
20/C5 **Denmark**
18/A2 **Denmark** (str.)
96/D3 **Denton**, Texas
93/F3 **Denver** (cap.), Colo.
98/F5 **Denville**, N.J.
23/G6 **Derby**, Eng.
96/E4 **De Ridder**, La.
95/G3 **Derry**, N.H.
93/J2 **Des Moines** (cap.), Iowa
99/Q15 **Des Plaines**, Ill.
26/G3 **Dessau**, Ger.
99/F7 **Detroit**, Mich.
92/C3 **Devils Postpile Nat'l Mon.**, Calif.
91/G5 **Devils Tower Nat'l Mon.**, Wyo.
87/S7 **Devon** (isl.), N.W.T.
62/E3 **Dhaka** (Dacca) (cap.), Bang.
62/B3 **Dhulia**, India
88/W13 **Diamond** (head), Hawaii
91/H4 **Dickinson**, N. Dak.
48/G10 **Diego Garcia** (isls.), Br. Ind. Oc. Terr.
65/C1 **Dien Bien Phu**, Viet.
30/A4 **Dieppe**, France
36/A3 **Dijon**, France
40/C3 **Dinaric Alps** (mts.), Bosnia
92/E2 **Dinosaur Nat'l Mon.**, U.S.
77/P6 **Dire Dawa**, Eth.
98/K8 **District of Columbia**, U.S.
86/C3 **Dixon Entrance** (str.), N. Amer.
94/B3 **Dixon**, Ill.
50/E2 **Diyarbakir**, Turkey
76/H3 **Djado** (plat.), Niger
66/C5 **Djakarta** (Jakarta), Indon.
77/P5 **Djibouti**
77/P5 **Djibouti** (cap.), Djibouti
66/D5 **Djokjakarta** (Yogyakarta), Indon.
18/G3 **Dnepr** (Dnieper) (riv.), Europe
44/E2 **Dneprodzerzhinsk**, Ukraine
44/E2 **Dnepropetrovsk**, Ukraine
44/D3 **Dnestr** (Dniester) (riv.), Europe
98/G4 **Dobbs Ferry**, N.Y.
50/A2 **Dodecanese** (isls.), Greece
93/G3 **Dodge City**, Kans.
50/D1 **Dogukaradeniz** (mts.), Turkey
52/F3 **Doha** (cap.), Qatar
33/J3 **Dolomite Alps** (mts.), Italy
104/F4 **Dominica**
104/D3 **Dominican Republic**
62/D6 **Dondra** (head), Sri Lanka
21/A3 **Donegal**, Ire.
44/F3 **Donetsk**, Ukraine
45/G2 **Donets** (riv.), Ukraine
61/G4 **Dongguan**, China
45/G3 **Don** (riv.), Russia
32/D4 **Dordogne** (riv.), France
28/B5 **Dordrecht**, Neth.
37/F3 **Dornbirn**, Austria
75/W18 **Dorsale** (mts.), Tun.
29/E5 **Dortmund**, Ger.
97/G4 **Dothan**, Ala.
76/G7 **Douala**, Cameroon
92/E5 **Douglas**, Ariz.
22/D3 **Douglas** (cap.), I. of Man
94/F4 **Dover** (cap.), Del.
25/H4 **Dover**, Eng.
30/A2 **Dover** (str.), Europe
95/G3 **Dover**, N.H.
98/F5 **Dover**, N.J.
99/P16 **Downers Grove**, Ill.
98/B3 **Downey**, Calif.
109/C8 **Drake** (passage)
81/E2 **Drakensburg** (range), S. Africa
40/C3 **Dráva** (riv.), Europe
27/G3 **Dresden**, Ger.
72/B4 **Drummond** (range), Austr.
53/G3 **Dubayyi** (Dubai), U.A.E.
97/H3 **Dublin**, Ga.
22/B5 **Dublin** (cap.), Ire.
40/D4 **Dubrovnik**, Croatia
93/K2 **Dubuque**, Iowa
24/D2 **Dudley**, Eng.
36/D6 **Dufourspitze** (mt.), Eur.
28/D6 **Duisburg**, Ger.
91/L4 **Duluth**, Minn.
98/G5 **Dumont**, N.J.
93/H4 **Duncan**, Okla.
98/K7 **Dundalk**, Md.
21/D2 **Dundee**, Scot.
97/H4 **Dunedin**, Fla.
71/R12 **Dunedin**, N.Z.
30/B1 **Dunkirk** (Dunkerque), France
92/F3 **Durango**, Colo.
100/D3 **Durango**, Mex.
93/H4 **Durant**, Okla.
81/E3 **Durban**, S. Africa
62/E3 **Durgapur**, India
23/G2 **Durham**, Eng.
95/G3 **Durham**, N.H.
97/J3 **Durham**, N.C.
46/G6 **Dushanbe** (cap.), Tajikistan
28/D6 **Düsseldorf**, Ger.
43/J3 **Dvina, Northern** (Dvina, Severnaya) (riv.), Russia
42/E5 **Dvina, Western** (Dvina Zapadnaya) (riv.), Belarus
42/J4 **Dzerzhinsk**, Russia
46/H5 **Dzhambul**, Kazakhstan

E

96/C4 **Eagle Pass**, Texas
25/H2 **East Anglia** (reg.), Eng.
98/F5 **East Brunswick**, N.J.
99/R16 **East Chicago**, Ind.
48/M6 **East China** (sea), Asia
69/Q7 **Easter** (isl.), Chile
62/C5 **Eastern Ghats** (mts.), India
28/D1 **East Frisian** (isls.), Ger.
94/C3 **East Lansing**, Mich.
94/D3 **East Liverpool**, Ohio
80/D4 **East London**, S. Africa
98/B2 **East Los Angeles**, Calif.
98/G5 **East Meadow**, N.Y.
98/E5 **Easton**, Pa.
98/F5 **East Orange**, N.J.
99/G7 **East Pointe**, Mich.
97/G3 **East Point**, Ga.
47/S2 **East Siberian** (sea), Russia
94/B4 **East St. Louis**, Ill.
94/B2 **Eau Claire**, Wis.
35/F2 **Ebro** (riv.), Spain
100/F5 **Ecatepec**, Mex.
99/F7 **Ecorse**, Mich.
106/C4 **Ecuador**
97/J2 **Eden**, N.C.
97/J2 **Edenton**, N.C.
96/D5 **Edinburg**, Texas
21/D3 **Edinburgh** (cap.), Scot.
98/F5 **Edison**, N.J.
99/C2 **Edmonds**, Wash.
90/E2 **Edmonton** (cap.), Alta.
95/G2 **Edmundston**, N.Br.
96/C4 **Edwards** (plat.), Texas
92/C4 **Edwards A.F.B.**, Calif.
94/B4 **Edwardsville**, Ill.
92/B3 **Eel** (riv.), Calif.
91/L5 **Effigy Mounds Nat'l Mon.**, Iowa
94/B4 **Effingham**, Ill.
71/R10 **Egmont** (mt.), N.Z.
77/L2 **Egypt**
28/C6 **Eindhoven**, Neth.
49/D5 **Elat** (Elath), Isr.
50/D2 **Elazig**, Turkey
38/B1 **Elba** (isl.), Italy
26/E2 **Elbe** (riv.), Ger.
92/F3 **Elbert** (mt.), Colo.
45/G4 **El'brus** (mt.), Russia
51/G2 **Elburz** (mts.), Iran
92/C4 **El Cajon**, Calif.
92/D4 **El Centro**, Calif.
76/D3 **El Djouf** (des.), Maur.
93/J4 **El Dorado**, Ark.
42/H5 **Elektrostal'**, Russia
104/B1 **Eleuthera** (isl.), Bah.
99/P15 **Elgin**, Ill.
97/J2 **Elizabeth City**, N.C.
98/F5 **Elizabeth**, N.J.
99/Q15 **Elk Grove Village**, Ill.
94/C3 **Elkhart**, Ind.
90/C4 **Ellensburg**, Wash.
87/T6 **Ellesmere** (isl.), N.W.T.
83/U **Ellsworth Land** (reg.), Antarc.
99/Q16 **Elmhurst**, Ill.
94/E3 **Elmira**, N.Y.
98/B2 **El Monte**, Calif.
99/Q16 **Elmwood Park**, Ill.
96/A4 **El Paso**, Texas
92/H4 **El Reno**, Okla.
102/D3 **El Salvador**
94/D3 **Elyria**, Ohio
98/E5 **Emmaus**, Pa.
93/H3 **Emporia**, Kans.
83/D **Enderby Land** (reg.), Antarc.
94/E3 **Endicott**, N.Y.
68/F3 **Enewetak** (atoll), Marshall Is.
21/D4 **England**, U.K.
98/G5 **Englewood**, N.J.
32/B2 **English** (chan.), Europe
93/H3 **Enid**, Okla.
28/D4 **Enschede**, Neth.
77/M8 **Entebbe**, Uganda
79/G5 **Enugu**, Nigeria
51/G2 **Enzeli** (Bandar-e Anzali), Iran
76/G7 **Equatorial Guinea**
26/F3 **Erfurt**, Ger.
94/D3 **Erie** (lake), N. Amer.
94/D3 **Erie**, Pa.
52/C5 **Eritrea**
26/G3 **Erzgebirge** (mts.), Europe
50/E2 **Erzurum**, Turkey
20/H3 **Esbo** (Espoo), Fin.
94/C2 **Escanaba**, Mich.
92/C4 **Escondido**, Calif.
51/G3 **Esfahān**, Iran
50/B2 **Eskişehir**, Turkey
68/F6 **Espiritu Santo** (isl.), Vanuatu
20/H3 **Espoo** (Esbo), Fin.
28/E6 **Essen**, Ger.
98/K7 **Essex**, Md.
42/E4 **Estonia**
77/N5 **Ethiopia**
38/D4 **Etna** (vol.), Italy
39/H3 **Euboea** (Évvoia) (isl.), Greece
94/D3 **Euclid**, Ohio
90/C4 **Eugene**, Oreg.
96/E4 **Eunice**, La.
50/F4 **Euphrates** (riv.), Asia
92/A2 **Eureka**, Calif.
18/* **Europe**
93/F3 **Evans** (mt.), Colo.
99/Q15 **Evanston**, Ill.
94/C4 **Evansville**, Ind.
62/E2 **Everest** (mt.), Asia
99/C2 **Everett**, Wash.
97/H5 **Everglades Nat'l Pk.**, Fla.
39/H3 **Évvoia** (isl.), Greece
24/C5 **Exeter**, Eng.
95/G3 **Exeter**, N.H.
70/F5 **Eyre** (lake), Austr.
70/F6 **Eyre** (pen.), Austr.

F

85/J3 **Fairbanks**, Alaska
98/J8 **Fairfax**, Va.
99/K10 **Fairfield**, Calif.
98/G4 **Fairfield**, Conn.
94/C4 **Fairfield**, Ohio
98/F5 **Fair Lawn**, N.J.
90/D4 **Fairmont**, W. Va.
85/L4 **Fairweather** (mt.), N. Amer.
64/B2 **Faisalabad**, Pak.
96/D5 **Falcon** (res.), N. Amer.
109/D7 **Falkland Islands**
95/G3 **Fall River**, Mass.
49/C2 **Famagusta**, Cyprus
69/K4 **Fanning** (Tabuaeran) (isl.), Kiribati
92/B3 **Farallon** (isls.), Calif.
91/J4 **Fargo**, N. Dak.
91/K5 **Faribault**, Minn.
92/E3 **Farmington**, N. Mex.
99/F7 **Farmington Hills**, Mich.
34/B4 **Faro**, Port.
18/C2 **Faroe** (isls.), Den.
93/J3 **Fayetteville**, Ark.
97/J3 **Fayetteville**, N.C.
99/C3 **Federal Way**, Wash.
59/F2 **Fengcheng**, China
46/H5 **Fergana**, Uzbekistan
91/K4 **Fergus Falls**, Minn.
33/J4 **Ferrara**, Italy
75/M13 **Fès**, Mor.
76/H2 **Fezzan** (reg.), Libya
81/H8 **Fianarantsoa**, Madag.
107/L6 **Fiera de Santana**, Braz.
68/G6 **Fiji**
94/D3 **Findlay**, Ohio
34/A1 **Finisterre** (cape), Spain
20/H2 **Finland**
42/E4 **Finland** (gulf), Europe
86/D3 **Finlay** (riv.), Br. Col.
98/G5 **Fire Isl. Nat'l Seashore**, N.Y.
33/J5 **Firenze** (Florence), Italy
40/B3 **Fiume** (Rijeka), Croatia
38/C2 **Fiumicino**, Italy
92/E4 **Flagstaff**, Ariz.
92/E2 **Flaming Gorge** (res.), U.S.
30/B2 **Flanders** (reg.), Eur.
90/B3 **Flattery** (cape), Wash.
26/E1 **Flensburg**, Ger.
73/D3 **Flinders** (isl.), Austr.
70/F6 **Flinders** (ranges), Austr.
99/E5 **Flint**, Mich.
98/G5 **Floral Park**, N.Y.
97/G3 **Florence**, Ala.
33/J5 **Florence** (Firenze), Italy
97/J3 **Florence**, S.C.
67/F5 **Flores** (isl.), Indon.
67/E5 **Flores** (sea), Indon.
108/B3 **Florianópolis**, Braz.
97/H5 **Florida** (bay), Fla.
97/H4 **Florida** (state), U.S.
93/K3 **Florissant**, Mo.
38/D2 **Foggia**, Italy
25/H4 **Folkestone**, Eng.
94/B3 **Fond du Lac**, Wis.
68/G5 **Fongafale** (cap.), Tuvalu
102/E3 **Fonseca** (gulf), Cent. Amer.
32/E2 **Fontainebleau**, France
98/C2 **Fontana**, Calif.
61/H3 **Foochow** (Fuzhou), China
33/K4 **Forlì**, Italy
109/L4 **Fortaleza**, Braz.
98/J8 **Ft. Belvoir**, Va.
92/F2 **Ft. Collins**, Colo.
104/F4 **Ft.-de-France** (cap.), Martinique
93/J2 **Ft. Dodge**, Iowa
21/D2 **Forth** (firth), Scot.
97/H5 **Ft. Lauderdale**, Fla.
98/G5 **Ft. Lee**, N.J.
90/E3 **Ft. Macleod**, Alta.
93/K2 **Ft. Madison**, Iowa
98/K7 **Ft. McHenry Nat'l Mon.**, Md.
86/E3 **Ft. McMurray**, Alta.
98/K7 **Ft. Meade**, Md.
97/H5 **Ft. Myers**, Fla.
90/G4 **Ft. Peck Lake** (res.), Mont.
97/H5 **Ft. Pierce**, Fla.
93/J4 **Ft. Smith**, Ark.
86/E2 **Ft. Smith**, N.W.T.
97/G4 **Ft. Walton Beach**, Fla.
94/C3 **Ft. Wayne**, Ind.
96/D3 **Ft. Worth**, Texas
94/D3 **Fostoria**, Ohio
98/C3 **Fountain Valley**, Calif.
76/C5 **Fouta Djallon** (reg.), Guinea
87/J2 **Foxe** (basin), N.W.T.
85/E5 **Fox** (isls.), Alaska
32/D3 **France**
91/J5 **Francis Case** (lake), S. Dak.
82/E5 **Francistown**, Botswana
94/C3 **Frankfort**, Ind.
94/C4 **Frankfort** (cap.), Ky.
26/E3 **Frankfurt am Main**, Ger.
27/H2 **Frankfurt an der Oder**, Ger.
86/D2 **Franklin** (mts.), N.W.T.
90/D3 **Franklin D. Roosevelt** (lake), Wash.
46/F2 **Franz Josef Land** (isls.), Russia
90/C3 **Fraser** (riv.), Br. Col.
99/G6 **Fraser**, Mich.
20/D5 **Fredericia**, Den.
94/E4 **Frederick**, Md.
94/E4 **Fredericksburg**, Va.
95/H2 **Fredericton** (cap.), N.Br.
20/D4 **Frederikshavn**, Den.
94/B3 **Freeport**, Ill.
98/G5 **Freeport**, N.Y.
78/D4 **Freetown** (cap.), S. Leone
36/D2 **Freiburg**, Ger.
90/B3 **Fremont**, Calif.
93/H2 **Fremont**, Nebr.
107/H3 **French Guiana**
69/M6 **French Polynesia**
92/C3 **Fresno**, Calif.
36/D4 **Fribourg**, Switz.
37/F2 **Friedrichshafen**, Ger.
73/B1 **Frome** (lake), Austr.
93/F2 **Front** (range), Colo., Wyo.
97/J2 **Front Royal**, Va.
46/H5 **Frunze** (Bishkek) (cap.), Kyrgyzstan
61/H3 **Fujian** (Fukien) (prov.), China
57/F3 **Fujisawa**, Japan
57/F3 **Fujiyama** (mt.), Japan
56/E2 **Fukui**, Japan
56/B4 **Fukuoka**, Japan
57/G2 **Fukushima**, Japan
56/C3 **Fukuyama**, Japan
98/C3 **Fullerton**, Calif.
93/K3 **Fulton**, Mo.
57/H7 **Funabashi**, Japan
35/V15 **Funchal**, Port.
95/H2 **Fundy** (bay), N. Amer.
95/H2 **Fundy Nat'l Pk.**, N.Br.
26/F4 **Fürth**, Ger.
58/B2 **Fushun**, China
37/G2 **Füssen**, Ger.
58/A1 **Fuxin**, China
61/H3 **Fuzhou**, China

G

76/H7 **Gabon**
80/D2 **Gaborone** (cap.), Bots.
97/G3 **Gadsden**, Ala.
97/H3 **Gaffney**, S.C.
97/H4 **Gainesville**, Fla.
97/H3 **Gainesville**, Ga.
70/F6 **Gairdner** (lake), Austr.
98/J7 **Gaithersburg**, Md.
16/E6 **Galápagos** (isls.), Ecua.
41/J3 **Galaţi**, Rom.
94/B3 **Galesburg**, Ill.
34/A1 **Galicia** (reg.), Spain
97/G2 **Gallatin**, Tenn.
62/D6 **Galle**, Sri Lanka
41/H5 **Gallipoli**, Turkey
92/E4 **Gallup**, N. Mex.
92/E4 **Galveston**, Texas
21/H7 **Galway**, Ire.
78/B3 **Gambia**
95/L1 **Gander**, Newf.
48/H7 **Ganges** (riv.), Asia
62/E2 **Gangtok**, India
33/J4 **Garda** (lake), Italy
93/G3 **Garden City**, Kans.
98/J5 **Garden City**, N.Y.
98/C3 **Garden Grove**, Calif.
98/F5 **Garfield**, N.J.
92/D3 **Garland**, Texas
37/H3 **Garmisch-Partenkirchen**, Ger.
32/D4 **Garonne** (riv.), France
99/R16 **Gary**, Ind.
95/H1 **Gaspé** (pen.), Que.
97/H3 **Gastonia**, N.C.
85/H2 **Gates of the Arctic Nat'l Pk.**, Alaska
98/F5 **Gateway Nat'l Rec. Area**, U.S.
63/F2 **Gauhati**, India
70/E6 **Gawler** (range), Austr.
62/E3 **Gaya**, India
49/D4 **Gaza Strip**
49/E1 **Gaziantep**, Turkey
27/K1 **Gdańsk**, Pol.
27/K1 **Gdańsk** (gulf), Pol.
27/K1 **Gdynia**, Pol.
73/C3 **Geelong**, Austr.
60/D4 **Gejiu**, China
28/E5 **Gelsenkirchen**, Ger.
36/C5 **Geneva** (Léman) (lake), Europe
94/E3 **Geneva**, N.Y.
36/C5 **Geneva**, Switz.
33/H4 **Genoa** (Genova), Italy
33/H5 **Genova** (gulf), It.
30/C1 **Gent**, Belg.
104/F2 **George Town** (cap.), Cayman Is.
106/G2 **Georgetown** (cap.), Guyana
66/B2 **George Town** (Pinang), Malaysia
45/G4 **Georgia**
90/C3 **Georgia** (str.), Br. Col.
97/G3 **Georgia** (state), U.S.
94/D2 **Georgian** (bay), Ont.
70/A5 **Geraldton**, Austr.
26/E3 **Germany**
94/E4 **Gettysburg**, Pa.
78/E4 **Ghana**
53/J2 **Ghazni**, Afghan.
34/C4 **Gibraltar**
34/C5 **Gibraltar** (str.)
70/D4 **Gibson** (des.), Austr.
57/E3 **Gifu**, Japan
34/C1 **Gijón**, Spain
92/D4 **Gila** (riv.), U.S.
92/E4 **Gila Cliff Dwellings Nat'l Mon.**, N. Mex.
68/G5 **Gilbert Is.** (Kiribati)
90/G4 **Gillette**, Wyo.
32/C4 **Gironde** (riv.), France
95/K2 **Glace Bay**, N.S.
86/G3 **Glacier Bay Nat'l Pk.**, Alaska
90/D2 **Glacier Nat'l Pk.**, Br. Col.
90/E3 **Glacier Nat'l Pk.**, Mont.
21/C3 **Glasgow**, Scot.
98/E6 **Glassboro**, N.J.
98/K7 **Glen Burnie**, Md.
92/E3 **Glen Canyon Nat'l Rec. Area**, U.S.
98/J5 **Glen Cove**, N.Y.
92/D4 **Glendale**, Ariz.
98/B2 **Glendale**, Calif.

95/F3 **Glens Falls,** N.Y.
99/Q15 **Glenview,** Ill.
27/K3 **Gliwice,** Pol.
24/D3 **Gloucester,** Eng.
62/B4 **Goa** (dist.), India
108/J7 **Goânia,** Braz.
54/E3 **Gobi** (des.), Asia
62/D4 **Godavari** (riv.), India
84/M3 **Godthåb** (Nuuk) (cap.), Greenl.
53/L1 **Godwin Austen** (K2) (mt.), Asia
49/D3 **Golan Heights,** Syria
72/D4 **Gold Coast,** Austr.
93/F3 **Golden,** Colo.
99/J11 **Golden Gate Nat'l Rec. Area,** Calif.
97/J3 **Goldsboro,** N.C.
44/D1 **Gomel',** Belarus
103/H2 **Gonâve** (isl.), Haiti
77/N5 **Gonder,** Eth.
80/B4 **Good Hope** (cape), S. Africa
92/B2 **Goose** (lake), U.S.
87/K3 **Goose Bay-Happy Valley,** Newf.
43/K4 **Gor'kiy** (Nizhniy Novgorod), Russia
62/D2 **Gorakhpur,** India
44/F2 **Gorlovka,** Ukraine
20/D4 **Göteborg,** Sweden
20/F4 **Gotland** (isl.), Sweden
29/G5 **Göttingen,** Ger.
28/B4 **Gouda,** Neth.
54/D3 **Govi Altayn** (mts.), Mong.
21/C2 **Grampian** (mts.), Scot.
34/D4 **Granada,** Spain
35/X17 **Gran Canaria** (isl.), Spain
105/C5 **Gran Chaco** (reg.), S. Amer.
59/D4 **Grand** (canal), China
104/B1 **Grand Bahama** (isl.), Bah.
92/D3 **Grand Canyon Nat'l Pk.,** Ariz.
103/F2 **Grand Cayman** (isl.), Cayman Is.
90/D2 **Grande Prairie,** Alta.
76/E1 **Grand Erg Occidental** (des.), Alg.
76/G1 **Grand Erg Oriental** (des.), Alg.
96/C4 **Grande, Rio** (riv.), N. Amer.
91/J4 **Grand Forks,** N. Dak.
93/H2 **Grand Island,** Nebr.
92/E3 **Grand Junction,** Colo.
95/H2 **Grand Manan** (isl.), N.Br.
94/B2 **Grand Portage Nat'l Mon.,** Minn.
94/C3 **Grand Rapids,** Mich.
90/F5 **Grand Teton Nat'l Pk.,** Wyo.
97/F2 **Granite City,** Ill.
92/F4 **Grants,** N. Mex.
90/C5 **Grants Pass,** Oreg.
33/G5 **Grasse,** France
25/G4 **Gravesend,** Eng.
33/L3 **Graz,** Austria
104/B1 **Great Abaco** (isl.), Bah.
70/D6 **Great Australian** (bight), Austr.
72/B1 **Great Barrier** (reef), Austr.
90/C2 **Great Basin** (basin), U.S.
92/D3 **Great Basin Nat'l Park,** Nev.
86/D2 **Great Bear** (lake), N.W.T.
93/H3 **Great Bend,** Kans.
21/E3 **Great Britain** (isl.), U.K.
71/H7 **Great Dividing** (range), Austr.
103/F1 **Greater Antilles** (isls.), N. Amer.
66/C4 **Greater Sunda** (isls.), Indon.
104/C2 **Great Exuma** (isl.), Bah.
90/F4 **Great Falls,** Mont.
104/C2 **Great Inagua** (isl.), Bah.
62/B2 **Great Indian** (Thar) (des.), India
93/G2 **Great Plains** (plains), U.S.
92/D2 **Great Salt** (lake), Utah
93/F3 **Great Sand Dunes Nat'l Mon.,** Colo.
77/K2 **Great Sand Sea** (des.), Egypt, Libya
70/C4 **Great Sandy** (des.), Austr.
86/E2 **Great Slave** (lake), N.W.T.
97/H3 **Great Smoky Mts. Nat'l Pk.,** Tenn.
70/D5 **Great Victoria** (des.), Austr.
59/B3 **Great Wall,** China
39/G3 **Greece**
93/F2 **Greeley,** Colo.
92/E3 **Green** (riv.), U.S.
94/B2 **Green Bay,** Wis.
97/H2 **Greeneville,** Tenn.
95/F3 **Greenfield,** Mass.
99/P14 **Greenfield,** Wis.
84/N2 **Greenland**
84/R2 **Greenland** (sea)
95/F3 **Green** (mts.), Vt.
21/C3 **Greenock,** Scot.
97/J2 **Greensboro,** N.C.
94/E3 **Greensburg,** Pa.
97/F3 **Greenville,** Miss.
97/J3 **Greenville,** N.C.
97/H3 **Greenville,** S.C.
98/G4 **Greenwich,** Conn.
97/F3 **Greenwood,** Miss.
97/H3 **Greenwood,** S.C.
72/A2 **Gregory** (range), Austr.
104/F5 **Grenada**
32/F4 **Grenoble,** France
97/F4 **Gretna,** La.
72/A5 **Grey** (range), Austr.
97/G3 **Griffin,** Ga.
42/E5 **Grodno,** Belarus
28/D2 **Groningen,** Neth.
99/G7 **Grosse Pointe Woods,** Mich.
33/K3 **Grossglockner** (mt.), Austria
45/H4 **Groznyy,** Russia
100/E4 **Guadalajara,** Mex.
34/D2 **Guadalajara,** Spain
68/E6 **Guadalcanal** (isl.), Sol. Is.
34/D4 **Guadalquivir** (riv.), Spain
96/B3 **Guadalupe** (mts.), U.S.
96/B4 **Guadalupe Mts. Nat'l Pk.,** Texas
104/F3 **Guadeloupe**
103/H4 **Guajira** (pen.), S. Amer.
68/D3 **Guam**
103/F1 **Guanabacoa,** Cuba
61/G3 **Guangdong** (prov.), China
61/G4 **Guangzhou** (Canton), China
103/H1 **Guantánamo,** Cuba
102/D3 **Guatemala**
102/D3 **Guatemala** (cap.), Guat.
106/B4 **Guayaquil,** Ecua.
106/B4 **Guayaquil** (gulf), Ecua.
94/D3 **Guelph,** Ont.
32/B2 **Guernsey** (isl.), Chan. Is.
106/F2 **Guiana Highlands** (range), S. Amer.
61/F3 **Guilin,** China
78/C4 **Guinea**
78/B3 **Guinea-Bissau**
76/F7 **Guinea** (gulf), Africa
60/E3 **Guiyang,** China
64/C1 **Gujranwala,** Pak.
62/C4 **Gulbarga,** India
96/D5 **Gulf Coastal** (plain), Texas
97/F4 **Gulf Isls. Nat'l Seashore,** Fla.
97/F4 **Gulfport,** Miss.
62/D4 **Guntur,** India
45/J3 **Gur'yev,** Kazakhstan
93/H4 **Guthrie,** Okla.
106/G3 **Guyana**
62/C2 **Gwalior,** India
82/E4 **Gweru,** Zim.
45/H4 **Gyandzhe,** Azerbaijan
40/C2 **Gyor,** Hung.

H

28/B4 **Haarlem,** Neth.
57/L10 **Habikino,** Japan
57/F3 **Hachioji,** Japan
98/F5 **Hackensack,** N.J.
98/E6 **Haddonfield,** N.J.
52/E5 **Hadhramaut** (reg.), Yemen
58/C3 **Haeju,** N. Korea
29/E6 **Hagen,** Ger.
94/E4 **Hagerstown,** Md.
28/B4 **Hague, The** (cap.), Neth.
49/D3 **Haifa,** Isr.
61/F4 **Haikou,** China
61/F5 **Hainan** (isl.), China
59/L9 **Haining,** China
65/D1 **Haiphong,** Viet.
103/H2 **Haiti**
55/N3 **Hakodate,** Japan
49/E1 **Halab** (Aleppo), Syria
88/T10 **Haleakala Nat'l Pk.,** Hawaii
95/J2 **Halifax** (cap.), N.S.
26/F3 **Halle,** Ger.
67/G3 **Halmahera** (isl.), Indon.
20/E4 **Hälsingborg,** Sweden
53/G3 **Hamadan,** Iran
49/E2 **Hamāh,** Syria
57/E3 **Hamamatsu,** Japan
28/G1 **Hamburg,** Ger.
70/B4 **Hamersley** (range), Austr.
58/E2 **Hamgyong** (mts.), N. Korea
58/D3 **Hamhung,** N. Korea
71/S10 **Hamilton,** N.Z.
94/C4 **Hamilton,** Ohio
94/E3 **Hamilton,** Ont.
20/G1 **Hammerfest,** Nor.
29/E5 **Hamm,** Ger.
98/R16 **Hammond,** Ind.
97/F4 **Hammond,** La.
94/E4 **Hampton,** Va.
99/F7 **Hamtramck,** Mich.
58/D4 **Han** (riv.), S. Korea
57/F3 **Hanchiōji,** Japan
59/C3 **Handan,** China
92/C3 **Hanford,** Calif.
54/D2 **Hangayn** (mts.), Mong.
59/L9 **Hangzhou** (Hangchow), China
93/K3 **Hannibal,** Mo.
29/G4 **Hannover,** Ger.
65/D1 **Hanoi** (cap.), Viet.
95/F3 **Hanover,** N.H.
54/F5 **Hanzhong,** China
82/F4 **Harare** (cap.), Zim.
55/K2 **Harbin,** China
77/P6 **Hargeysa,** Somalia
96/D5 **Harlingen,** Texas
95/E4 **Harpers Ferry Nat'l Hist. Site,** W. Va.
99/G7 **Harper Woods,** Mich.
94/E3 **Harrisburg** (cap.), Pa.
94/E4 **Harrisonburg,** Va.
98/G5 **Harrison,** N.Y.
94/C4 **Harrodsburg,** Ky.
95/F3 **Hartford** (cap.), Conn.
99/Q16 **Harvey,** Ill.
29/H5 **Harz** (mts.), Ger.
93/H2 **Hastings,** Nebr.
97/F4 **Hattiesburg,** Miss.
103/F1 **Havana** (cap.), Cuba
92/D4 **Havasu** (lake), U.S.
95/G3 **Haverhill,** Mass.
90/F3 **Havre,** Mont.
88/U11 **Hawaii** (isl.), Hawaii
88/S10 **Hawaii** (state), U.S.
69/H2 **Hawaiian** (isls.), U.S.
88/U11 **Hawaii Volcanoes Nat'l Pk.,** Hawaii
52/E3 **Hawalli,** Kuwait
98/B3 **Hawthorne,** Calif.
86/E2 **Hay River,** N.W.T.
93/H3 **Hays,** Kans.
99/K11 **Hayward,** Calif.
99/F7 **Hazel Park,** Mich.
90/A2 **Hazleton** (mts.), Br. Col.
94/F3 **Hazleton,** Pa.
59/G6 **Hebei** (Hopei) (prov.), China
21/B2 **Hebrides, Inner** (isls.), Scot.
21/B2 **Hebrides, Outer** (isls.), Scot.
49/D4 **Hebron,** West Bank
59/D5 **Hefei,** China
57/L2 **Hegang,** China
26/E4 **Heidelberg,** Ger.
20/N7 **Hekla** (mt.), Iceland
90/F4 **Helena** (cap.), Mont.
53/H2 **Helmand** (riv.), Afghan.
20/H3 **Helsinki** (cap.), Fin.
98/G5 **Hempstead,** N.Y.
59/B4 **Henan** (Honan) (prov.) China
97/G2 **Henderson,** Ky.
92/D3 **Henderson,** Nev.
97/J2 **Henderson,** N.C.
61/G3 **Hengyang,** China
53/H2 **Herat,** Afghan.
49/D3 **Hermon** (mt.), Asia
100/C2 **Hermosillo,** Mex.
29/E5 **Herne,** Ger.
26/E3 **Hesse** (state), Ger.
97/H5 **Hialeah,** Fla.
91/K4 **Hibbing,** Minn.
97/H3 **Hickory,** N.C.
98/G5 **Hicksville,** N.Y.
57/L10 **Higashi-Osaka,** Japan
99/Q15 **Highland Park,** Ill.
99/F7 **Highland Park,** Mich.
97/H3 **High Point,** N.C.
52/C3 **Hijāz, Jabal al** (mts.), Saudi Arabia
90/C4 **Hillsboro,** Oreg.
98/F5 **Hillside,** N.J.
88/U11 **Hilo,** Hawaii
48/G6 **Himalaya** (mts.), Asia
56/D3 **Himeji,** Japan
49/E2 **Ḥimṣ,** Syria
53/J1 **Hindu Kush** (mts.), Asia
99/Q16 **Hinsdale,** Ill.
56/D3 **Hirakata,** Japan
55/N3 **Hirosaki,** Japan
56/C3 **Hiroshima,** Japan
104/C2 **Hispaniola** (isl.), W. Indies
57/G2 **Hitachi,** Japan
73/C4 **Hobart,** Austr.
93/G4 **Hobbs,** N. Mex.
98/F5 **Hoboken,** N.J.
65/D4 **Ho Chi Minh City** (Saigon), Viet.
99/P15 **Hoffman Estates,** Ill.
59/B2 **Hohhot,** China
55/N3 **Hokkaidō** (isl.), Japan
103/G1 **Holguin,** Cuba
94/C3 **Holland,** Mich.
97/H5 **Hollywood,** Fla.
49/D3 **Holon,** Isr.
95/F3 **Holyoke,** Mass.
97/H5 **Homestead,** Fla.
102/E3 **Honduras**
102/D2 **Honduras** (gulf), Cent. Amer.
61/G4 **Hong Kong**
68/E5 **Honiara** (cap.), Sol. Is.
88/T10 **Honolulu** (cap.), Hawaii
55/M5 **Honshu** (isl.), Japan
90/C4 **Hood** (mt.), Oreg.
92/D3 **Hoover** (dam), U.S.
96/E3 **Hope,** Ark.
94/E4 **Hopewell,** Va.
94/B4 **Hopkinsville,** Ky.
109/C8 **Horn** (cape), Chile
94/E3 **Hornell,** N.Y.
96/E3 **Hot Springs Nat'l Park,** Ark.
97/F4 **Houma,** La.
96/E4 **Houston,** Texas
92/E3 **Hovenweep Nat'l Mon.,** U.S.
62/E3 **Howrah,** India
27/H3 **Hradec Králové,** Czech Rep.
61/J3 **Hsinchu,** Taiwan
59/D4 **Huainan,** China
106/C6 **Huancayo,** Peru
55/H4 **Huang He** (Yellow) (riv.), China
105/B3 **Huascarán** (mt.), Peru
62/C4 **Hubli-Dharwar,** India
23/G4 **Huddersfield,** Eng.
87/H2 **Hudson** (bay), Can.
87/J2 **Hudson** (str.), Can.
94/F3 **Hudson** (riv.), U.S.
34/B4 **Huelva,** Spain
65/D2 **Hue,** Viet.
82/B4 **Huila** (plat.), Angola
23/H4 **Hull,** Eng.
94/F2 **Hull,** Que.
23/H4 **Humber** (riv.), Eng.
92/E4 **Humphreys** (peak), Ariz.
61/F2 **Hunan** (prov.), China
40/D2 **Hungary**
58/D3 **Hŭngnam,** N. Korea
55/K3 **Hunjiang,** China
94/C3 **Huntington,** Ind.
98/G5 **Huntington,** N.Y.
94/D4 **Huntington,** W. Va.
98/C3 **Huntington Beach,** Calif.
98/B3 **Huntington Park,** Calif.
97/G3 **Huntsville,** Ala.
96/E4 **Huntsville,** Texas
94/D2 **Huron** (lake), N. Amer.
91/J4 **Huron,** S. Dak.
93/H3 **Hutchinson,** Kans.
59/E5 **Huzhou,** China
98/K8 **Hyattsville,** Md.
62/C4 **Hyderabad,** India
53/J3 **Hyderabad,** Pak.

I

41/H2 **Iaşi,** Rom.
79/F5 **Ibadan,** Nigeria
106/C3 **Ibagué,** Col.
35/F3 **Ibiza** (isl.), Spain
20/N7 **Iceland**
59/B5 **Ichang** (Yichang), China
57/H7 **Ichikawa,** Japan
56/E3 **Ichinomiya,** Japan
90/E5 **Idaho** (state), U.S.
90/E5 **Idaho Falls,** Idaho
30/B2 **Ieper,** Belg.
79/G5 **Ife,** Nigeria
105/D5 **Iguazú** (falls), S. Amer.
76/D2 **Iguidi, Erg** (des.), Alg.
28/C3 **IJsselmeer** (lake), Neth.
76/F6 **Ilesha,** Nigeria
85/G4 **Iliamna** (lake), Alaska
94/B3 **Illinois** (riv.), Ill.
94/B4 **Illinois** (state), U.S.
67/F1 **Iloilo,** Phil.
79/G4 **Ilorin,** Nigeria
60/B3 **Imphal,** India
58/D4 **Inch'ŏn,** S. Korea
93/J3 **Independence,** Kans.
93/J3 **Independence,** Mo.
48/G7 **India**
94/E3 **Indiana,** Pa.
94/C3 **Indiana** (state), U.S.
99/R16 **Indiana Dunes Nat'l Lakeshore,** Ind.
94/C4 **Indianapolis** (cap.), Ind.
17/N6 **Indian Ocean**
47/Q3 **Indigirka** (riv.), Russia
92/C4 **Indio,** Calif.
65/C1 **Indochina** (reg.), Asia
66/E4 **Indonesia**
62/C3 **Indore,** India
48/F7 **Indus** (riv.), Asia
98/B3 **Inglewood,** Calif.
99/F7 **Inkster,** Mich.
33/K2 **Inn** (riv.), Europe
21/B2 **Inner Hebrides** (isls.), Scot.
54/G3 **Inner Mongolia** (reg.), China
37/H3 **Innsbruck,** Austria
60/C5 **Insein,** Burma
90/B2 **Interior** (plat.), Br. Col.
91/H3 **International Peace Garden,** N. Amer.
85/M2 **Inuvik,** N.W.T.
71/Q12 **Invercargill,** N.Z.
21/C2 **Inverness,** Scot.
21/B2 **Iona** (isl.), Scot.
39/F3 **Ionian** (sea), Eur.
39/F3 **Ionian** (isls.), Greece
93/K2 **Iowa City,** Iowa
93/J2 **Iowa** (state), U.S.
66/B3 **Ipoh,** Malaysia
25/H2 **Ipswich,** Eng.
87/K2 **Iqaluit,** N.W.T.
106/D4 **Iquitos,** Peru
39/J5 **Iráklion,** Greece
48/E6 **Iran**
101/E4 **Irapuato,** Mex.
50/E3 **Iraq**
60/B5 **Irawaddy** (riv.), Burma
49/D3 **Irbid,** Jordan
51/F2 **Irbil,** Iraq
21/A4 **Ireland**
21/B3 **Ireland, Northern,** U.K.
67/J4 **Irian Jaya** (reg.), Indon.
22/C4 **Irish** (sea), Europe
54/E1 **Irkutsk,** Russia
94/D4 **Ironton,** Ohio
60/B5 **Irrawaddy** (riv.), Burma
46/G4 **Irtysh** (riv.), Russia
98/C3 **Irvine,** Calif.
92/D3 **Irving,** Texas
98/F5 **Irvington,** N.J.
38/C2 **Ischia** (isl.), Italy
57/E3 **Ise,** Japan
32/F4 **Isère** (riv.), France
49/E1 **Iskenderun,** Turkey
64/B1 **Islamabad** (cap.), Pak.
22/D3 **Isle of Man,** U.K.
94/B1 **Isle Royale** (isl.), Mich.
94/B2 **Isle Royale Nat'l Pk.,** Mich.
98/G5 **Islip,** N.Y.
49/C4 **Ismailia,** Egypt
49/D3 **Israel**
50/B1 **Istanbul,** Turkey
18/E4 **Italy**
94/E3 **Ithaca,** N.Y.
42/J4 **Ivanovo,** Russia
78/D5 **Ivory Coast**
57/G2 **Iwaki,** Japan
68/D2 **Iwo Jima** (isl.), Japan
43/M4 **Izhevsk,** Russia
50/A2 **Izmir,** Turkey
41/J5 **Izmit,** Turkey

J

62/C3 **Jabalpur,** India
94/C3 **Jackson,** Mich.
97/F3 **Jackson** (cap.), Miss.
97/F3 **Jackson,** Tenn.
96/E3 **Jacksonville,** Ark.
97/H4 **Jacksonville,** Fla.
94/B4 **Jacksonville,** Ill.
97/J3 **Jacksonville,** N.C.
64/G4 **Jaffna,** Sri Lanka
62/C2 **Jaipur,** India
66/C5 **Jakarta** (cap.), Indon.
101/N7 **Jalapa Enriquez,** Mex.
103/G2 **Jamaica**
66/B4 **Jambi,** Indon.
87/H3 **James** (bay), Can.
94/E4 **James** (riv.), Va.
91/J4 **Jamestown,** N. Dak.
94/E3 **Jamestown,** N.Y.
64/C1 **Jammu,** India
53/K2 **Jammu & Kashmir** (state), India
62/B3 **Jamnagar,** India
62/E3 **Jamshedpur,** India
94/B3 **Janesville,** Wis.
18/C1 **Jan Mayen** (isl.), Nor.
55/M4 **Japan**
55/L4 **Japan** (sea), Asia
57/E3 **Japanese Alps** (mts.), Japan
60/D5 **Jars** (plain), Laos
69/J5 **Jarvis** (isl.), Pacific
66/C5 **Java** (isl.), Indon.
66/D5 **Java** (sea), Indon.
93/J3 **Jefferson City** (cap.), Mo.
94/C4 **Jeffersonville,** Ind.
34/B4 **Jerez de la Frontera,** Spain
49/D4 **Jericho,** West Bank
32/B2 **Jersey** (isl.), Chan. Is.
98/F5 **Jersey City,** N.J.
49/D4 **Jerusalem** (cap.), Isr.
95/N6 **Jésus** (isl.), Que.
91/H5 **Jewel Cave Nat'l Mon.,** S. Dak.
64/B2 **Jhang Sadar,** Pak.
62/C2 **Jhansi,** India
55/L2 **Jiamusi,** China
59/E5 **Jiaxing,** China
52/C4 **Jiddah,** Saudi Arabia
55/K3 **Jilin,** China
59/D3 **Jinan** (Tsinan), China
61/H2 **Jingdezhen,** China
61/H2 **Jinhua,** China
59/E2 **Jinzhou,** China
55/L2 **Jixi,** China
107/M5 **João Pessoa,** Braz.
62/B2 **Jodhpur,** India
80/D2 **Johannesburg,** S. Africa
90/C4 **John Day** (riv.), Oreg.
97/H2 **Johnson City,** Tenn.
94/E3 **Johnstown,** Pa.
66/B3 **Johor Baharu,** Malaysia
99/P16 **Joliet,** Ill.
97/F3 **Jonesboro,** Ark.
20/E4 **Jönköping,** Sweden
95/G1 **Jonquière,** Que.
93/J3 **Joplin,** Mo.
50/D4 **Jordan**
49/D4 **Jordan** (riv.), Asia
92/D4 **Joshua Tree Nat'l Mon.,** Calif.
90/B3 **Juan de Fuca** (str.), N. Amer.
105/A6 **Juan Fernández** (isls.), Chile
31/G8 **Judaea** (reg.), Asia
108/D2 **Juiz de Fora,** Braz.
64/C2 **Jullundur,** India
93/H3 **Junction City,** Kans.

108/C2 **Jundiaí**, Braz.
85/M4 **Juneau** (cap.), Alaska
36/D4 **Jungfrau** (mt.), Switz.
36/B4 **Jura** (mts.), Europe
103/K7 **Juventud** (isl.), Cuba

K

53/L1 **K2** (mt.), Asia
53/J2 **Kabul** (cap.), Afghan.
82/E3 **Kabwe**, Zambia
79/G4 **Kaduna**, Nigeria
58/D3 **Kaesŏng**, N. Korea
56/B5 **Kagoshima**, Japan
88/T10 **Kahoolawe** (isl.), Hawaii
50/D2 **Kahramanmaras**, Turkey
54/G5 **Kaifeng**, China
88/T10 **Kailua**, Hawaii
31/G5 **Kaiserslautern**, Ger.
88/T10 **Kaiwi** (chan.), Hawaii
62/D4 **Kakinada**, India
84/N2 **Kalaallit Nunaat** (Greenland)
82/D5 **Kalahari** (des.), Africa
94/C3 **Kalamazoo**, Mich.
59/C2 **Kalgan** (Zhangjiakou), China
66/D4 **Kalimantan** (reg.), Indon.
42/D5 **Kaliningrad** (Königsberg), Russia
42/H5 **Kaliningrad**, Moscow Oblast, Russia
42/H5 **Kaluga**, Russia
57/H7 **Kamakura**, Japan
47/R4 **Kamchatka** (pen.), Russia
90/C3 **Kamloops**, Br. Col.
77/M7 **Kampala** (cap.), Uganda
65/D3 **Kampuchea** (Cambodia)
82/D2 **Kananga**, Zaire
57/E2 **Kanazawa**, Japan
62/E2 **Kanchenjunga** (mt.), Asia
62/D6 **Kandy**, Sri Lanka
88/T10 **Kaneohe**, Hawaii
58/C2 **Kangnam** (mts.), N. Korea
43/K2 **Kanin** (pen.), Russia
94/C3 **Kankakee**, Ill.
97/H3 **Kannapolis**, N.C.
79/H3 **Kano**, Nigeria
62/D2 **Kānpur**, India
93/H3 **Kansas** (riv.), Kans.
92/D2 **Kansas** (state), U.S.
93/J3 **Kansas City**, Kans.
93/J3 **Kansas City**, Mo.
61/J4 **Kaohsiung**, Taiwan
82/B4 **Kaokoveld** (mts.), Namibia
78/A3 **Kaolack**, Sen.
46/G2 **Kara** (sea), Russia
45/K4 **Kara-Bogaz-Gol** (gulf), Turkmenistan
53/J4 **Karachi**, Pak.
46/H5 **Karaganda**, Kazakhstan
51/G3 **Karaj**, Iran
53/K1 **Karakoram** (mts.), Asia
54/E2 **Karakorum** (ruins), Mong.
45/L5 **Karakumy** (des.), Turkmenistan
82/E4 **Kariba** (lake), Africa
26/E4 **Karlsruhe**, Ger.
50/A3 **Kárpathos** (isl.), Greece
82/D2 **Kasai** (riv.), Zaire
51/G3 **Kashan**, Iran
47/H6 **Kashi** (Kashgar), China
29/G6 **Kassel**, Ger.
95/G2 **Katahdin** (mt.), Maine
82/D2 **Katanga** (reg.), Zaire
62/E2 **Kathmandu** (cap.), Nepal
85/G4 **Katmai Nat'l Pk.**, Alaska
27/K3 **Katowice**, Pol.
20/D4 **Kattegat** (str.), Europe
88/S10 **Kauai** (chan.), Hawaii
88/S9 **Kauai** (isl.), Hawaii
42/D5 **Kaunas**, Lithuania
57/F3 **Kawagoe**, Japan
57/F3 **Kawaguchi**, Japan
57/F3 **Kawasaki**, Japan
50/C2 **Kayseri**, Turkey
46/G5 **Kazakhstan**
43/L5 **Kazan'**, Russia
93/H2 **Kearney**, Nebr.
98/F5 **Kearny**, N.J.
40/D2 **Kecskemét**, Hun.
66/D5 **Kediri**, Indon.
61/J3 **Keelung**, Taiwan
95/F3 **Keene**, N.H.
66/B3 **Kelang**, Malaysia
90/D3 **Kelowna**, Br. Col.
90/C4 **Kelso**, Wash.
46/J4 **Kemerovo**, Russia
85/J3 **Kenai Fjords Nat'l Pk.**, Alaska
97/H5 **Kendall**, Fla.
75/L13 **Kenitra**, Mor.
95/S10 **Kenmore**, N.Y.
97/F4 **Kenner**, La.
90/D4 **Kennewick**, Wash.
99/Q14 **Kenosha**, Wis.
94/D3 **Kent**, Ohio
94/B4 **Kentucky** (lake), U.S.
94/C4 **Kentucky** (state), U.S.
74/F4 **Kenya**
77/M8 **Kenya** (Batian) (mt.), Kenya
93/K2 **Keokuk**, Iowa
64/F3 **Kerala** (state), India
44/F3 **Kerch**, Ukraine
39/F3 **Kérkira** (Corfu) (isl.), Greece
68/G7 **Kermadec** (isls.), N.Z.
51/J4 **Kerman**, Iran
92/D4 **Kerrville**, Texas
85/M4 **Ketchikan**, Alaska
94/C4 **Kettering**, Ohio
94/B2 **Keweenaw** (pen.), Mich.
94/C2 **Keweenaw** (pt.), Mich.
97/H5 **Key West**, Fla.
55/M2 **Khabarovsk**, Russia
44/F2 **Khar'kov**, Ukraine
62/E3 **Kharagpur**, India
52/B5 **Khartoum** (cap.), Sudan
44/E3 **Kherson**, Ukraine
91/K3 **Khíos** (isl.), Greece
44/C2 **Khmel'nitskiy**, Ukraine
51/G3 **Khorramabad**, Iran
51/G4 **Khorramshahr**, Iran
62/E3 **Khulna**, Bang.
53/K2 **Khyber** (pass), Asia
27/L3 **Kielce**, Pol.
26/F1 **Kiel**, Ger.
44/D2 **Kiev** (cap.), Ukraine
82/F1 **Kigali** (cap.), Rwanda
82/C2 **Kikwit**, Zaire
96/E3 **Kilgore**, Texas
82/G1 **Kilimanjaro** (mt.), Tanz.
21/B4 **Kilkenny**, Ire.
21/H7 **Killarney**, Ire.
96/D4 **Killeen**, Texas
70/D3 **Kimberley** (plat.), Austr.
80/D3 **Kimberley**, S. Africa
73/C3 **King** (isl.), Austr.
92/D4 **Kingman**, Ariz.
92/C3 **Kings Canyon Nat'l Pk.**, Calif.
97/H2 **Kingsport**, Tenn.
103/G2 **Kingston** (cap.), Jam.
94/F3 **Kingston**, N.Y.
104/F4 **Kingstown** (cap.), St. Vinc. & Grens.
96/D5 **Kingsville**, Texas
82/C1 **Kinshasa** (cap.), Zaire
97/J3 **Kinston**, N.C.
68/H5 **Kiribati**
50/C2 **Kirikkale**, Turkey
69/K4 **Kiritimati** (isl.), Kiribati
99/C2 **Kirkland**, Wash.
93/J2 **Kirksville**, Mo.
51/F3 **Kirkuk**, Iraq
45/H4 **Kirovakan**, Armenia
44/E2 **Kirovograd**, Ukraine
57/F2 **Kiryu**, Japan
77/L7 **Kisangani**, Zaire
41/J2 **Kishinev** (cap.), Moldova
56/D3 **Kishiwada**, Japan
77/M8 **Kisumu**, Kenya
56/B4 **Kitakyushu**, Japan
94/D3 **Kitchener**, Ont.
82/E3 **Kitwe**, Zambia
82/E1 **Kivu** (lake), Africa
20/E2 **Kjølen** (Kölen) (mts.), Europe
42/D5 **Klaipeda**, Lithuania
92/B2 **Klamath** (mts.), Calif., Oreg.
90/C5 **Klamath Falls**, Oreg.
85/K3 **Kluane Nat'l Pk.**, Yukon
97/H3 **Knoxville**, Tenn.
56/D3 **Kobe**, Japan
31/G3 **Koblenz**, Ger.
85/G2 **Kobuk** (riv.), Alaska
85/G2 **Kobuk Valley Nat'l Pk.**, Alaska
56/C4 **Kochi**, Japan
85/H4 **Kodiak** (isl.), Alaska
41/H2 **Kodry** (hills), Moldova
57/F3 **Kofu**, Japan
94/C3 **Kokomo**, Ind.
42/H1 **Kola** (pen.), Russia
31/F2 **Köln** (Cologne), Ger.
42/H5 **Kolomna**, Russia
68/E4 **Kolonia** (cap.), Micronesia
82/E3 **Kolwezi**, Zaire
47/R3 **Kolyma** (range), Russia
55/M1 **Komsomol'sk**, Russia
53/J1 **Kondūz**, Afghan.
50/C2 **Konya**, Turkey
90/D3 **Kootenai** (riv.), U.S.
43/P5 **Kopeysk**, Russia
58/D2 **Korea, North**
58/D4 **Korea, South**
56/A4 **Korea** (str.), Japan, S. Korea
57/G2 **Koriyama**, Japan
68/C4 **Koror** (cap.), Palau
48/R3 **Koryak** (range), Russia
73/D3 **Kosciusko** (mt.), Austr.
27/L4 **Košice**, Slovakia
50/A2 **Kos** (isl.), Greece
76/D6 **Kossou** (lake), Iv. Coast
42/J4 **Kostroma**, Russia
66/B2 **Kota Baharu**, Malaysia
62/C2 **Kota**, India
67/E2 **Kota Kinabalu**, Malaysia
62/C6 **Kotte**, Sri Lanka
85/E2 **Kotzebue** (sound), Alaska
42/J4 **Kovrov**, Russia
61/G4 **Kowloon**, Hong Kong
65/B4 **Kra** (isth.), Thai.
66/C5 **Krakatau** (isl.) Indon.
27/K3 **Kraków**, Pol.
44/F2 **Kramatorsk**, Ukraine
44/F3 **Krasnodar**, Russia
46/K4 **Krasnoyarsk**, Russia
28/D6 **Krefeld**, Ger.
44/E2 **Kremenchug**, Ukraine
20/C4 **Kristiansand**, Nor.
44/E3 **Krivoy Rog**, Ukraine
65/C3 **Krung Thep** (Bangkok), Thai.
66/B3 **Kuala Lumpur** (cap.), Malaysia
66/B2 **Kuala Terengganu**, Malaysia
66/D3 **Kuching**, Malaysia
77/K3 **Kufrah** (oasis), Libya
56/B4 **Kumamoto**, Japan
79/E5 **Kumasi**, Ghana
45/G4 **Kumayri**, Armenia
46/H6 **Kunlun** (mts.), Asia
60/D3 **Kunming**, China
58/D5 **Kunsan**, S. Korea
56/C3 **Kurashiki**, Japan
51/E2 **Kurdistan** (reg.), Asia
56/C3 **Kure**, Japan
43/Q5 **Kurgan**, Russia
47/P5 **Kuril** (isls.), Russia
62/C4 **Kurnool**, India
44/F2 **Kursk**, Russia
56/B4 **Kurume**, Japan
55/N3 **Kushiro**, Japan
85/G3 **Kuskokwim** (mts.), Alaska
85/F3 **Kuskokwim** (riv.), Alaska
43/P5 **Kustanay**, Kazakhstan
45/G4 **Kutaisi**, Georgia
62/A3 **Kutch, Rann of** (salt marsh), India
51/F4 **Kuwait**
45/J1 **Kuybyshev** (Samara), Russia
68/F4 **Kwajalein** (atoll), Marshall Is.
58/D5 **Kwangju**, S. Korea
82/C1 **Kwango** (riv.), Ang., Zaire
82/N7 **Kyoga** (lake), Uganda
58/C4 **Kyŏnggi** (bay), S. Korea
58/E5 **Kyŏngju**, S. Korea
56/D3 **Kyoto**, Japan
46/H5 **Kyrgyzstan**
56/B5 **Kyushu** (isl.), Japan
54/C1 **Kyzyl**, Russia
46/G5 **Kyzyl-Kum** (des.), Uzbekistan
46/G5 **Kzyl-Orda**, Kazakhstan

L

76/C2 **Laayoune**, W. Sahara
87/K3 **Labrador** (dist.), Newf.
87/L3 **Labrador** (sea), Can.
62/B5 **Laccadive** (Cannanore) (isls.), India
73/A3 **Lacepede** (bay), Austr.
95/S10 **Lackawanna**, N.Y.
95/G3 **Laconia**, N.H.
34/A1 **La Coruña**, Spain
94/B3 **La Crosse**, Wis.
53/L2 **Ladakh** (mts.), Asia
42/F3 **Ladoga** (lake), Russia
68/D5 **Lae**, Papua N.G.
94/C3 **Lafayette**, Ind.
96/E4 **Lafayette**, La.
79/F5 **Lagos**, Nigeria
90/D4 **La Grande**, Oreg.
97/G3 **La Grange**, Ga.
98/C3 **La Habra**, Calif.
64/C2 **Lahore**, Pak.
96/E4 **Lake Charles**, La.
86/A2 **Lake Clark Nat'l Pk.**, Alaska
99/Q15 **Lake Forest**, Ill.
92/D4 **Lake Havasu City**, Ariz.
97/H4 **Lakeland**, Fla.
90/D3 **Lake Louise**, Alta.
92/D4 **Lake Mead Nat'l Rec. Area**, U.S.
98/B3 **Lakewood**, Calif.
98/F5 **Lakewood**, N.J.
97/H5 **Lake Worth**, Fla.
34/D3 **La Mancha** (reg.), Spain
76/H8 **Lambaréné**, Gabon
98/B3 **La Mirada**, Calif.
88/T10 **Lanai** (isl.), Hawaii
92/C4 **Lancaster**, Calif.
23/F3 **Lancaster**, Eng.
94/D4 **Lancaster**, Ohio
94/E3 **Lancaster**, Pa.
24/A6 **Land's End** (prom.), Eng.
99/Q16 **Lansing**, Ill.
94/C3 **Lansing** (cap.), Mich.
61/H2 **Lanxi**, China
54/E4 **Lanzhou** (Lanchow), China
65/C2 **Laos**
106/E7 **La Paz** (cap.), Bol.
55/N2 **La Pérouse** (str.), Asia
20/F1 **Lapland** (reg.), Europe
105/D6 **La Plata**, Arg.
94/C3 **La Porte**, Ind.
47/M2 **Laptev** (sea), Russia
98/C2 **La Puente**, Calif.
90/G5 **Laramie** (mts.), U.S.
90/G5 **Laramie**, Wyo.
96/D5 **Laredo**, Texas
97/H5 **Largo**, Fla.
39/H3 **Lárisa**, Greece
92/F4 **Las Cruces**, N. Mex.
35/X16 **Las Palmas de Gran Canaria**, Spain
92/B2 **Lassen Volcanic Nat'l Pk.**, Calif.
92/C3 **Las Vegas**, Nev.
93/F4 **Las Vegas**, N. Mex.
49/D2 **Latakia**, Syria
42/E4 **Latvia**
73/C4 **Launceston**, Austr.
98/K7 **Laurel**, Md.
97/F4 **Laurel**, Miss.
94/C1 **Laurentian** (plat.), Can.
36/C5 **Lausanne**, Switz.
92/B2 **Lava Beds Nat'l Mon.**, Calif.
95/F2 **Laval**, Que.
98/C2 **La Verne**, Calif.
98/B3 **Lawndale**, Calif.
93/J3 **Lawrence**, Kans.
95/G3 **Lawrence**, Mass.
93/H4 **Lawton**, Okla.
93/J3 **Leavenworth**, Kans.
49/D3 **Lebanon**
94/E3 **Lebanon**, Pa.
23/G4 **Leeds**, Eng.
104/F3 **Leeward** (isls.), W. Indies
32/D2 **Le Havre**, France
25/E1 **Leicester**, Eng.
28/B4 **Leiden**, Neth.
22/B5 **Leinster** (reg.), Ire.
26/G3 **Leipzig**, Ger.
61/F4 **Leizhou** (pen.), China
32/D2 **Le Mans**, France
47/N3 **Lena** (riv.), Russia
42/F4 **Leningrad** (St. Petersburg), Russia
46/J4 **Leninsk-Kuznetskiy**, Russia
101/E4 **León**, Mex.
102/E3 **León**, Nic.
34/C1 **León**, Spain
37/E5 **Lepontine Alps** (mts.), Italy, Switz.
35/F2 **Lérida**, Spain
60/D2 **Leshan**, China
80/D3 **Lesotho**
104/E3 **Lesser Antilles** (isls.), W. Indies
90/E2 **Lesser Slave** (lake), Alta.
39/J3 **Lésvos** (isl.), Greece
98/G5 **Levittown**, N.Y.
90/E3 **Lewis** (range), Mont.
21/B1 **Lewis** (isl.), Scot.
21/B1 **Lewis, Butt of** (prom.), Scot.
90/D4 **Lewiston**, Idaho
95/G2 **Lewiston**, Maine
94/C4 **Lexington**, Ky.
97/H3 **Lexington**, N.C.
60/A2 **Lhasa**, China
35/G2 **L'Hospitalet**, Spain
59/D4 **Lianyungang**, China
59/E2 **Liaodong** (gulf), China
59/E3 **Liaodong** (pen.), China
59/F2 **Liaoyuan**, China
93/G3 **Liberal**, Kans.
78/C5 **Liberia**
76/G7 **Libreville** (cap.), Gabon
77/J2 **Libya**
77/K2 **Libyan** (des.), Africa
77/K1 **Libyan** (plat.), Egypt, Libya
37/F3 **Liechtenstein**
31/E2 **Liège**, Belg.
33/H5 **Ligurian** (sea), Italy
88/S10 **Lihue**, Hawaii
30/C2 **Lille**, France
82/F3 **Lilongwe** (cap.), Malawi
106/C6 **Lima** (cap.), Peru
94/C3 **Lima**, Ohio
49/C2 **Limassol**, Cyprus
21/A4 **Limerick**, Ire.
32/D4 **Limoges**, France
82/F5 **Limpopo** (riv.), Africa
61/H3 **Linchuan**, China
94/B3 **Lincoln**, Ill.
93/H2 **Lincoln** (cap.), Nebr.
99/F7 **Lincoln Park**, Mich.
98/G5 **Lindenhurst**, N.Y.
98/F5 **Linden**, N.J.
69/K4 **Line** (isls.), Kiribati
20/E4 **Linköping**, Sweden
33/L2 **Linz**, Austria
35/H1 **Lions** (gulf), France
38/D3 **Lipari** (isls.), Italy
44/F1 **Lipetsk**, Russia
28/D5 **Lippe** (riv.), Ger.
34/A3 **Lisbon** (cap.), Port.
42/D5 **Lithuania**
90/G4 **Little Big Horn Nat'l Mon.**, Mont.
103/F2 **Little Cayman** (isl.), Cayman Is.
92/E4 **Little Colorado** (riv.), U.S.
85/E2 **Little Diomede** (isl.), Alaska
93/J4 **Little Rock** (cap.), Ark.
61/F3 **Liuzhou**, China
99/L11 **Livermore**, Calif.
23/F5 **Liverpool**, Eng.
23/E5 **Liverpool** (bay), Eng.
98/F5 **Livingston**, N.J.
90/E3 **Livingstone** (range), Alb.
82/E4 **Livingstone**, Zambia
99/F7 **Livonia**, Mich.
33/J5 **Livorno** (Leghorn), Italy
40/B2 **Ljubljana** (cap.), Slovenia
96/C3 **Llano Estacado** (plain), U.S.
109/C1 **Llullaillaco** (vol.), Chile
94/E3 **Lockport**, N.Y.
99/M10 **Lodi**, Calif.
49/F8 **Lod** (Lydda), Isr.
27/K3 **Łódź**, Pol.
20/D2 **Lofoten** (isls.), Nor.
85/K3 **Logan** (mt.), Yukon
94/C3 **Logansport**, Ind.
92/E2 **Logan**, Utah
32/C3 **Loire** (riv.), France
76/C6 **Loma** (mts.), S. Leone
109/E3 **Lomas de Zamora**, Arg.
99/P16 **Lombard**, Ill.
33/J4 **Lombardy** (reg.), Italy
79/F5 **Lomé** (cap.), Togo
21/C2 **Lomond** (lake), Scot.
92/B4 **Lompoc**, Calif.
22/A2 **Londonderry**, N. Ire.
25/F3 **London** (cap.), U.K.
94/D3 **London**, Ont.
108/B2 **Londrina**, Braz.
104/C2 **Long** (isl.), Bah.
98/G5 **Long** (isl.), N.Y.
98/B3 **Long Beach**, Calif.
98/G5 **Long Beach**, N.Y.
98/G5 **Long Branch**, N.J.
95/G2 **Longfellow** (mts.), Maine
98/G5 **Long Island** (sound), U.S.
93/F2 **Longmont**, Colo.
95/K2 **Long Range** (mts.), Newf.
96/E3 **Longview**, Texas
90/C4 **Longview**, Wash.
47/R4 **Lopatka** (cape), Russia
54/C3 **Lop Nur** (Lop Nor) (dry lake), China
94/D3 **Lorain**, Ohio
71/K6 **Lord Howe** (isl.), Austr.
31/E5 **Lorraine** (reg.), Fr.
93/F4 **Los Alamos**, N. Mex.
99/K12 **Los Altos**, Calif.
98/B2 **Los Angeles**, Calif.
65/C2 **Louangphrabang**, Laos
96/E4 **Louisiana** (state), U.S.
94/C4 **Louisville**, Ky.
32/C5 **Lourdes**, France
93/F2 **Loveland**, Colo.
95/G3 **Lowell**, Mass.
46/K3 **Lower Tunguska** (riv.), Russia
69/V12 **Loyalty** (isls.), New Caledonia
82/E1 **Lualaba** (riv.), Zaire
82/B2 **Luanda** (cap.), Angola
82/F3 **Luangwa** (riv.), Moz., Zambia
82/E3 **Luanshya**, Zambia
96/C3 **Lubbock**, Texas
26/F2 **Lübeck**, Ger.
27/M3 **Lublin**, Pol.
82/E3 **Lubumbashi**, Zaire
37/E3 **Lucerne** (lake), Switz.
37/E3 **Lucerne** (Luzern), Switz.
62/D2 **Lucknow**, India
58/A3 **Lüda** (Dalian), China
64/C2 **Ludhiana**, India
26/E4 **Ludwigshafen**, Ger.
96/E4 **Lufkin**, Texas
44/F2 **Lugansk**, Ukraine
82/G3 **Lugenda** (riv.), Moz.
97/J3 **Lumberton**, N.C.
61/F3 **Luoyang**, China
82/G3 **Lúrio** (riv.), Moz.
82/E4 **Lusaka** (cap.), Zambia
25/F3 **Luton**, Eng.
44/C2 **Lutsk**, Ukraine
31/E4 **Luxembourg**
31/F4 **Luxembourg** (cap.), Lux.
52/B3 **Luxor**, Egypt
61/H5 **Luzon** (isl.), Phil.
44/C2 **Lviv** (L'vov), Ukraine
24/C5 **Lyme** (bay), Eng.
98/G5 **Lynbrook**, N.Y.
97/J2 **Lynchburg**, Va.
95/G3 **Lynn**, Mass.
98/B3 **Lynwood**, Calif.
36/A6 **Lyon**, France
44/F1 **Lyubertsy**, Russia

M

20/H1 **Maanselkä** (mts.), Fin.
26/D3 **Maas** (riv.), Neth.
31/E2 **Maastricht**, Neth.
107/H3 **Macapa**, Braz.
61/G4 **Macau**
70/E4 **Macdonnell** (ranges), Austr.
39/G2 **Macedonia**
107/L5 **Maceió**, Braz.
57/H7 **Machida**, Japan
85/N2 **Mackenzie** (riv.), N.W.T.
94/B3 **Macomb**, Ill.
97/H3 **Macon**, Ga.
73/C1 **Macquarie** (riv.), Austr.
49/D4 **Ma'daba**, Jordan
81/H8 **Madagascar**
106/F5 **Madeira** (riv.), Braz.
35/U14 **Madeira** (isl.), Port.
94/B3 **Madison** (cap.), Wis.
99/F6 **Madison Heights**, Mich.
66/D5 **Madiun**, Indon.
62/D5 **Madras**, India

100/D3 Madre Occidental, Sierra (range), Mex.
101/F4 Madre Oriental, Sierra (range), Mex.
34/D2 Madrid (cap.), Spain
64/G4 Madurai, India
57/F2 Maebashi, Japan
47/R4 Magadan, Russia
95/J2 Magdalen (isls.), Que.
106/D3 Magdalena (riv.), Col.
26/F2 Magdeburg, Ger.
109/B7 Magellan (str.), S. Amer.
37/E6 Maggiore (lake), Europe
43/N5 Magnitogorsk, Russia
76/H5 Maiduguri, Nigeria
26/E4 Main (riv.), Ger.
95/G3 Maine (gulf), U.S.
95/G2 Maine (state), U.S.
31/H3 Mainz, Ger.
35/G3 Majorca (isl.), Spain
68/G4 Majuro (atoll), Marshall Is.
67/E4 Makassar (str.), Indon.
44/F3 Makeyevka, Ukraine
45/H4 Makhachkala, Russia
62/B5 Malabar (coast), India
76/G7 Malabo (cap.), Equat. Guin.
65/B5 Malacca (str.), Asia
34/C4 Málaga, Spain
66/D5 Malang, Indon.
82/C2 Malange, Angola
50/D2 Malatya, Turkey
82/F3 Malawi
47/B2 Malay (pen.), Asia
66/B3 Malaya (reg.), Malaysia
47/C2 Malaysia
48/G9 Maldives
48/G9 Male (cap.), Maldives
62/B3 Malegaon, India
76/E4 Mali
31/F3 Malmédy, Belg.
20/E5 Malmö, Sweden
38/D5 Malta
98/G5 Mamaroneck, N.Y.
94/C4 Mammoth Cave Nat'l Pk., Ky.
67/F3 Manado, Indon.
102/E3 Managua (cap.), Nic.
52/F3 Manama (cap.), Bahrain
94/E4 Manassas, Va.
106/F4 Manaus, Braz.
23/F5 Manchester, Eng.
95/G3 Manchester, N.H.
55/J3 Manchuria (reg.), China
60/C4 Mandalay, Burma
91/H4 Mandan, N. Dak.
77/P5 Mandeb, Bab el (str.)
62/B5 Mangalore, India
93/H3 Manhattan, Kans.
98/B3 Manhattan Beach, Calif.
48/M8 Manila (cap.), Phil.
50/A2 Manisa, Turkey
22/D3 Man, Isle of (isl.)
86/F3 Manitoba (prov.), Can.
94/D2 Manitoulin (isl.), Ont.
94/C2 Manitowoc, Wis.
106/C2 Manizales, Col.
91/K5 Mankato, Minn.
62/C6 Mannar (gulf), India, Sri Lanka
26/E4 Mannheim, Ger.
94/D3 Mansfield, Ohio
33/J4 Mantova, Italy
71/R10 Manukau, N.Z.
98/F5 Maplewood, N.J.
81/F2 Maputo (cap.), Moz.
106/D1 Maracaibo, Ven.
106/E1 Maracay, Ven.
109/E4 Mar del Plata, Arg.
104/E5 Margarita (isl.), Ven.
103/F1 Marianao, Cuba
40/B2 Maribor, Slovenia
83/T Marie Byrd Land (reg.), Antarc.
97/G3 Marietta, Ga.
94/C3 Marion, Ind.
94/D3 Marion, Ohio
33/G4 Maritime Alps (mts.), Europe
44/F3 Mariupol', Ukraine
94/E3 Markham, Ont.
50/B1 Marmara (sea), Turkey
32/E2 Marne (riv.), France
69/M5 Marquesas (isls.), Fr. Poly.
94/C2 Marquette, Mich.
76/D1 Marrakech, Mor.
32/F5 Marseille, France
96/E3 Marshall, Texas
68/G3 Marshall Islands
93/J2 Marshalltown, Iowa
95/G3 Martha's Vineyard (isl.), Mass.
104/F4 Martinique
94/E4 Maryland (state), U.S.
95/L2 Marystown, Newf.
82/G1 Masai Steppe (grsld.), Tanz.
58/E5 Masan, S. Korea
67/F1 Masbate (isl.), Phil.
80/D3 Maseru (cap.), Lesotho
53/G1 Mashhad, Iran
93/J2 Mason City, Iowa
95/F3 Massachusetts (state), U.S.
98/G5 Massapequa, N.Y.
32/E4 Massif Central (plat.), Fr.
94/D3 Massillon, Ohio
82/B2 Matadi, Zaire
96/D4 Matagorda (isl.), Texas
101/F3 Matamoros, Mex.
95/H1 Matane, Que.
68/H6 Mata Utu (cap.), Wallis & Futuna
107/G6 Mato Grosso (plat.), Braz.
57/H7 Matsudo, Japan
57/E2 Matsumoto, Japan
56/C4 Matsuyama, Japan
94/B4 Mattoon, Ill.
106/F2 Maturín, Ven.
88/T10 Maui (isl.), Hawaii
88/U11 Mauna Kea (mt.), Hawaii
88/U11 Mauna Loa (mt.), Hawaii
76/C4 Mauritania
81/S15 Mauritius
95/F4 May (cape), N.J.
85/L3 Mayo, Yukon
81/H6 Mayotte
99/Q16 Maywood, Ill.
53/J1 Mazar-i-Sharif, Afghan.
100/D4 Mazatlán, Mex.
27/L2 Mazury (reg.), Pol.
81/E2 Mbabane (cap.), Swaziland
77/J7 Mbandaka, Zaire
82/F2 Mbeya, Tanz.
82/D2 Mbuji-Mayi, Zaire
93/J4 McAlester, Okla.
96/D5 McAllen, Texas
17/N8 McDonald (isls.), Austr.
94/E3 McKeesport, Pa.
85/H3 McKinley (mt.), Alaska
86/F1 M'Clintock (chan.), N.W.T.
87/R7 M'Clure (str.), N.W.T.
92/D3 Mead (lake), U.S.
52/C4 Mecca, Saudi Arabia
26/F2 Mecklenburg-Western Pomerania (state), Ger.
66/A3 Medan, Indon.
106/C2 Medellín, Col.
90/C5 Medford, Oreg.
92/F2 Medicine Bow (range), Wyo.
90/F3 Medicine Hat, Alta.
52/C4 Medina, Saudi Arabia
17/K4 Mediterranean (sea)
62/C2 Meerut, India
49/G6 Megiddo, Isr.
75/M14 Meknès, Mor.
65/D4 Mekong (riv.), Asia
66/B3 Melaka (Malacca), Malaysia
68/E5 Melanesia (reg.), Pacific
73/C3 Melbourne, Austr.
97/H4 Melbourne, Fla.
44/E3 Melitopol, Ukraine
70/E2 Melville (isl.), Austr.
87/R7 Melville (isl.), N.W.T.
87/H2 Melville (pen.), N.W.T.
97/F3 Memphis, Tenn.
88/B3 Mendocino (cape), Calif.
109/C3 Mendoza, Arg.
99/K12 Menlo Park, Calif.
94/B3 Menominee Falls, Wis.
94/D3 Mentor, Ohio
92/B3 Merced, Calif.
99/C2 Mercer Island, Wash.
65/B4 Mergui (arch.), Burma
101/H4 Mérida, Mex.
97/F3 Meridian, Miss.
109/E3 Merlo, Arg.
52/B5 Meroe (ruins), Sudan
98/G5 Merrick, N.Y.
23/F5 Mersey (riv.), Eng.
49/D1 Mersin, Turkey
92/E4 Mesa, Ariz.
92/E3 Mesa Verde Nat'l Pk., Colo.
51/E3 Mesopotamia (reg.), Iraq
96/D3 Mesquite, Texas
38/D3 Messina, Italy
33/K4 Mestre, Italy
97/F4 Metairie, La.
31/F5 Metz, France
32/F1 Meuse (riv.), Europe
84/G7 Mexico
84/H7 Mexico (gulf), N. Amer.
101/K7 Mexico City (cap.), Mex.
97/H5 Miami, Fla.
97/H5 Miami Beach, Fla.
60/E2 Mianyang, China
61/E2 Mianyang, China
43/P5 Miass, Russia
94/C2 Michigan (lake), U.S.
94/C2 Michigan (state), U.S.
94/C3 Michigan City, Ind.
94/C2 Michipicoten (isl.), Ont.
68/E3 Micronesia (reg.), Pacific
95/F3 Middlebury, Vt.
23/G2 Middlesbrough, Eng.
98/F5 Middletown, N.J.
94/C3 Midland, Mich.
94/E2 Midland, Ont.
96/C4 Midland, Texas
68/H2 Midway Islands
93/H4 Midwest City, Okla.
39/J4 Mikonos (isl.), Greece
33/H4 Milan, Italy
98/G4 Milford, Conn.
88/U13 Mililani Town, Hawaii
98/F5 Millburn, N.J.
91/K4 Mille Lacs (lake), Minn.
99/L12 Milpitas, Calif.
99/Q13 Milwaukee, Wis.
21/C1 Minch, The (sound), Scot.
67/F2 Mindanao (isl.), Phil.
67/F1 Mindoro (isl.), Phil.
98/G5 Mineola, N.Y.
91/K4 Minneapolis, Minn.
89/K4 Minnesota (state), U.S.
35/H2 Minorca (Menorca) (isl.), Sp.
34/A1 Miño (riv.), Spain
91/H3 Minot, N. Dak.
44/C1 Minsk (cap.), Belarus
39/H4 Mirtóön (sea), Greece
94/C3 Mishawaka, Ind.
40/E1 Miskolc, Hung.
76/J1 Mişrātah, Libya
96/D5 Mission, Texas
92/C4 Mission Viejo, Calif.
97/F4 Mississippi (riv.), U.S.
97/F3 Mississippi (state), U.S.
90/E4 Missoula, Mont.
93/J3 Missouri (riv.), U.S.
93/J3 Missouri (state), U.S.
106/D7 Misti, El (mt.), Peru
102/B2 Mitla (ruin), Mex.
57/G2 Mito, Japan
82/E2 Mitumba (mts.), Zaire
56/B5 Miyazaki, Japan
97/F4 Mobile, Ala.
33/J4 Modena, Italy
92/B3 Modesto, Calif.
77/Q7 Mogadishu (cap.), Somalia
44/D1 Mogilev, Belarus
92/C4 Mojave (des.), Calif.
58/D5 Mokp'o, S. Korea
94/B3 Moline, Ill.
88/T10 Molokai (isl.), Hawaii
67/G3 Moluccas (isls.), Indon.
82/G1 Mombasa, Kenya
104/D3 Mona (passage), W. Indies
33/G5 Monaco
90/D3 Monashee (mts.), Br. Col.
31/F1 Monchengladbach, Ger.
95/H2 Moncton, N. Br.
54/D2 Mongolia
96/E3 Monroe, La.
94/D3 Monroe, Mich.
98/C2 Monrovia, Calif.
78/C5 Monrovia (cap.), Liberia
30/C3 Mons, Belg.
90/F4 Montana (state), U.S.
98/F5 Montclair, N.J.
98/B2 Montebello, Calif.
38/B1 Montecristo (isl.), Italy
40/D4 Montenegro (rep.), Yugo.
92/B3 Monterey, Calif.
101/E3 Monterrey, Mex.
98/B2 Monterey Park, Calif.
109/E3 Montevideo (cap.), Urug.
97/G3 Montgomery (cap.), Ala.
94/F2 Mont-Laurier, Que.
95/G2 Montmagny, Que.
32/E5 Montpellier, France
95/F2 Montpelier (cap.), Vt.
94/F2 Montréal, Que.
95/N6 Mont-Royal, Que.
104/F3 Montserrat
33/H4 Monza, Italy
69/K6 Moorea (isl.), Fr. Poly.
93/H4 Moore, Okla.
91/J4 Moorhead, Minn.
95/G2 Moosehead (lake), Maine
90/G3 Moose Jaw, Sask.
62/C1 Moradabad, India
27/J4 Morava (riv.), Europe
39/G1 Morava (riv.), Yugo.
27/J4 Moravia (reg.), Czech Rep.
21/D2 Moray (firth), Scot.
101/E5 Morelia, Mex.
92/C4 Moreno Valley, Calif.
97/F4 Morgan City, La.
94/E4 Morgantown, W. Va.
55/N4 Morioka, Japan
76/C1 Morocco
67/F2 Moro (gulf), Phil.
109/E3 Morón, Arg.
81/G5 Moroni (cap.), Comoros
98/F5 Morristown, N.J.
97/H2 Morristown, Tenn.
90/D4 Moscow, Idaho
42/H5 Moscow (cap.), Russia
31/G3 Mosel (riv.), Ger.
33/G2 Moselle (riv.), France
90/D4 Moses Lake, Wash.
103/E4 Mosquito Coast (reg.), Nic.
103/F4 Mosquitos (gulf), Pan.
97/F4 Moss Point, Miss.
51/E2 Mosul, Iraq
60/C5 Moulmein, Burma
99/K12 Mountain View, Calif.
99/C2 Mountlake Terrace, Wash.
95/L2 Mount Pearl, Newf.
99/Q15 Mount Prospect, Ill.
90/C4 Mount Rainier Nat'l Pk., Wash.
93/G2 Mount Rushmore Nat'l Mem., S. Dak.
94/B4 Mount Vernon, Ill.
98/G5 Mount Vernon, N.Y.
94/D3 Mount Vernon, Ohio
90/C3 Mount Vernon, Wash.
82/G4 Mozambique
74/G6 Mozambique (chan.), Africa
82/F3 Muchinga (mts.), Zambia
55/K3 Mudanjiang, China
82/E3 Mufulira, Zambia
99/J11 Muir Woods Nat'l Mon., Calif.
34/D4 Mulhacén (mt.), Spain
36/D2 Mülheim, Ger.
36/D2 Mulhouse, France
64/A2 Multan, Pak.
94/C3 Muncie, Ind.
55/K3 Mundanjiang, China
99/P15 Mundelein, Ill.
37/H1 Munich (München), Ger.
29/E5 Münster, Ger.
99/Q16 Munster, Ind.
35/E4 Murcia, Spain
41/G2 Mureş (riv.), Rom.
97/G3 Murfreesboro, Tenn.
42/G1 Murmansk, Russia
33/L3 Mur (Mura) (riv.), Europe
73/A2 Murray (riv.), Austr.
73/C2 Murrumbidgee (riv.), Austr.
51/H5 Musandam, Ras (cape), Oman
53/G4 Muscat (cap.), Oman
70/E5 Musgrave (ranges), Austr.
94/C3 Muskegon, Mich.
93/J4 Muskogee, Okla.
82/F4 Mutare, Zim.
82/F1 Mwanza, Tanz.
82/E2 Mweru (lake), Africa
97/J3 Myrtle Beach, S.C.
62/C5 Mysore, India

N

43/M5 Naberezhnye Chelny, Russia
49/D3 Nabulus, West Bank
96/E4 Nacogdoches, Texas
63/F2 Nagaland (state), India
57/F2 Nagano, Japan
57/F2 Nagaoka, Japan
56/A4 Nagasaki, Japan
64/F4 Nagercoil, India
57/E3 Nagoya, Japan
62/C3 Nagpur, India
68/B2 Naha, Japan
77/M8 Nairobi (cap.), Kenya
52/D3 Najd (reg.), Saudi Arabia
45/G4 Nalchik, Russia
46/H5 Namangan, Uzbekistan
63/J3 Nam Dinh, Viet.
82/B5 Namib (des.), Namibia
82/C5 Namibia
90/D5 Nampa, Idaho
58/C3 Namp'o, N. Korea
90/C3 Nanaimo, Br. Col.
61/G2 Nanchang, China
60/E2 Nanchong, China
31/F6 Nancy, France
53/K1 Nanga Parbat (mt.), Pak.
59/D4 Nanjing (Nanking), China
61/F4 Nanning, China
32/C3 Nantes, France
59/E4 Nantong, China
95/G3 Nantucket (isl.), Mass.
99/K10 Napa, Calif.
99/P16 Naperville, Ill.
97/H5 Naples, Fla.
38/D2 Naples, Italy
56/D3 Nara, Japan
62/C3 Narmada (riv.), India
95/G3 Nashua, N.H.
97/G2 Nashville (cap.), Tenn.
62/B4 Nasik, India
104/B1 Nassau (cap.), Bah.
106/L5 Natal, Braz.
97/F4 Natchez, Miss.
96/E4 Natchitoches, La.
92/C4 National City, Calif.
92/E3 Natural Bridges Nat'l Mon., Utah
100/F5 Naucalpan, Mex.
68/F5 Nauru
92/E3 Navajo Nat'l Mon., Ariz.
47/T3 Navarin (cape), Russia
34/D1 Navarre (reg.), Spain
39/J4 Náxos (isl.), Greece
49/D3 Nazareth, Isr.
76/J5 N'Djamena (cap.), Chad
82/E3 Ndola, Zambia
22/B2 Neagh (lake), N. Ire.
93/G2 Nebraska (state), U.S.
26/E4 Neckar (riv.), Ger.
94/B2 Neenah, Wis.
50/D4 Negev (reg.), Isr.
109/D5 Negro (riv.), Arg.
67/F2 Negros (isl.), Phil.
54/G3 Nei Monggol (plat.), China
106/C3 Neiva, Col.
90/D3 Nelson, Br. Col.
86/G3 Nelson (riv.), Man.
62/D2 Nepal
98/F5 Neptune City, N.J.
21/C2 Ness (lake), Scot.
26/C3 Netherlands
104/D5 Netherlands Antilles
101/N10 Netzahualcóycotl, Mex.
34/D4 Nevada, Sierra (mts.), Spain
92/C3 Nevada, Sierra (mts.), U.S.
92/C3 Nevada (state), U.S.
104/F3 Nevis (isl.), St. Kitts & Nevis
94/C4 New Albany, Ind.
99/K11 Newark, Calif.
98/F5 Newark, N.J.
94/D3 Newark, Ohio
95/G3 New Bedford, Mass.
99/P14 New Berlin, Wis.
97/J3 New Bern, N.C.
96/D4 New Braunfels, Texas
95/F3 New Britain, Conn.
68/D5 New Britain (isl.), Papua N.G.
95/H2 New Brunswick (prov.), Can.
98/F5 New Brunswick, N.J.
68/F6 New Caledonia
98/G4 New Canaan, Conn.
73/D2 Newcastle, Austr.
94/C4 New Castle, Ind.
95/H2 Newcastle, N. Br.
94/D3 New Castle, Pa.
23/G2 Newcastle upon Tyne, Eng.
98/G4 New City, N.Y.
62/C2 New Delhi (cap.), India
87/K3 Newfoundland (prov.), Can.
95/L1 Newfoundland (isl.), Newf.
68/E5 New Georgia (isl.), Sol. Is.
95/J2 New Glasgow, N.S.
67/J4 New Guinea (isl.), Pacific
95/G3 New Hampshire (state), U.S.
68/D5 New Hanover (isl.), Papua N.G.
95/F3 New Haven, Conn.
96/F4 New Iberia, La.
68/E5 New Ireland (isl.), Papua N.G.
94/F3 New Jersey (state), U.S.
95/F3 New London, Conn.
94/E2 Newmarket, Ont.
92/F4 New Mexico (state), U.S.
97/F4 New Orleans, La.
94/C4 Newport, Ky.
95/G3 Newport, R.I.
98/C3 Newport Beach, Calif.
94/E4 Newport News, Va.
104/B1 New Providence (isl.), Bah.
98/G5 New Rochelle, N.Y.
47/P2 New Siberian (isls.), Russia
73/C1 New South Wales (state), Austr.
93/H3 Newton, Kans.
95/G3 Newton, Mass.
91/K4 New Ulm, Minn.
90/C3 New Westminster, Br. Col.
98/G5 New York, N.Y.
94/F3 New York (state), U.S.
71/Q10 New Zealand
57/L10 Neyagawa, Japan
65/E3 Nha Trang, Viet.
94/E3 Niagara Falls, N.Y.
94/E3 Niagara Falls, Ont.
95/R9 Niagara (riv.), N. Amer.
79/F3 Niamey (cap.), Niger
66/A3 Nias (isl.), Indon.
103/E3 Nicaragua
35/G5 Nice, France
63/F6 Nicobar (isls.), India
49/C2 Nicosia (cap.), Cyprus
76/G4 Niger
76/G6 Nigeria
79/G5 Niger (riv.), Africa
57/F2 Niigata, Japan
88/R10 Niihau (isl.), Hawaii
28/C5 Nijmegen, Neth.
44/D3 Nikolayev, Ukraine
77/M2 Nile (riv.), Africa
99/Q15 Niles, Ill.
94/D3 Niles, Ohio
32/F5 Nimes, France
61/J2 Ningbo (Ningpo), China
86/F3 Nipawin, Sask.
94/B1 Nipigon (lake), Ont.
94/E2 Nipissing (lake), Ont.
57/L10 Nishinomiya, Japan
40/E4 Niš, Yugo.
108/D2 Niteroi, Braz.
69/J7 Niue
43/K4 Nizhniy Novgorod, Russia
43/N4 Nizhniy Tagil, Russia
76/G7 N'Kongsamba, Cameroon
92/E5 Nogales, Ariz.
85/E3 Nome, Alaska
20/H1 Nordkapp (cape), Nor.
71/M5 Norfolk I. (terr.), Austr.
93/H2 Norfolk, Nebr.
94/E4 Norfolk, Va.
46/J3 Noril'sk, Russia
94/B3 Normal, Ill.
93/H4 Norman, Okla.
86/D2 Norman Wells, N.W.T.
98/E5 Norristown, Pa.
20/F4 Norrköping, Sweden
18/D3 North (sea), Europe
71/R10 North (isl.), N.Z.
84/* North America

25/F2 **Northampton**, Eng.
95/F3 **Northampton**, Mass.
90/F2 **North Battleford**, Sask.
94/F2 **North Bay**, Ont.
98/F5 **North Bergen**, N.J.
99/Q15 **Northbrook**, Ill.
98/F5 **North Brunswick**, N.J.
97/H3 **North Carolina** (state), U.S.
90/C3 **North Cascades Nat'l Pk.**, Wash.
97/J3 **North Charleston**, S.C.
99/Q15 **North Chicago**, Ill.
91/H4 **North Dakota** (state), U.S.
21/B3 **Northern Ireland**, U.K.
70/E3 **Northern Territory**, Austr.
91/K4 **Northfield**, Minn.
26/E1 **North Frisian** (isls.), Europe
99/M9 **North Highlands**, Calif.
58/D2 **North Korea**
92/D3 **North Las Vegas**, Nev.
93/J4 **North Little Rock**, Ark.
84/G2 **North Magnetic Pole**, N.W.T.
98/F5 **North Plainfield**, N.J.
93/G2 **North Platte**, Nebr.
93/G2 **North Platte** (riv.), U.S.
97/G3 **Northport**, Ala.
90/F2 **North Saskatchewan** (riv.), Can.
95/S9 **North Tonawanda**, N.Y.
95/J2 **Northumberland** (str.), Can.
86/D4 **North Vancouver**, Br. Col.
70/A4 **North West** (cape), Austr.
86/E2 **Northwest Territories**, Can.
94/C3 **Norton Shores**, Mich.
85/E3 **Norton** (sound), Alaska
98/B3 **Norwalk**, Calif.
98/G4 **Norwalk**, Conn.
20/C3 **Norway**
18/C 2 **Norwegian** (sea), Europe
25/H1 **Norwich**, Eng.
95/G2 **Notre Dame** (mts.), Que.
23/G6 **Nottingham**, Eng.
78/A2 **Nouakchott** (cap.), Mauritania
69/V13 **Nouméa** (cap.), New Caledonia
108/D2 **Nova Iguaçu**, Braz.
95/J2 **Nova Scotia** (prov.), Can.
99/J10 **Novato**, Calif.
46/E2 **Novaya Zemlya** (isls.), Russia
42/F4 **Novgorod**, Russia
99/F7 **Novi**, Mich.
40/D3 **Novi Sad**, Yugo.
44/G3 **Novocherkassk**, Russia
46/J4 **Novokuznetsk**, Russia
44/F1 **Novomoskovsk**, Russia
44/F3 **Novorossiysk**, Russia
46/J4 **Novosibirsk**, Russia
52/B4 **Nubian** (des.), Sudan
96/D4 **Nueces** (riv.), Texas
69/H7 **Nuku'alofa** (cap.), Tonga
70/D6 **Nullarbor** (plain), Austr.
57/F3 **Numazu**, Japan
85/E4 **Nunivak** (isl.), Alaska
26/F4 **Nürnberg**, Ger.
98/F5 **Nutley**, N.J.
84/M3 **Nuuk** (cap.), Greenl.
82/F3 **Nyasa** (lake), Africa
40/E2 **Nyíregyháza**, Hung.

O

91/H4 **Oahe** (lake), U.S.
88/S10 **Oahu** (isl.), Hawaii
99/Q14 **Oak Creek**, Wis.
99/Q16 **Oak Forest**, Ill.
99/K11 **Oakland**, Calif.
99/Q16 **Oak Lawn**, Ill.
99/Q16 **Oak Park**, Ill.
99/F7 **Oak Park**, Mich.
97/G3 **Oak Ridge**, Tenn.
95/Q9 **Oakville**, Ont.
102/B2 **Oaxaca de Juárez**, Mex.
28/D6 **Oberhausen**, Ger.
55/N3 **Obihiro**, Japan
46/G3 **Ob'** (riv.), Russia
97/H4 **Ocala**, Fla.
92/C4 **Oceanside**, Calif.
98/G5 **Oceanside**, N.Y.
20/D5 **Odense**, Den.
27/H2 **Oder** (Odra) (riv.), Europe
96/C4 **Odessa**, Texas
44/D3 **Odessa**, Ukraine
49/G4 **Ogaden** (reg.), Eth.
79/G4 **Ogbomosho**, Nigeria
92/E2 **Ogden**, Utah
94/B4 **Ohio** (riv.), U.S.
94/B4 **Ohio** (state), U.S.
40/E5 **Ohrid** (lake), Europe
30/B5 **Oise** (riv.), France
56/B4 **Oita**, Japan
109/C2 **Ojos del Salado** (mt.), S. Amer.
56/C3 **Okayama**, Japan
57/E3 **Okazaki**, Japan
97/H5 **Okeechobee** (lake), Fla.
47/Q4 **Okhotsk** (sea), Russia
48/M7 **Okinawa** (isl.), Japan
93/H4 **Oklahoma City** (cap.), Okla.
93/H4 **Oklahoma** (state), U.S.
93/J4 **Okmulgee**, Okla.
20/F4 **Öland** (isl.), Sweden
93/J3 **Olathe**, Kans.
98/F5 **Old Bridge**, N.J.
29/F2 **Oldenburg**, Ger.
94/E3 **Olean**, N.Y.
107/M5 **Olinda**, Braz.
27/L2 **Olsztyn**, Pol.
99/B3 **Olympia** (cap.), Wash.
90/C4 **Olympic** (mts.), Wash.
90/B4 **Olympic Nat'l Pk.**, Wash.
39/H2 **Olympus** (mt.), Greece
93/J2 **Omaha**, Nebr.
53/G4 **Oman**
53/G4 **Oman** (gulf), Asia
52/B5 **Omdurman**, Sudan
57/G2 **Omiya**, Japan
46/H4 **Omsk**, Russia
46/B4 **Omuta**, Japan
42/G3 **Onega** (lake), Russia
79/G5 **Onitsha**, Nigeria
98/C2 **Ontario**, Calif.
86/H3 **Ontario** (prov.), Can.
94/E3 **Ontario** (lake), N. Amer.
97/G3 **Opelika**, Ala.
96/E4 **Opelousas**, La.
27/J3 **Opole**, Pol.
40/E2 **Oradea**, Rom.
75/Q16 **Oran**, Alg.
80/B3 **Orange** (riv.), Africa
73/D2 **Orange**, Austr.
98/C3 **Orange**, Calif.
98/F5 **Orange**, N.J.
96/E4 **Orange**, Texas
94/D3 **Orangeville**, Ont.
59/B3 **Ordos** (des.), China
44/E3 **Ordzhonikidze**, Ukraine
20/E4 **Örebro**, Sweden
90/C4 **Oregon** (state), U.S.
92/B2 **Oregon Caves Nat'l Mon.**, Oreg.
90/C4 **Oregon City**, Oreg.
44/F1 **Orel**, Russia
92/E2 **Orem**, Utah
45/K2 **Orenburg**, Russia
94/E2 **Orillia**, Ont.
106/F2 **Orinoco** (riv.), S. Amer.
43/D3 **Orissa** (state), India
97/H4 **Orlando**, Fla.
32/D3 **Orléans**, France
95/H2 **Oromocto**, N. Br.
95/G2 **Orono**, Maine
49/E2 **Orontes** (riv.), Syria
45/L2 **Orsk**, Russia
51/F2 **Orūmīyah** (Urmia), Iran
106/E7 **Oruro**, Bol.
56/D3 **Osaka**, Japan
94/E3 **Oshawa**, Ont.
55/M3 **Oshima** (pen.), Japan
94/B2 **Oshkosh**, Wis.
46/H5 **Osh**, Kyrgyzstan
79/G5 **Oshogbo**, Nigeria
40/D3 **Osijek**, Croatia
20/D3 **Oslo** (cap.), Nor.
29/F4 **Osnabrück**, Ger.
98/G4 **Ossining**, N.Y.
27/K4 **Ostrava**, Czech Rep.
94/E3 **Oswego**, N.Y.
39/F2 **Otranto** (str.), Europe
56/D3 **Otsu**, Japan
94/F2 **Ottawa** (cap.), Can.
94/E2 **Ottawa** (riv.), Can.
93/J2 **Ottumwa**, Iowa
96/E3 **Ouachita** (mts.), Ark., Okla.
79/E3 **Ouagadougou** (cap.), Burk. Faso
75/P13 **Oujda**, Mor.
31/F4 **Our** (riv.), Europe
21/B2 **Outer Hebrides** (isls.), Scot.
95/N6 **Outremont**, Que.
93/J3 **Overland Park**, Kans.
34/C1 **Oviedo**, Spain
94/C4 **Owensboro**, Ky.
94/D2 **Owen Sound**, Ont.
25/E3 **Oxford**, Eng.
98/A2 **Oxnard**, Calif.
79/F5 **Oyo**, Nigeria
93/J3 **Ozarks, Lake of the** (lake), Mo.
93/J3 **Ozarks** (mts.), U.S.

P

99/K11 **Pacifica**, Calif.
16/B4 **Pacific Ocean**
90/B3 **Pacific** (ranges), Br. Col.
66/B4 **Padang**, Indon.
29/F5 **Paderborn**, Ger.
33/J4 **Padova** (Padua), Italy
96/D5 **Padre Island Nat'l Seashore**, Texas
94/B4 **Paducah**, Ky.
69/H6 **Pago Pago** (cap.), Amer. Samoa
66/B3 **Pahang** (riv.), Malaysia
92/E4 **Painted** (des.), Ariz.
21/C3 **Paisley**, Scot.
53/H3 **Pakistan**
99/P15 **Palatine**, Ill.
68/C4 **Palau**
66/B4 **Palembang**, Indon.
38/C3 **Palermo**, Italy
35/G3 **Palma de Mallorca**, Spain
78/D5 **Palmas** (cape), Liberia
97/H4 **Palm Bay**, Fla.
98/B1 **Palmdale**, Calif.
106/C3 **Palmira**, Col.
92/C4 **Palm Springs**, Calif.
99/K12 **Palo Alto**, Calif.
46/H6 **Pamir** (plat.), Asia
97/J3 **Pamlico** (sound), N.C.
109/D4 **Pampas** (reg.), Arg.
96/C3 **Pampa**, Texas
34/E1 **Pamplona**, Spain
103/F4 **Panama**
103/G4 **Panamá** (cap.), Pan.
103/G4 **Panama** (gulf), Pan.
97/G4 **Panama City**, Fla.
67/F1 **Panay** (isl.), Phil.
58/D4 **P'anmunjŏm**, Korea
69/X15 **Papeete** (cap.), Fr. Poly.
68/D5 **Papua New Guinea**
93/K3 **Paragould**, Ark.
105/D5 **Paraguay**
109/E1 **Paraguay** (riv.), S. Amer.
107/G3 **Paramaribo** (cap.), Suriname
98/B3 **Paramount**, Calif.
98/F5 **Paramus**, N.J.
109/D3 **Paraná**, Arg.
108/B3 **Paraná** (state), Braz.
105/D5 **Paraná** (riv.), S. Amer.
106/F1 **Paria** (gulf)
30/B6 **Paris** (cap.), France
96/E3 **Paris**, Texas
94/D4 **Parkersburg**, W. Va.
99/Q15 **Park Ridge**, Ill.
98/K7 **Parkville**, Md.
33/J4 **Parma**, Italy
94/D3 **Parma**, Ohio
39/H3 **Parnassós** (Parnassus) (mt.), Greece
39/J4 **Páros** (isl.), Greece
86/F1 **Parry** (chan.), N.W.T.
94/D2 **Parry Sound**, Ont.
93/J3 **Parsons**, Kans.
98/B2 **Pasadena**, Calif.
96/E4 **Pasadena**, Texas
97/F4 **Pascagoula**, Miss.
90/D4 **Pasco**, Wash.
98/F5 **Passaic**, N.J.
106/C3 **Pasto**, Col.
109/B6 **Patagonia** (reg.), Arg.
98/F5 **Paterson**, N.J.
64/D2 **Patiala**, India
62/E2 **Patna**, India
39/G3 **Pátrai**, Greece
46/H4 **Pavlodar**, Kazakhstan
95/G3 **Pawtucket**, R.I.
86/E3 **Peace** (riv.), Can.
88/W13 **Pearl City**, Hawaii
88/V13 **Pearl** (harb.), Hawaii
43/M2 **Pechora** (riv.), Russia
97/G5 **Pecos** (riv.), Texas
96/C4 **Pecos**, Texas
40/D2 **Pécs**, Hung.
63/G3 **Pegu**, Burma
42/E4 **Peipus** (lake), Russia
59/D3 **Peking** (Beijing) (cap.), China
94/B3 **Pekin**, Ill.
94/D3 **Pelée** (pt.), Ont.
104/F4 **Pelée** (vol.), Martinique
90/E2 **Pelican** (mts.), Alb.
85/M3 **Pelly** (riv.), Yukon
39/G4 **Peloponnisos** (reg.), Greece
108/A4 **Pelotas**, Braz.
82/G 2 **Pemba** (isl.), Tanz.
94/E2 **Pembroke**, Ont.
90/D4 **Pendleton**, Oreg.
90/D4 **Pend Oreille** (lake), Idaho
94/E2 **Penetanguishene**, Ont.
61/H4 **Penghu** (isls.), Taiwan
23/F2 **Pennine Chain** (range), Eng.
98/E6 **Pennsauken**, N.J.
94/E3 **Pennsylvania** (state), U.S.
97/G4 **Pensacola**, Fla.
90/D3 **Penticton**, Br. Col.
45/H1 **Penza**, Russia
94/B3 **Peoria**, Ill.
95/H1 **Percé**, Que.
106/C3 **Pereira**, Col.
32/D4 **Périgueux**, France
52/D6 **Perim** (isl.), Yemen
43/N4 **Perm'**, Russia
32/E5 **Perpignan**, France
52/E3 **Persian** (gulf), Asia
98/F5 **Perth Amboy**, N.J.
70/B6 **Perth**, Austr.
94/E2 **Perth**, Ont.
21/D2 **Perth**, Scot.
106/C5 **Peru**
38/C1 **Perugia**, Italy
61/H4 **Pescadores** (Penghu) (isls.), Taiwan
38/D1 **Pescara**, Italy
53/K2 **Peshawar**, Pak.
49/D3 **Petah Tiqwa**, Isr.
99/J10 **Petaluma**, Calif.
25/F1 **Peterborough**, Eng.
94/E2 **Peterborough**, Ont.
94/E4 **Petersburg**, Va.
95/H2 **Petitcodiac**, N. Br.
49/D4 **Petra** (ruins), Jordan
92/E4 **Petrified Forest Nat'l Pk.**, Ariz.
47/R4 **Petropavlovsk-Kamchatskiy**, Russia
46/G4 **Petropavlovsk**, Kazakhstan
42/G3 **Petrozavodsk**, Russia
96/D5 **Pharr**, Texas
97/G3 **Phenix City**, Ala.
98/E6 **Philadelphia**, Pa.
48/M8 **Philippines**
65/D4 **Phnom Penh** (cap.), Camb.
92/D4 **Phoenix** (cap.), Ariz.
69/H5 **Phoenix** (isls.), Kiribati
30/B4 **Picardy** (reg.), Fr.
98/B3 **Pico Rivera**, Calif.
97/H3 **Piedmont** (plat.), U.S.
33/G4 **Piedmont** (reg.), Italy
91/H4 **Pierre** (cap.), S. Dak.
95/N7 **Pierrefonds**, Que.
81/E3 **Pietermaritzburg**, S. Africa
93/F3 **Pike's** (peak), Colo.
98/K7 **Pikesville**, Md.
105/C5 **Pilcomayo** (riv.), S. Amer.
27/G4 **Pilsen** (Plzeň), Czech Rep.
39/G2 **Pindus** (mts.), Greece
93/J4 **Pine Bluff**, Ark.
59/C4 **Pingdingshan**, China
61/J4 **Pingtung**, China
92/B3 **Pinnacles Nat'l Mon.**, Calif.
103/F1 **Pinos** (Juventud) (isl.), Cuba
44/C1 **Pinsk**, Belarus
92/D3 **Pipe Spring Nat'l Mon.**, Ariz.
91/J2 **Pipestone Nat'l Mon.**, Minn.
94/C3 **Piqua**, Ohio
39/H4 **Piraiévs**, Greece
33/J5 **Pisa**, Italy
98/F5 **Piscataway**, N.J.
69/N7 **Pitcairn** (isl.), Pacific
41/G3 **Piteşti**, Rom.
99/L10 **Pittsburg**, Calif.
94/D3 **Pittsburgh**, Pa.
93/J3 **Pittsburg**, Kans.
95/F3 **Pittsfield**, Mass.
106/B5 **Piura**, Peru
98/C3 **Placentia**, Calif.
98/F5 **Plainfield**, N.J.
98/G5 **Plainview**, N.Y.
96/C3 **Plainview**, Texas
96/D3 **Plano**, Texas
97/H5 **Plantation**, Fla.
109/E3 **Plata, Rio de la** (est.), S. Amer.
93/H2 **Platte** (riv.), Nebr.
94/F2 **Plattsburgh**, N.Y.
99/K11 **Pleasant Hill**, Calif.
99/L11 **Pleasanton**, Calif.
65/E3 **Pleiku**, Viet.
41/G4 **Pleven**, Bulg.
41/H3 **Ploieşti**, Rom.
42/G4 **Plovdiv**, Bulg.
104/F3 **Plymouth** (cap.), Montserrat
24/B6 **Plymouth**, Eng.
90/E5 **Pocatello**, Idaho
42/H5 **Podol'sk**, Russia
58/E4 **P'ohang**, S. Korea
68/E4 **Pohnpei** (isl.), Micronesia
95/N7 **Pointe-Claire**, Que.
82/B1 **Pointe-Noire**, Congo
94/D3 **Pointe Pelée Nat'l Pk.**, Ont.
27/K2 **Poland**
44/E2 **Poltava**, Ukraine
69/J3 **Polynesia** (reg.), Pacific
27/H2 **Pomerania** (reg.), Europe
27/H2 **Pomerania** (reg.), Pol.
98/C2 **Pomona**, Calif.
97/H5 **Pompano Beach**, Fla.
38/D2 **Pompei** (ruins), Italy
93/H3 **Ponca City**, Okla.
104/E3 **Ponce**, P. Rico
64/G3 **Pondicherry**, India
97/F4 **Pontchartrain** (lake), La.
99/F6 **Pontiac**, Mich.
66/C4 **Pontianak**, Indon.
38/C2 **Ponziane** (isls.), Italy
62/B4 **Poona** (Pune), India
106/E7 **Poopó** (lake), Bol.
93/K3 **Poplar Bluff**, Mo.
85/K2 **Porcupine** (riv.), N. Amer.
33/J4 **Po** (riv.), Italy
20/H1 **Porsangen** (fjord), Nor.
91/J3 **Portage la Prairie**, Man.
94/C3 **Portage**, Mich.
90/B3 **Port Alberni**, Br. Col.
90/B3 **Port Angeles**, Wash.
96/E4 **Port Arthur**, Texas
103/H2 **Port-au-Prince** (cap.), Haiti
97/H5 **Port Charlotte**, Fla.
98/G4 **Port Chester**, N.Y.
80/D4 **Port Elizabeth**, S. Africa
79/G5 **Port Harcourt**, Nigeria
95/J2 **Port Hawkesbury**, N.S.
99/H6 **Port Huron**, Mich.
95/G3 **Portland**, Maine
90/B4 **Portland**, Ore.
81/S15 **Port Louis** (cap.), Mauritius
68/D5 **Port Moresby** (cap.), Papua N.G.
108/B4 **Porto Alegre**, Braz.
104/F5 **Port-of-Spain** (cap.), Trin. & Tob.
79/F5 **Porto-Novo** (cap.), Benin
34/A2 **Porto** (Oporto), Port.
106/F5 **Porto Velho**, Braz.
49/C4 **Port Said**, Egypt
25/E5 **Portsmouth**, Eng.
95/G3 **Portsmouth**, N.H.
94/D4 **Portsmouth**, Ohio
94/E4 **Portsmouth**, Va.
52/C5 **Port Sudan**, Sudan
34/A3 **Portugal**
94/E4 **Potomac** (riv.), U.S.
26/G2 **Potsdam**, Ger.
94/F3 **Pottstown**, Pa.
94/F3 **Poughkeepsie**, N.Y.
92/E3 **Powell** (lake), U.S.
90/B3 **Powell River**, Br. Col.
61/G2 **Poyang** (lake), China
27/J2 **Poznań**, Pol.
27/H3 **Prague** (Praha) (cap.), Czech Rep.
92/D4 **Prescott**, Ariz.
95/G2 **Presque Isle**, Maine
23/F4 **Preston**, Eng.
21/C3 **Prestwick**, Scot.
80/E2 **Pretoria** (cap.), S. Africa
85/D4 **Pribilof** (isls.), Alaska
97/F5 **Prichard**, Ala.
90/G2 **Prince Albert**, Sask.
87/J2 **Prince Charles** (isl.), N.W.T.
95/J2 **Prince Edward Island** (prov.), Can.
17/L8 **Prince Edward** (isls.), S. Africa
90/C2 **Prince George**, Br. Col.
86/G1 **Prince of Wales** (isl.), N.W.T.
87/R7 **Prince Patrick** (isl.), N.W.T.
85/M4 **Prince Rupert**, Br. Col.
98/F5 **Princeton**, N.J.
40/E4 **Priština**, Yugo.
46/J4 **Prokop'yevsk**, Russia
95/G3 **Providence** (cap.), R.I.
103/F3 **Providencia** (isl.), Col.
92/E2 **Provo**, Utah
85/J1 **Prudhoe** (bay), Alaska
41/J2 **Prut** (riv.), Europe
42/F4 **Pskov**, Russia
101/L7 **Puebla de Zaragoza**, Mex.
93/F3 **Pueblo**, Colo.
104/E5 **Puerto La Cruz**, Ven.
104/E3 **Puerto Rico**
90/C4 **Puget** (sound), Wash.
69/J6 **Pukapuka** (atoll), Cook Is.
90/D4 **Pullman**, Wash.
64/B2 **Punjab** (plain), India
64/C2 **Punjab** (state), India
64/B2 **Punjab** (prov.), Pak.
109/B7 **Punta Arenas**, Chile
106/F4 **Purus** (riv.), S. Amer.
58/E5 **Pusan**, S. Korea
42/F4 **Pushkin**, Russia
99/C3 **Puyallup**, Wash.
58/C3 **P'yŏngyang** (cap.), N. Korea
34/E1 **Pyrenees** (mts.), Europe

Q

87/T7 **Qaanaaq**, Greenl.
76/G1 **Qafsah**, Tun.
53/J2 **Qandahār**, Afghan.
52/F3 **Qatar**
50/A4 **Qattâra** (depr.), Egypt
51/G2 **Qazvin**, Iran
87/L2 **Qeqertarsuaq**, Greenl.
54/D4 **Qilian** (mts.), China
59/E3 **Qingdao** (Tsingtao), China
54/D4 **Qinghai** (lake), China
55/J2 **Qiqihar**, China
49/D3 **Qiryat Shemona**, Isr.
55/L2 **Qitaihe**, China
51/G3 **Qom** (Qum), Iran
90/G3 **Qu'Appelle** (riv.), Sask.
95/G2 **Québec** (cap.), Que.
87/J3 **Québec** (prov.), Can.
86/C3 **Queen Charlotte** (isls.), Br. Col.
87/Q7 **Queen Elizabeth** (isls.), N.W.T.
83/A **Queen Maud Land** (reg.), Antarc.
98/G5 **Queens** (borough), N.Y.
71/G4 **Queensland** (state), Austr.
101/E4 **Querétaro**, Mex.
90/C2 **Quesnel**, Br. Col.
53/J2 **Quetta**, Pak.
59/D4 **Qufu**, China
94/B4 **Quincy**, Ill.
95/G3 **Quincy**, Mass.
65/E3 **Qui Nhon**, Viet.
106/C4 **Quito** (cap.), Ecua.
61/H2 **Quzhou**, China

R

75/L13 **Rabat** (cap.), Mor.
68/E5 **Rabaul**, Papua N.G.
87/L4 **Race** (cape), Newf.
99/Q14 **Racine**, Wis.
27/L3 **Radom**, Pol.
98/F5 **Rahway**, N.J.

92/E3 **Rainbow Bridge Nat'l Mon.**, Utah
90/C4 **Rainier** (mt.), Wash.
91/K3 **Rainy** (lake), N. Amer.
62/D3 **Raipur**, India
62/D4 **Rajahmundry**, India
62/B3 **Rajkot**, India
97/J3 **Raleigh** (cap.), N.C.
49/D3 **Ramat Gan**, Isr.
62/E3 **Ranchi**, India
98/C2 **Rancho Cucamonga**, Calif.
98/K7 **Randallstown**, Md.
65/B2 **Rangoon** (cap.), Burma
94/B3 **Rantoul**, Ill.
69/L7 **Rapa** (isl.), Fr. Poly.
91/H4 **Rapid City**, S. Dak.
94/E4 **Rappahannock** (riv.), Va.
98/F5 **Raritan** (riv.), N.J.
69/J7 **Rarotonga** (isl.), Cook Is.
77/N5 **Ras Dashen Terara** (mt.), Eth.
51/G2 **Rasht**, Iran
52/F3 **Ra's Tannūrah** (cape), Saudi Arabia
33/K4 **Ravenna**, Italy
37/F2 **Ravensburg**, Ger.
64/B2 **Ravi** (riv.), Asia
64/B1 **Rawalpindi**, Pak.
90/G5 **Rawlins**, Wyo.
95/K2 **Ray** (cape), Newf.
25/F4 **Reading**, Eng.
94/F3 **Reading**, Pa.
107/M5 **Recife**, Braz.
60/E4 **Red** (riv.), Asia
93/J5 **Red** (riv.), U.S.
34/C4 **Red** (sea)
90/E2 **Red Deer**, Alta.
90/F3 **Red Deer** (riv.), Alta.
92/B2 **Redding**, Calif.
98/C2 **Redlands**, Calif.
99/C2 **Redmond**, Wash.
98/B3 **Redondo Beach**, Calif.
91/J4 **Red River of the North** (riv.), U.S.
79/E4 **Red Volta** (riv.), Africa
99/K12 **Redwood City**, Calif.
92/A2 **Redwood Nat'l Pk.**, Calif.
21/A4 **Ree** (lake), Ire.
26/G4 **Regensburg**, Ger.
38/D3 **Reggio di Calabria**, Italy
33/J4 **Reggio nell'Emilia**, Italy
91/G3 **Regina** (cap.), Sask.
30/D5 **Reims**, France
86/F3 **Reindeer** (lake), Can.
94/E2 **Renfrew**, Ont.
32/C2 **Rennes**, France
92/C3 **Reno**, Nev.
59/D3 **Renqiu**, China
99/C3 **Renton**, Wash.
93/H2 **Republican** (riv.), U.S.
109/E2 **Resistencia**, Arg.
87/K2 **Resolution** (isl.), N.W.T.
98/H8 **Reston**, Va.
81/R15 **Réunion**
37/F1 **Reutlingen**, Ger.
90/D3 **Revelstoke**, Br. Col.
100/B5 **Revillagigedo** (isls.), Mex.
90/F5 **Rexburg**, Idaho
20/N7 **Reykjavík** (cap.), Iceland
37/F5 **Rhaetian Alps** (mts.), Europe
26/C3 **Rhine** (riv.), Europe
95/G3 **Rhode Island** (state), U.S.
41/F4 **Rhodope** (mts.), Europe
32/F4 **Rhône** (riv.), Europe
21/B2 **Rhum** (isl.), Scot.
98/C2 **Rialto**, Calif.
66/B3 **Riau** (arch.), Indon.
108/C2 **Ribeirão Preto**, Braz.
90/D4 **Richland**, Wash.
99/K11 **Richmond**, Calif.
94/C4 **Richmond**, Ind.
94/C4 **Richmond**, Ky.
94/E4 **Richmond** (cap.), Va.
98/F5 **Ridgewood**, N.J.
91/H3 **Riding Mtn. Nat'l Pk.**, Man.
75/M13 **Rif, Er** (mts.), Mor.
42/E4 **Riga** (cap.), Latvia
42/D4 **Riga** (gulf), Latvia
67/H2 **Rīgestan** (des.), Afghan.
40/B3 **Rijeka**, Croatia
33/K4 **Rimini**, Italy
95/G1 **Rimouski**, Que.
108/D2 **Rio de Janeiro**, Braz.
96/C4 **Rio Grande** (riv.), N. Amer.
98/C3 **Riverside**, Calif.
97/H5 **Riviera Beach**, Fla.
95/G2 **Rivière-du-Loup**, Que.
52/E4 **Riyadh** (cap.), Saudi Arabia
59/D4 **Rizhao**, China
104/E3 **Road Town** (cap.), V.I. (Br.)
94/E4 **Roanoke**, Va.
97/J2 **Roanoke Rapids**, N.C.
95/F1 **Roberval**, Que.
91/K4 **Rochester**, Minn.
95/G3 **Rochester**, N.H.
94/E3 **Rochester**, N.Y.
94/B3 **Rockford**, Ill.
72/C3 **Rockhampton**, Austr.
97/H3 **Rock Hill**, S.C.
94/B3 **Rock Island**, Ill.
90/F5 **Rock Springs**, Wyo.
98/J7 **Rockville**, Md.
98/G5 **Rockville Centre**, N.Y.
84/E4 **Rocky** (mts.), N. Amer.
97/J3 **Rocky Mount**, N.C.
90/E2 **Rocky Mountain House**, Alta.
93/F2 **Rocky Mountain Nat'l Pk.**, Colo.
93/J3 **Rogers**, Ark.
41/F3 **Romania**
97/G3 **Rome**, Ga.
38/C2 **Rome** (cap.), Italy
94/F3 **Rome**, N.Y.
83/W **Ronne Ice Shelf**, Antarc.
83/N **Roosevelt** (isl.), Antarc.
106/F6 **Roosevelt** (riv.), Braz.
109/D3 **Rosario**, Arg.
104/F4 **Roseau** (cap.), Dominica
90/C5 **Roseburg**, Oreg.
49/B4 **Rosetta** (Rashīd), Egypt
99/G6 **Roseville**, Mich.
83/P **Ross** (sea), Antarc.
83/P **Ross Ice Shelf**, Antarc.
26/G1 **Rostock**, Ger.
44/F3 **Rostov**, Russia
93/F4 **Roswell**, N. Mex.
28/B5 **Rotterdam**, Neth.
68/G6 **Rotuma** (isl.), Fiji
30/A5 **Rouen**, France
94/E1 **Rouyn-Noranda**, Que.
44/C2 **Rovno**, Ukraine
92/D2 **Roy**, Utah
99/F6 **Royal Oak**, Mich.
52/E5 **Rub' al Khali** (des.), Asia
82/G2 **Rufiji** (riv.), Tanz.
27/G1 **Rügen** (isl.), Ger.
28/D6 **Ruhr** (riv.), Ger.
82/F2 **Rukwa** (lake), Tanz.
104/C2 **Rum** (cay), Bah.
94/E1 **Rupert** (riv.), Que.
41/G4 **Ruse**, Bulg.
46/H3 **Russia**
96/E3 **Ruston**, La.
95/F3 **Rutland**, Vt.
82/G3 **Ruvuma** (riv.), Tanz.
82/E1 **Rwanda**
44/F1 **Ryazan'**, Russia
42/H4 **Rybinsk**, Russia
48/M7 **Ryukyu** (isls.), Japan

S

90/C3 **Saanich**, Br. Col.
31/F5 **Saarbrücken**, Ger.
42/D4 **Saaremaa** (isl.), Estonia
42/D4 **Saarland** (state), Ger.
35/G2 **Sabadell**, Spain
67/E2 **Sabah** (reg.), Malaysia
96/E4 **Sabine** (riv.), U.S.
95/H3 **Sable** (cape), N.S.
95/J3 **Sable** (isl.), N.S.
95/H2 **Sackville**, N. Br.
92/B3 **Sacramento** (cap.), Calif.
99/L10 **Sacramento** (riv.), Calif.
93/F4 **Sacramento** (mts.), N. Mex.
76/H1 **Safāqis** (Sfax), Tun.
56/B4 **Saga**, Japan
57/F3 **Sagamihara**, Japan
98/G5 **Sagamore Hill Nat'l Hist. Site**, N.Y.
94/D3 **Saginaw**, Mich.
92/E4 **Saguaro Nat'l Mon.**, Ariz.
95/G1 **Saguenay** (riv.), Que.
76/G3 **Sahara** (des.), Africa
53/L3 **Saharanpur**, India
65/D4 **Saigon** (Ho Chi Minh City), Viet.
90/E2 **St. Albert**, Alta.
97/H4 **St. Augustine**, Fla.
94/E3 **St. Catharines**, Ont.
93/K3 **St. Charles**, Mo.
99/G7 **St. Clair** (lake), N. Amer.
99/G6 **St. Clair Shores**, Mich.
91/K4 **St. Cloud**, Minn.
104/E3 **St. Croix** (isl.), V.I. (U.S.)
91/K4 **St. Croix** (riv.), U.S.
81/R15 **St-Denis** (cap.), Réunion
94/F2 **Ste-Agathe-des-Monts**, Que.
95/G2 **Ste-Foy**, Que.
86/B2 **St. Elias** (mt.), Alaska
95/N6 **Ste-Thérèse**, Que.
32/F4 **St-Étienne**, France
95/N6 **St-Eustache**, Que.
33/H3 **St. Gallen**, Switz.
95/K1 **St. George** (cape), Newf.
21/B5 **St. George's** (chan.), Europe
104/F4 **St. George's** (cap.), Grenada
16/J6 **St. Helena & Dependencies**
90/C4 **St. Helens** (mt.), Wash.
32/B2 **St. Helier** (cap.), Jersey, Chan. Is.
95/F2 **St-Hyacinthe**, Que.
95/F1 **St-Jean** (lake), Que.
95/F2 **St-Jerôme**, Que.
95/H2 **St. John**, N. Br.
95/H2 **St. John** (riv.), N. Amer.
104/E3 **St. John** (isl.), V.I. (U.S.)
104/F3 **St. Johns** (cap.), Ant. & Bar.
95/L2 **St. John's** (cap.), Newf.
93/J3 **St. Joseph**, Mo.
73/F5 **St. Kilda**, Austr.
104/F3 **St. Kitts & Nevis**
104/F3 **St. Kitts** (isl.), St. Kitts & Nevis
95/P6 **St-Lambert**, Que.
95/J1 **St. Lawrence** (gulf), Can.
85/D3 **St. Lawrence** (isl.), Alaska
95/G1 **St. Lawrence** (riv.), N. Amer.
95/N6 **St-Léonard**, Que.
93/K3 **St. Louis**, Mo.
104/F4 **St. Lucia**
95/F2 **St-Maurice** (riv.), Que.
32/B3 **St-Nazaire**, France
91/K4 **St. Paul** (cap.), Minn.
32/B2 **St. Peter Port** (cap.), Guernsey, Chan. Is.
97/H5 **St. Petersburg**, Fla.
42/F4 **St. Petersburg**, Russia
95/K2 **St. Pierre & Miquelon**
97/H4 **St. Simons** (isl.), Ga.
95/H2 **St. Stephen**, N. Br.
94/D3 **St. Thomas**, Ont.
104/E3 **St. Thomas** (isl.), V.I. (U.S.)
104/F4 **St. Vincent & the Grenadines**
68/D3 **Saipan** (isl.), N. Marianas
57/L10 **Sakai**, Japan
91/H4 **Sakakawea** (lake), N. Dak.
47/Q4 **Sakhalin** (isl.), Russia
109/D2 **Salado** (riv.), Arg.
34/C2 **Salamanca**, Spain
16/D7 **Sala y Gómez** (isl.), Chile
90/C4 **Salem** (cap.), Oreg.
64/G3 **Salem**, India
95/G3 **Salem**, N.H.
94/D4 **Salem**, Va.
38/D2 **Salerno**, Italy
93/H3 **Salina**, Kans.
92/B3 **Salinas**, Calif.
93/F4 **Salinas Nat'l Mon.**, N. Mex.
94/F4 **Salisbury**, Md.
90/E4 **Salmon** (riv.), Idaho
90/E4 **Salmon River** (mts.), Idaho
108/C1 **Salta**, Arg.
101/E3 **Saltillo**, Mex.
92/E2 **Salt Lake City** (cap.), Utah
92/C4 **Salton Sea** (lake), Calif.
97/H3 **Saluda** (riv.), S.C.
107/L6 **Salvador**, Braz.
60/C5 **Salween** (riv.), Asia
33/K3 **Salzburg**, Austria
45/J1 **Samara**, Russia
49/G7 **Samaria** (reg.), West Bank
67/E4 **Samarinda**, Indon.
48/M8 **Samar** (isl.), Phil.
46/G6 **Samarkand**, Uzbekistan
50/A2 **Sámos** (isl.), Greece
39/J2 **Samothráki** (isl.), Greece
50/D1 **Samsun**, Turkey
52/D5 **Sanaa** (San'a) (cap.), Yemen
103/F3 **San Andrés** (isl.), Col.
96/C4 **San Angelo**, Texas
96/D4 **San Antonio**, Texas
98/C2 **San Bernardino**, Calif.
98/C2 **San Bernardino** (mts.), Calif.
99/K11 **San Bruno**, Calif.
92/C4 **San Clemente** (isl.), Calif.
68/F6 **San Cristobal** (isl.), Solomon Is.
103/H5 **San Cristóbal**, Ven.
92/C4 **San Diego**, Calif.
94/D3 **Sandusky**, Ohio
98/F5 **Sandy Hook** (spit), N.J.
97/G3 **Sandy Springs**, Ga.
92/E2 **Sandy**, Utah
98/B2 **San Fernando**, Calif.
97/H4 **Sanford**, Fla.
95/G3 **Sanford**, Maine
97/J3 **Sanford**, N.C.
99/K11 **San Francisco** (bay), Calif.
99/K11 **San Francisco**, Calif.
98/B2 **San Gabriel**, Calif.
93/F3 **Sangre de Cristo** (mts.), U.S.
99/L10 **San Joaquin** (riv.), Calif.
99/L12 **San Jose**, Calif.
103/E4 **San José** (cap.), C. Rica
108/C2 **San José dos Campos**, Braz.
109/C3 **San Juan**, Arg.
104/E3 **San Juan** (cap.), P. Rico
92/E3 **San Juan** (riv.), U.S.
99/K11 **San Leandro**, Calif.
100/C4 **San Lucas** (cape), Mex.
92/B4 **San Luis Obispo**, Calif.
101/E4 **San Luis Potosí**, Mex.
96/D4 **San Marcos**, Texas
33/K5 **San Marino**
99/K11 **San Mateo**, Calif.
102/D3 **San Miguel**, El Sal.
108/C2 **San Miguel de Tucumán**, Arg.
92/C4 **San Nicolas** (isl.), Calif.
102/D3 **San Pedro Sula**, Hond.
99/J11 **San Rafael**, Calif.
104/C1 **San Salvador** (isl.), Bah.
102/D3 **San Salvador** (cap.), El Sal.
34/E1 **San Sebastián**, Spain
98/C3 **Santa Ana**, Calif.
102/D3 **Santa Ana**, El Sal.
98/A2 **Santa Barbara**, Calif.
92/C4 **Santa Catalina** (isl.), Calif.
99/L12 **Santa Clara**, Calif.
103/G1 **Santa Clara**, Cuba
98/B2 **Santa Clarita**, Calif.
106/F7 **Santa Cruz**, Bol.
92/B3 **Santa Cruz**, Calif.
35/X16 **Santa Cruz de Tenerife**, Spain
68/F6 **Santa Cruz** (isls.), Sol. Is.
109/D3 **Santa Fe**, Arg.
93/F4 **Santa Fe** (cap.), N. Mex.
93/B4 **Santa Maria**, Calif.
106/D1 **Santa Marta**, Col.
98/B2 **Santa Monica**, Calif.
34/D1 **Santander**, Spain
92/B3 **Santa Rosa**, Calif.
97/J3 **Santee** (riv.), S.C.
109/B3 **Santiago** (cap.), Chile
103/H1 **Santiago de Cuba**, Cuba
104/D3 **Santiago**, Dom. Rep.
96/C4 **Santiago** (mts.), Texas
108/C2 **Santo Andre**, Braz.
104/D3 **Santo Domingo** (cap.), Dom. Rep.
108/C2 **Santos**, Braz.
108/C2 **São Bernardo do Campo**, Braz.
107/K4 **São Luís**, Braz.
32/F3 **Saône** (riv.), France
108/C2 **São Paulo**, Braz.
76/F7 **São Tomé and Príncipe**
76/G7 **São Tomé** (cap.), São T. & Pr.
34/A4 **São Vincent** (cape), Port.
55/N3 **Sapporo**, Japan
35/E2 **Saragossa**, Spain
40/D4 **Sarajevo** (cap.), Bosn.
45/H1 **Saransk**, Russia
66/D3 **Sararwak** (reg.), Malaysia
97/H5 **Sarasota**, Fla.
99/K12 **Saratoga**, Calif.
94/F3 **Saratoga Springs**, N.Y.
45/H2 **Saratov**, Russia
38/A2 **Sardinia** (isl.), Italy
64/B1 **Sargodha**, Pak.
32/B2 **Sark** (isl.), Chan. Is.
94/D3 **Sarnia**, Ont.
56/A4 **Sasebo**, Japan
86/F3 **Saskatchewan** (prov.), Can.
91/G2 **Saskatchewan** (riv.), Can.
90/G3 **Saskatoon**, Sask.
41/F2 **Satu Mare**, Rom.
52/D4 **Saudi Arabia**
94/C2 **Sault Ste. Marie**, Mich.
94/C2 **Sault Ste. Marie**, Ont.
99/K11 **Sausalito**, Calif.
97/H3 **Savannah**, Ga.
97/H3 **Savannah** (riv.), U.S.
40/C3 **Sava** (riv.), Yugo.
82/F5 **Save** (riv.), Moz.
67/F5 **Savu** (sea), Indon.
92/F3 **Sawatch** (range), Colo.
92/D1 **Sawtooth** (mts.), Idaho
26/F3 **Saxony-Anhalt** (state), Ger.
98/F5 **Sayreville**, N.J.
98/G4 **Scarsdale**, N.Y.
99/P15 **Schaumburg**, Ill.
94/F3 **Schenectady**, N.Y.
26/E1 **Schleswig-Holstein** (state), Ger.
88/V12 **Schofield Barracks**, Hawaii
26/F3 **Schweinfurt**, Ger.
21/B5 **Scilly** (isls.), Eng.
94/D4 **Scioto** (riv.), Ohio
98/F5 **Scotch Plains**, N.J.
83/W **Scotia** (sea), Antarc.
21/C2 **Scotland**, U.K.
92/G2 **Scottsbluff**, Nebr.
97/G3 **Scottsboro**, Ala.
92/E4 **Scottsdale**, Ariz.
94/F3 **Scranton**, Pa.
39/F1 **Scutari** (lake), Europe
98/B3 **Seal Beach**, Calif.
90/C4 **Seattle**, Wash.
93/J3 **Sedalia**, Mo.
34/C2 **Segovia**, Spain
32/D2 **Seine** (riv.), France
79/E5 **Sekondi**, Ghana
90/D3 **Selkirk** (mts.), Br. Col.
91/J3 **Selkirk**, Man.
97/G3 **Selma**, Ala.
106/E5 **Selvas** (for.), Braz.
66/D5 **Semarang**, Indon.
46/H4 **Semipalatinsk**, Kazakhstan
56/B5 **Sendai**, Japan
78/B3 **Senegal**
78/B2 **Senegal** (riv.), Africa
58/D4 **Seoul** (cap.), S. Korea
95/H1 **Sept-Îles**, Que.
92/C3 **Sequoia Nat'l Pk.**, Calif.
40/E4 **Serbia** (rep.), Yugo.
42/H5 **Serpukhov**, Russia
75/U17 **Sétif**, Alg.
34/A2 **Setúbal**, Port.
34/A3 **Setúbal** (bay), Port.
44/E3 **Sevastopol'**, Ukraine
47/K2 **Severnaya Zemlya** (isls.), Russia
98/K7 **Severn** (riv.), Md.
24/D3 **Severn** (riv.), U.K.
42/H2 **Severodvinsk**, Russia
92/D3 **Sevier** (riv.), Utah
34/C4 **Seville**, Spain
85/J3 **Seward**, Alaska
85/E2 **Seward** (pen.), Alaska
75/H5 **Seychelles**
28/B4 **'s Gravenhage** (The Hague) (cap.), Neth.
59/B4 **Shaanxi** (Shensi) (prov.), China
62/C2 **Shahjahanpur**, India
59/D3 **Shandong** (Shantung) (prov.), China
59/C4 **Shanghai**, China
61/H2 **Shangrao**, China
21/H7 **Shannon** (riv.), Ire.
63/G3 **Shan** (plat.), Burma
61/H4 **Shantou** (Swatow), China
59/B3 **Shanxi** (Shansi) (prov.), China
61/J2 **Shaoxing**, China
94/D3 **Sharon**, Pa.
92/B2 **Shasta** (lake), Calif.
92/B2 **Shasta** (mt.), Calif.
50/F4 **Shatt-al-'Arab** (riv.), Asia
95/F2 **Shawinigan**, Que.
93/H4 **Shawnee**, Okla.
94/C3 **Sheboygan**, Wis.
23/G5 **Sheffield**, Eng.
97/H3 **Shelby**, N.C.
47/R3 **Shelekhov** (gulf), Russia
94/E4 **Shenandoah Nat'l Pk.**, Va.
58/B2 **Shenyang** (Mukden), China
95/G2 **Sherbrooke**, Que.
90/G4 **Sheridan**, Wyo.
96/D3 **Sherman**, Texas
28/C5 **'s Hertogenbosch**, Neth.
90/E2 **Sherwood Park**, Alta.
45/J4 **Shevchenko**, Kazakhstan
91/J4 **Sheyenne** (riv.), N. Dak.
59/C3 **Shijiazhuang**, China
56/C4 **Shikoku** (isl.), Japan
57/F3 **Shimizu**, Japan
56/B4 **Shimonoseki**, Japan
51/H4 **Shiraz**, Iran
54/F4 **Shizuishan**, China
57/F3 **Shizuoka**, Japan
62/C4 **Sholapur**, India
96/E3 **Shreveport**, La.
55/L2 **Shuangyashan**, China
50/B4 **Shubrā al Khaymah**, Egypt
64/C1 **Sialkot**, Pak.
65/C3 **Siam** (Thailand)
46/K3 **Siberia** (reg.), Russia
41/G2 **Sibiu**, Rom.
60/D2 **Sichuan** (Szechwan) (prov.), China
38/C3 **Sicily** (isl.), Italy
75/Q16 **Sidi Bel-Abbès**, Alg.
76/J1 **Sidra** (gulf), Libya
31/H2 **Siegen**, Ger.
78/B4 **Sierra Leone**
92/C3 **Sierra Nevada** (mts.), U.S.
92/E5 **Sierra Vista**, Ariz.
62/E2 **Sikkim** (state), India
27/H3 **Silesia** (reg.), Pol.
98/J7 **Silver Spring**, Md.
45/J1 **Simbirsk**, Russia
94/E2 **Simcoe** (lake), Ont.
94/D3 **Simcoe**, Ont.
44/E3 **Simferopol'**, Ukraine
98/B2 **Simi Valley**, Calif.
70/F4 **Simpson** (des.), Austr.
50/C4 **Sinai** (pen.), Egypt
53/J3 **Sind** (reg.), Pak.
66/B3 **Singapore**
66/B3 **Singapore** (cap.), Sing.
58/C2 **Sinŭiju**, N. Korea
93/H2 **Sioux City**, Iowa
91/J5 **Sioux Falls**, S. Dak.
38/D4 **Siracusa** (Syracuse), Italy
85/L4 **Sitka**, Alaska
50/D2 **Sivas**, Turkey
77/L2 **Siwah** (oasis), Egypt
62/D2 **Siwalik** (range), India, Nepal
20/D4 **Skagerrak** (str.), Europe
86/D3 **Skeena** (mts.), Br. Col.
86/D3 **Skeena** (riv.), Br. Col.
75/V17 **Skikda**, Alg.
99/Q15 **Skokie**, Ill.
40/E5 **Skopje** (cap.), Macedonia
21/B2 **Skye** (isl.), Scot.
99/D2 **Skykomish** (riv.), Wash.
84/F3 **Slave** (riv.), Can.
40/C3 **Slavonia** (reg.), Croatia
97/F4 **Slidell**, La.
21/A3 **Sligo**, Ire.
27/K4 **Slovakia**
40/B3 **Slovenia**
90/B2 **Smithers**, Br. Col.
94/E2 **Smiths Falls**, Ont.
93/G3 **Smoky Hill** (riv.), Kans.
42/G5 **Smolensk**, Russia
97/G3 **Smyrna**, Ga.
90/D5 **Snake** (riv.), U.S.
99/D2 **Snoqualmie** (riv.), Wash.
22/D5 **Snowdon** (mt.), Wales
44/R4 **Sochi**, Russia
69/K6 **Society** (isls.), Fr. Poly.
75/H3 **Socotra** (isl.), Yemen
41/F4 **Sofia** (cap.), Bulg.
58/C3 **Sŏjosŏn** (bay), N. Korea
31/G1 **Solingen**, Ger.
68/E6 **Solomon Islands**
68/E5 **Solomon** (sea)
22/E2 **Solway** (firth), U.K.
77/Q6 **Somalia**
86/G1 **Somerset** (isl.), N.W.T.

30/A3 **Somme** (riv.), France
59/F1 **Songhua** (riv.), China
63/H6 **Songkhla**, Thai.
58/D4 **Sŏngnam**, S. Korea
95/F2 **Sorel**, Que.
108/C2 **Sorocaba**, Braz.
27/K3 **Sosnowiec**, Pol.
95/J2 **Souris**, P.E.I.
91/H3 **Souris** (riv.), N. Amer.
71/R11 **South** (isl.), N.Z.
82/D6 **South Africa**
105/* **South America**
25/E5 **Southampton**, Eng.
87/H2 **Southampton** (isl.), N.W.T.
70/E5 **South Australia** (state), Austr.
94/C3 **South Bend**, Ind.
95/F2 **South Burlington**, Vt.
97/H3 **South Carolina** (state), U.S.
48/L8 **South China** (sea), Asia
91/H4 **South Dakota** (state), U.S.
25/G3 **Southend-on-Sea**, Eng.
71/Q11 **Southern Alps** (mts.), N.Z.
99/F7 **Southfield**, Mich.
98/B3 **South Gate**, Calif.
99/F7 **Southgate**, Mich.
83/X **South Georgia** (isl.), Antarc.
99/Q16 **South Holland**, Ill.
64/D4 **South Korea**
92/C3 **South Lake Tahoe**, Calif.
99/Q14 **South Milwaukee**, Wis.
83/W **South Orkney** (isls.), Antarc.
98/F5 **South Plainfield**, N.J.
93/G2 **South Platte** (riv.), U.S.
83/A **South Pole**
83/Y **South Sandwich** (isl.), Antarc.
99/K11 **South San Francisco**, Calif.
90/F3 **South Saskatchewan** (riv.), Can.
80/D2 **Soweto**, S. Africa
34/C2 **Spain**
92/C3 **Sparks**, Nev.
97/H3 **Spartanburg**, S.C.
46/B2 **Spitsbergen** (isl.), Nor.
40/C4 **Split**, Cro.
90/D4 **Spokane**, Wash.
27/H2 **Spree** (riv.), Ger.
93/J3 **Springdale**, Ark.
94/B4 **Springfield** (cap.), Ill.
94/E3 **Springfield**, Mass.
93/J3 **Springfield**, Mo.
94/D4 **Springfield**, Ohio
90/C4 **Springfield**, Oreg.
94/F3 **Springfield**, Vt.
95/H2 **Springhill**, N.S.
73/G5 **Springvale**, Austr.
98/F4 **Spring Valley**, N.Y.
90/C3 **Squamish**, Br. Col.
62/D6 **Sri Lanka**
53/K2 **Srinagar**, India
98/G4 **Stamford**, Conn.
109/E7 **Stanley** (cap.), Falkland Is.
77/L8 **Stanley** (falls), Zaire
47/N4 **Stanovoy** (range), Russia
98/C3 **Stanton**, Calif.
41/G4 **Stara Zagora**, Bulg.
97/F3 **Starkville**, Miss.
94/E3 **State College**, Pa.
98/F5 **Staten** (isl.), N.Y.
97/H3 **Statesboro**, Ga.
97/H3 **Statesville**, N.C.
94/E4 **Staunton**, Va.
45/G3 **Stavropol'**, Russia
93/G2 **Sterling**, Colo.
99/F6 **Sterling Heights**, Mich.
45/K1 **Sterlitamak**, Russia
94/D3 **Steubenville**, Ohio
94/B2 **Stevens Point**, Wis.
71/Q12 **Stewart** (isl.), N.Z.
93/H3 **Stillwater**, Okla.
20/F4 **Stockholm** (cap.), Sweden
23/F5 **Stockport**, Eng.
99/M11 **Stockton**, Calif.
96/C4 **Stockton** (plat.), Texas
23/G2 **Stockton-on-Tees**, Eng.
23/F5 **Stoke-on-Trent**, Eng.
95/Q9 **Stoney Creek**, Ont.
36/D1 **Strasbourg**, France
38/G4 **Stratford**, Conn.
94/D3 **Stratford**, Ont.
25/E2 **Stratford-upon-Avon**, Eng.
38/D3 **Stromboli** (isl.), Italy
72/A5 **Sturt** (des.), Austr.
93/K4 **Stuttgart**, Ark.
26/E4 **Stuttgart**, Ger.
40/D2 **Subotica**, Yugo.
106/E7 **Sucre** (cap.), Bol.
77/L5 **Sudan**
76/H5 **Sudan** (reg.), Africa
94/D2 **Sudbury**, Ont.
15/H3 **Sudeten** (mts.), Europe
49/C5 **Suez**, Egypt
49/C4 **Suez** (canal), Egypt
50/C4 **Suez** (gulf), Egypt
94/E4 **Suffolk**, Va.
57/L10 **Suita**, Japan
98/K8 **Suitland-Silver Hill**, Md.
53/J3 **Sukkur**, Pak.
67/E4 **Sulawesi** (Celebes) (isl.), Indon.
93/J5 **Sulphur**, La.
67/E2 **Sulu** (sea), Asia
67/F3 **Sulu** (arch.), Phil.
66/B4 **Sumatra** (isl.), Indon.
67/E5 **Sumba** (isl.), Indon.
67/E5 **Sumbawa** (isl.), Indon.
45/J4 **Sumgait**, Azerbaijan
95/J2 **Summerside**, P.E.I.
98/F5 **Summit**, N.J.
97/H3 **Sumter**, S.C.
44/E2 **Sumy**, Ukraine
66/B5 **Sunda** (str.), Indon.
23/G2 **Sunderland**, Eng.
99/K12 **Sunnyvale**, Calif.
92/E4 **Sunset Crater Nat'l Mon.**, Ariz.
73/F5 **Sunshine**, Austr.
56/B4 **Suo** (sea), Japan
94/C2 **Superior** (lake), N. Amer.
94/A2 **Superior**, Wis.
66/D5 **Surabaya**, Indon.
66/D5 **Surakarta**, Indon.
62/B3 **Surat**, India
107/G3 **Suriname**
90/C3 **Surrey**, Br. Col.
75/X18 **Sūsah**, Tun.
94/E4 **Susquehanna** (riv.), U.S.
68/G6 **Suva** (cap.), Fiji
97/H4 **Suwannee** (riv.), U.S.
58/D4 **Suwŏn**, S. Korea
59/E5 **Suzhou**, China
46/B2 **Svalbard** (isls.), Nor.
43/P4 **Sverdlovsk** (Yekaterinburg Russia
87/R7 **Sverdrup** (isls.), N.W.T.
103/F2 **Swan** (Santanilla) (isls.), Hond.
24/C3 **Swansea**, Wales
81/E2 **Swaziland**
20/E3 **Sweden**
96/C3 **Sweetwater**, Texas
90/F5 **Sweetwater** (riv.), Wyo.
90/G3 **Swift Current**, Sask.
36/D4 **Switzerland**
73/D2 **Sydney**, Austr.
95/J2 **Sydney**, N.S.
94/E3 **Syracuse**, N.Y.
46/G5 **Syrdar'ya** (riv.), Kazakhstan
50/D3 **Syria**
50/D3 **Syrian** (des.), Asia
45/J1 **Syzran'**, Russia
27/H2 **Szczecin**, Pol.
60/D2 **Szechwan** (Sichuan), China
40/E2 **Szeged**, Hung.
40/D2 **Székesfehérvár**, Hung.

T

90/E3 **Taber**, Alta.
82/F2 **Tabora**, Tanz.
51/F2 **Tabriz**, Iran
69/K4 **Tabuaeran** (isl.), Kiribati
99/C3 **Tacoma**, Wash.
76/H2 **Tadrart** (mts.), Africa
58/D3 **T'aebaek** (mts.), N. Korea
58/E5 **Taegu**, S. Korea
58/D4 **Taejŏn**, S. Korea
44/F3 **Taganrog**, Russia
34/B3 **Tagus** (riv.), Europe
69/L6 **Tahiti** (isl.), Fr. Poly.
92/C3 **Tahoe** (lake), U.S.
59/D3 **Tai'an**, China
61/J3 **Taichung**, China
61/J3 **Taichung**, Taiwan
61/J4 **Tainan**, Taiwan
39/H4 **Tainaron, Ákra** (cape), Greece
61/J3 **Taipei** (cap.), Taiwan
61/J3 **Taiwan** (Rep. of China)
61/H3 **Taiwan** (str.), Asia
59/C3 **Taiyuan**, China
50/D6 **Ta'izz**, Yemen
46/H6 **Tajikistan**
56/D3 **Takamatsu**, Japan
57/E2 **Takaoka**, Japan
57/F2 **Takasaki**, Japan
48/H6 **Takla Makan** (des.), China
79/E5 **Takoradi**, Ghana
109/B4 **Talca**, Chile
109/B4 **Talcahuano**, Chile
97/G3 **Talladega**, Ala.
97/G4 **Tallahassee** (cap.), Fla.
42/E4 **Tallinn** (cap.), Estonia
76/E6 **Tamale**, Ghana
45/G1 **Tambov**, Russia
97/H5 **Tampa**, Fla.
20/G3 **Tampere**, Fin.
101/F4 **Tampico**, Mex.
77/N5 **Tana** (lake), Eth.
70/E3 **Tanami** (des.), Austr.
85/J3 **Tanana** (riv.), Alaska
109/E4 **Tandil**, Arg.
76/E3 **Tanezrouft** (des.), Africa
82/F2 **Tanganyika** (lake), Africa
82/G2 **Tanga**, Tanz.
75/M13 **Tangier**, Mor.
59/D3 **Tangshan**, China
66/C5 **Tanjungkarang**, Indon.
49/B4 **Tanta**, Egypt
82/F2 **Tanzania**
93/F3 **Taos**, N. Mex.
102/C3 **Tapachula**, Mex.
49/D2 **Tarabulus** (Tripoli), Leb.
38/E2 **Taranto**, Italy
68/G4 **Tarawa** (atoll), Kiribati
47/J5 **Tarim He** (riv.), China
27/L4 **Tarnów**, Pol.
97/H4 **Tarpon Springs**, Fla.
35/F2 **Tarragona**, Spain
49/D1 **Tarsus**, Turkey
42/E4 **Tartu**, Estonia
46/G5 **Tashkent** (cap.), Uzbekistan
68/E8 **Tasman** (sea), Pacific
73/C4 **Tasmania** (state), Austr.
55/N2 **Tatar** (str.), Russia
63/G3 **Taunggyi**, Burma
24/C4 **Taunton**, Eng.
95/G3 **Taunton**, Mass.
49/B 1 **Taurus** (mts.), Turkey
64/B1 **Taxila** (ruins), Pak.
21/D2 **Tay** (firth), Scot.
99/F7 **Taylor**, Mich.
46/K2 **Taymyr** (pen.), Russia
45/H4 **Tbilisi** (cap.), Georgia
98/F5 **Teaneck**, N.J.
76/G1 **Tébessa**, Alg.
75/W18 **Tebessa** (mts.), Africa
23/G2 **Tees** (riv.), Eng.
102/E3 **Tegucigalpa** (cap.), Hond.
51/G3 **Tehran** (cap.), Iran
34/B3 **Tejo** (Tagus) (riv.), Port.
49/D3 **Tel Aviv-Yafo**, Isr.
75/Q16 **Tell Atlas** (mts.), Alg.
92/E4 **Tempe**, Ariz.
96/D4 **Temple**, Texas
109/B4 **Temuco**, Chile
35/X16 **Tenerife** (isl.), Spain
97/F3 **Tennessee** (riv.), U.S.
97/G3 **Tennessee** (state), U.S.
100/D4 **Tepic**, Mexico
107/K5 **Teresina**, Braz.
67/G3 **Ternate**, Indon.
38/C1 **Terni**, Italy
95/L1 **Terra Nova Nat'l Pk.**, Newf.
35/F2 **Terrassa**, Spain
94/C4 **Terre Haute**, Ind.
76/D1 **Tétouan**, Mor.
96/E3 **Texarkana**, Ark.
96/E3 **Texarkana**, Texas
96/C4 **Texas** (state), U.S.
96/E4 **Texas City**, Texas
28/B2 **Texel** (isl.), Neth.
65/C3 **Thailand**
63/H6 **Thailand** (gulf), Asia
64/A2 **Thal** (des.), India
25/G3 **Thames** (riv.), Eng.
94/D3 **Thames** (riv.), Ont.
62/B4 **Thana**, India
64/G3 **Thanjavur**, India
62/B2 **Thar** (Great Indian) (des.), India
39/J2 **Thásos** (isl.), Greece
90/C4 **The Dalles**, Oreg.
92/E4 **Theodore Roosevelt** (lake), Ariz.
91/G4 **Theodore Roosevelt Nat'l Pk.**, N. Dak.
91/H2 **The Pas**, Man.
39/H2 **Thessaloniki**, Greece
95/G2 **Thetford Mines**, Que.
97/F4 **Thibodeaux**, La.
78/A3 **Thiés**, Sen.
62/E2 **Thimphu** (cap.), Bhutan
97/H4 **Thomasville**, Ga.
97/H3 **Thomasville**, N.C.
65/C3 **Thon Buri**, Thai.
98/B2 **Thousand Oaks**, Calif.
39/J2 **Thracian** (sea), Greece
94/B1 **Thunder Bay**, Ont.
36/D4 **Thun**, Switz.
26/F3 **Thüringer Wald** (for.), Ger.
26/F3 **Thuringia** (state), Ger.
59/D3 **Tianjin** (Tientsin), China
46/H 5 **Tian Shan** (mts.), Asia
49/D3 **Tiberias**, Isr.
38/C1 **Tiber** (riv.), Italy
76/J3 **Tibesti** (mts.), Africa
62/E2 **Tibet** (reg.), China
59/D3 **Tientsin** (Tianjin), China
109/C7 **Tierra del Fuego** (isl.), S. Amer.
94/D3 **Tiffin**, Ohio
97/H4 **Tifton**, Ga.
51/F4 **Tigris** (riv.), Asia
28/C5 **Tilburg**, Neth.
71/R11 **Timaru**, N.Z.
78/E2 **Timbuktu** (Tombouctou), Mali
40/E3 **Timişoara**, Rom.
94/D1 **Timmins**, Ont.
67/F5 **Timor** (isl.), Indon.
67/G5 **Timor** (sea), Indon.
68/D3 **Tinian** (isl.), N. Marianas
99/Q16 **Tinley Park**, Ill.
21/A4 **Tipperary**, Ire.
39/F2 **Tiranë** (Tirana) (cap.), Albania
41/J2 **Tiraspol'**, Moldova
41/G3 **Tirgovişte**, Rom.
41/G2 **Tirgu Mureş**, Rom.
33/J3 **Tirol** (reg.), Austria
64/G3 **Tiruchchirappalli**, India
106/E7 **Titicaca** (lake), S. Amer.
40/D4 **Titograd**, Yugo.
97/H4 **Titusville**, Fla.
100/F5 **Tlalnepantla**, Mex.
75/Q16 **Tlemcen**, Alg.
81/J7 **Toamasina** (Tamatave), Madag.
104/F5 **Tobago** (isl.), Trin. & Tob.
46/G4 **Tobol'sk**, Russia
77/K1 **Tobruk**, Libya
79/F4 **Togo**
92/C3 **Toiyabe** (range), Nev.
69/H5 **Tokelau**
56/D3 **Tokushima**, Japan
57/F3 **Tokyo** (cap.), Japan
41/H4 **Tolbukhin**, Bulg.
94/D3 **Toledo**, Ohio
34/C3 **Toledo**, Spain
102/B2 **Toluca**, Mex.
45/J1 **Tol'yatti**, Russia
55/N3 **Tomakomai**, Japan
97/F4 **Tombigbee** (riv.), U.S.
78/E2 **Tombouctou** (Timbuktu), Mali
46/J4 **Tomsk**, Russia
95/S9 **Tonawanda**, N.Y.
69/H7 **Tonga**
69/K5 **Tongareva** (atoll), Cook Is.
55/K3 **Tonghua**, China
58/E3 **Tongjosŏn** (bay), N. Korea
65/D2 **Tonkin** (gulf), Asia
65/C3 **Tonle Sap** (lake), Camb.
92/D2 **Tooele**, Utah
72/C4 **Toowoomba**, Austr.
93/J3 **Topeka** (cap.), Kans.
33/G4 **Torino** (Turin), Italy
94/E3 **Toronto** (cap.), Ont.
24/C5 **Torquay**, Eng.
98/B3 **Torrance**, Calif.
70/F6 **Torrens** (lake), Austr.
100/E3 **Torreón**, Mex.
68/D6 **Torres** (str.)
18/C2 **Tórshavn**, Faroe Is.
104/E3 **Tortola** (isl.), V.I. (Br.)
27/K2 **Toruń**, Pol.
56/D3 **Tottori**, Japan
32/F5 **Toulon**, France
32/D5 **Toulouse**, France
30/C2 **Tournai**, Belg.
32/D3 **Tours**, France
72/B2 **Townsville**, Austr.
98/K7 **Towson**, Md.
57/E2 **Toyama**, Japan
57/E3 **Toyohashi**, Japan
57/L10 **Toyonaka**, Japan
57/N9 **Toyota**, Japan
50/D1 **Trabzon**, Turkey
34/B4 **Trafalgar** (cape), Spain
21/H7 **Tralee**, Ire.
83/W **Transantarctic** (mts.), Antarc.
40/F3 **Transylvanian Alps** (mts.), Rom.
41/F2 **Transylvania** (reg.), Rom.
94/C2 **Traverse City**, Mich.
27/K4 **Trencín**, Slovakia
98/F5 **Trenton** (cap.), N.J.
99/F7 **Trenton**, Mich.
31/F4 **Trier**, Ger.
33/K4 **Trieste**, Italy
104/F5 **Trinidad and Tobago**
93/F3 **Trinidad**, Colo.
104/F5 **Trinidad** (isl.), Trin. & Tob.
92/B2 **Trinity** (riv.), Calif.
95/L2 **Trinity** (bay), Newf.
96/E4 **Trinity** (riv.), Texas
76/H1 **Tripoli** (cap.), Libya
49/D1 **Tripolitania** (reg.), Libya
49/D2 **Tripoli** (Tarabulus), Leb.
16/J7 **Tristan da Cunha** (isl.), St. Helena
64/F4 **Trivandrum**, India
95/F2 **Trois-Rivières**, Que.
20/D3 **Trondheim**, Nor.
99/F6 **Troy**, Mich.
94/F3 **Troy**, N.Y.
106/C5 **Trujillo**, Peru
68/E4 **Truk** (isls.), Micronesia
98/G4 **Trumbull**, Conn.
46/H4 **Tselinograd**, Kazakhstan
69/L6 **Tuamotu** (arch.), Fr. Poly.
37/F1 **Tübingen**, Ger.
69/K7 **Tubuai** (Austral) (isls.), Fr. Poly.
92/E4 **Tucson**, Ariz.
92/C3 **Tulare**, Calif.
44/F1 **Tula**, Russia
97/G3 **Tullahoma**, Tenn.
93/H3 **Tulsa**, Okla.
92/E5 **Tumacacori Nat'l Mon.**, Ariz.
75/X17 **Tunis** (cap.), Tun.
75/X17 **Tunis** (gulf), Tun.
76/G1 **Tunisia**
97/F3 **Tupelo**, Miss.
33/G4 **Turin**, Italy
77/N7 **Turkana** (lake), Africa
46/G5 **Turkestan**, Kazakhstan
50/C2 **Turkey**
46/F6 **Turkmenistan**
104/C2 **Turks & Caicos Is.**
20/G3 **Turku**, Fin.
92/B3 **Turlock**, Calif.
97/G3 **Tuscaloosa**, Ala.
33/J5 **Tuscany** (reg.), Italy
97/G3 **Tuskegee**, Ala.
64/G4 **Tuticorin**, India
69/H6 **Tutuila** (isl.), Amer. Samoa
68/G5 **Tuvalu**
43/G4 **Tver'**, Russia
90/E5 **Twin Falls**, Idaho
94/C2 **Two Rivers**, Wis.
27/K3 **Tychy**, Poland
96/E3 **Tyler**, Texas
49/D3 **Tyre** (Sur), Leb.
38/B2 **Tyrrhenian** (sea), Italy
43/Q4 **Tyumen**, Russia

U

77/J7 **Ubangi** (riv.), Africa
56/B4 **Ube**, Japan
108/C1 **Uberaba**, Braz.
108/B1 **Uberlândia**, Braz.
106/D5 **Ucayali** (riv.), Peru
62/B3 **Udaipur**, India
43/M5 **Ufa**, Russia
77/M7 **Uganda**
92/E2 **Uinta** (mts.), Utah
62/C3 **Ujjain**, India
67/E5 **Ujung Pandang** (Makassar), Indon.
44/D2 **Ukraine**
54/F2 **Ulaanbaatar** (cap.), Mong.
54/F1 **Ulan-Ude**, Russia
62/B4 **Ulhasnagar**, India
37/F1 **Ulm**, Ger.
58/E5 **Ulsan**, S. Korea
22/A3 **Ulster** (reg.), Ire.
45/J1 **Ul'yanovsk** (Simbirsk), Russia
38/C1 **Umbria** (reg.), Italy
90/C5 **Umpqua** (riv.), Oreg.
87/K3 **Ungava** (bay), Que.
87/J2 **Ungava** (pen.), Que.
98/F5 **Union**, N.J.
99/K11 **Union City**, Calif.
98/F5 **Union City**, N.J.
97/F2 **Union City**, Tenn.
52/F4 **United Arab Emirates**
18/C3 **United Kingdom**
88/* **United States**
94/C2 **Upper** (pen.), Mich.
94/D3 **Upper Arlington**, Ohio
90/C5 **Upper Klamath** (lake), Oreg.
78/E3 **Upper Volta** (Burkina Faso)
20/F4 **Uppsala**, Sweden
51/F4 **Ur** (ruins), Iraq
46/F5 **Ural** (riv.), Asia
46/F3 **Ural** (mts.), Russia
45/J2 **Ural'sk**, Kazakhstan
57/F3 **Urawa**, Japan
94/B3 **Urbana**, Ill.
50/D2 **Urfa**, Turkey
51/F2 **Urmia** (lake), Iran
109/E3 **Uruguay**
109/E2 **Uruguay** (riv.), S. Amer.
54/B3 **Ürümqi** (Urumchi), China
55/L2 **Ussuri** (Wusuli) (riv.), Asia
46/J4 **Ust-Kamenogorsk**, Kazakhstan
92/E3 **Utah** (state), U.S.
94/F3 **Utica**, N.Y.
28/C4 **Utrecht**, Neth.
57/F2 **Utsunomiya**, Japan
96/D4 **Uvalde**, Texas
101/H4 **Uxmal** (ruins), Mex.
46/G5 **Uzbekistan**

V

80/C3 **Vaal** (riv.), S. Africa
20/G3 **Vaasa**, Fin.
99/L10 **Vacaville**, Calif.
37/F3 **Vaduz** (cap.), Liechtenstein
85/J3 **Valdez**, Alaska
109/B4 **Valdivia**, Chile
97/H4 **Valdosta**, Ga.
35/E3 **Valencia**, Spain
35/F3 **Valencia** (gulf), Sp.
106/E1 **Valencia**, Ven.
34/C2 **Valladolid**, Spain
99/K10 **Vallejo**, Calif.
38/D5 **Valletta** (cap.), Malta
98/G5 **Valley Stream**, N.Y.
109/B3 **Valparaíso**, Chile
94/C3 **Valparaiso**, Ind.
93/J4 **Van Buren**, Ark.
90/C3 **Vancouver**, Br. Col.
90/A3 **Vancouver** (isl.), Br. Col.
90/C4 **Vancouver**, Wash.
94/B4 **Vandalia**, Ill.
92/B4 **Vandenberg A.F.B.**, Calif.
20/E4 **Vänern** (lake), Sweden
20/H3 **Vantaa**, Fin.
68/F6 **Vanuatu**
62/D2 **Varanasi**, India
41/H4 **Varna**, Bulg.
20/F4 **Västeras**, Sweden
38/C2 **Vatican City**
62/C5 **Vellore**, India
33/J4 **Veneto** (reg.), Italy
33/K4 **Venezia** (gulf), It.
106/E2 **Venezuela**
97/H5 **Venice**, Fla.

Venice – Zwolle

33/K4 **Venice** (Venezia), Italy
98/A2 **Ventura**, Calif.
101/F5 **Veracruz**, Mex.
76/B5 **Verde** (cape), Sen.
31/E5 **Verdun-sur-Meuse**, France
47/P3 **Verkhoyansk**, Russia
47/N3 **Verkhoyansk** (range), Russia
91/J5 **Vermillion**, S. Dak.
95/F2 **Vermont** (state), U.S.
97/H5 **Vero Beach**, Fla.
33/J4 **Verona**, Italy
30/B6 **Versailles**, France
38/D2 **Vesuvius** (vol.), Italy
33/J4 **Vicenza**, Italy
32/E3 **Vichy**, France
97/F3 **Vicksburg**, Miss.
74/F5 **Victoria** (lake), Africa
73/C3 **Victoria** (state), Austr.
90/C4 **Victoria** (cap.), Br. Col.
61/G4 **Victoria** (cap.), Hong Kong
82/E4 **Victoria** (Mosi-Oa-Tunya) (falls), Africa
86/E1 **Victoria** (isl.), N.W.T.
96/D4 **Victoria**, Tex.
33/M2 **Vienna** (cap.), Austria
98/J8 **Vienna**, Va.
65/C2 **Vientiane** (cap.), Laos
65/D2 **Vietnam**
34/A1 **Vigo**, Spain
62/D4 **Vijayawada**, India
68/F6 **Vila** (cap.), Vanuatu
101/G5 **Villahermosa**, Mex.
99/Q16 **Villa Park**, Ill.
42/E5 **Vilnius** (cap.), Lithuania
109/B3 **Viña del Mar**, Chile
94/C4 **Vincennes**, Ind.
94/F4 **Vineland**, N.J.
63/J4 **Vinh**, Viet.
44/D2 **Vinnitsa**, Ukraine
83/U **Vinson Massif** (mt.), Antarc.
91/K4 **Virginia**, Minn.
94/E4 **Virginia** (state), U.S.
94/F4 **Virginia Beach**, Va.
104/E3 **Virgin Is.** (Br.)
104/E3 **Virgin Is. Nat'l Pk.** V.I. (U.S.)
104/E3 **Virgin Is.** (U.S.)
62/D4 **Visakhapatnam**, India
92/C3 **Visalia**, Calif.
92/C4 **Vista**, Calif.
42/F5 **Vitebsk**, Belarus
108/D2 **Vitória**, Braz.
34/D1 **Vitoria**, Spain
45/H4 **Vladikavkaz**, Russia
42/J4 **Vladimir**, Russia
55/L3 **Vladivostok**, Russia
28/A6 **Vlissingen**, Neth.
27/H4 **Vltava** (riv.), Czech Rep.
81/H9 **Vohimena** (cape), Madag.
46/E5 **Volga** (riv.), Russia
45/H2 **Volgograd**, Russia
42/H4 **Vologda**, Russia
78/E5 **Volta** (lake), Ghana
108/C2 **Volta Redonda**, Braz.
45/H2 **Volzhskiy**, Russia
46/G3 **Vorkuta**, Russia
44/F2 **Voronezh**, Russia
44/F2 **Voroshilovgrad** (Lugansk), Ukraine
36/C2 **Vosges** (mts.), France
91/K3 **Voyageurs Nat'l Pk.**, Minn.
43/L4 **Vyatkha**, Russia

W

94/C4 **Wabash** (riv.), U.S.
96/D4 **Waco**, Tex.
88/V13 **Wahiawa**, Hawaii
88/T10 **Wailuku**, Hawaii
88/S10 **Waipahu**, Hawaii
46/D3 **Wakayama**, Japan
68/F3 **Wake** (isl.), Pacific
27/J3 **Walbrzych**, Pol.
21/C4 **Wales**, U.K.
90/D4 **Walla Walla**, Wash.
68/G6 **Wallis & Futuna**
92/E4 **Walnut Canyon Nat'l Mon.**, Ariz.
99/K11 **Walnut Creek**, Calif.
24/D1 **Walsall**, Eng.
82/B5 **Walvis Bay**, Namibia
61/F2 **Wanxian**, China
62/C4 **Warangal**, India
97/H3 **Warner Robins**, Ga.
72/B4 **Warrego** (range), Austr.
99/F6 **Warren**, Mich.
94/D3 **Warren**, Ohio
93/J3 **Warrensburg**, Mo.
23/F5 **Warrington**, Eng.
27/L2 **Warsaw** (cap.), Pol.
95/G3 **Warwick**, R.I.
92/E2 **Wasatch** (range), U.S.
95/G2 **Washington** (mt.), N.H.
94/D3 **Washington**, Pa.
90/C4 **Washington** (state), U.S.
98/J8 **Washington, D.C.** (cap.), U.S.
21/F4 **Wash, The** (bay), Eng.
95/F3 **Waterbury**, Conn.
21/B4 **Waterford**, Ire.
93/J2 **Waterloo**, Iowa
94/F3 **Watertown**, N.Y.
91/J4 **Watertown**, S. Dak.
94/B3 **Watertown**, Wis.
95/G2 **Waterville**, Maine
104/C1 **Watling** (San Salvador) (isl.), Bah.
92/B3 **Watsonville**, Calif.
99/Q15 **Waukegan**, Ill.
99/P13 **Waukesha**, Wis.
94/B2 **Wausau**, Wis.
99/P13 **Wauwatosa**, Wis.
97/H4 **Waycross**, Ga.
99/F7 **Wayne**, Mich.
98/F5 **Wayne**, N.J.
83/W **Weddell** (sea), Antarc.
94/D3 **Weirton**, W. Va.
95/R10 **Welland**, Ont.
71/R11 **Wellington** (cap.), N.Z.
90/C4 **Wenatchee**, Wash.
61/J3 **Wenzhou**, China
29/F1 **Weser** (riv.), Ger.
80/D2 **Wes-Rand**, S. Africa
99/P13 **West Allis**, Wis.
49/G7 **West Bank**
94/B3 **West Bend**, Wis.
98/E6 **West Chester**, Pa.
98/C2 **West Covina**, Calif.
70/C4 **Western Australia** (state), Austr.
64/F3 **Western Ghats** (mts.), India
76/B3 **Western Sahara**
69/H6 **Western Samoa**
94/D3 **Westerville**, Ohio
91/J4 **West Fargo**, N. Dak.
98/F5 **Westfield**, N.J.
84/L7 **West Indies**
98/F7 **Westland**, Mich.
93/K4 **West Memphis**, Ark.
98/B3 **Westminster**, Calif.
23/F3 **Westmorland** (reg.), Eng.
98/F5 **West Orange**, N.J.
97/H5 **West Palm Beach**, Fla.
98/G4 **Westport**, Conn.
95/S10 **West Seneca**, N.Y.
92/E2 **West Valley City**, Utah
94/D4 **West Virginia** (state), U.S.
99/P16 **Wheaton**, Ill.
99/Q15 **Wheeling**, Ill.
94/D3 **Wheeling**, W. Va.
94/E3 **Whitby**, Ont.
94/C4 **White** (riv.), Ind.
42/H2 **White** (sea), Russia
85/L3 **Whitehorse** (cap.), Yukon
77/M5 **White Nile** (riv.), Africa
98/G4 **White Plains**, N.Y.
92/F4 **White Sands Nat'l Mon.**, N. Mex.
92/C3 **Whitney** (mt.), Calif.
98/B3 **Whittier**, Calif.
93/H3 **Wichita**, Kans.
93/H4 **Wichita** (mts.), Okla.
96/D3 **Wichita Falls**, Tex.
33/M2 **Wien** (Vienna), Austria
31/H3 **Wiesbaden**, Ger.
25/E5 **Wight** (isl.), Eng.
29/F2 **Wilhelmshaven**, Ger.
94/F3 **Wilkes-Barre**, Pa.
83/J **Wilkes Land** (reg.), Antarc.
90/B4 **Willamette** (riv.), Oreg.
104/D4 **Willemstad** (cap.), Neth. Ant.
94/E4 **Williamsburg**, Va.
94/E3 **Williamsport**, Pa.
98/F5 **Willingboro**, N.J.
91/H3 **Williston**, N. Dak.
91/K4 **Willmar**, Minn.
99/Q15 **Wilmette**, Ill.
98/E6 **Wilmington**, Del.
97/J3 **Wilmington**, N.C.
97/J3 **Wilson**, N.C.
98/G4 **Wilton**, Conn.
25/E4 **Winchester**, Eng.
94/E4 **Winchester**, Va.
91/H5 **Wind Cave Nat'l Pk.**, S. Dak.
82/C5 **Windhoek** (cap.), Namibia
99/F7 **Windsor**, Ont.
104/F4 **Windward** (isls.), W. Indies
93/H3 **Winfield**, Kans.
94/B3 **Winnebago** (lake), Wis.
99/Q15 **Winnetka**, Ill.
91/J3 **Winnipeg** (cap.), Man.
91/J3 **Winnipeg** (lake), Man.
91/H2 **Winnipegosis** (lake), Man.
91/L4 **Winona**, Minn.
92/E4 **Winslow**, Ariz.
97/H2 **Winston-Salem**, N.C.
97/H4 **Winter Haven**, Fla.
97/H4 **Winter Park**, Fla.
37/E3 **Winterthur**, Switz.
94/B2 **Wisconsin** (state), U.S.
94/B2 **Wisconsin** (riv.), Wis.
94/B2 **Wisconsin Rapids**, Wis.
26/G3 **Wittenberg**, Ger.
73/D2 **Wollongong**, Austr.
24/D2 **Wolverhampton**, Eng.
58/D4 **Wŏnju**, S. Korea
58/D3 **Wŏnsan**, N. Korea
98/F5 **Woodbridge**, N.J.
86/E2 **Wood Buffalo Nat'l Pk.**, Can.
99/L9 **Woodland**, Calif.
99/P16 **Woodridge**, Ill.
91/K3 **Woods, Lake of the** (lake), N. Amer.
94/D3 **Wooster**, Ohio
24/D2 **Worcester**, Eng.
95/G3 **Worcester**, Mass.
16/* **World**
26/E4 **Worms**, Ger.
91/K5 **Worthington**, Minn.
85/K3 **Wrangell** (mts.), Alaska
85/K3 **Wrangell-St. Elias Nat'l Pk.**, Alaska
27/J3 **Wroclaw**, Pol.
59/C5 **Wuhan**, China
59/D5 **Wuhu**, China
92/E4 **Wupatki Nat'l Mon.**, Ariz.
29/E6 **Wuppertal**, Ger.
26/E4 **Würzburg**, Ger.
55/L2 **Wusuli** (Ussuri) (riv.), Asia
59/L8 **Wuxi**, China
94/C3 **Wyoming**, Mich.
90/F5 **Wyoming** (state), U.S.

X

94/D4 **Xenia**, Ohio
61/H3 **Xiamen** (Amoy), China
61/H3 **Xiamen**, China
61/G3 **Xiangtan**, China
54/F5 **Xi'an** (Sian), China
59/B4 **Xi Jiang** (riv.), China
107/H4 **Xingu** (riv.), Braz.
54/E4 **Xining**, China
59/C3 **Xinji**, China
46/J5 **Xinjiang** (reg.), China
59/C4 **Xinxiang**, China
61/G3 **Xinyu**, China
59/D4 **Xuzhou** (Süchow), China

Y

54/E6 **Ya'an**, China
54/F1 **Yablonovyy** (range), Russia
90/C4 **Yakima**, Wash.
47/N3 **Yakut Aut. Rep.**, Russia
47/N3 **Yakutsk**, Russia
55/J3 **Yalu** (riv.), Asia
57/G1 **Yamagata**, Japan
78/D5 **Yamoussoukro** (cap.), Iv. Coast
62/D2 **Yamuna** (riv.), India
61/H2 **Yangtze** (Chang Jiang) (riv.), China
91/J5 **Yankton**, S. Dak.
59/E3 **Yantai**, China
57/L10 **Yao**, Japan
76/H7 **Yaoundé** (cap.), Cameroon
68/C4 **Yap** (isl.), Micronesia
42/H4 **Yaroslavl'**, Russia
51/H4 **Yazd**, Iran
97/F3 **Yazoo City**, Miss.
43/P4 **Yekaterinburg**, Russia
55/J4 **Yellow** (sea), Asia
55/H4 **Yellow** (Huang He) (riv.), China
86/E2 **Yellowknife** (cap.), N.W.T.
90/G4 **Yellowstone** (riv.), U.S.
90/F4 **Yellowstone Nat'l Pk.**, U.S.
52/E5 **Yemen**
46/J3 **Yenisey** (riv.), Russia
45/H4 **Yerevan** (cap.), Armenia
59/B5 **Yichang**, China
55/K2 **Yichun**, China
54/F4 **Yinchuan**, China
61/G2 **Yingcheng**, China
66/D5 **Yogyakarta**, Indon.
56/E3 **Yokkaichi**, Japan
57/F3 **Yokohama**, Japan
57/F3 **Yokosuka**, Japan
98/G5 **Yonkers**, N.Y.
98/C3 **Yorba Linda**, Calif.
70/G2 **York** (cape), Austr.
23/G4 **York**, Eng.
94/E4 **York**, Pa.
94/E4 **York** (riv.), Va.
92/C3 **Yosemite Nat'l Pk.**, Calif.
58/D5 **Yŏsu**, S. Korea
94/D3 **Youngstown**, Ohio
99/E7 **Ypsilanti**, Mich.
101/H5 **Yucatán** (pen.), Mex.
61/G2 **Yueyang**, China
40/E3 **Yugoslavia**
86/B2 **Yukon** (riv.), N. Amer.
85/L2 **Yukon** (terr.), Can.
92/D4 **Yuma**, Ariz.
60/D3 **Yunnan** (prov.), China
59/E5 **Yuyao**, China

Z

28/B4 **Zaandam**, Neth.
27/K3 **Zabrze**, Pol.
40/C3 **Zagreb** (cap.), Croatia
82/F2 **Zagros** (mts.), Iran
74/E5 **Zaire**
82/F4 **Zambezi** (riv.), Africa
82/F3 **Zambia**
67/F2 **Zamboanga**, Phil.
94/D4 **Zanesville**, Ohio
82/G2 **Zanzibar** (isl.), Tanz.
82/G2 **Zanzibar**, Tanz.
59/D4 **Zaozhuang**, China
42/E3 **Zaporozh'ye**, Ukraine
35/E2 **Zaragoza** (Saragossa), Spain
79/G4 **Zaria**, Nigeria
59/C2 **Zhangjiakou** (Kalgan), China
59/D4 **Zhanjiang**, China
59/C4 **Zhengzhou** (Chengchow), China
44/D2 **Zhitomir**, Ukraine
61/G3 **Zhuzhou**, China
59/D3 **Zibo**, China
60/E2 **Zigong**, China
82/E4 **Zimbabwe**
99/Q15 **Zion**, Ill.
92/D3 **Zion Nat'l Pk.**, Utah
37/E3 **Zug**, Switz.
37/H3 **Zugspitze** (mt.), Europe
37/E3 **Zürich**, Switz.
26/G3 **Zwickau**, Ger.
28/D4 **Zwolle**, Neth.